The Old Southwest, 1795–1830

The Old Southwest, 1795–1830

Frontiers in Conflict

Thomas D. Clark and John D. W. Guice

Foreword by Howard R. Lamar

UNIVERSITY OF OKLAHOMA PRESS
NORMAN AND LONDON

Library of Congress Cataloging-in-Publication Data

Clark, Thomas Dionysius, 1903–
    [Frontiers in conflict]
    The Old Southwest, 1795–1830 : frontiers in conflict / Thomas D.
Clark and John D.W. Guice ; foreword by Howard R. Lamar.
        p.   cm.
    Originally published: Frontiers in conflict. Albuquerque :
University of New Mexico Press, 1989. (Histories of the American
frontier).
    Includes bibliographical references and index.
    ISBN 0-8061-2836-4 (alk. paper)
    1. Southern States—History—1775–1865.   2. Southwest, Old—
History.   3. Gulf States—History.   4. Frontier and pioneer life—
Southern States.   5. Frontier and pioneer life—Southwest, Old.
6. Frontier and pioneer life—Gulf States.   I. Guice, John D. W.
II. Title.
F213.C56   1996
975′.03—dc20
                                                                    95-42772
                                                                    CIP

Original edition titled Frontiers in Conflict: The Old Southwest, 1795–1830.

1 2 3 4 5 6 7 8 9 10

To the pioneers of the Old Southwest,
and particularly the Clarks who trekked
from Virginia and South Carolina and
settled in the virgin forest of the
Dancing Rabbit country;
and to the Guices who from Pennsylvania
ventured through the Carolinas to Natchez
when it was still a British province
to fulfill dreams of land.

Contents

Maps

Foreword

Historians writing about North American frontiers almost inevitably find themselves describing distinctive phases or periods of development. They begin with an "international" phase, during which Euroamericans engage in conflicting assertions of sovereignty over newly discovered lands and native peoples. This first phase is succeeded by a "national" one in which settlement takes place, often after wars with Indians. The extension of laws, expansion of land and Indian policies, and establishment of state and local governments round out the national phase. Frederick Jackson Turner's apt remark that the frontier played a crucial role in the process of "nation building" is especially true for the early national period in American history.

Paralleling this national effort was a more subtle, but equally important, "region-building" process: the almost accidental development of a distinctive regional economy and society, created from the interaction of different peoples with a unique landscape. Thus, rather early on, terms such as the Appalachian and Kentucky frontiers, the Old Northwest, and the Old Southwest took on meanings far beyond the initial territorial designations.

Of these early national frontiers, none has a richer, more complex, and intriguing history than that of the Old Southwest. Just as the Old Northwest embraced the future states of Ohio, Indiana, Illinois, Michigan, Wisconsin, and a part of Minnesota, the Old Southwest comprised the Creek-dominated region of Georgia west of the Ocmulgee River and the area south of the Tennessee River. This included the territory of the future states of Alabama and Mississippi westward to the Mississippi River and southward as far as the Gulf of Mexico.

This vast area was famous (or infamous, depending upon one's viewpoint) for the complex, never-ending international and Indian-white rivalries that occurred within its borders. On the boundary between Georgia and Spanish Florida, Americans, Creeks, Spanish officials, British traders, and the emerging Seminoles competed for control until 1819, when Spain finally ceded control of Florida to the United States through the Adams-Onís Treaty. Even then, not until the United States had fought in the Seminole War (1835–1842) could the Americans assert that they really controlled this area.

Similarly, American settlers clashed with Spanish officials for control of West Florida until that region also was secured by the Adams-Onís Treaty. These international rivalries were complicated further by the fact that five independent Indian "nations"—the Cherokee, Chickasaw, Choctaw, Creek, and emerging Seminole peoples—not only occupied the Old Southwest but also resisted white occupation and conquest.

After suffering military defeat during the American Revolution, the originally pro-British Cherokees decided to pursue a policy of cultural assimilation and peaceful accommodation with the United States, even to the point of establishing a constitutional government based on American models. Similarly, for more than three decades—until they were forced to remove to Indian Territory—the Choctaws and Chickasaws pursued brilliant policies of neutrality, accommodation, and retreat. An uneasy peace between the Creeks and white settlers dating back to the American Revolution was broken during the War of 1812, when a number of Creeks joined Tecumseh in a war against the whites. In revenge for the Creek massacre of more than two hundred white settlers at Fort Mims in 1813, Andrew Jackson attacked and defeated the Creeks at the Battle of Horseshoe Bend.

Preceding and paralleling the Indian removals of the 1830s, white settlers, accompanied by thousands of black slaves, swarmed into Alabama and Mississippi Territories to raise cotton both on the scale of large, commercial plantation enterprises and on small family farms. Thanks to recent studies by John Guice, Terry Jordan, Jr., and Forrest McDonald and Grady McWhiney, we now know that other settlers also introduced to the Old Southwest an important open-range cattle industry that expanded westward to meet and mingle with Spanish-Mexican ranching systems that had spread from Mexico.

Until now the fascinating story of the Old Southwest had been told selectively, rather than in its entirety, by many popular narrators and professional historians. We have excellent and moving histories of the

Five Civilized tribes and their removal. Andrew Jackson's biographers have vividly portrayed his role in defeating the Creeks and driving the British from New Orleans. Thomas Perkins Abernethy has traced settlement patterns and land policy intrigues in great detail. More recently, Malcolm Rohrburgh and others have given us a careful narrative of the concurrent expansion of cotton and slavery across the southwest into Texas and Arkansas.

To tell the complex, multifaceted story of the Old Southwest frontier in a single volume, more than a decade ago Ray Allen Billington, founder of the Histories of the American Frontier Series, persuaded Thomas D. Clark and John D. W. Guice to write a book entitled *Frontiers in Conflict: The Old Southwest, 1795–1830*. It is that volume which is here being reprinted in paperback under a new title.

Thomas D. Clark, having pursued a distinguished career as a scholar and teacher at the University of Kentucky, is especially well known for his *History of Kentucky* and his popular text, *Frontier America* (in which the Southern frontier is given excellent coverage). These and many other works have been augmented by his study of business entrepreneurs on the frontier in *Pills, Petticoats and Plows,* and by his thoughtful volume, *The Emerging South,* which examines the twentieth-century history of the region. For his scholarly accomplishments and leadership in his field, Clark was elected president of the Southern History Association in 1947 and served as editor of the *Journal of Southern History* between 1948 and 1952. After his retirement from the University of Kentucky in 1968, he was named the Distinguished Service Emeritus Professor of History at Indiana University.

John D. W. Guice's interests in southern and western frontier history nicely complement those of Clark. Although he is a Mississippian who has spent most of his academic career teaching at the University of Southern Mississippi, his first book, *The Rocky Mountain Bench,* was a pioneering study of how federal courts functioned in western territories. Subsequently he has published seminal articles on cattle raising in the Old Southwest, and now he is working on a history of the Natchez Trace. It would be difficult to find two more appropriate scholars to coauthor a succinct, fresh new history of the frontiers of the Old Southwest.

One of the original features of this volume is that it acknowledges the importance of geography and climate in making the Old Southwest a unique American region. It was, the authors observe, a land beset with physical obstacles: scores of rivers, thousands of creeks and streams, moccasin-ridden swamps, impenetrable canebrakes, and desolate pine barrens. Yet despite its reputation as a dangerous environment because of the presence of malaria and yellow fever, unbearable summer heat, and destructive storms, the Old Southwest was also a land of incredibly fertile soil, whether in the Black Belt of Alabama or in the delta region of the Mississippi. Not only did it support some 100,000 largely agricultural Native Americans, but it also was destined to become the center of the Cotton Kingdom of the Old South. It is the often violent contest for these rich lands between both Indian and white slave-owning planters and the yeoman farmers—"Nabobs and Nobodies," the authors call them—and between different local and national political visions that is the focus of *The Old Southwest, 1795–1830: Frontiers in Conflict*.

Finally, Clark and Guice have not hesitated to question some older interpretations. They believe, for example, that the older accounts of both Thomas Jefferson's and Andrew Jackson's Indian policies are in need of revision. In recounting the impressive presence of non-slave-owning settlers and the piney woods open-range cattle raisers, they question the assumption that the institution of slavery and the cotton economy entirely shaped the history of the Old Southwest. Perhaps most significant of all, they see the Old Southwest as a frontier that endured, in pockets at least, long after most other regions had evolved beyond the frontier phase. Indeed, one of the authors discovered an area in rural Alabama where a frontier lifestyle and economy still survived in twentieth century America!

When this book first was published, in 1989, by the University of New Mexico Press, reviewers, while praising the volume, sometimes asked: was it frontier, southern, or western history? The answer is that the volume is all three, hence its title and its crucial value as a new synthesis. Not only does it stand on its own as a valuable general history, the volume complements the veritable renaissance of valuable Carolina and Piedmont backcountry studies that have appeared in the past decade. The University of Oklahoma Press is to be especially congratulated on the timely publication of this new paperback edition. It is a volume that will continue to interest students of frontier, southern, regional, and western history for many years to come.

Howard R. Lamar
Yale University

Summer 1995

Acknowledgments

Obviously, it is impossible to identify, much less thank individually, all of the persons who contributed to our effort to portray the Old Southwest during the opening decades of the republic. Without the pioneers who braved that wilderness, without the concern of the usually nameless souls who preserved the records of the era, and without the assistance of the institutions and professionals who now are the custodians of such treasures, there would be no book to write. Despite the hackneyed ring of the words, we nevertheless express our heartfelt thanks to all of the known and unknown persons who made this book possible. We especially thank the innumerable librarians and archivists—literally from one edge of the continent to the other—who assisted us in our research.

In every project, however, there are institutions and individuals whose contributions deserve special tribute. We express appreciation for the grant from the Huntington Library which supported a summer's research by Tom Clark in the unique environment of the Huntington. We are indebted to the staff of the Manuscript Department of the William R. Perkins Library at Duke University for making so accessible to both of us the extensive papers of the late William B. Hamilton whose works and papers we cite so often. Likewise, we acknowledge the help of the staffs of the Mississippi Department of Archives and History and the Tennessee State Library and Archives.

Particular thanks are due fellow historian Robert V. Haynes who read the entire manuscript and who generously shared with us his considerable knowledge of the Old Southwest. We cite frequently his excellent dissertation as well as his numerous published works. Dr. Samuel J. Wells, former student, friend, and colleague of John Guice, contributed significantly to our project. His assistance was considerably greater than one might suspect from the several citations to his publications. Three other graduates of the University of Southern Mississippi deserve mention. Michael F. Beard shared with us his expertise on Natchez and Natchez Under-the-Hill. Dr. G. Douglas Inglis, now a resident of Seville, Spain, made available copies of numerous documents from the Archivo General de Indias in Seville and offered several important suggestions which are incorporated in Chapter 3. The late Richard S. Lackey—an entrepreneur-scholar in the tradition of the nineteenth century that he understood so well—left his imprint on our work through his insights as a premier genealogist and family historian.

For his confidence and council, we express our appreciation posthumously to Ray Allen Billington who invited us to write *Frontiers in Conflict*, and of course, we are indebted to the Series co-editors, Howard R. Larmar, Martin Ridge and David J. Weber. Each of them offered helpful and useful advice; the fault is ours if we have not followed it carefully. It is difficult to credit adequately David Holtby for his expeditious, diplomatic, and effective editing.

Finally, we express our appreciation to the University of Southern Mississippi for its generous support of our research and writing. John Guice received two Summer Research Grants in addition to several grants from research funds administered by Dr. Karen Yarbrough, Vice President for Research and Extended Services. On the recommendation of its Faculty Subvention Committee and with the approval of Dr. Yarbrough, the University of Southern Mississippi provided to the University of New Mexico Press a subvention grant to underwrite the cost of the maps herein. For this considerable assistance from the University and for the supportive role of Dr. Yarbrough we express our gratitude.

Thomas D. Clark
Lexington, KY

John D. W. Guice
Hattiesburg, MS
Spring 1989

The Old Southwest, 1795–1830

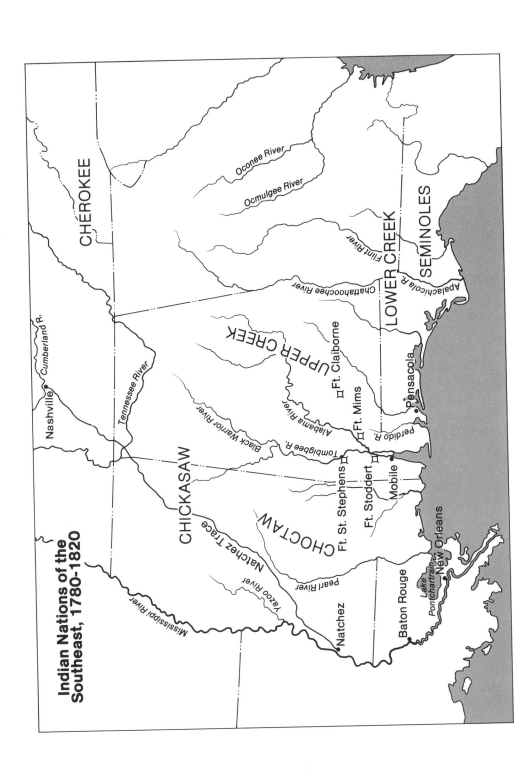

Indian Nations of the
Southeast, 1780–1820

CHEROKEE

CHICKASAW

CHOCTAW

UPPER CREEK

LOWER CREEK

SEMINOLES

Mississippi River

Yazoo River

Natchez Trace

Cumberland R.

Nashville

Tennessee River

Black Warrior River

Alabama River

Tombigbee R.

Pearl River

Natchez

Baton Rouge

Lake Pontchartrain

New Orleans

Mobile

Ft. Stoddert

Ft. St. Stephens

Ft. Mims

Ft. Claiborne

Perdido R.

Pensacola

Chattahoochee River

Apalachicola R.

Flint River

Ocmulgee River

Oconee River

1

"The lands here lie in a very curious manner"

"The lands here lie in a very curious manner," young Seargent Smith Prentiss wrote back home to Maine.[1] Prentiss, destined to become one of Mississippi's best known orators and statesmen, had just encountered the series of parallel rivers running out of fertile valleys into the Gulf of Mexico on America's southwestern frontier. More often than not, the arterial rivers were interlaced with numerous bayous and boggy swamps. The Old Southwest—that irregular region embraced in the great natural envelope south of the Tennessee River, west of the Ocmulgee River in Georgia, east of the Mississippi, and above the Gulf of Mexico—was as vast as it was curious. Five hundred miles of wilderness separated Natchez from the Creek Agency on the Ocmulgee; the Tennessee River was over 300 miles north of the Gulf Coast; the Mississippi Territory created in 1798 was 375 miles wide as the crow flew, not as the horse trotted. At that time the Old Southwest was inhabited by five major tribes of Indians and several widely scattered pockets of Euro-Americans, some with their African slaves. The rising Federal bureaucracy in Washington had only the haziest knowledge of this portion of the nation's frontier which constituted the vital southwestern quadrant of the young republic.

In addition to being a curious land topographically, the Old Southwest was, since de Soto's violent introduction of the Europeans to the Native Americans in 1540, a region marked by conflict. From the early sixteenth century Spain had considered herself guardian of the northern shore of the Gulf of Mexico—indeed, the original definition of *Florida* for Spain had meant an area from Virginia south to the Florida Keys and west all the way to New Mexico. That claim shrank steadily, however, and at the turn of the eighteenth century Spain had found her guardianship contested by France and Great Britain. This three-cornered struggle among

1

the Spanish, French, and British, with only intermittent pauses, gradually intensified until it climaxed in the French and Indian War, which concluded with the Peace of Paris of 1763. That treaty gave East and West Florida to England and the vast Mississippi empire—including New Orleans—to Spain.

Meanwhile, these three European powers had implicated the Indian tribes in their contest for mercantilistic dominance of North America by spinning an intricate web of international rivalries around the indigenous population. After 1763 events unfolded quickly: the American Revolution; Spanish recapture of the Floridas in 1779–80; the Paris Peace of 1783 ending the War for American Independence; conflicts with Spain over the boundary of West Florida, incitement of the Indians, navigation of the Mississippi, and separatist intrigues; the 1795 Treaty of San Lorenzo with Spain resolving these problems; the creation of the Mississippi Territory in 1798; the Louisiana Purchase in 1803; the War of 1812; and controversies surrounding statehood for Louisiana, Mississippi, and Alabama.[2] The curiosities of the land and the conflicts among its inhabitants are outlined in the paragraphs below. In subsequent chapters they will be analyzed in considerable detail.

The Old Southwest was largely defined by rivers and swamps, even in the upland sections that drained to the Gulf coastal areas. The broad slanting face of the region was sharply marked by numerous streams of potential navigable width and depth, and all of them provided access into the interior. To the east, the Ocmulgee and Altamaha rivers on the western Georgia frontier in the early 1800s comprised a boundary between the pressures of a spreading Anglo-American settlement line and the domain of the Creek Indians. Deeper into the frontier the Chattahoochee gathered its headstreams in the folds of the southernmost reaches of the Appalachian range and emptied its waters into the Gulf of Mexico. In its course southward this river formed a fairly broad valley which drained the heartland of the great pine barrens. Early in the history of the region the Chattahoochee constituted a north-south artery of penetration into the western Indian country, and later it was to form a natural boundary between Georgia and Alabama.

In the great expanse between the Chattahoochee and the Mississippi there flowed the Alabama with its Coosa, Tallapoosa, and Cahaba headstreams. The Alabama poured its waters ultimately into the Gulf through Mobile Bay. Above Mobile and west of the Alabama, the Tombigbee slashed its winding channel southward through present-day Mississippi and the fertile black belt of Alabama; its lateral, the Black Warrior, drained central western Alabama. The geography of the area immediately above Mobile is confusing. The Alabama flowing southwestward and the Tombigbee flowing southeastward merge and form for just a few miles a confluence known as the "Cut-off."

Below the "Cut-off," in an almost mysterious separation, the current of water from the Alabama River becomes the Tensaw, and the Tombigbee current creates the Mobile. Between these short twin rivers—the Mobile and the Tensaw east of it—is an oblong stretch of land known as Tensaw Island. The handful of French families who for many generations had eked out a living in the vicinity of Mobile were joined during the Revolutionary Era by scattered Tories and Whigs from Georgia and the Carolinas. Add to this mixture some Scotsmen and other Indian traders, their mixed-blood progeny, and a few hardy cattle raisers—also from Georgia and the Carolinas—and you have a composite of the small population there in 1795.

To the west of the Tombigbee the sluggish Pascagoula and the Pearl meandered toward the Gulf with their intricate systems of headstreams. All of these formed fertile alluvial deltas which in time were to exert considerable economic, social, and political influence by attracting American yeoman farmers and in some instances planters to their locale. A few descendants of the original French emigrants lived in the coastal strip between the mouths of these streams. A short distance to the east of Mobile Bay, the Perdido River ran across the Florida panhandle and emptied into the Gulf of Mexico. Situated immediately east of the Perdido was Pensacola with its natural deep-water harbor.

Of all these rivers, with the exception of the Mississippi, none was more significant historically than the Tennessee. Forming the boundary between white and Indian civilizations, this vigorous fresh-water stream originated in the Appalachian highlands. For unrecorded centuries it had bored its determined way through rocky barriers toward the Mississippi. In doing so it inevitably lost its surge and instead followed a circuitous channel of serpentine elbows and bends before emptying into the Ohio River just thirty miles above its confluence with the Mississippi. Its course outward was broken in the extreme northeast corner of present-day Alabama by the rocky Muscle Shoals which severely impeded navigation. The Tennessee in its Great Bend deposited annual burdens of alluvial sedimentation to create one of the richest farming areas on the southern frontier.[3]

No internal stream in the Old Southwest formed so precise a geopolitical divisional line in the history of the westward movement as did this one. The Tennessee Valley with its towering ridges had long been the homeground of the Cherokee, Creek, and Chickasaw Indians. The wide triangle formed by the Tennessee, Wolfe, and Mississippi Rivers was the upper homeland of the Chickasaw. The white settlers of this region were thus involved in a national drive to acquire full possession of the eastern bank of the Mississippi. The Tennessee laced into a cultural whole the southern portion of the westward movement during the opening decades of the nineteenth century.

Like the rivers of the ancient eastern world, those of the Old Southwest with their wide shouldering deltas exerted an enormous influence on the human history of their regions. Once the full tide of the population movement into the Old Southwest broke over the region, bottom cotton lands were gobbled up by planters in something akin to a "gold rush." They planted on these lands their own peculiar social, political, and economic systems—systems that discolored or camouflaged the frontier life style of most frontiersmen. For the nation as a whole, the flow of the southern streams toward the Gulf of Mexico created delicate problems of diplomacy and eventually sectional politics. From the outset the official records pertaining to the Old Southwest document eloquently the early sectional problems that arose.[4]

Unfortunately their shallowness and seasonal fluctuations of flow kept many of the smaller streams from becoming dependable commercial channels. On this score, Judge Harry Toulmin wrote from Fort St. Stephens in 1805 to Mississippi territorial delegate Dr. William Lattimore: "The current of the Tombigby, as you know, is remarkably placid—and its banks are admirably adapted to the purpose of moving boats by the strength of horses."[5] The territorial judge, who thought the Federal government should retain possession of strips on either bank of the stream for tow paths, concluded that the gangling Tombigbee could be converted into an important commercial water route, even if its depth was inadequate in the dry months. The recently completed Tennessee-Tombigbee Waterway fulfills Toulmin's prediction.

By no means were all the intricate internal stream systems in the Old Southwest of a positive nature. Seasonal inundations often threatened life and property located within their flood plains, and in many cases actually devastated large areas of land. Consequently, the lower three fourths of the Old Southwest were pockmarked by countless bayous, sloughs, cypress ponds, stagnant lakes, and abandoned river beds all conducive to the breeding of the malaria-bearing mosquitoes that menaced settlers each summer. During the first half of the nineteenth century it was a rare swamp-dweller who did not develop a sallow complexion, sunken cheeks, and a loss of energy because of recurring attacks of malaria.

While contemporary observers commented on the disease and death associated with the swamplands, they also recognized the potential for tillage. "If effectually drained and embanked," argued a contributor to *DeBow's Review*, "the soil of the delta of the Nile or Mississippi would not surpass them in fertility, or perhaps equal them in the variety of fruits which they would be capable of yielding. . . . Health, too, would probably reign where pestilence now abides."[6] It took the southern population more than a century, however, to drain the pools, control the flood waters, and eradicate the mosquitoes, but eventually considerable areas of these previously unproductive and uninhabitable areas would be placed under cultivation.

Nature provided other obstacles to settlement of the Old Southwest in the form of fierce tornadoes and hurricanes that came out of the Gulf of Mexico. Evidences of their destructiveness were the tangles of uprooted timber which often blocked trails or choked streams, and it was almost a certainty that during spring and fall of any year the region would suffer damage from the merciless blows.

Because many of the more important trails and roads into the Old Southwest ran diagonally across the rivers and creeks, travelers encountered hundreds of fords and ferries. Often immigrants were held up for long periods on stream banks waiting for the waters to recede or building rafts to be used in crossing. Consequently, famous crossing places cropped up such as Shallow Ford on the Chattahoochee, Tookabatchie on the Tallapoosa, Cahaba Old Town on the Alabama, Cotton Gin Port on the Tombigbee, the famous Alabama–Tombigbee Cut-off just below Fort Stoddert, John Ford's Stand on the lower Pearl in Mississippi Territory, Grindstone ford at Bayou Pierre on the Natchez Trace, and the Tennessee ferriage at Colbert's and Ditto's landings.[7]

While en route from Boston to New Orleans, William Richardson suffered a more or less common experience of travelers when he attempted to cross the Tennessee at Colbert's Ferry in March of 1815. Richardson had traveled all day in the rain; one of the pack horses had bolted through the woods strewing corn everywhere. Finally when the party arrived at the river, the ferryman would not brave the storm to carry them across. During his anxious wait, Richardson endured a heavy hailstorm that injured his horse! Exasperated, the traveler waded through the downpour to Colbert's house only to find that there was no stable to shelter his mount. The following day started out no better when his horse fell into the water, causing a great commotion.[8]

This melancholic experience was repeated thousands of times in the Old Southwest at stream crossings, sometimes with much more tragic results. No historian can adequately convey a sense of the anxieties of migrant families as they huddled beside a swollen river wondering if they could ever negotiate it in safety. A universal feature of extant accounts of travel in the Old Southwest is the constancy of references to the crossing of streams. Attitudes varied according to the age, health, and responsibility of the reporter, but these events always deserved notice. Paradoxically, the streams were at once inlets and barriers to the pioneers.

Dramatic loess bluffs which both captivated and bored river travelers formed the banks of the Mississippi River near the confluence of the Wolfe River in western Tennessee, and from Vicksburg to Natchez. Inland there were the sharper contrasts of almost bottomless alluvial soils, interspersed with oak flats, sandy "pine barrens," and sandstone-based highlands. The hills of Mississippi, West Tennessee, and Alabama were composites of fertile and sterile ridge soils growing both lush and scrub forest trees. The sandy rock faces of the tapering Appalachians spread out into separating hogback ridges of lands which in time would also exert their peculiar isolative impacts on the South.[9]

No doubt the most notable of the geographical features of the Old Southwest were the monotonous pine barrens which spread westward from the Georgia coast to well beyond the Mississippi, including the famous Gulf Coast long-leaf pine belt which would in later days become so productive of top-grade lumber. Interspersed were stands of oak, hickory, gum, and other hardwoods which experienced frontiersmen viewed as indicators of fertile soil. To the earliest settlers and tourists, the woodlands appeared almost impenetrable—endless and challenging, if not frightening and forbidding. Travelers viewed the virgin forests alternately as spiritually uplifting and as depressive.[10]

In 1804, Ephraim Kirby, the Mississippi Territorial Land Commissioner, mentioned the prevalence of pine trees in a letter to Thomas Jefferson: "The country on the west side of the Mobile and Tombigbie is generally a Pine-baren of great extent, and will not for a considerable length of time become otherwise useful, than as range for cattle and healthy positions for habitations."[11] Kirby could have written the same thing about the pine barrens stretching eastward from the Alabama and Tombigbee Rivers to the Ocmulgee in Georgia.

Of course, "a considerable length of time" is a relative term. Compared to the age of the forests in the Old Southwest, four decades represents only a momentary pause. It was, however, only that length of time before Natchez editor J. F. L. Claiborne, after a tour of the Piney Woods of southeastern Mississippi, predicted in 1841 a more immediate economic exploitation of the magnificent stands of pines. After a number of fascinating observations of the Piney Woods and its inhabitants, Claiborne concluded:

But the great source of wealth in this country must ultimately be—for it is now scarcely thought of—the lumber trade. The whole east is thickly planted with an almost unvaried forest of yellow pine. Finer, straighter, loftier trees the world does not produce. For twenty miles at a stretch in places you may ride through these ancient woods and see them as they have been for countless years untouched by the hand of man and only scratched by the lightning or the flying tempest. This growth of giant pines is unbroken on the route we pursued for an hundred miles or more, save where rivers or large water courses intervene.[12]

Within forty years after Claiborne penned these words, timber companies had begun the stripping of the virgin forests.

The forests abounded in beautiful shrubs and flowering trees, such as azalea and dogwood. Philadelphia naturalist William Bartram, who traveled from the Ocmulgee River in western Georgia to the Mississippi in the early summer of 1776, described dozens of them in the most glowing terms. After walking through "stately columns of Magnolia" Bartram wrote:

What a sylvan scene is here! the pompous Magnolia, reigns sovereign of the forests; how sweet the aromatic Illisium groves! how gaily flutters the radiated wings of the Magnolia auriculata! each branch supporting an expanded umbrella, superbly crested with a silver plume, fragrant blossom, or crimson studded strobile and fruits![13]

Not all land lay under forest cover in the Old Southwest, however. There were many of what eighteenth-century visitors called "plains" or "meadows," and frequently there appeared Indian cornfields hacked out of the woods. Near the Alabama River, for instance, Bartram encountered "expansive illuminated grassy plains" over twenty miles long and nearly half as wide. Bartram, who never neglected an opportunity to comment on pristine beauty, noted that the vast fields against a background of high forests presented "a magnificent and pleasing sylvan landscape of primitive, uncultivated nature."[14] Even to the untrained eye these occasional prairies must have offered a welcome relief from the endless miles of pines.

Travelers—and the few pioneers who wrote journals or reminiscences—never failed to comment on the monstrous canebrakes growing throughout the Old Southwest. Bartram, for instance, found near the Flint River in Georgia an abundance of cane ("*Arunda gigantea*") of "great height and thickness," and noted that the "cane swamps afforded excellent food and range for our horses."[15] At other times the naturalist wrote of cane meadows. Frontiersmen, however, more often called these matted and dense thickets "canebrakes." On the positive side, however, they offered rich winter browse for deer and bear, and when herdsmen arrived, their cattle and hogs relished the nutritious young shoots. For many immigrant families moving into the region, however, the canebrakes were impenetrable barriers—hiding places for hostile Indians and outlaws. Scalpel-sharp cane stubble crippled man and beast alike, and the growth provided shelter for deadly snakes. The clearing of a canebrake challenged the strength and fortitude of the hardiest pioneer. Though the dried cane readily burned, only persistent chopping could destroy the interwoven roots of tremendous viability and tensile strength.

Not only did settlers in the Old Southwest have to overcome topographical barriers and endure dangerous natural phenomena, but they also had to reconcile themselves to the presence of many frightening and perilous vermin, reptiles, and insects. In the woods and canebrakes of the region at least four species and numerous subspecies of venomous snakes thrived in menacing numbers. They had been so threatening to the Indian population that some of the serpents, especially the rattlesnakes, had come to be regarded as indestructible evil spirits.[16] In the swamps and canebrakes and among the rocky hills were five or six subspecies of rattlesnakes varying in length from one to eight feet. In addition, there were the smaller and thus less visible copperheads, the aggressive cottonmouth water moccasins, and the deadly coral snakes. Surveyors, hunters and travelers alike could not free themselves from the anxiety of stepping on one of these creatures.

"All the varieties of the rattlesnake, *crotalus horribus*, are seen, in some places in pernicious abundance," wrote geographer Timothy Flint in 1828.

The yellow rattlesnake is the largest of the species. They are sometimes seen, as large as a man's leg, and from six to nine feet in
length. A species of small rattlesnake is sometimes seen in great
numbers on the prairies (eastern Mississippi and central Alabama). . . . There is a very troublesome species, called snappers,
or ground rattlesnakes. They travel in the night, and frequent
roads and house paths. The copperhead is a terrible serpent,
deemed to inflict a more dangerous bite than the rattlesnake. They
inhabit the same region but are not so common, as the . . . moc-
casin snake. There are three or four varieties of this serpent inhabiting the southern country.[17]

Flint might well have added that some of the streams were inhabited
by alligators which, despite their awesome appearance, posed less of an
actual danger.

While snakes threatened the peace of mind and safety of travelers
in the southern woodlands and swamps, the lowlands swarmed with
insects of almost every known American species. Especially offensive
were the mosquitoes, deerflies, chiggers or redbugs, many kinds of
gnats, fleas, and a variety of ticks. For nine months out of the year these
insects made human life dreadfully uncomfortable in much of the Old
Southwest. Though there are no statistics or contemporaneous entomol-
ogical treatises describing this pestilence, travelers frequently complained of insects, and the personal journals and memoirs of early settlers
generally contain references to this unpleasantness—a fact easily understood by anyone who has ever lived and worked in the southern out-
doors.[18]

In time, a veritable army of observers crossed the southern frontier: some
enamored with it; others bored and disenchanted. Fortescue Cuming,
an Irish traveler, quoted a British sailor who had helped him disembark
in the Natchez District in 1809:

And is it here you stop, and is this the country to which so many
poor ignorant devils remove, to make their fortunes? D—n my
precious eyes if I would not rather be at allowance of a mouldy
biscuit a day in any part of old England, or even New York, Pennsylvania, or Maryland, than I would be obliged to live in such a
country two years, to own the finest cotton plantation, and the
greatest gang of negroes in the territory.[19]

Many others shared his opinion, but migration figures prove that thousands did not.

A decade later New England missionary Timothy Flint praised the alluvial soil of the bottom lands as highly fertile and productive, with the humus-rich hammocks ranking especially high on the scale of American soil qualities and durability.[20] Even the sterile pine lands he considered excellent ranges for cattle and hogs. On the Tombigbee, Flint noticed that greedy speculators grabbed up the first-rate lands as fast as they could be pried away from the government, selling some plots for as much as fifty dollars an acre. Obviously, in the long range, Flint's positive view dominated.

Of all the natural circumstances that determined the destiny of the Old Southwest, none had a more overpowering influence than the presence of five of the most populous, powerful, and culturally advanced tribes of Indians in North America.[21] Whoever the international claimants may have been throughout the post-Columbian era, in 1795 this portion of the continent was the ancestral home of nearly 100,000 Cherokee, Creek, Chickasaw, Choctaw, and Seminole Indians. They were town-dwelling agriculturalists who were advanced in pottery and religion. Some were fierce warriors, others were shrewd diplomats. Quickly they learned how to use the tools and weapons of the white men. At the time of the European intrusion, of course, numerous other smaller tribes resided there, including the aristocratic and ceremonious Natchez whom the French literally decimated as a tribe in 1731. From the birth of the American republic until well after the War of 1812, the formulation and administration of a workable Indian policy consumed no small portion of the energy of the nation's leadership. When George Washington was inaugurated, these Indians were still in such control of their homelands that the Natchez District was the only part of the nation's southwestern domain not claimed and occupied by them.

Ages before Europeans began the contest for empire, the Native Americans of the Old Southwest had subdivided the area into a veritable patchwork of loosely defined tribal and sub-tribal territories. In places boundaries were vague, but the tribesmen recognized them. In some instances, neutral plots separated hunting grounds; in others there were war-provoking overlappings. As early as 1785 the United States Government had begun through treaty negotiations the process of identifying and rearranging the vast checkerboard of tribal boundaries. From that date until the completion of the removal process, successive administrations had pieced together heterogeneous Indian policies dealing with pacification, acculturation, boundaries, land acquisition, roads, defense, trade, and other expediencies.

From the time of the planting of the first European banner in the Old Southwest, the region had become a pawn in a complicated high-stake succession of territorial and commercial controversies. At different times, France, Spain and England had claimed it. Each had plastered on an overlay of ownership which ignored and superseded Indian possession and which had given to the Old Southwest a troubled legacy of conflicting land claims and inscrutable land laws. In this process, the entire Gulf Coastal plain had become the scene of trade rivalries, with the grossest sort of human chicanery, and bizarre commercial practices. It is ironic, for instance, that the Spanish licensed a British trading firm—Panton, Leslie, and Company—to operate out of Pensacola after Spain reoccupied West Florida during the American Revolution. Panton, Leslie and Company dominated trade with the Choctaw, Creek, and Seminole Indians until the establishment of United States Government trading posts among the Creeks in 1795 and the Choctaw in 1802.

No part of the American frontier was more conducive to smuggling than the accessible coastal fringe of the Old Southwest. The maze of rivers leading up from the Gulf of Mexico were open channels for illicit traders to pass almost unobserved behind the impenetrable screen of forest and swamp undergrowth. Behind this screen awaited abundant caches of Indian trade commodities—primarily peltry—which so tantalized French, Spanish, English, and Scottish merchants. William Bowen, the assistant factor at Fort Hawkins, in a letter in 1817 refers to such long-established practices:

> Indian traders or rather smugglers in the Creek Nation are constantly introducing their merchandize among the Indians. Most of them cross the [Chattahoochee] river high up to avoid suspicion or give time to detect them; Scarcely a week but I hear of some person going through the Nation selling their merchdze & collecting Peltries &ca. Any force at this place cannot Effectually stop them before they are apprized thereof, made sales of their goods and are gone off with their Peltries.[22]

Largely because of the intense European rivalries, the traders made few or no maps, surveyed no great tracts of land, left almost no detailed travel journals, and opened few permanent arterial roads.

Instead, the European traders memorialized their presence through their large broods of mixed-blood children—a legacy far more significant and lasting than books and roads. Often bearing Scotch surnames and displaying the marks of the highlands in their faces and personalities, these mixed bloods created invigorating as well as disruptive forces on the frontier. Because of the matrilineal social structure of the tribes, the progeny of white traders and other Euro-Americans who took Indian wives quickly acquired social prominence and political power. With their understanding of European ways, the mixed bloods served as catalysts of acculturation. Eventually, however, tribal factionalism caused in part by their growing dominance accelerated the cultural dissolution and deterioration of the Indian tribes of the Old Southwest.[23] The Native Americans thus played a role as significant as it was complex in the history of the Old Southwest. Accordingly, four of the following chapters pertain to them.

In 1789 when George Washington took the first presidential oath of office, Spanish forces occupied the Old Southwest between the Mississippi and the Chattahoochee as far north as present-day Vicksburg— or along an east-west line drawn through the mouth of the Yazoo River. Since the United States claimed the thirty-first parallel, the northern boundary of Spanish West Florida, as its southern boundary, the dispute over this huge parcel of land loomed as the most important of the four major sources of friction between the young republic and the Spanish Empire. The other three were the closure of the Mississippi River to free commerce, the incitement of the Indians, and the instigation of separatist intrigues with frontier leaders in Tennessee and Kentucky. As will be discussed in considerable detail in Chapter 3, these festering issues were largely resolved in 1795 by the extremely popular Treaty of San Lorenzo, which the U.S. Senate unanimously ratified. If not considered so by the entire nation, certainly to the big-time land speculators and eager pioneers in the South, the San Lorenzo agreement, also known as Pinckney's Treaty, was the crowning diplomatic achievement of the Washington Administration.[24]

When Congress created the Mississippi Territory in 1798, the Federal government inherited several wearisome problems in the Old Southwest. Weighed in human terms, the most important and persistent has already been mentioned—the development of a policy to guide relations with the Native Americans. A second problem was the establishment of a skeletonized defense force that could be strategically located and effectively maneuvered in the wilderness. The establishment and maintenance of mail service between the national seat of government and this far distant corner of the republic provided another challenge. Even for agents of the

Federal government, crossing the wilderness proved to be a severe challenge. If they were not sent from the eastern seaboard around the Florida peninsula and up the Mississippi River to Natchez, dispatches had to be carried across the Appalachians to either the Ohio or the Tennessee River and down one of the tributaries to the Mississippi. Messengers who braved the Indian path from Nashville to Natchez—soon to be improved and known as the Natchez Trace—had to ride through portions of the Cherokee, Chickasaw, and Chocktaw Nations.

To many immigrants, the most vexatious of all problems in the Old Southwest related to the management of the public domain. Indeed, the life force of Anglo-American pioneering in the Old Southwest was the process of land distribution. Reams of official correspondence, legislative actions, administrative directives, surveyor and land office reports, and other legal records of eternal squabbling survive to document this paramount issue.

There were several types of claimants among the some 6,000 people, exclusive of the Native Americans, who lived in the scattered settlements of the Mississippi Territory at the time of its organization. The earliest settlers had occupied the land under French, Spanish, and English dispensations, and, understandably, they or their descendants held steadfastly to claims made under all these colonial governments. In addition to these hopelessly complicated and confused claims of foreign derivation were those created by Georgia who did not relinquish her claim to the land from the Yazoo River Line to the southern border of Tennessee until 1803.

In 1785, the Georgia legislature had created out of its western empire a colossal district called Bourbon County, only to repeal the act in 1788. To make matters worse, in 1789 and again in 1795 the Georgia legislature involved itself in the most grandiose speculative schemes ever concocted in a nation known for its agrarian cupidity—namely, the Yazoo Frauds. In 1795 the Georgia legislature, which had succumbed to bribery, granted 35 million acres of its western lands between the Alabama and Mississippi Rivers for a cent and a half an acre to four companies controlled primarily by northern speculators. After shouts of indignation and revulsion from across the nation pressured the Georgia legislature to rescind the sale a year later, protracted litigation ensued. The incredible tenacity of the claimants under these schemes finally paid off in 1814 when Congress, after some of the most acrimonious debates in its turbid history, voted to distribute among them $5,000,000 from the proceeds of land sales in the Mississippi Territory. Though the Bourbon County and

Yazoo ventures enriched a bevy of lawyers and speculators—and financially decimated others—few claimants settled in the Old Southwest. The promotional impact and litigational legacies of these Georgian designs, however, were not insignificant.

By far the largest contingent of claimants of the land were the immigrants who arrived after the Treaty of San Lorenzo. These frontiersmen grounded their ownership on United States statutes. Even so, throughout the territorial years they flooded the Congress and administrative officials with emotional petitions and other outcries in efforts to legitimatize their landholdings. Indeed, not until 1803 did Congress enact a general land law establishing guidelines for the disposition of public land below the Tennessee River and opening two land offices in the Mississippi Territory. In view of the fact that countless families before and after 1803 squatted on land before the Indian title had been extinguished and before it had been properly surveyed, there was no end to the land tangles. An effort to explain them, at least partially, will be made in Chapter 4.

Although the United States in its brief existence before 1800 had gained considerable experience at coping with the bothersome territorial questions which beset it, the Old Southwest represented a supreme challenge. Such a vast stretch of virginal territory in a fermentative national age generated issues with an almost unheard of constancy and intensity. There was not at hand either the necessary legal means or the technical assistance necessary for developing an orderly process of survey, land distribution, and settlement of a growing population. Also lacking was a military force sufficiently strong to permit firm administrative control of affairs in the area and to discourage European powers from exploiting the western river system.

Despite the fact that there were on the Federal statute books ordinances and other legislation pertaining to land survey and distribution, often they were not applicable in the Old Southwest. Because of the conditions summarized above, no general survey brought immediately under Federal control the distribution of lands which might be freed from Indian possession. In a sense, every administrative proclamation, order, letter of instruction, or directive after 1798 became an instrument of emerging public policy for the new territory. Nevertheless, the basic governmental structure outlined in the Northwest Ordinance of 1787 worked reasonably well in the Old Southwest, as it did, with refinements, in the trans-Mississippi territories.

Throughout the Old Southwest soils varied sharply from the thin sand-clay washed areas of the frontal Appalachian ridges of northern Georgia and Alabama to the central black prairies to the deep alluvial soils of the many river basins. Nearly all of the southwestern soils historically produced an impressive variety of field crops and grasses. Especially significant, however, was the suitability of large areas to the growing of short staple cotton. This fact prompted James D. B. DeBow, the perceptive New Orleans editor, to observe that "in the United States of America there is a small parcel of ground destined to supply the world with *Cotton.*"[25] Obviously, DeBow was comparing his "small parcel" to the surface of the planet Earth, for he defined it as "the little strip of land composing South Carolina, Georgia, Florida, Alabama, Mississippi, Louisiana, Arkansas, and Texas and a very small portion of Tennessee." DeBow's prediction helps us to comprehend the later errant enthusiasm of secessionists and Confederate leaders who would crown cotton as king.

One cannot calculate the amount of physical energy necessary to bring under cultivation sizable fields of crops and pasturage. There existed on the southwestern frontier, as noted above, some scattered Indian corn patches, but these were small, widely dispersed tracts, and not available to the early settlers who cleared their own fields. Consequently, the immigrants flooding into the Old Southwest viewed the hardwood forests not as resources, but as undesirable cover that absorbed the sun's life-giving rays and prevented them from farming potentially productive soil. On arrival, one of their first tasks was the removal of the shade-producing trees, principally with axe and fire.

In his informative, colorful chapter on "Backwoods Times," Alabama historian Albert Burton Moore describes in his classic 1927 history just a few of the endless tasks facing frontier settlers.

> Agriculture was, of course, a universal pursuit, and the fine soils and climate were exceptionally inviting, but to clear away the dense forests and the jungles of cane-brakes, vines, briers, and brush wood was a huge undertaking. When this was accomplished, the trouble was by no means over. Rails must be split, fences built around the fields, and for several years the trunks and limbs of trees that had been deadened must be piled up and burned.[26]

Another major challenge was to break the new ground with an iron share plow with a wooden moldboard—a profanity-provoking device that busted human chins and limbs as well as sod and tree roots. Work consumed the life of early settlers—at times literally before they had lived many decades. For it was not uncommon for a man to wear himself out improving and selling several farms in rapid succession.

While thousands of white immigrant yeomen performed this backbreaking labor, black slaves provided much of the muscle power required to transform forests into farms, a fact reflected from the outset in regional population statistics. Never in the history of African slavery in North America was there a greater demand for field hands than for the clearing away of the southern forests, the raising of crude homes and barns, and the cultivation of stubborn new grounds, especially in the "flush times" of the 1830s. In Mississippi Territory the number of slaves increased from 3,489 in 1800 to 17,088 in 1810; by 1820 the total in Mississippi and Alabama, formerly one territory, reached 74,693, a number that had increased to 183,208 in 1830.

As the early observer noted, the land in the Old Southwest did, indeed, "lie in a very curious manner." Had he returned several decades later, he could have made the same observation about society there. It had developed in an equally curious manner. In the interior of the Old Southwest three distinctly different frontier types lived side by side in apparent detachment from each other: planters, yeoman farmers, and herdsmen. Amidst them lived increasingly large numbers of African slaves, and on the Gulf Coast, where Frenchmen gathered products from the sea, made naval stores, and grazed cattle, another entirely different type of Euro-American frontier society persisted. In some ways, the process of folk occupation and settlement on the southwestern frontier differed little from that in other areas of the American frontier. In other ways, it differed considerably. An obscuring and differentiating element in the Old Southwest, after the invention of the cotton gin, was the advance of the cotton culture—a culture emulated to a surprising degree by the Native Americans. The presence of so many slaves has led some historians to describe this frontier as "more South than West." If one has to choose only from those terms, it probably was more "West than South" or at least "as West as South." Actually the Old Southwest, though similar in some ways to other frontiers in North America, was unique.

To a large extent, the story of any frontier is the story of conflict. Indeed, many historians see international conflict as the prevailing theme of American colonial history—a theme also woven through the history of its expansion westward. Of the various segments of the American frontier, the Old Southwest lays claim, if not to the greatest numbers of conflicts, at least to some of the most peculiar.

In a sense, the region provides a study of macro- as well as micro-conflicts. At the macro level were two world powers, Spain and the United States, in a contest for control of a frontier that was in a state of disequilibrium. Stated in oversimplified terms, the southwestern frontier of the expansionistic young United States was pushing aside the North American frontier of the crumbling Spanish empire. As with many frontiers, the lines separating the two were not neat. Even after the thirty-first parallel was defined as the northern boundary of Florida, a wide assortment of characters filtered or flowed back and forth across that arbitrarily established border. Vestiges of the French empire in Louisiana as well as British interference—actual and feared—gave the scene a turbidity that matched that of the waters flowing out of the Mississippi River.

No part of the North American borderlands history is more complex and less studied than the Isle of Orleans and West Florida on which frontiersmen of the Old Southwest focused so much of their attention. The Spanish frontier encountered there represented a passive-defensive borderland designed as a buffer to the more important colonial possessions of an empire on the brink of forced disintegration. Spain's energies at this time were being dissipated by European political strife; accordingly, her American empire was in a holding pattern, to use an anachronistic figure of speech. Had Spain not been so distracted at home, one might argue, she would have slapped down forthwith her challengers in the Americas.

Measuring these two frontiers with a United States yardstick is unfair. From the Spanish perspective, West Florida—occupied in 1810 by the United States by presidential proclamation—represented a minimal investment of men and resources and was insignificant compared to the gold and silver producing areas such as Mexico and Peru. The opposite was true for the United States. In the eyes of the early presidential administrations of the emerging republic, the southwest was vital, and by comparison its capital city lay in reasonable proximity. Another major difference was the character of the on-the-scene representatives of the competing nations. Overseeing the interests of Spain were professional bureaucrats thousands of miles across the seas from Madrid. But the pioneers pushing southwestward had a personal stake in shoving aside the Spaniards. If ever the United States had a locally oriented and popular frontier, it was in the Old Southwest. Thus many individuals molded national policy to suit their own desires.

The litany of the other conflicts examined in this book is too long to recite here. For everywhere one turned in the Old Southwest, a dichotomy was encountered. Sometimes there were more than two sides, parties, or participants involved in the issue. The Indian question, for example, defies simplistic dichotomous description in terms of Anglo-Americans versus Native Americans. There were whites of many nationalities, predilections, and motivations. The same was true of the Indians of both pure and mixed blood. In the presence of so many nuances, the positing of generalities regarding Indian relationships becomes difficult.

Almost as complex were the sectional rivalries that emerged during the territorial period and erupted in full force during the quest for statehood. As many differences as miles, figuratively speaking, separated the Natchez and Tombigbee residents. The Gulf Coast and the Great Bend were 300 miles apart and quite different. Conflict also surrounded land titles, land laws, law enforcement, proportionate representation, commerce, the War of 1812, filibustering, the thirty-first parallel, politics, education, statehood, and boundaries. The list could go on and on and it belies the region's pristine beauty. Not only did the Old Southwest "lie in a very curious manner" as Seargent S. Prentiss noted, but on that land were a number of distinct, even curious frontiers in conflict.

2

Changing Empires

At the beginning of the nineteenth century, the region we now call the Old Southwest was one of rapidly shifting human patterns. Though the forces eroding the foundation of Native American culture first appeared with the arrival of De Soto in 1540, they greatly intensified with the growth of the Anglo-American population and government. In 1795, the Federal government dealt with the tribes as powerful nations, and the Indians vastly outnumbered white immigrants in the region. Within the span of a single lifetime, however, the tables were turned and the societies indigenous to the region were substantially reduced in number, nature, and influence. To a large extent, the history of the Old Southwest is an account of this process.[1]

Occupying most of the young nation's fertile southwestern domain were the Creek, Chickasaw, Choctaw, and Seminole tribes, who belonged to the Muskhogean linguistic family. The other major Indian group was the Cherokee, whose language indicated that they were of Iroquoian stock. Despite their cultural similarities, each tribe gained a reputation for its own special characteristics: the Cherokee for law and polity, the Creeks as peacemakers and diplomats, the Choctaw for excellence in agriculture and trade, the Chickasaw as warriors and hunters, and the Seminole for their disaccordance and nonconformity. These tribes shared a common culture that was flexible and resilient enough to adapt to white ways—even to writing political constitutions—and because of their adaptability they came to be called the "five civilized tribes."

At the time of European intrusion, numerous smaller tribes shared the coastal plains and river valleys with the large tribes, but by the late colonial period they had either become extinct or been absorbed by the dominant tribes. Indeed, the Natchez shared a similar fate. Approximately

the same size as the Chickasaw prior to European intrusion, their principal town stood on the banks of the Mississippi River at the site of the city
now bearing their name. The Natchez revolted in 1729 against the French
who had constructed a fort in their midst, but the tribe paid dearly for
the blood they spilled. For in 1731 the French and their Indian allies almost
annihilated them, leaving but a few of the Natchez to tell the tale.[2]

While these tribes were marked by natural and social differences, to a
large extent they shared a common culture based on the cultivation of
maize. Though hunting and gathering were certainly important to them
as sources of sustenance and shelter, they were primarily town-dwelling
agriculturalists. In addition to separate household gardens, the villagers
generally planted communal crops in meadows or plots laboriously cleared
from forests by girdling the trees. Between the hills of corn were planted
beans, pumpkins, peas, melons, sunflowers, and tobacco. Some grew
wild rice along river banks. Weeding and cultivation were considered
work for women and children, but the heavy planting and the harvest
were communal projects in which the men fully participated. Since maize
was the most important staple, much depended on a successful corn harvest. Excess grain was bartered with other tribes and, after the introduction of cattle by Europeans, fed to livestock.[3]

Despite the primacy of agriculture, the tribesmen oriented their lives
to a large extent toward the forests. Deer, bear, (and earlier, bison) meat
comprised a basic part of all tribal diets. Byproducts—hides, bones,
antlers, entrails, sinews, and claws—were important in fashioning clothing, implements, weapons, and ceremonial ornaments. A portion of the
meat was eaten fresh; the balance was dried or smoked. Heavy bearskins
made excellent robes, blankets, moccasins, and boots, and bear oil was a
highly prized commodity widely used in cooking and in grooming the
hair and body.

Because the streams, bayous, and lakes often abounded in scale and
shell fish, they were an important source of food. Fish were trapped,
netted, speared, shot, and even caught by hand. Women and children
gathered numerous varieties of nuts, wild mulberries, strawberries, black-
berries, grapes, plums, persimmons, and onions, as well as edible fungi.
Honey was a welcome treat; licks and springs provided salt which some
tribes secured through barter. Aboriginal Mississippians concocted numerous potions, teas, poultices, emetics, and other remedies from a host of
leaves, barks, roots, herbs, and berries. Just as they sought the flesh of
admired animals, such as deer and bear, the natives avoided eating certain creatures considered unclean or unworthy such as wolves, panthers,

foxes, mice, rats, and particularly moles. The avoidance of this possible food supply reflects the abundance of the land and the advanced stages of their cultures.

Ingenious craftsmen, natives of the area, molded clay pottery for cooking, eating, and storage. They sewed garments of finely tanned deerskins, using thread spun from the inner bark of trees, animal fur, or shredded sinew. Construction of housing varied according to climatic zones; in the mountainous regions, summer and winter shelters were used alternately, while farther south homes were occupied year around. Houses often were constructed of log-framed walls covered with woven branches or cane with roofs of thatched grass. In some instances, walls were finished on both sides with clay plaster. Crude beds and stools were common furnishings, and the homes were sometimes illuminated with pitch torches.

Indians of the Old Southwest enhanced their economies and life styles through trade with each other. The items exchanged were numerous and varied according to their needs and surpluses. Choctaw commerce, for instance, depended on their surplus of corn. Each of the tribes, however, traveled great distances for highly prized items. The European intrusion intensified the tribes' existing commercial activities. Parodoxically, this trade both enriched and impoverished the Indians. Certainly the natives did not realize that white traders were actually harbingers of doom. So they innocently plunged into an active trade, exchanging primarily deerskins and Indian slaves for accouterments of European society. Cloth, guns, powder, shot, beads, knives, hatchets, and kettles were exchanged for the pelts and for slaves destined for Carolina and West Indian plantations. The resulting competition for hunting grounds and the increased demand for slaves intensified warfare, complicated Indian-white diplomacy, and exposed the Native Americans to a ruinous credit system—one which in time would cost some of them their land. Powerful commercial firms such as Panton, Leslie, & Company operating out of Pensacola allowed the Indians to purchase on credit, and then they used the resulting indebtedness as leverage for control of tribal relationships and policies. As will be discussed later, some critics of American policy accused the government of following suit. This trade also formed the basis of complex and ultimately destructive alliances with European powers.

A matrilineal social order generally characterized each of the five civilized tribes which were divided into two major moieties. In turn, the moieties were subdivided into clans. The basic unit of government, a reflection of the sedentary life style, was the town council above which was a pyramid of councils whose number and location depended on the size of each tribe. Most matters were decided at the town level with only the gravest concerns discussed by the highest council. Meetings on all levels were marked by open debate. Since progeny of the unions of Europeans and Indian women inherited the prestige and status of their mothers, mixed bloods rapidly rose to power. By the nineteenth century, the large number of mixed bloods in leadership positions caused dissension within all the tribes. This tension, which heightened during the tribal debates over the cession treaties, is addressed in Chapter 12.

Religion permeated aboriginal life in the Old Southwest. Most natural phenomena—especially the mysteries of birth, puberty, maturation, and death—were explained in religious terms. Since the sun, the Great Holy Fire Above, had a central place in their hierarchy of deities, sacred fires tended by a priest burned in most towns. Even their games had spiritual overtones, and festivals celebrated important natural events such as the corn harvest. Though burial customs reflected different attitudes toward the journey after death, the tribesmen believed in life hereafter. Monogamous marriages prevailed, although polygamy was accepted under proper social and economic conditions. Many taboos were related to women who were required to isolate themselves during menstruation, at childbirth, and for a time during the postnatal period.

The Indians of the Old Southwest maintained such a close-knit relationship to the land that they felt a "oneness with the earth." Consequently, they claimed vast game preserves. Because the Anglo-American settlers viewed this practice as wasteful and sinful, many conflicts developed over Indian-white approaches to land utilization. By European standards, Indian agriculture seemed inefficient, and the tribesmen demonstrated no sense of permanent occupation and improvement. The concepts of homestead and personal descent of property were unknown to the Native Americans in the Old Southwest, though others (in the Pacific Northwest, for example) displayed a very real sense of property ownership.

The Cherokee occupied lands in the western Carolinas, southeastern Tennessee, and northeastern Alabama. Below them were the most variegated of the five tribes, the Creeks. Occupying central and west Georgia, northern Florida, and much of Alabama, the Creek Nation was comprised of numerous small tribes satellite to the Muskogees, Hitchitis, Alabamas, and Euchees, which were the major Creek tribes. Though the division of the confederation into geographical groups—the Lower and the Upper Creeks—belies ethnic complexities, those terms were widely employed. Below the Creeks and associated closely with them lived the

Seminole who were not recognized as a separate tribe until the close of the eighteenth century. That nation was an amalgamation of dissident Creeks and other small Florida tribes.

The Chickasaw lived in what is now northern Mississippi and the northwestern tip of Alabama. However, their ancient domain included western Tennessee as well as the southwestern corner of Kentucky. By 1800 their population, which never exceeded 5,000, included bloodlines of various Yazoo River tribes, whom they had decimated, and of surviving Natchez whom they had absorbed after the French destruction of that tribe in 1731. Largest of any tribes in the Old Southwest except the Cherokee, the 20,000 Choctaw lived below the Chickasaw in the southern three quarters of Mississippi and in southwestern Alabama. In their veins also ran the blood of smaller Mississippi tribes which had become extinct by the early national period.[4]

The greater acceptance of blacks by the Seminole and their greater consideration of them illustrates their individuality for which they were later to pay a high price. Each of the above tribal tendencies explains, to an extent, the variance in their relations with European intruders. Thus the vast domain acquired by the United States in 1783 sustained complex indigenous human elements each of which had its own social and political institutions.

The need for a policy to guide relations with Native Americans who inhabited the vast domain to the west of the thirteen states was immediately apparent to members of the Continental Congress. Though both the Patriots and the British began the Revolutionary War with protestations of neutrality toward the Indians, the tribesmen quickly became embroiled in the War for Independence just as they had in the century of wars concluded by the Peace of Paris of 1763. Generally speaking, the Native Americans sided with England. Of the Indians in the Old Southwest, however, only the Cherokee and the Chickasaw actively entered the fray. The Cherokee paid a considerable price in both casualties and land cessions for supporting the British, but the Chickasaw, who had closed off the Mississippi River to traffic of the patriots, suffered less for their transgression. Because of French and Spanish assistance in the war, the Americans enjoyed the good will of most of the Choctaw and Creeks.

The Continental Congress created a standing committee on Indian affairs, which divided Indian areas into three departments: northern, middle, and southern. The southern department included the Cherokee and all tribes to the south of them. Though it named several commissioners to collectively oversee the tribes in each department, Congress had virtually no resources to expend on either gifts or arms for its few Indian allies. The Articles of Confederation became effective in 1781 and shortly thereafter the fighting ended. Congress immediately appointed commissioners to negotiate treaties with the Indians. As it implemented the Articles of Confederation, Congress eventually asserted national supremacy over Indian affairs, and created in 1786 a southern and a northern Indian Department with the Ohio River dividing them. The two superintendents reported to the Secretary of War. Though the new government shared many prerogatives with the states pertaining to the Indians, it wasted no time in asserting itself with the natives inhabiting its newly acquired domain. Top priorities of the Congress were an Indian acknowledgment of American sovereignty and the development of a national Indian policy.[5]

The pattern of paternalism and pacification adopted by Congress under the Articles of Confederation and later by the early Presidents under the Constitution was inherited from the European powers, especially from the British but also from the Spanish and French as well. All of them had sought to neutralize the various tribes and to exploit them to varying degrees. While American exploitation may have been disguised and/or delayed, the new nation adhered to the principle of pacification through so-called legal treaties. In time official reports of Indian affairs and the text of United States Statutes were to be filled with records of treaty negotiations reflecting this policy, and the map of the Old Southwest soon became checkered with outlines of cessions and grants of roadways.[6]

The first were the landmark treaties of Hopewell negotiated late in 1785 with the Cherokee and early in 1786 with the Choctaw and Chickasaw on the Keowee River in South Carolina. Through these agreements, Commissioners Benjamin Hawkins, Andrew Pickens, and Joseph Martin sought to resolve one of the most vexing issues of Indian relations in the Old Southwest by establishing fixed boundaries among the tribes. Besides defining boundaries of the Indian Nations, these treaties contained an acknowledgment of the protection of the United States and granted that Nation exclusive right to regulate trade with the Native Americans. A virtually identical treaty was signed by the Creeks in 1790 in New York. According to the latter, the government gratuitously agreed to furnish the Creeks with domestic animals and implements in order that they might become "herdsmen and cultivators," thereby achieving a "greater degree of civilization." At Hopewell, the Choctaw relinquished three plots six miles square and the Chickasaw one small circular reserve for future American trading posts.[7]

As they negotiated on the Keowee River in South Carolina late in 1785 and in 1786, the Americans were quite mindful that Spanish troops controlled the Gulf Coast and the Natchez District. Hence, a major goal was neutralization of Spanish influence among the bellicose Creek confederation and the vacillating Choctaw. The Chickasaw, who switched their allegiance from the British to the Americans, had traditionally disdained the French and Spanish. But the Choctaw fealty was not so steadfast; that nation displayed a partiality toward the Spanish which was particularly evident in the southern Choctaw towns. The Creeks also remained generally loyal to the Spanish, though they also harbored considerable pro-British sympathy.

A measure of the national concern with Indian affairs was the willingness with which the states abdicated control in that area at the Constitutional Convention in Philadelphia in 1787. The new Constitution placed in the hands of Congress responsibility for all matters relating to the Indian tribes. Considering that the Native Americans controlled most of the national domain, Indian policy was of no little interest to the frontier-minded Americans. In 1790, when the Congress organized the executive branch of government, it entrusted the Department of War to oversee such matters pertaining to the Indians as directed by the President. Each tribe was dealt with as a separate nation through treaties, a process which placed the initiative for Indian policy in the hands of the President who constitutionally was assigned the conduct of foreign affairs. Relations with the Indians was one area in which the Congress sought strong executive leadership, and fortunately President George Washington and Secretary of War Henry Knox were well prepared to cope with that responsibility by virtue of their experience, interest, and good judgment.

The Federalist Administration of President Washington—and later of President John Adams—continued a program of pacification and paternalism aptly summarized by Secretary Knox, who wrote in a letter to Governor William Blount:

> It is the most ardent desire of the President of the United States, and the general government, that a firm peace should be established with all the neighbouring tribes of Indians on such pure principles of justice and moderation. . . . The Indians have constantly had their jealousies and hatred excited by the attempts to obtain their lands. I hope in God that all such designs are suspended for a long period. We may therefore now speak to them with the confidence of men conscious of the fairest motives toward their happiness and interest in all respects. A little perseverance

in such a system will teach the Indians to love and reverence the power which protects and cherishes them. The reproach which our country has sustained will be obliterated and the protection of the helpless, ignorant Indians, while they demean themselves peaceably, will adorn the character of the United States.[8]

Washington's primary objectives were the maintenance of peace through negotiations, protection against white encroachment beyond defined boundaries, and development of a fair trade. The treaties signed at Hopewell and in New York prior to Washington's inauguration provided the President with a good foundation for such a policy with the Native Americans of the Old Southwest.

Under the Federalists a system of carefully controlled government trading houses—known as factories—was established in 1795 in response to Washington's insistence that the Indians be protected from unscrupulous traders.[9] Peaceful natives required less of a military presence. It is significant that the first factories were located among the Creeks and Cherokee in 1795 and the next two in 1802 among the Choctaw and the Chickasaw, the former at Fort St. Stephens and the latter at Chickasaw Bluffs, site of present-day Memphis.[10] Clearly, Federal attention was focused on the Old Southwest.

The purposes of the factory system were multifold: *diplomatic* in the elimination of foreign influence over the Indians; *economic* in the wresting of profitable trade from British merchants; *military* as a mechanism of control of the native population; and *humane* in the provision of goods that had become vitally necessary to the greatly altered Indian life style. Depending on priorities and conditions, various administrations emphasized different goals. The trade and intercourse acts provided a welcome relief from the abuses of private traders, but they never created a government monopoly. Throughout the twenty-seven-year life of the factory system it suffered from its temporary character and a rather limited capital structure. Generally, the factories were fairly and frugally managed. However, the factors were severely handicapped by strict limitations on stock levels and accounts receivable. Finally its enemies, especially the American Fur Company, garnered sufficient political clout to persuade Congress to abolish the system in 1822.[11] It is interesting that this government venture into business did not precipitate criticism from strict constructionists who voiced such loud disapproval of a national bank as unconstitutional. Perhaps they construed factories as a national security matter.

President Washington began to implement his policy through a series of treaties with Indians in the Northwest and in the Southwest where his aides concluded important agreements with the Cherokee and Creeks. North Carolina's cession in 1790 of her western lands extending to the Mississippi necessitated clarification of boundaries, particularly with the Cherokee. So on July 2, 1791, William Blount, Governor of the Territory South of the River Ohio and Superintendent of Indian Affairs for the Southern District, signed for the United States a treaty of "perpetual peace and friendship" with Cherokee leaders assembled on the bank of the Holston River near the mouth of the French Broad. Signing for their tribe was a small army of chiefs and warriors who bore such fetching names as "King Fisher," "Slave Catcher," "Chickasaw Killer," "Bloody Fellow," "Bear-at-Home," and "Standing Turkey."[12]

In addition to its expressions of amity, the Holston Treaty provided for the surrender of all prisoners then held by each side, defined national boundaries, and granted a right-of-way and free use of a road across the nation which would connect Washington and Nashville. The United States was to regulate trade in the Cherokee Nation and to forbid persons to enter Cherokee territory without official passports. The Indians promised to surrender all white criminals that they harbored, and the United States agreed to punish whites found guilty of crimes against the Cherokee. Finally there were to be no retaliatory acts for past crimes. The treaty encouraged the Cherokee to gain a "greater degree of civilization" by becoming "herdsmen and cultivators" through use of gratuitously furnished implements of husbandry. On February 17, 1792, the treaty was amended to increase annuities from $1,000 to $1,500.[13]

Three years after the Holston Treaty, its terms were clarified and amplified in an agreement negotiated on June 26, 1794, in Philadelphia. At this meeting, terms of the Holston Treaty were reaffirmed and procedures spelled out for the marking of the previously defined boundaries. In addition, compensation for lands ceded by the Cherokees at Hopewell and Holston was increased from a $1,000 cash annuity to an annual distribution of goods valued at $5,000. Furthermore, the Cherokee committed themselves to cease the thievery of horses or suffer a reduction of annuity in the amount of $50 per horse stolen and not returned within three months.[14]

At Coleraine, Georgia, on June 29, 1796, another major treaty of amity was signed with the Creeks by commissioners Benjamin Hawkins, George Clymer, and Andrew Pickens, all experienced in Indian affairs. After reaffirming the terms of the New York Treaty of 1790, the Creeks recognized the boundaries of the Chickasaw, Choctaw, and Cherokee outlined in the Hopewell and Holston Treaties.They also agreed to the marking of specified lines, granted to the United States five-acre plots for trading houses or military posts, and arranged the release of prisoners. For these concessions, the Creeks received goods valued at $6,000 plus the services of two blacksmiths accompanied by helpers, known as "strikers," and supplied with the necessary tools.[15]

The final treaty of the 1790s signed with Indians of the Old Southwest was negotiated on October 2, 1798, with the Cherokee at Tellico on the Tennessee River. Though it confirmed past treaties, its primary purpose was the extraction of a cession of Cherokee land along the Tennessee River. For this tract, the right to mark its boundaries, and for free passage on the road to the Cumberland River the government paid $5,000 in goods plus an increase of $1,000 in the value of items to be delivered annually to the Cherokee.[16]

Consistent with the Federalist policy of pacification and paternalism, this series of Indians treaties did not seek cessions of large blocks of land so much as friendship, fealty, regulation of trade, definition of boundaries, rights-of-way through the nations, and locations for trading and military posts. Regardless of Washington's insistence on justice and integrity as a basis for the nation's Indian relations, his policy was more expedient than permanent. However, the pressures of an ever-expanding frontier west of the Appalachians necessitated the formulation of a more comprehensive Indian policy by the beginning of the nineteenth century. Even as recently as 1789 when the Constitution was implemented, no one had realized just how rapidly the citizens of the young republic would risk a move across the Appalachians.

By 1800, when Thomas Jefferson was elected to the presidency, one million Americans—approximately one out of five—lived beyond the mountain barrier. New laws offering public land at two dollars an acre on credit attracted immigrants at an even greater pace during his first term, and many of them would soon begin raising cash crops in the West. Kentucky entered the union in 1792 and in 1796 Tennessee became a state. Even without international complications, the West would have demanded much of the new President's attention. However, French acquisition of Louisiana by the Treaty of San Ildefonso in 1800, the subsequent suspension of the right of deposit in New Orleans in 1802, and the Spanish presence in West Florida compounded the urgency for a comprehensive Indian policy to deal with the five formidable Indian Nations in possession of most of the Old Southwest. Not only did they control the routes of communication to the growing islands of settlement there, but they had a history of alliances with European powers. One of these powers, France, held title to New Orleans through which most western commerce flowed; another, Spain, still governed that port.

Another factor further complicating Jefferson's task as a formulator of Indian policy was the restlessness and uneasiness which characterized the tribes at the beginning of the nineteenth century. After three centuries of contact with Europeans, their culture was disintegrating at an alarming and ever-increasing rate. Factionalism within the five civilized tribes intensified as the Native Americans dealt with a host of disruptive factors such as the growing dominance of the mixed bloods and the schisms left by debates over tribal alliances with intruding European nations. The President remained sensitive to the concerns of a proud indigenous people who viewed their Nations as sovereign, but at the same time he realized that they represented a considerable military threat.

Considering these conditions and his long interest in the culture and language of the Native Americans, it is not surprising that no President figured more prominently in the formation of Federal Indian policy than Thomas Jefferson. Unfortunately, historians tend to offer descriptions of his policy that are as simplistic as their explanations of his motivations. Few keep in mind the historical context in which the events unfolded or the intellectual dispositions of statesmen directing national responses to them. Francis Paul Prucha, noted historian of American Indian policy, correctly suggests that critics of Jefferson often fail to appreciate his Enlightenment mind, and thus they arrive at the simplistic conclusions that he only desired to gain Indian land and that he actually had little concern for their welfare.[17]

As Washington's first Secretary of State and Adams' Vice President, Jefferson was deeply involved in Indian affairs from the beginning. Hence it is logical that he continued to stress pacification and paternalism, although he more heavily emphasized the desire of civilizing the Indian.[18] Indeed, instructions to the agents from every level of his Administration stressed the urgency of civilizing the Native Americans—of recasting them in the mold of the yeoman farmer. Secretary of War Henry Dearborn carefully explained this policy in 1802 to Silas Dinsmoor, a native of New Hampshire and the newly appointed agent to the Choctaw:

> The motives of the Government for sending agents to reside with the Indian Nations, are the cultivation of peace and harmony between the U. States, and the Indian Nations generally; the

detection of any improper conduct in the Indians, or the Citizens of the U. States, or other relating to the Indians, or their lands, and the introduction of the Arts of husbandry, and domestic manufactures, as means of producing, and diffusing the blessings attached to a well regulated civil Society: To effect the foregoing important objects of your Agency, you will use all the prudent means in your power.[19]

No term appears as frequently in the official correspondence concerning Indians during Jefferson's Administration as *civilize*—used as a verb, noun, or adjective! The witty, good-natured Dinsmoor was the right man in the right place to implement Jefferson's policy. Formerly agent to the Cherokee, this sensitive New Englander made good use in his new post of his knowledge of surveying and his earlier experience as a purser.

Long before reaching the White House, Jefferson had concluded that Indians were not only educable but that they were equal to whites in terms of their physical and mental endowments.[20] Indeed, to him the Native Americans seemed superior to Africans in their ability to adapt themselves to European ways. In these views lay the roots of Jefferson's goal of civilization, which was an essential step in the amalgamation of the tribesmen with the Anglo-Americans who otherwise would eventually encroach upon all of their land.[21] Naive though it seems in hindsight, his belief in coexistence and gradualism was nevertheless well intentioned. Moreover, without an understanding of Jefferson, his design appears to have been merely a rouge for the acquiescence of his and later Administrations to agrarian cupidity. Indeed, this view is shared by numerous historians, particularly those most influenced by the Indianist sentiments of the 1960s.[22] It is not unusual to find historians tracing the antecedents of Jackson's removal policy to Jefferson, but they generally base their conclusion on his assertion that the tribes stood a greater chance of survival if protected from voracious settlers.[23]

Both the Washington and Adams Administrations pacified the Indians with gifts and liberal trading practices, and despite Jefferson's continuation of the appeasement policies of his two predecessors, his Administration stepped up the negotiation of cession treaties. Consequently, his policy is often described as one of land greed.[24] However, the facts belie this misinterpretation. His three early treaties with the Choctaw primarily formalized existing boundaries agreed upon with the British. These cessions, as well as those in 1802 by the Creeks and in 1804 by the Cherokee, reflect the President's desire to avoid conflicts between the growing number of Anglo-Americans and the indigenous population.

Even more misunderstood, however, are acquisitions of Indian land during Jefferson's second Administration—acquisitions prompted by his strong fear of foreign manipulation of the Indians in the Old Southwest. As will be discussed more fully below, the serious threat of international involvement along the wide sweep of the Gulf Coast and the Mississippi River, rather than satiation of the yeoman's appetite for land, guided Jefferson's Indian policy in the years preceding the War of 1812.[25] Of course, motivations of national leaders in the postwar period related more directly to the increasing American rapacity for land.

In the first treaty of Jefferson's Administration, the Chickasaw agreed to permit the United States to open a trace through their nation designed to connect Natchez with Nashville. The Indians agreed to "a high way for the citizens of the United States, and the Chickasaws," but they wisely stipulated that "the necessary ferries over the water courses crossed by said road shall be held and deemed to be the property of the Chickasaw nation."[26] Signed on October 24, 1801, at Chickasaw Bluffs overlooking the Mississippi, the brief treaty was negotiated by General James Wilkinson, Benjamin Hawkins, and Andrew Pickens. As customary, it contained a promise that the American government would protect the tribesmen from encroachments by their white neighbors and a profession of friendship. The Chickasaw representatives collectively received goods valued at $700 for the expense and inconvenience of treating with the American commissioners; six of the seventeen principal men and warriors signing for the Chickasaw Nation bore either Scottish, British, or French surnames.

Some two months later downriver at Fort Adams, the same commissioners signed with the Choctaw the second treaty of the Jefferson Administration by which that tribe ceded to the United States over 2.5 million acres in the southwestern corner of the Mississippi Territory. Rather than a diminution of their domain, however, this 1801 treaty merely formalized the lines of demarcation earlier agreed upon by the Choctaw and the British—lines forming the area long known as the Natchez District. In addition, the Treaty of Fort Adams granted the United States the right to open the southern portion of the Natchez Trace through the Choctaw nation. For these concessions Indian signatories received gifts valued at $2,000 "net cost of Philadelphia," plus "three sets of blacksmith's tools."[27]

The long itinerary of Commissioners Wilkinson, Hawkins, and Pickens reveals that conditions in the Old Southwest remained on Jefferson's mind. A few months later they were on the banks of the Oconee River in

Georgia near Fort Wilkinson treating with Creek leaders in the vicinity of present-day Milledgeville. When Georgia ceded its domain between the present state boundary and the Mississippi River in April of 1802, it had extracted a commitment from the Federal government that it would extinguish Indian title to much of the land remaining in western Georgia, particularly the tract between the Oconee and Ocmulgee Rivers. Jefferson took this compact seriously. Hence, in June of 1802, the commissioners bargained for a strip of land along the western bank of the Oconee River.[28] This stream lies to the east of the Ocmulgee and with it forms the Altamaha, which eventually runs into the Atlantic Ocean. Georgia's frontiersmen, particularly the cattle raisers, were quick to press into Creek land. Thus peace as well as national honor was at stake.

From the Oconee, the ubiquitous James Wilkinson made his way westward to the Tombigbee where at Fort Confederation he concluded, this time without the assistance of Hawkins and Pickens, a treaty which formalized the southern Choctaw boundary between the Chickasawhay and Tombigbee Rivers. As in the case at Fort Adams, this line had been "established by and between his Britannic majesty and the said Choctaw nation."[29] The Fort Confederation Treaty in October of 1802 stipulated that this line would form the boundary between the Indian Nation and the expanding republic.

In August of the next year Wilkinson signed another agreement with the Choctaw whereby they ceded over 800,000 acres lying between the Tombigbee and Chickasawhay north of Mobile. This ceremony took place on a bluff known as Hoe Buckintoopa, the site of Fort St. Stephens midway between the thirty-first and thirty-second parallels on the Tombigbee below Fort Confederation. As a consideration, the Choctaw negotiators received "fifteen pieces of strouds [a course woolen blanket], three rifles, one hundred and fifty blankets, two hundred and fifty pounds of powder, two hundred and fifty pounds of lead, one bridle, one man's saddle, and one black silk handkerchief."[30] Rather than a boundary clarification, this treaty involved the first actual diminution of the Choctaw domain at the hands of the Americans.

Since five formidable Indian tribes occupied most of the republic's southwestern quadrant, the War Department could not focus its attention exclusively along foreign borders. Conflict between encroaching frontiersmen had to be minimized and communications with the distant settlements improved. Consequently Jefferson's Administration found itself constantly involved with the Cherokee whose ancestral lands stretched across the mountains and valleys of eastern Tennessee and western North

Carolina. They controlled not only some of the most fertile lands of the great Tennessee Valley but also the most direct routes to the entire region. This Indian nation, like most of the others, was divided into several components. Some of them were Appalachian highlanders whose villages were locked in the vastness of the Great Smoky and Blue Ridge mountain ranges. Others occupied the arable valleys of the numerous creeks and rivers of the Tennessee system. Hence, Cherokee land was the object of constant negotiation.

In late summer of 1804, Thomas Jefferson appointed two master Indian managers and sharp traders as commissioners to seek transfer of Indian lands in eastern Tennessee, northern Georgia, and northern Alabama. Daniel Smith and Return Jonathan Meigs were to pursue, nag, bribe, and cajole the Cherokee relentlessly in season and out. Like Meigs and Smith, the Cherokee chiefs also were canny, if somewhat less skillful, bargainers. In many respects their people had made the greatest advances in adopting the agrarian lifestyle promoted so fervently by Jefferson's policy. No other tribe in the Old Southwest had experienced such constant, mostly hostile, contact with Anglo-Americans.

On October 24, 1804, at the Tellico Garrison in southeast Tennessee, the two commissioners signed a treaty with the Cherokee for the cession of a narrow strip of land in northeastern Georgia known as the Wafford Plantation.[31] The consideration was a one-time payment of $5,000 plus an annuity of $1,000—both to be paid in either merchandise or cash at the option of the Indians. Meigs and Smith had driven an opening wedge, and now other cessions followed in quick order.

Neighbors of the Cherokee in Tennessee and northern Alabama were the Chickasaw who in some areas claimed common land. At a site simply labeled "in the Chickasaw country," commissioners James Robertson and Silas Dinsmoor in late July of 1805 struck a bargain with the Chickasaw for a tadpole-shaped parcel of land extending all the way from the Ohio River down into Alabama. The tail of the tadpole touched the Ohio River near Paducah, Kentucky, and its nose extended just below Huntsville, Alabama. For the cession, the United States paid the nation $20,000 cash—part of which was owed to merchants—and remitted $1000 each to George Colbert and Chief O'Koy, two of the signatories. Chinubee Mingo, listed as king of the Nation in the document, received a lifetime annuity of $100.[32]

The following October at Tellico, Meigs and Smith signed a pair of treaties with the Cherokee—one on the 25th and another on the 27th. In the first, the Cherokee relinquished title to a portion of the lands ceded three months earlier by the Chickasaw, lands to which they also had claimed ownership. They also ceded a large expanse of their lands in the upper Tennessee Valley, while reserving several small tracts for tribal use.[33] In actuality, these reservations were intended for specific individuals, the most notable of them being a chief named Doublehead, who leased or sold land for speculative purposes.[34] (Buried in War Department correspondence files are the details of these enterprising ventures, which reflect the complexity of Indian-white relationships.) This treaty also guaranteed American citizens "free and unmolested use" of proposed roads to Georgia and the Tombigbee settlements. The second of these tandem treaties relinquished title to minute parcels of land on the upper Tennessee River and provided free use of the road from Tellico to Tombigbee.[35]

Constant though the pressure on the Cherokee may have been, in no part of the Old Southwest was there more potential for conflict than in Georgia. Indeed, it is difficult to realize just how close the frontier of that state remained to the seaboard. Frontiersmen on its westernmost fringes, many of them cattle raisers perennially anxious for more grazing room, were as rowdy, voracious, and vociferous as any with whom Jefferson had to deal. Consequently, he gave a lot of thought to their demands, particularly in light of the government's commitment in 1802 to extinguish Indian titles in western Georgia.

The President revealed these thoughts in a remarkably tactful letter to the Creek Indian agent, Benjamin Hawkins, on February 18, 1803. As so many of his letters did, this particular communication illustrates just how small the bureaucracy remained and how intimately Jefferson knew members of his Administration. After sharing the political news with Hawkins, he eased into the subject of Indian relations, repeating his theme of the need for their adoption of agriculture and industry and the resulting uselessness to the Creeks of vast forest areas: "While they are learning to do better on less land, our increasing numbers will be calling for more land, and thus a coincidence of interests will be produced between those who have lands to spare, and want other necessaries, and those who have such necessaries to spare, and want lands."[36]

Unless one remembers Jefferson's fascination with nature, his next analogy will appear bizarre. "The wisdom of the animal which amputates and abandons to the hunter the parts for which he is pursued should be theirs, with this difference, that the former sacrifices what is useful, the latter what is not."[37] (Forests are no longer useful to Indians behind the plow.) Once more, Jefferson repeated that to find happiness the Indians must "intermix" with the Anglo-Americans and "become one people."

Finally, the chief executive revealed the real purpose of his letter when he emphasized, with reference to agrarian cupidity, that "from no quarter is there at present so strong a pressure on this subject as from Georgia for the residue of the fork of the Oconee and Oakmulgee."[38] After a plea for Hawkins to use his influence for the relief of this pressure, Jefferson teased the agent about his gout. "I did not expect that Indian cookery or Indian fare would produce that; but it is considered as a security for good health otherwise."[39]

No doubt the Virginia republican heaved a sigh of relief when finally, late in 1805, his Secretary of the War, Henry Dearborn, signed a treaty with Creek leaders assembled in Washington, D.C. By its terms, the Creeks granted to the United States the long-sought lands between the Oconee and Ocmulgee Rivers as well as the right of American citizens to pass freely along a horse path through the Creek Nation from the Ocmulgee to Mobile. Other clauses dealt with fishing privileges and permission for an American post and trading house. In exchange, the Creek Nation received a $12,000 annuity to be paid in either goods or cash for eight years, after which it would drop to $11,000 for another ten years. In addition, the Federal government was to supply for eight years two blacksmiths and strikers in lieu of previous commitments concerning smiths.[40]

As concerned as Jefferson was over pacification of the Georgia and Tennessee frontiers, he never permitted himself to become distracted from his even greater concern for the security of the western border with European powers. If his policy in the Old Southwest had a central or underlying theme, it was national defense. The republic must be defended.[41] He lectured Congress as well as his own Administrators on the need for "the establishment of a strong front on our western boundary," and he insisted that acquisition of Indian lands bordering the Mississippi River was crucial to achieving that goal.[42] In particular the President desired the Chickasaw and Choctaw lands along the Mississippi, though his eyes were also on territory even farther to the north.

In March of 1805, Secretary Dearborn appointed the famous old Tennessee border soldier and land speculator James Robertson and the New Hampshire Yankee Silas Dinsmoor as special commissioners to treat with the Chickasaw and Choctaw. Although instructed to deal with the problems related to Indian debts to traders, their main objective was procurement of lands along the river. Jefferson was most anxious to acquire the acreage from the mouth of the Big Black northward to the Chickasaw boundary. The desired area included most of today's priceless Yazoo–

Mississippi Delta, land which Henry Dearborn predicted would probably never be inhabited because it was "overflown every year."[43]

Negotiations for the river land began late in the spring of 1805 at Fort St. Stephens above Mobile, and in many respects it must have been one of the most luxurious Indians councils ever held in North America. Silas Dinsmoor had ordered from New Orleans a long list of gourmet foods, premium cigars, fine whiskies, and the best wines. Over to this wilderness fort were carried victuals befitting the table of the most handsome antebellum Natchez mansion. It is difficult to visualize old Watauga Indian fighter James Robertson dining on such delicacies as "anchovies, raisins, almonds, hyson tea, coffee, mustard, preserves, English Cheese, Segars, brandy, wine, etc., etc., etc." The menu so shocked Secretary Dearborn that he expressed his "mortification on the subject" and declared that "such accounts of expenses at an Indian Treaty, have I presume, never before been exhibited to our government and, it is to be wished that we may never have a second exhibition of the kind."[44] No matter how sumptuous the spread may have been, however, the council recessed in failure.

Later that same year—and on a far more austere diet—Dinsmoor and Robertson resumed negotiations at Mount Dexter in the heart of Choctaw country.[45] There, on November 16, 1805, the Choctaw signed a treaty which diminished their domain by over 5 million acres. The Mount Dexter cession was a rectangular strip running some 150 miles along the northern side of the thirty-first parallel from the Natchez District eastward to the highlands between the Tombigbee and Alabama Rivers above Mobile. In exchange, the government paid the Choctaw $50,000 plus an annuity in goods of $3000. Also, three chiefs or Mingoes each received $500 and life-time annuities of $150. Intriguing reservations of 2,560 acres each were set aside for two daughters of former Choctaw agent Samuel Mitchell by Molly, a Choctaw woman, and the United States was requested to recognize the claim of one John M'Grew to a 1,500-acre plot donated to him earlier by the tribe. Another curious provision in the agreement is the payment of $2,500 to John Pitchlynn, a white man, for "certain losses sustained in the Chaktaw country, and as a grateful testimonial of the nation's esteem." Until recently, historians assumed that this amounted to a pay-off to the official interpreter to the tribe for influencing its leaders to dispose of their territory. Now, however, it is known that Pitchlynn did indeed suffer losses at the hands of an alcohol-plying trader who intrigued to have his property blown up.[46] A handsome gentleman known for his ever-pleasant countenance, for a half century John Pitchlynn played an important role among the Indians of the old Southwest. From the negotiation of the Treaty of Hopewell in 1786 until after the signing of the Treaty of Dancing Rabbit Creek in 1830 Pitchlynn was a ubiquitous figure in his role of interpreter. When still a young man, John Pitchlynn had married a Choctaw maiden from an influential family. The best known of his five mixed-blood sons, Peter, later became a chief of the Choctaw and was the delegate to Congress from the Indian Territory.[47]

President Jefferson delayed submission of the Mount Dexter treaty to the Senate for ratification for over two years. Why? The answer probably relates to Jefferson's disappointment that the ceded lands were not along the east bank of the Mississippi, an area that he hoped would soon be sufficiently populated to support an effective militia. Jefferson seemed obsessed with the need for military preparedness along borders shared with European powers.

Of all the Indian treaties signed during Jefferson's Administration, none has received so much scrutiny as this Mount Dexter Treaty. Historians often focus on the fact that $48,000 of the $50,000 paid for the cession actually went to Panton, Leslie, and Company to liquidate a long-standing Choctaw debt to that British trading company which operated out of West Florida. His detractors view this payment to Panton, Leslie as evidence that Jefferson was a heartless land grabber who took advantage of the Indians' inability to cope with the credit system.[48] Actually, Jefferson was extracting the Indians from the clutches of a foreign firm with the hope that henceforth the Choctaw would trade with government factories where profits were marginal and credit was discouraged.

New factories had been established at Fort St. Stephens and at Chickasaw Bluff early in the Administration of Jefferson, who was enthusiastic in his support of that system for several reasons. Not only did it protect the Indians from the rascality of private traders, but more importantly, it effectively promoted his primary goal of civilizing the tribesmen. Having observed the inability of the Indians to cope with the credit system employed by private traders—most notably Panton, Leslie, and Company— the President realistically observed that their inability to handle credit would eventually lead to the dissolution of their empires. Most frequently cited as substantiation of Jefferson's deceitful use of the factory system is his suggestion to William Henry Harrison, Governor of Indiana Territory, that "when these debts get beyond what the individuals can pay, they become willing to lop them off by a cession of lands."[49] Jefferson offered a similar rationale to Congress in his discussion of the need to acquire land along the Mississippi from the Chickasaw.[50]

To suggest that entrapment of the Indians through the factory system was a high priority of Jefferson's is to misread his many letters on Indian relations and the voluminous War Department correspondence outlining his policy. Indeed, the quotations most often cited are extracted from comments primarily discussing defense needs. Besides, he offered ample evidence that government factories protected the Indians from the many abuses of scurrilous traders and hastened the ultimate assimilation of the Indians into American society. His remarks to Harrison more likely were a comment on eventualities rather than an expression of a strategy. More importantly, operation of the factories belies Indian indebtedness as a motivation. Prices were low; so was profit.[51] Tight restrictions on factory capitalization prohibited accumulation of large accounts receivable. Had the factories been part of a land-grabbing scheme, they would have been funded and operated in a different manner.[52]

If Jefferson was a heartless land-grabber eager to take advantage of Choctaw indebtedness to British traders, why did he delay sending the Mount Dexter treaty to the Senate until January of 1808, just three weeks after his message advocating the embargo? The President's sudden request for Senate ratification of the 1805 treaty in the midst of his pursuit of an anti-British foreign policy of "peaceable coercion" unquestionably ties his change in Indian policy to concerns over foreign relations and national security. His words to the Senate leave little doubt.

> Progressive difficulties, however, in our foreign relations, have brought into view considerations other than those which then prevailed. It is now, perhaps, become as interesting to obtain footing for a strong settlement of militias, along our southern frontier, eastward of the Mississippi, as on the west of that river; and more so than higher up the river itself. The consolidation of the Mississippi territory, and the establishing a barrier of separation between the Indians and our southern neighbors, are also important objects.[53]

Here Jefferson was introducing the concept of defensive settlement, reminiscent of Spain's colonial borderland concept. An interesting question is raised by Jefferson's reference to Panton, Leslie as "certain mercantile characters" in his Senate message. Considering his anti-mercantilistic bias and colloquialistic use of the term *character*, that may have been a mild denigration. If so, his language weakens the argument that indebtedness of the Indians was the motivation for support of the factory system.[54]

All quarters of the Old Southwest demanded attention, but Jefferson focused his main attention on the security of the national borders along the Mississippi River and the Florida boundary. Less than two months after the Mount Dexter ceremony, for instance, Secretary Dearborn affixed his signature on January 7, 1806, to a treaty with the Cherokee in Washington.[55] There, tribal representatives relinquished title to lands lying north of the Tennessee and south of the Duck River, the eastern portion of which had already been ceded by the Chickasaw in the July 23, 1805, treaty mentioned above. It is doubtful whether or not the Cherokee believed they actually had a valid claim to all of this land for which they received $2,000 in cash plus a four-year annuity of $2,000. Perhaps both sides looked upon this payment partly as a bribe to secure agreement to the Cherokee–Chickasaw boundary south of the Tennessee River specified therein. As did so many of the Jeffersonian treaties, this one stipulated gifts to the Nation which would enhance the civilization process. In this case, the United States agreed to construct for the Cherokee a gristmill and a "machine for cleaning cotton." In an elucidation of this treaty the cession was enlarged to include a tract along the Elk River in order to include some 200 squatter families already settled there.[56]

While most of the Jeffersonian treaties in the Old Southwest follow a well-defined pattern, the special convention signed with the Cherokee in December of 1807 provides an interesting exception. This Hiwassee cession made one of the few allusions to mineral deposits. In exchange for $5,000 and 1,000 bushels of corn, the Cherokee ceded a six-mile-square tract at the mouth of Chickamauga Creek in the extreme northwestern corner of Georgia. The land was to be used for the establishment of an iron works to exploit the surrounding ore beds.

Not until after the Creek War in 1814 would another treaty be struck with Indians in the Old Southwest. Indeed, in the entire United States, only nine were concluded during this period. The perils to American neutrality during the Napoleonic struggles and the subsequent prosecution of the War of 1812 consumed every ounce of Jefferson's energy, and his successor's, James Madison, as well. Indeed, events in the early years of Madison's Administration vindicated Jefferson's concern for national security.

3

A Perimeter of Conflict

During the first decade of the nineteenth century, peace and conflict hung in delicate balance along the sprawling Gulf Coast perimeter, which extended from Pensacola to New Orleans and up the Mississippi past Baton Rouge to Natchez, and up the Tombigbee to Fort St. Stephens. In addition to Indian problems, the region was caught up in an intricate web of international politics, border tensions, United States domestic pressures, and human chicanery. Most aspects of the conflict related in some way to the southern boundary between the United States and Spanish West Florida, which had been established at the thirty-first parallel by the Treaty of San Lorenzo in 1795. This line, however, neither followed a natural topographical boundary nor did it logically divide populations of Native Americans and whites. Since the Treaty of San Lorenzo set Florida's western boundary at the Mississippi, and since several other navigable rivers flowed southward across the thirty-first parallel through West Florida into the Gulf of Mexico, the right of free navigation and deposit produced interminable and often bitter disputes between the two nations. Akin to these difficulties and closely related to previously discussed Indian problems was the widespread American concern for national security. For these and other reasons, it took immense diplomatic energy to settle the ticklish issues on which hinged the peace and prosperity of the Old Southwest.

If one places the history of Europe in juxtaposition to that of the Old Southwest, there is nothing unusual in the fact that the five major rivers which flowed southward in watery parallels to the Gulf of Mexico were a primary source of conflict. Even so, few rivers of the Old World generated so much upstream economic and trading pressure as did the Mississippi and Tombigbee–Alabama systems whose estuaries lay in Spanish Florida.

41

Since the economic weight of the central part of the continent bore down upon them, the President, Congress, and the Spanish officials as well, felt considerable political pressure to open these two gigantic waterways even more freely to commercial intercourse than the terms of Pinckney's treaty seemed to guarantee. Residents upstream from Mobile particularly objected to the fact that the treaty failed to guarantee free navigation of the rivers flowing into Mobile Bay or the right of deposit in Mobile.[1]

The United States was determined to view these rivers as international waterways. Secretary of War Henry Dearborn indicated as much when he wrote General James Wilkinson, September 14, 1802.

> When you go to New Orleans it may not be improper to mention our intentions of establishing a Trading House on the Tombigby, with a view of sounding the present feelings of the Government [Spain] on the subject of our navigating the Mobile. It should be taken for granted that those rivers which empty themselves out of the U. States into the ocean through a small part of the Spanish Territory, are common highways but should be used in such a manner as not to injure our neighbours.[2]

Dearborn was cognizant of the American diplomatic efforts in Spain and France to open the rivers of Spanish West Florida to free navigation by settlers north of the thirty-first parallel. In addition, the machinations in Europe caused by Napoleon's designs for Louisiana weighed heavily on the minds of Jefferson and his Cabinet members. In this light, Dearborn's comment was restrained. The "Mississippi question" had been a thorny one since Spain originally had closed that river to free navigation in 1784. American officials had thought they resolved it with Pinckney's popular Treaty of San Lorenzo in 1795.[3]

To reiterate a point stressed in the preceding chapter, President Jefferson was equally concerned with the related issue of national security. The Choctaw and Creek Indian frontier along the lengthy West Florida boundary provided easy access to unlicensed traders and other troublemakers, and a similar danger was posed by the international border along the Mississippi. His request in 1807 for ratification of the Treaty of Mount Dexter had the important purpose of moving the Indians back from international boundaries and from direct contact with foreign powers. Henry Dearborn wrote James Wilkinson on this subject as early as February 21, 1803, saying that he believed the Choctaw in the lower towns would be willing to part with their lands located so strategically between the Tombigbee and Alabama Rivers.[4] While the Choctaw had transferred title to land along the thirty-first parallel at Mount Dexter, Jefferson clearly had designs as well on their lands along the Mississippi.

Early in Jefferson's Administration, Congress favored a policy designed to protect the nation's western empire from international intervention—a policy most effectively manifested through control of the Indian trade. The Intercourse Act of 1802, which served as the basic law governing Indian relations until 1834, restated the temporary laws of 1796 and 1799.[5] Not only did the 1802 act prohibit foreigners from trading on American soil, but also it authorized the use of military force in the seizure of foreign trade goods and of items such as peltry which had been exchanged illicitly. Within a month after passage of the Intercourse Act, Silas Dinsmoor was appointed Choctaw Indian Agent, succeeding John McKee whose responsibilities as a subordinate to Benjamin Hawkins had never been defined. The detailed instructions of the Secretary of War to the new agent reflected the Administration's intentions to monitor closely Indian affairs on the border and to generally tighten the chain of command. Dinsmoor was instructed to prohibit persons from entering Choctaw country without a pass, keep squatters out, maintain vigilance against meddling foreign agents, and communicate when appropriate with Benjamin Hawkins, agent to the Creeks, who then also served as "principal Temporary Agent for Indian affairs south of the Ohio."[6]

Conditions under which frontier diplomats negotiated land-cession treaties with Indian tribes contrasted sharply with those encountered by more sophisticated diplomats abroad who dealt with issues of southwestern boundaries, territorial possessions, and trade rights. Though both groups sought the common objective of secure borders, peace was not so readily obtainable. Socially, politically, and economically, the boundary drawn at San Lorenzo in 1795 was unrealistic. Because of past shiftings of international occupants and claimants to the country east of the Mississippi and immediately north of the Gulf of Mexico, settlements had neither established nor precisely recognized international delineations. After 1783 when an official boundary was proposed it arbitrarily cut through social and national allegiances, homesteads, and political attachments—facts which created constant friction. Also, the physical nature of the region invited filibusters and adventurers to stir up troubles. Indeed, until 1810 the thirty-first parallel remained more a line of contention than of clarification.

The lack of tranquility along this border must be seen, however, in light of the heterogeneity of the inhabitants. From the first appearance of Anglo-Americans above the thirty-first parallel, a dichotomy between the eastern and western regions of the Mississippi Territory emerged. During the colonial and early national periods along the Atlantic Seaboard, antipathies often developed between the frontier, or western, regions and the older, or eastern, regions. In the Mississippi Territory, however, directions were reversed. On the western edge of this frontier zone sat Natchez—comparable, on a smaller scale, to Boston, New York, Williamsburg, or Charleston—while the newer, more isolated frontier later appeared along its more eastern river valleys. By the time Commissioner Andrew Ellicott ran the line separating West Florida from Mississippi Territory, a third cluster of largely Anglo-American settlers lived just south of it in an area known as Feliciana. Actually, a trichotomy rather than a dichotomy had developed—namely, the Natchez District, Feliciana (below the thirty-first parallel just south of the Natchez District), and the Tombigbee settlements above Mobile. The turbulence that eventually evolved into a rebellion against the Spanish must be traced in a "particular" rather than in a "linear" manner. In other words, unrest in the east was not always a continuation of or even related to that in the west. Indeed, the roots of dissension above the thirty-first parallel north of Mobile differed from those to the west in the vicinity of Baton Rouge.

Consider the contrast between conditions in Natchez and those in the Tombigbee region. Life in Natchez, and in Washington six miles away, was relatively urban, sophisticated, and cosmopolitan compared with that in the scattered settlements in the river valleys above Mobile. Squatters along the Tombigbee lived equidistant from Georgia and Natchez and they more closely resembled the stereotypical frontiersmen than did most residents of the Natchez District. In addition to sectional differences, after the Treaty of San Lorenzo in 1795, the Tombigbee settlers continued to have serious grievances against the Spanish authorities who persisted in taxing their commerce. To the frontiersmen above Mobile, the "Tombigbee question" loomed as large as the "Mississippi question" and both led to the Louisiana Purchase. Hence, for an assortment of sometimes unrelated and sometimes interrelated reasons, the thirty-first parallel constituted a large segment of the perimeter of conflict.

Casting a much longer shadow than that of a casual, international, political good neighbor, the United States actually exercised an enormous influence in West Florida with respect to such matters as Indian affairs, river trade, border transgressions, and the presence of the Federal author-

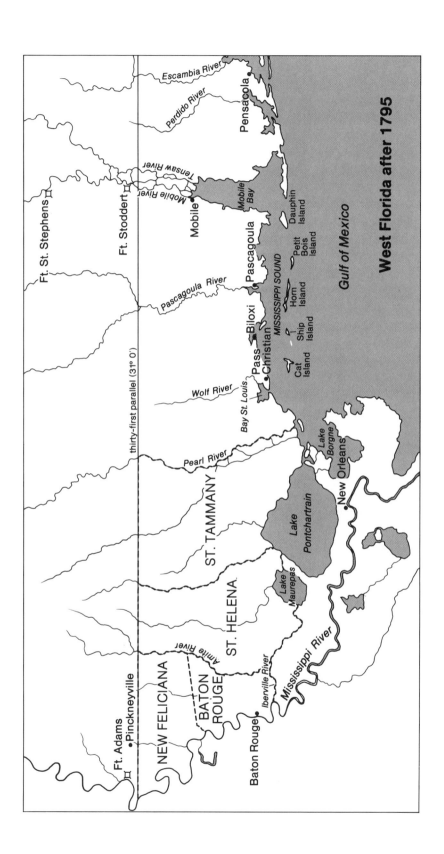

West Florida after 1795

ity in the Orleans and Mississippi territories. A highly confused but important issue was that of clarifying the eastern boundaries of the Louisiana Purchase, an issue which deeply involved West Florida and which remained unsettled until the Adams-Onís treaty of 1819.[7] Residents of the Old Southwest never wavered in their contention that the Louisiana Purchase included West Florida as far to the east as the Perdido River. Annexation of that part of West Florida was not to be accomplished without the generation of endless rumors, anxieties, administrative ineptness on both sides of the border, international complications involving four nations, individual opportunism, and out-and-out freebooting.[8] After the congressional prohibition of the international slave trade became effective in 1808, the smuggling of slaves through Florida into the United States became another factor adding to the tension along the border.

The most dramatic of the transborder incidents affecting this part of the frontier were those centering on the attempted development of a block of land in Feliciana owned by United States Senator John Smith, a prominent Cincinnati merchant and land speculator. Smith's holdings were located just south of the Spanish-American border along the Mississippi. There he proposed to organize and promote among Americans a village to be called New Valentia. To carry out his plans he sent three Kemper brothers to the area as his representatives. Reuben, Samuel, and Nathan Kemper were sons of a Baptist preacher from Fauquier County, Virginia. Like so many of their Old Dominion neighbors, they had followed the westward movement of population into the Ohio Valley where they had become associated with Senator Smith. Once in New Valentia, however, the Kempers proved to be highly untrustworthy, and Senator Smith was soon of the opinion that their management was unprofitable, due in all probability to their gross maladministration of his affairs. After referring their wrongdoings to a committee of neighbors, he secured a judgment against them and forcibly removed the defalcating agents from his Bayou Sara property in June of 1804.[9]

The Kempers then settled in Mississippi Territory near Pinckneyville, a hamlet sitting almost astride the international boundary. In August of 1804, there occurred the first of several Kemper-inspired raids into Spanish territory. An altercation had occurred in June between *Alcalde* Alexander Sterling and Nathan Kemper in the vicinity of Bayou Sara, followed by several skirmishes between militia patrols and border rowdies. In retaliation, Nathan and Samuel Kemper and a party of some thirty armed ruffians crossed the border, captured several local officials, burned a home and a cotton gin, and marched to Baton Rouge shouting for Floridian freedom. Unsuccessful in its efforts to capture Carlos de Grand-Pré, commanding officer at Baton Rouge, the band retreated to the environs of Bayou Sara where it continued to maraud on both sides of the line. Grand-Pré soon marshaled sufficient volunteers, however, to contain the rebels for the time being.[10]

The motivation of the Kempers undoubtedly was complex, and its exact nature may never be determined. It is likely, however, that they were pawns of a sort—not innocent ones, to be sure, but pawns nevertheless. Just as the Kempers were agents of speculator Senator John Smith so they may also have been agents of Virginia emigrant Edward Randolph of Pinckneyville and his partner, an influential New Orleans merchant named Daniel Clark. After all, during the August raid, the Kemper company carried Randolph's proclamation of Floridian independence and a banner of seven white and blue stripes with two white stars in a field of red.[11] While the symbolism of the American colors of red, white, and blue is obvious, the reasons for seven stripes and two stars remain to be explained. The presence, however, of such a sophisticated flag clearly indicates the intentions of the Kempers and their cohorts to establish an insurrectionary government.

This early siege of the Spanish seat on the Mississippi at Baton Rouge failed, but it stirred further enmity between the officials of the Spanish province and those of the Orleans and Mississippi territories. The Spanish contended that the raid, if not actually instigated by, at least had been encouraged by Mississippi territorial officials, who then found ample reasons for not extraditing the offenders. His Catholic Majesty's officers tightened security and sought assistance from their faltering home government. They recognized the grave danger that an incident of this sort might touch off an attack upon Spanish officials by western frontiersmen, especially by the Tennessee and Kentucky farmers and boatmen who felt harassed by Spanish interference with their use of New Orleans harbor.[12]

Though he attempted to display only minor concern over the Kemper affair, Governor W. C. C. Claiborne revealed his uneasiness to President Jefferson. He admitted that there were many Frenchmen "who encourage discontents, and who derive assistance from the Spanish Agents" and observed that the Louisianians were an "amiable" though "credulous" people.[13] Nevertheless, he promised that "Public' tranquil'ity here will be preserved." Despite Claiborne's pessimism over the possibility of lengthy negotiations with Spain, the President found his assurances comforting. Claiborne went on to write:

> But if a Rupture should unfortunately ensue, I believe our Government will find her Citizens united, and she may confidently rely upon the prompt and persevering efforts of the Western People to support the claims and maintain the Glory of our Country.—
> I speak of the Western *people* more particularly, because in the event of a War with Spain, *they* would probably be the first called upon to act.—
> I find Kemper's Riot, for it cannot fairly be called an Insurrection, is viewed to the northward, as an important Affair, and that it has been used by the Spanish Minister among others, as a pretext for calumniating our administration.[14]

The governor stressed that he had assured local Spanish officials that the American government had not encouraged Kemper and that his personal desire was "to see the United States at Peace with all the World." Claiborne may have been sincere in *his* pacifist declaration, but a large segment of Americans along the border were anxious to see American dominion over West Florida.

A second dramatic episode involving the Kempers occurred on the night of September 3, 1805, apparently with Spanish cooperation. A party of twelve whites and seven Negro slaves from below the line broke into the Kemper Tavern near Pinckneyville and seized Reuben Kemper while he was asleep. Nathan also was abducted from his bedroom and his wife was threatened with death. In a like manner Samuel Kemper fell captive to other raiders, and the three prisoners were bound, dragged across the border, and turned over to Captain Solomon Alston, leader of a Spanish detachment. En route down the Mississippi to Baton Rouge, Captain Alston and his crew allowed the pirogue bearing the prisoners to drift too close to the river bank, and the Kempers shouted word of their plight to an American patrol which immediately seized the boat and its occupants. The Spanish soldiers were briefly detained at Fort Adams, and the Kempers were sent up to the territorial capital in Washington. There Judge Thomas Rodney placed the Kempers under a peace bond, but he refused to extradite them on the ground that the Spanish had illegally abducted them.[15] Though Mississippi's territorial governor alerted the entire militia and ordered two companies to patrol the border of West Florida, a brief interlude of calm settled over the southwestern corner of the Old Southwest.

The tranquility was short-lived, however. The escapades of the Kempers and others revealed that the population on the east bank of the Mississippi River was in a state of unrest, if not in actual rebellion against the

Spanish rule. In 1805 the two governments realized that it would take no more than a minor incident to touch off the aggressive wrath of the Kentuckians, Tennesseans, and their Ohio Valley neighbors—not to mention the Mississippians—against Spanish control of the lower Mississippi.[16] Both sides constantly were placed in awkward relationships by the border disturbances along the thirty-first parallel and in Louisiana. There, after the transition to American dominion, troubles developed involving escaped and stolen slaves and incitement of Indians. Though tangential to the West Florida controversy, such incidents in the newly acquired Louisiana Territory and the eastern fringes of Texas must have frayed further the nerves of all concerned and thus added to international tensions.[17] Border eruptions would have evoked greater response had Spain not been so preoccupied with the Napoleonic struggles which threatened her very existence.

Originally settled by a small number of Frenchmen, the population of West Florida by this time was overwhelmingly Scotch and English. Nevertheless, the West Floridians were a heterogeneous people who had immigrated for a variety of political, social, and economic reasons over a period of several decades. Residents included the old Tories who had fled to the region during the American Revolution in order to avoid persecution at the hands of patriots, early settlers who had followed the natural drift of the rivers from Kentucky and West Tennessee to settle there, and land-hungry immigrants only recently arrived in the country.[18] It may also have been true, as some claimed, that there was a generous sprinkling of "banditti" among the settlers. Whatever their time and place of origin or moral character, all these groups had specific economic interests in the land and river trade and in the possession of slaves under the most casual domestic laws. To date they had developed no unified political philosophy. Nevertheless, any threat from the outside, or inside for that matter, to their perceived self-interests aroused an almost militant response.[19] Interestingly, royal policy precluded any significant migration of Spanish subjects into the area.

Clear indication of the depth of the turmoil in West Florida was the issuance by Governor Claiborne on December 16, 1806, of a stern proclamation against filibusters and their attempts to usurp the authority of either the United States or Spain. Claiborne cited the United States law against treason, a crime punishable by death, and proclaimed that anybody convicted of usurping the powers of Spain in West Florida faced imprisonment and a fine not to exceed $3,000.[20] These laws, however, did not deter rebellious persons within the Mississippi and Orleans Territories from fomenting political change, if not outright revolution, on the Spanish side of the border.

One of the major reasons for the complexity of the situation in the Old Southwest was the ubiquitous presence of James Wilkinson. Wilkinson participated constantly in both the making and the execution of United States policies. Yet he kept a foot in both national camps, wearing the uniform of an American commanding general while on the Spanish payroll. Of course his meddling hand was felt in the West Florida controversy. At one point he recommended to Governor Vicente Folch that he protest a presidential claim to West Florida.[21] It would be impossible to assess fully the mischief against the United States done by this wily officer, partly because much of what he did and said was cast in terms of implications and innuendoes.[22] Wilkinson's name appears thousands upon thousands of times on manuscripts in the Departments of War and State as well as in documents in state repositories, not to mention the Archives of the Indies in Seville.

At the turn of the century, West Florida provided the kind of milieu in which Wilkinson, the Kempers, and other schemers could operate most successfully. None of them worked alone. In New Orleans, for instance, the influential Daniel Clark, former U.S. Consul, was an old master at manipulating coastal and river affairs. His intimacy with Burr, his speculation in land in West Florida, and his reputation as an Anglophile caused the Spanish to view Clark with suspicion. Later, he published an extensive revelation of the questionable activities of Wilkinson and other officials of the region.[23]

Given all these crosscurrents and turbulences, at best Spain's hold on West Florida after 1803 was tenuous. Her administration suffered from a lack of a Spanish population, a shortage of supplies, inadequate financial support, friction among Spanish provincial officials, French interference, and tremendous pressures exerted by American filibusters. From the consummation of the Louisiana Purchase until the American flag was hoisted over Fort Charlotte in Mobile on April 15, 1813, by Wilkinson's forces, this region was the constant scene of border disturbances.[24] Meanwhile, the rising potential of American assumption of authority increased annually. After 1808 various assemblies took place in the Bayou Sara and Baton Rouge vicinities, ostensibly for the purposes of strengthening Spanish rule and addressing economic problems. These meetings, however, proved to be separation conventions.[25]

Meanwhile, above the thirty-first parallel in the Mississippi Territory, another political drama was unfolding. There, impatient and apprehensive petitioners representing widely separated settlements with differing motivations clamored for Congress to create two states out of the huge territory. Though territorial residents living on both sides of the Pearl River sought annexation of West Florida, they in fact represented rival—when not hostile—sectional factions. In a masterfully composed petition of November 11, 1809, settlers east of the Pearl, who were primarily clustered north of Mobile, sought resolution of their long-suffered abuses by creation of a separate state combining the eastern half of Mississippi Territory with the above-mentioned portion of West Florida. The existing territory, they argued, was "already too unwieldy for the purposes of good government" and "one half of West Florida naturally belongs to the District East of Pearl river, and can never conveniently be united with any other Territory."[26]

A veritable litany of grievances, loyalties, and proposals, this petition from settlers east of the Pearl beautifully illustrated the sectional rivalry between the Tombigbee settlements and those in the Natchez District. Petitioners along the Tombigbee spoke, for example, of their need for protection against "the plundering spirit of the savages" and the "artful machinations or daring outrages of the worthless & proscribed citizens of other states." In sum, the Bigbee settlers viewed themselves as "an unrepresented portion of the American nation" suffering under "a heavy burthen of foreign oppression," a reference to taxes on commerce extracted by the Spanish estimated at 24 percent. In a powerful interrogatory, the petitioners asked:

> —Are we Americans or Spaniards?—Shall we support the Republic of the United States, or the Spanish Monarchy?—Our principles,—our habits,—our affections,—our hearts, drive us to you,—but you,—shall we say it,—dare we pronounce the dreadful curse,—drive us back again to the Spaniards!—No: you do not:—we will not believe it:—we will not indulge the idea that we pay taxes to an European Monarchy.[27]

After reciting some taunting observations of attitudes of the neighboring Creeks toward apparent American weakness, the petitioners closed with a statement of great confidence that relief would be forthcoming.

In a relatively brief petition some two years later, 250 residents of Mississippi Territory who lived west of the Pearl asked Congress to create a state by attaching West Florida to the Mississippi Territory. After pointing out that the combined populations would meet requirements for the granting of statehood, the petitioners reasoned as follows:

> The people of W. F. are all Americans by birth and we believe in principle. Their political sentiments are republican and their political creed, the Federal constitution.
>
> The sameness of our local interests is also an argument in favor of the coallition. The productions of the soil are the same and the pursuits of the inhabitants similar. Nearly all the navigable streams whose sources are in the Miss. Ter. pass through Florida and either discharge themselves into Lake Ponchartrain, or into the Mississippi—hence it follows that if the two territories were united all our produce &c would concentre in our own ports.[28]

Despite their sectional differences, it is evident that these rival factions within the territory recognized that West Florida naturally complemented Mississippi Territory.

Back of this claim of communality were many complicated factors. Even after the Louisiana Purchase from Napoleon, both Spanish and American interests in West Florida felt threatened by French and British invasions. The European wars preyed on their minds, and the reign of Napoleon's brother, Joseph Bonaparte, on the Spanish throne from 1808 to 1814 created considerable confusion in West Florida as it did throughout the empire. For several years preceding the Baton Rouge Rebellion, it became a distinct political liability in West Florida for a Spanish official to have anything to do with a Frenchman in fear that he might be an "agent." Carlos de Grand-Pré learned this hard lesson in 1808. In July of that year he entertained the unprincipled opportunist Octaviano Davilmar, a French filibuster and adventurer who had entered West Florida under the pretension of trade. When the visitor moved on to Texas, Grand-Pré permitted him to leave a trunk behind in storage. In these times, an aura of distrust and suspicion hung over the the District of Baton Rouge. Grand-Pré, the chief Spanish official there, was suspect among his superiors, and he was fearful—rightfully so—of the activities in Feliciana above Baton Rouge. The presence of the trunk created suspicion of Grand-Pré's disloyalty, and prior to his departure from Baton Rouge, he was forced to open the trunk in the presence of his successor, Carlos Dehault de Lassus. It contained nothing more harmful than some French uniforms and books, unless a copy of Machiavelli's *Prince* be considered seditious. Grand-Pré's innocent association with Davilmar and the storage of the trunk contributed to Grand-Pré's recall and perhaps hastened his death.[29]

Grand-Pré's administration had been far too mild to strengthen Spanish rule of West Florida, but he had had little choice. He was generally popular with the non-Spanish inhabitants, a popularity that his successor Carlos Dehault de Lassus never enjoyed. De Lassus, viewed as too officious by many residents, became commandant at Baton Rouge late in 1808 at a moment when the American commercial embargo against England and France was having its most stringent effects. Anglo-American farmers and merchants, who constituted an overwhelming majority of the West Florida population, were hard pressed by Jefferson's embargo which had closed the port of New Orleans. Indeed, the American policy of "peaceable coercion" severely curtailed commerce on both sides of the border, and British agents tempted businessmen from Mississippi Territory as well as West Florida to engage in illicit trade through various ports along the Gulf.[30]

For West Florida the die was cast by 1808. Spain's fight for independence from French occupation plus the effort to oust Joseph Bonaparte absorbed all of her military and economic resources. Spain could not spare even one additional soldier for West Florida. Certainly along the eastern Gulf coast of North America she was too weak to contest the gathering forces of self-government among its constituents. The assemblies mentioned earlier were attended by selected representatives and syndics from the various jurisdictions in the Grand-Pré–De Lassus era. These meetings were conducted more within the context of American republicanism than under the colonial rule of the faltering Spanish Empire.[31]

The Spanish colonial system, based on a centralized enlightened despotism, stifled the development of local political leadership. Even so, under Carlos de Grand-Pré, and subsequently Carlos Dehault de Lassus, the internal pressures of Spanish rule were fairly light and casual. The purchase of Louisiana with its international tensions and changes had a radical effect on that part of West Florida immediately along the east bank of the Mississippi. With the expansion of America's official influence in Orleans Territory there quickly emerged in West Florida the federalistic force of the so-called Insurgency Convention. Some fourteen men who represented four divisions in the Baton Rouge district first assembled in late July of 1810. Although the convention maintained an outward appearance of support for Spanish authority, it was organizing a revolt.[32]

In Baton Rouge during the summer of 1810 Carlos Dehault de Lassus and lesser officials were in a state of administrative paralysis. They lacked supplies, troops, and money, and were without local political understanding or support. The territory west of the Pearl also was rapidly approaching an island status with the move to organize the State of Louisiana. Never short of gossip, West Florida by 1810 had become a veritable rumor mill. Nevertheless, some of the rumors were well founded. Spain's inability to defend Baton Rouge, for instance, was an obvious fact. The fort overlooking the river stood in disrepair with an almost nonexistent garrison manning it. Nor did De Lassus expect support from Pensacola, Havana, Mexico, or Madrid. The convention, meanwhile, had met a second time in mid-August and by the twenty-fifth had adopted a lengthy "Ordinance Providing for the Public Safety and for the Better Administration of Justice within the Jurisdiction of Baton-Rouge" to which De Lassus affixed his signature of approval. He would not, however, agree to the appointment of Fulwar Skipwith to the supreme court nor that of Philemon Thomas as brigadier general of the militia.[33]

Why the insurgents put down their pens and took up arms may never be known. Was De Lassus stalling for time? Were Spanish reinforcements en route from Pensacola? Were American Tories actually marching down river to thwart republicanism? These were only some of the rumors. Whatever the reasons, in the early hours of the morning on September 23, 1810, a group of Floridians forcibly seized His Catholic Majesty's fortress at Baton Rouge. Accounts of the attack vary. The most interesting account attributes the lack of American casualties to the craftiness of an illiterate Kentuckian, Larry Moore, who led mounted troops through a tiny opening on the back side of the fort used by the cattle to reach their pasture. It took little effort for the cavalrymen to overpower the defenders and open the main gates. Ironically, one of the few Spanish casualties was Luis de Grand–Pré, eldest son of the former governor, who sacrificed his life in a display of bravado, which he evidently felt was expected of him.[34] After hoisting the Lone Star Flag, the jubilant Floridians dragged the red and yellow Spanish banner through the streets and confined De Lassus to house arrest.

Just thirty-four days later, President James Madison proclaimed American dominion over West Florida, and without delay Governor Claiborne occupied Baton Rouge and prepared to annex the region to Orleans Territory. In his October 27 proclamation, Madison reiterated American claims to West Florida as part of the Louisiana Purchase, explained that acquiescence to "temporary continuance" of Spanish authority was not an abandonment of our claim, and admitted that "a satisfactory adjustment" had been "too long delayed."[35] Moreover, he continued:

A failure of the United States to take the said territory into its possession may lead to events ultimately contravening the views of both parties, whilst in the meantime the tranquillity and security of our adjoining territories are endangered and new facilities given to violations of our revenue and commercial laws and of those prohibiting the introduction of slaves.[36]

Since inaction might be construed as a dereliction of title, the President ordered possession taken of the disputed territory with the understanding that "it will not cease to be a subject of fair and friendly negotiation and adjustment."

The revolt at Baton Rouge placed Floridians west of the Perdido in a state of governmental limbo, exposing the defenseless coastal settlements to considerable jeopardy. Governor Folch at Mobile faced demands which he could not meet; the insurgents, or conventioneers, strove to stabilize their local governing authority. Protection of lives and property—especially a wide diversity of land titles—and establishment of relations with the United States were their first priorities. In Washington, D.C., American officials faced a diplomatic and political dilemma. Among the unresolved questions were the boundaries of Orleans Territory, the creation of the State of Louisiana, the approaching crisis with Great Britain, the dissipating French influence in the territory, tightening controls on the sprawling Indian frontier, and surveillance of the slave population on both sides of the border. Most vital of all was the development of a policy dealing with the West Florida Convention forces without incurring Spanish and British accusations of American intervention.

Though the Baton Rouge rebels and their supporters generally favored annexation to the United States, there were several problems connected with such a move—many of which demanded immediate resolution. The most pressing needs were for a sufficient supply of money, the establishment of credit, and organization of local government. West Florida was an open door to the lawless, if not to the outright banditti, and to all sorts of adventurers who sought to skirt the law for selfish purposes. In November of 1810 an embryonic republic was organized in Baton Rouge. Fulmer Skipwith, who had lost a fortune speculating in France and who was a friend of James Monroe, was chosen governor, and a two-house legislative assembly was organized.[37] It was obvious that this temporary government looked to Washington for guidance while it wrestled with the multiplying internal problems. In addition, the West Florida issue created a considerable amount of friction between the rival governors of Mississippi and Orleans territories.[38]

Not all the contention in West Florida centered on Baton Rouge, however. Two hundred miles to the east, strong discontent had fermented for over a decade. Serious trouble had begun in 1799, after the Spanish commander at Fort St. Stephens had ceremoniously surrendered his keys to a mixed-blood Tombigbee resident named Richard Brashears.[39] Even though the Spaniards had evacuated this portion of the land north of the thirty-first parallel as stipulated in the treaty of San Lorenzo, her officials continued to control Mobile. As early as 1800, they began to impose tariffs on shipments across the thirty-first parallel—in the minds of Americans an outrage which annually grew more grievous. Though imposition of duties by officials of His Catholic Majesty remained at the core of their disaffection, it was exacerbated by numerous other problems, including location of the Choctaw factory at St. Stephens, unresolved land claims, rustling of cattle, illicit slave trade, and various unsavory border incidents. Such conditions, for example, led Aaron Burr to believe that he would be well received in the Bigbee country subsequent to his escape from authorities in the Natchez District. There Burr was recaptured, and from there he was escorted to Richmond to answer to the charge of treason. Here the name of the ubiquitous Reuben Kemper—whose civil loyalties were as fluid as Pearl River swamp water—surfaced once again.

It was against this background that Spanish officials in June of 1810 expressed their alarm to Colonel Richard Sparks, commander of Fort Stoddert, after learning of the organization by some Anglo-Americans of a society known as the "Expedition of Mobile" which planned to capture Mobile and destroy its house of commerce.[40] Named as its leader was Joseph P. Kennedy, vociferous leader of the local bar. Without delay, Sparks notified Secretary of War William Eustis of this, explaining that he had tried to placate the Spaniards with assurances that it was not the policy of the United States to act unjustly toward other nations. He informed Secretary Eustis that indeed a powerful combination was being formed to proceed against Mobile and possibly Pensacola. In addition, rumors had reached him of a plan to seize the army post at Fort Stoddert with its supply of ammunition. Recent harsh treatment by Spanish officials of Kentucky and West Tennessee emigrants entering the Tombigbee country by way of Mobile had greatly excited discontent. Sparks reiterated the continuing unhappiness over high Spanish duties, an unhappiness intensified by the sight of Indians freely trading up and down the rivers. The commander closed with a plea for reinforcements, explaining that "Deaths, Desertions, and Discharges, will soon leave me almost without men."[41] In a postscript as fascinating as it is lengthy, Sparks offered a character sketch of Joseph P. Kennedy. In part he warned, "He is a young man, educated in the Eastern States, ambitious, and intriguing, and popular; and although without *real* talents, yet in a seditious intrigue, or for the low arts that secure popularity, he must be acknowledged eminent."[42]

In a letter of twenty-four lengthy paragraphs to President Madison, territorial Judge Harry Toulmin corroborated Colonel Sparks' appraisal of the situation above Mobile. In addition to the role of Kennedy, Toulmin mentioned the leadership of the brothers James and John Caller.[43] Meanwhile, on July 31, 1810, David Holmes, Governor of Mississippi Territory, wrote to James Caller, requesting him to reconsider his resignation as Sixth Territorial Regiment commander and imploring him not to participate in "lawless aggressions upon the adjacent Province of West Florida." Such an attempt, warned Holmes, "would ruin the individuals who might engage in it—injure the reputation of the country, and be productive of much mischief."[44] So concerned was Holmes that he wrote Toulmin a series of letters urging him to impress upon the Bigbee residents the dangers to their nation of an expedition against Mobile.[45]

Not all the disturbance was confined to one side of the eastern border. When Governor Vicente Folch gathered Choctaw Indians from the Six Towns to defend Mobile against the anticipated Tombigbee raiders, Governor Holmes protested. He emphatically stated that Indians residing within the United States national borders were under government protection and in return they owed it their allegiance. Indian relations were tender matters about which Americans were most apprehensive, particularly if they suspected interference by an outside power. Consequently, Governor Holmes expressed to Folch the belief that on sober reflection the Spanish officials would forgo any plans to form an alliance with the Choctaw.[46]

Rumors of an impending foray by the settlers of Washington County against Mobile became so prevalent that Governor Holmes in September of 1810 requested Judge Harry Toulmin to persuade the leading citizens to halt such action. He also wrote to James Caller, Joseph Carson, and James Patton, regimental militia leaders, in the same vein. Holmes believed that their direct action would sacrifice the sanctity of the Constitution and "would have a tendency to retard rather than to facilitate the object of their wishes."[47] Holmes had reason to hope that Congress at its next session would consider the matter and effect a happy termination of the issue. Therefore the governor admonished that parties to aggression would "hazard both their fortunes and reputations," and he pleaded with them to aid in suppression of such "delusions." Governor Holmes's warning reflected fears of the Federal administration that overt action against the Spanish might provoke British intervention on the Gulf Coast. Even had relations between England and the United States not been so strained, American officials realized only too well that British—not Spanish—traders conducted commerce from West Florida with Choctaw and Creek Indians and that England had a keen interest in the maintenance of the *status quo* south of the thirty-first parallel.

Judge Toulmin, a prolific writer, kept the President informed through frequent and voluminous letters and, at the same time, tried earnestly to frustrate the efforts of the "Expedition of Mobile" as Holmes had urged. The judge's correspondence indicates that he busied himself with tours on both sides of the border as well as with quill and ink. His forceful communiqué to the militia captains of Washington County—the southeasternmost in Mississippi Territory—echoed the stern warnings of Governor Holmes in substance and verbiage.[48] The citizenry of Mobile were as agitated as the settlers upstream, particularly over the exaggerated rumor that a sixteen hundred-man force was en route from Baton Rouge supposedly to bolster the society led by Kennedy and the Callers.

On November 22, after touring the district east of the Pearl, Toulmin prepared a lengthy report for President Madison.[49] Earlier suspicions had "ripened into certainty." A tense feeling of alarm prevailed among the people around Mobile. There Toulmin met and talked with James Innerarity of John Forbes & Co. and suggested that an infallible way to avert disaster in the crisis would be for the officials of West Florida to propose that the United States take possession of the region. Innerarity assured Toulmin that the mere hint of such a thing from within Mobile would be considered an act of treason. Nevertheless Governor Folch was a man of practicality, and he might respond to an official suggestion if directed to him personally. As he closed his report, Toulmin requested that Colonel Sparks be instructed to break up the Kemper–Kennedy–Caller Mobile cabal in order that harmony might prevail between the two governments.

In October, the committee of public safety of the West Florida Convention had dispatched Reuben Kemper as a commissioner to Mobile and Pensacola. He was assigned the task of uniting their brethren in those communities in the rebellion. As one might have expected, Kemper and Kennedy immediately became confederates who shared a common contempt for authority on both sides of the thirty-first parallel. Toulmin's opposition seemed to make Kemper more determined than ever to march against Mobile, and possibly Pensacola. When he and Kennedy launched their expedition in late November of 1810, they did so with signs of doubts and uncertainty, a condition created by the influence and power of Judge Harry Toulmin whom Kemper called a "base Devil filled with deceptive and Bloody Rascality."[50] Despite the apparent popular support for the filibusters, the expedition made slow advance southward. It lacked supplies, organization and, most important of all, manpower.

In the meantime, Folch, pressured by Innerarity to place West Florida in the trusteeship of the United States pending a formal treaty, agreed instead to abolish duties and to discontinue all forms of commercial discrimination if the American officials, both territorial and national, would repudiate both Kemper and the Convention support. Rather than relying upon Innerarity or Toulmin, Governor Folch depended upon his old friend John McKee, an experienced agent to the Choctaw, as an intermediary to convey his veiled proposal for abdicating Spanish control in the area. In his January (1811) reply to the letter delivered by McKee, Secretary of State Robert Smith assured Folch that arrangements for the delivery of West Florida to the United States would be "advantageous to all parties concerned."[51] President Madison had appointed McKee and General George Matthews to meet with Folch and receive possession of the region. A delicate moment in the resolution of the Florida question was at hand.

No one possessed a keener awareness of the precarious state of affairs than Judge Toulmin, who interposed his authority and influence at times with considerable personal risk. Through the powers of his office, Toulmin impeded Kennedy and Kemper, but he could not prevent them from recruiting some one hundred followers from along the Tombigbee and Alabama Rivers.[52] Few men of property enlisted in this ragtag army which had no realistic chance of overrunning the Spanish fort at Mobile. Nevertheless, its descent downriver in late November of 1810, coupled with rumors of as many as 500 to 1,000 sympathizers marching from Baton Rouge, stirred considerable excitement. Camping opposite Mobile on McCurtin's Bluff, which they dubbed "Bunkers Hill," the insurrectionists "occasioned a general terror" among nearby residents.[53]

It is amazing that this foray did not result in greater casualties than the deaths of six men—two of Folch's and four of the invaders—and a handful of wounded before the West Florida Convention banner waved by the Bigbee upstarts had been carried back upstream. Shortly after the Kemper–Kennedy expedition had encamped on the eastern bank of Mobile

Bay, a boatload of supplies, which included several casks of whiskey, arrived from Baton Rouge. During the ensuing celebration Kemper and Kennedy raised the spirits of their followers even higher with a barrage of oratory, but cold rains and internal dissension soon led them to move their campaign across the bay. Some of the men crossed by boat to Sawmill Creek twelve miles north of Mobile while Kemper headed around the bay with his horse company. In the advance camp, whiskey flowed and fiddlers bowed. Meanwhile, Folch, who had been informed of the frolic, ordered a party of 200 soldiers and volunteers to attack the vulnerable invaders. Shortly before midnight on December 10, 1810, the Spanish forces surprised the Americans, who were still frolicking. They killed four, wounded several, and captured ten who soon found themselves in a Havana prison where they remained for five years.[54]

While territorial officials labored to resolve this conflict, diplomats in Washington and in Madrid followed the West Florida developments with keen interest. Spanish Minister Luís de Onís, though forced to communicate through intermediaries in Washington because he had not yet been recognized, nevertheless displayed little temerity as he complained of American manipulation of the Floridians and voiced fears of impending French intervention. The British chargé J. P. Morier was even more effective in championing the Spanish cause. His vociferous support of Onís increased American apprehension of possible British interference. Federalist editors, sympathetic to Spain, added pressure by accusing Republican officials of provoking war with England. Such outcries failed to deter President James Madison who in 1811 dismissed Robert Smith as Secretary of State and boldly denied charges of American duplicity made by British minister Augustus J. Foster.[55]

Meanwhile the United States took more positive steps to mitigate the Florida crises. On December 21, 1810, Secretary of War William Eustis ordered Colonel Thomas Cushing, en route to Fort Stoddert from Natchez via the Mississippi and the Gulf, to garrison posts abandoned by Spanish forces within West Florida.[56] On January 3, 1811, after a forty-nine-day passage marred by adverse winds, Cushing sailed unchallenged into Mobile Bay. In the meantime, Colonel Sparks, in response to letters from Governors Claiborne and Holmes of Louisiana and Mississippi Territories, had ordered Captain Edmund Pendleton Gaines to Mobile to demand the surrender of the town. An attack planned by Sparks on refusal of surrender was canceled by Cushing because of a lack of materials and arms.[57] Judge Toulmin, who felt the pressure of threats of violence against his person, opined that the timely arrival of Cushing "has really saved this country from becoming a scene of plunder and desolation."[58]

Though the most intense and prolonged turmoil centered around Baton Rouge and Mobile, the predominantly French settlement near the mouth of the Pascagoula River—eventually to be known as the town of Pascagoula, Mississippi—also experienced considerable commotion late in 1810. The brigandlike actions of Sterling Dupree, a despicable freebooter who took advantage of the confusion caused by the revolt, caused particular distress. Operating under a commission from James Caller, Joseph P. Kennedy, and Reuben Kemper, and displaying the lone star banner of the convention, Dupree plundered the peaceful French community. So great was his booty that he commandeered several schooners to carry his loot, which included large inventories of stolen goods and a number of valuable slaves to the relative safety of the Tombigbee area above the Florida boundary.[59] Although vigilantes inflicted some casualties upon Dupree's confederates, neither the posse nor Federal troops recovered significant amounts of the loot nor brought to justice the brigands, who had found a haven in Washington County, which extended from the Pearl River to the Georgia boundary. Within a few weeks, however, both the American flag and tranquility reigned over the Gulf Coast between the Pearl and the Pascagoula.

It would be some time before Judge Toulmin enjoyed a similar interlude of peace. Post riders were kept busy as he and the insurrectionists exchanged bitter recriminations in lengthy letters to President Madison and other Administration officials.[60] Indeed, the years preceding the War of 1812 were one of the most frantic periods in the fascinating career of this unique frontier official who was as complex as he was competent. With a Christian minister for a father and a bookseller for a mother, Toulmin came by his intellectualism and verbosity naturally before migrating from England to Virginia in 1792. His republican tendencies were strengthened by his acquaintance with Thomas Jefferson, James Madison, and other Virginia free thinkers before he migrated to Kentucky where he became president of Transylvania Seminary in 1794, later serving as secretary of state from 1796 to 1802. Editor and compiler of a number of historical and legal works, Toulmin left Kentucky where his dissenting religious views were out of tune with the fundamentalist majority. His roles were as numerous as his contacts. The complexity of his life was reflected in the marriages of his children: one daughter to Edmund Pendleton Gaines, a commander of Ft. Stoddert; another to a son of General James Wilkinson, and a son to a daughter of James Caller! What a shame— but little wonder—that no significant collection of his private papers is extant![61]

The West Florida struggle resembled a ponderous gothic drama played out on broad natural and diplomatic stages. The strands of its history were numerous, varicolored, and inextricably intertwined. Outwardly at least the United States was bound by a proclaimed policy of nonaggression, yet the pressures to extend the American frontier to the coastal shores created problems too numerous and provocative to be ignored. Spain was too weak and preoccupied with European matters to defend its colonial interests in the region; France and Great Britain threatened intolerable intervention, especially with western commerce. Thus the four nations were drawn into an ominous web of intrigues, conspiracies, and violations of principles. Indeed, the dividing line between neutrality and belligerency with Spain was at times scarcely more than an imaginary one, and had it not been for the embroilment with Great Britain it might have vanished completely.

Spain's destiny in West Florida was writ large in retreat. Given Spain's involvement in Europe's strife of the time (alliances with France, then against France, occupation by a French army, and then Spain's own war to liberate itself from the French), West Florida must be considered a minor Spanish concern, whose importance diminished rapidly as time passed. Nevertheless the Captain General of Cuba in Havana felt a grave concern for any reverses in West Florida, for he was the primary officer responsible for its defense. Cuba had experienced a couple of its own upheavals in this period which further removed the importance of West Florida from Spanish consideration.

Spanish officials in West Florida obviously gave great weight to the events there, and Cuba's officials responded—but in proportion to their own concerns. Meanwhile the Court in Madrid, and later the Cortes de Cádiz, and all the officials involved in negotiation with the United States, employed the West Florida situation as they saw fit, perhaps to gain an advantage or two at the bargaining table. But the larger questions of Spain's defense and Spanish dependence upon flour from the United States were the real interests of Madrid. After the Louisiana Purchase, Spain viewed the Floridas for what they were: untenable provinces or colonies to be bargained away at the best price possible.[62] Once again the adage applies: "Europe's distresses spelled America's diplomatic successes."[63]

Spain was unwilling to supply the necessary defense for the geographical and political island which suddenly had become such a vital link in westward American expansion. From the moment Spanish authorities suspended the right of deposit at New Orleans in 1802 Spain was confronted with the militant determination of western farmers and boatmen, especially those of Kentucky and West Tennessee, to maintain free access to the Gulf via New Orleans. Lack of support by Louisiana's inhabitants and the rising threat of the United States were complicating factors. Spain's problems were also exacerbated by the unrecognized status of Luis de Onís as the Spanish Minister to the United States, which necessitated negotiation through intermediaries, while failures of Napoleon's European campaigns increased the possibility of British intervention along the Gulf Coast. American policy precluded recognition of diplomats of rival governments in Spain. Onís represented the nationalist *Junta Central* which opposed the rule of Joseph Bonaparte, who had been planted on the Spanish imperial throne in 1808 by his brother Napoleon.

In addition, the West Florida stage was crowded with as varied an assortment of Spanish, French, and American characters as ever appeared on an American frontier. It was difficult, if not impossible, to separate brigand from trustworthy pioneer. In a superficial view, there was substantial truth in the ofttimes partisan contentions of Mississippi territorial officials that the population south of the thirty-first parallel was made up of fugitives, rascals, troublemakers, land speculators, and adventurers! Carlos de Grand-Pré, Carlos Dehault de Lassus, and Vicente Folch also may have shared this opinion.

That expansionist forces, often blamed for the War of 1812, were at work in this "perimeter of conflict" was obvious. There was less certainty, however, regarding their definition and intensity. For instance, what was the relative importance of the factors of expansionism and national security? Considerable evidence points to the presence of a persistent tone of nascent Manifest Destiny in American actions and reactions. It was discernible in the presidential proclamation of annexation, numerous petitions from inhabitants of West Florida, speeches of congressmen, anxieties over land claims, cries by squatters and pre-emptioners for support, and rivalry between Federal territories for acquired land. Similarly, much of the correspondence also contained a tone of the Protestant sense of mission in descriptions of the country and in observations that neither the Spanish nor the French had fully developed it. One detects in the documents the existence of a nascent Manifest Destiny.

On the other hand, concern for the defense of national borders remained constantly on the minds of Federal officials at every level. Geographically and strategically, the mouth of the Perdido, Mobile Bay, the Pearl estuary, and the great sprawling embouchure of the Mississippi were interrelated. No United States boundary was so nakedly exposed to invasion and occupation by a strong naval power as the Gulf coastal fringe of the Old Southwest which contained no imposing American fortifications. Forts Stoddert and St. Stephens on the Tombigbee River were anchorages against Indian attacks, not against invasion by a sophisticated European force. Fort Charlotte at Mobile, though neither well-manned nor adequately fortified, remained a Spanish toehold. And American defenses of the Mississippi and New Orleans were in about the same degree of disarray as General James Wilkinson's rhetoric on the subject. Besides, the United States War Department had neither the tactical understanding nor the fiscal capability to remedy the situation. In a sense, such a weak military posture in the Old Southwest, exemplified by American anxiety over the Spanish presence in Mobile, suggests that the strength of expansionistic forces in the early nineteenth century have been exaggerated.

The continuing historical debate over the nature of American expansionism will not alter the fact that President Madison's proclamation of 1810 assured the advance of the young republic to the Gulf Coast. Congressional acts creating the State of Louisiana and dividing West Florida between the newly created state and the Territory of Mississippi prior to the declaration of war in June of 1812, merely validated Madison's assertion of American dominion over the area.

By mid-March of 1813, General Wilkinson in New Orleans had received orders from Secretary of War John Amstrong to occupy Mobile. Within two weeks the general encamped with seven companies of infantry and one of artillery at Pass Christian on the Gulf Coast, roughly midway between New Orleans and Mobile. Although the news of this troop movement caused alarm among Spanish officials in Mobile and Pensacola, they could only make a defensive gesture by stationing a small garrison on Dauphine Island at the entrance to Mobile Bay.[64]

At Pass Christian Wilkinson suffered several delays. One was a boating accident in which he narrowly escaped an "unprofessional end" by drowning. But his fortune soon changed for the better and he pressed forward smoothly with the Mobile campaign which, in the words of historian Isaac Cox, "constituted a dress parade for Wilkinson."[65] Prior to his departure for Mobile, Wilkinson ordered ten gunboats to blockade the city and instructed Colonel John Bowyer to march down from Fort Stoddert to the east shore of Mobile Bay.

By the time Wilkinson arrived, United States gunboats controlled Mobile Bay and Bowyer's troops secured the land route from Mobile to Pensacola. The Dauphine Island Spanish contingent fled to Pensacola on the approach of the American forces from Pass Christian. On April 12, Wilkinson asked Captain Cayetano Pérez, Spanish commandant of Fort Charlotte in Mobile, to peacefully retire with his garrison to Pensacola so that the Americans could occupy the post located within the "legitimate limits" of the United States. Though Fort Charlotte was well constructed and armed with sixty-two cannon, Pérez had only sixty poorly provisioned men to defend it. Camped below Fort Charlotte were Wilkinson's 600 men; just above the thirty-first parallel was Fort Stoddert; guarding the east bank of Mobile Bay was Bowyer's command.

So it is not surprising that Pérez sent his reply before the sun had set. It contained a protest and a promise to evacuate the fort provided that his men could take their possessions with them and that Wilkinson would supply transports. The question of territorial sovereignty, Pérez admitted, rested with their respective governments. The following day, April 13, the Spanish commander and an aide to Wilkinson signed articles of agreement on the procedures for Spanish evacuation. Spain would reimburse the United States for costs of transportation and provisions; the American government would be held accountable for the Spanish cannon and munitions. On April 15, 1813, the Spanish detachment departed without incident, and at five o'clock that afternoon General Wilkinson's forces hoisted the Stars and Stripes over Fort Charlotte as ships and land batteries fired salutes. Wilkinson had captured Mobile, according to his boast, "without the effusion of a drop of blood," and now the American flag waved over West Florida as far east as the Perdido River.[66]

Given all that had taken place along the perimeter of conflict, the transfer of Mobile to the American forces under General Wilkinson on April 15, 1813, was anticlimactic.

4

Land of Speculation

"Were I to characterize the *United States,* it should be by the appellation of the *land of speculation,*" quipped William Priest, a perceptive British tourist, in 1796.[1] Clearly, he had captured the essence of the American spirit at the close of the eighteenth century. So dominant were the forces of speculation that they may be described as centrifugal. And in no section of the young republic was this spirit more evident than in the Old Southwest. There, on the shifting sands of national titles and transfers, took place some of the most avaricious episodes of land grabbing, political corruption, and moral effrontery in the history of the nation.

During the colonial era, France, Spain, and Great Britain had each at one time or other enjoyed dominion over all or most of the Old Southwest. Each of them had awarded land grants which varied not only in clarity of title but also in many instances overlapped in terms of their bounds. To complicate matters further, Georgia claimed most of the area which eventually became the states of Alabama and Mississippi, and its legislature on three occasions between 1785 and 1795 issued huge land grants in that region.[2] By the time the Mississippi Territory was organized in 1798, only a few persons claimed French grants, but there seemed to be no end to the number of claimants who traced their titles back to concessions of the governments of Great Britain, Spain, or Georgia.

Many of the land tangles in the Old Southwest stemmed from the British acquisition of Florida from Spain in 1763 at the conclusion of the French and Indian War. As she had done in most of her other colonies, England encouraged migration to her newly acquired possession which she divided into East and West Florida. Indeed, during this era, West Florida, especially the Natchez District, attracted a number of Loyalists, particularly from New England. Great Britain, stationing troops as far north as the

Yazoo River, governed the Floridas until Spain conquered them in 1779. Prior to Spanish occupation, the British Crown rather freely granted large parcels of land to settlers as well as to veterans and court favorites. Many of the latter group, however, failed to perfect their titles by making the required improvements. Otherwise, the confusion surrounding land titles in the Old Southwest would have been even greater, if that is possible to imagine.[3]

After Spain regained permanent control of East and West Florida by the Treaty of Paris in 1783, her officials instituted a more rigidly controlled land policy that applied even to the disputed territory occupied by Spanish officials as far north as Vicksburg, then known as Walnut Hills. In an effort to curtail speculation, grants were made only to bona fide settlers, and a registry was begun in hopes of ascertaining the status of titles, the availability of vacant lands, and the presence of squatters. However, the signing of the Treaty of San Lorenzo between Spain and the United States on October 27, 1795, not only ended Spain's attempt to restore order, but set in motion events that would cause untold expense and anguish to generations of landowners in the Southwest. Spanish officials delayed transfer of the region to the United States, while granting a number of land titles which they dated *prior* to October 27, 1795.[4]

It would seem that the southwestern frontier north of the thirty-first parallel had enough confusion and anxiety for one section, but yet another complication was to be injected into this Pandora's box of claims and counterclaims. In 1785, Georgia created in its western domain a political gossamer named Bourbon County. This gigantic county stretched northward from the thirty-first parallel to the Yazoo River and as far west as the Mississippi. The four commissioners dispatched to Natchez by Georgia to establish a seat of government overstepped the bounds of their instructions. Rumors of plans for a show of force prompted quick reaction from Governor Esteban Miró as well as residents of Natchez, and Miró ordered the commissioners out of the district.[5]

On February 1, 1788, the Georgia legislature repealed the Bourbon County Act, and in the same measure attempted to cede to the United States a 140-mile-wide tract of land north of the thirty-first parallel and between the Chattahoochee and Mississippi Rivers. However, the Federal government rejected the cession, which included Natchez, because the act demanded a guarantee to Georgia of the unceded portion of her claim which extended up to the Tennessee line. Unfortunately for future clarification of land issues, the Bourbon County Act was in force just long enough to leave a legacy which would haunt the Old Southwest for years to come.

The South Carolina Yazoo Company was a descendant of Bourbon County traced through the lineage of John Wood. An Indian trader, Wood convinced the Choctaw in 1786 to grant him some two million acres of land which included the strategic settlement of Walnut Hills. Because the Bourbon Act stipulated that land was to be sold only to persons securing Indian claims, Wood's Choctaw cession had sufficient legitimacy that he was able to dispose of it to an unprincipled Georgia speculator known as Thomas Washington, whose surname actually was Walsh. Washington, who would be hanged in South Carolina in 1792 for counterfeiting financial instruments, aligned himself in 1789 with three financial associates.[6]

The three South Carolinians who associated themselves with Washington were William Clay Snipes, Isaac Huger, and Alexander Moultrie, a brother of Governor William Moultrie. This group commissioned the famous Kentucky Indian fighter, John Holder, to recruit 400 families from the Blue Grass state to found a settlement at Walnut Hills, a mission which proved abortive. Soon they expanded their association to a total of twenty, adopted the name South Carolina Yazoo Company, and in November of 1789 petitioned the Georgia legislature to confirm its speculative activities. By then two similar groups—the Virginia Yazoo Company led by Patrick Henry and Joseph Martin and the Tennessee Yazoo Company inspired by Zachariah Cox and John Sevier and cheered on by William Blount—also sought concessions. Evidently, the appellation of "Yazoo" became popular for several reasons. The original focus of speculative interest was on the site of the present town of Vicksburg—then known as Walnut Hills—where the Yazoo River flowed into the Mississippi. Though no Indian towns were located there, it was an ideal place for a trading center. Also, the Yazoo River meandered through much of the fertile area now known as the Mississippi Delta. For these reasons undoubtedly the name "Yazoo" caught on. Also, it was an easily pronounced Indian word that had the kind of mystique about it that appealed to promoters.

For an average price of less than one cent an acre, the Georgia legislature four days before Christmas of 1789 sold more than 25 million acres to these three compaines: over 10 million acres to the South Carolina Company for $66,964; 11.4 million acres to the Virginia Company for $93,741; and 4 million acres to the Tennessee Company for $46,875.

Georgia's 1789 Christmas gift to the three Yazoo Companies opened a drama of land speculation unequaled in American history. The actors included Georgia governors and legislators, future Presidents of the United States, Senators and congressmen, Supreme Court Justices and the Court

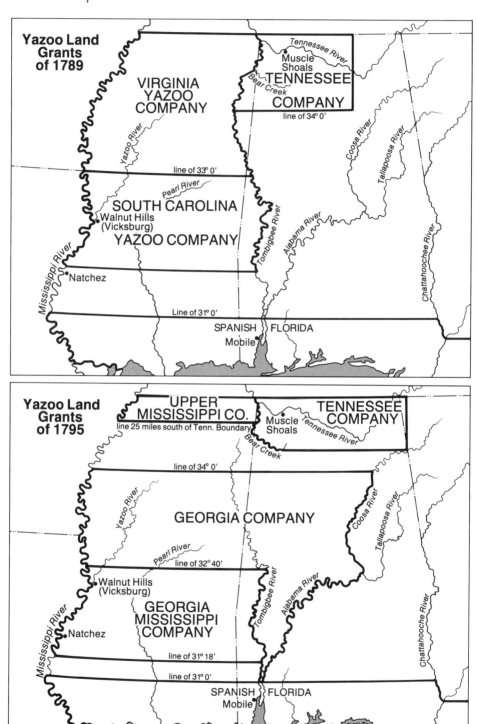

Yazoo Land Grants of 1789

VIRGINIA YAZOO COMPANY

TENNESSEE COMPANY

Tennessee River

Muscle Shoals

Bear Creek

line of 34° 0'

Yazoo River

Coosa River

Tallapoosa River

line of 33° 0'

Pearl River

SOUTH CAROLINA

Walnut Hills (Vicksburg)

YAZOO COMPANY

Tombigbee River

Alabama River

Chattahoochee River

Mississippi River

Natchez

Line of 31° 0'

SPANISH   FLORIDA
Mobile

Yazoo Land Grants of 1795

UPPER MISSISSIPPI CO.

TENNESSEE COMPANY

line 25 miles south of Tenn. Boundary

Muscle Shoals

Tennessee River

Bear Creek

line of 34° 0'

Yazoo River

GEORGIA COMPANY

Coosa River

Tallapoosa River

Pearl River

line of 32° 40'

Walnut Hills (Vicksburg)

Tombigbee River

Alabama River

Chattahoochee River

Mississippi River

Natchez

GEORGIA MISSISSIPPI COMPANY

line of 31° 18'

line of 31° 0'

SPANISH   FLORIDA
Mobile

itself, and several special commissions. Before the final curtain fell, Congress was paralyzed by prolonged spells of furious debate and recriminations, and many men were left bankrupt politically, morally, and financially. A few of them were even injured or killed in duels over related Yazoo issues. Ultimately, the United States was shamed by the gross fraud, and as often was the case, the Indian tribes suffered irreparable damage.

Of the three ventures, the South Carolina Company, which initiated the most activity and caused the most concern diplomatically, involved several fascinating characters. Of these, no one was more colorful than Dr. James O'Fallon, who replaced Holder as its field agent and who rivaled James Wilkinson in his duplicity. In part, O'Fallon's instructions included the fulfillment of Holder's assignment to settle 400 families at Walnut Hills. This native of Ireland, who had completed two years of medical training at the University of Edinburgh, undoubtedly embellished the already grandiose dreams of the investors. As Thomas P. Abernethy summarized, "It was thus with high hopes that O'Fallon, endowed with an uninhibited tongue and a vivid imagination, set out to found a new empire on the Lower Mississippi."[7]

The design of an independent state which would serve as a barrier between the United States and Spain was not entirely a figment of O'Fallon's imagination. Correspondence between Moultrie and Thomas Washington clearly reveals plans for a comprehensive commercial center at Walnut Hills from which the sale of slaves, Indian trade, land transactions, and other activities would be conducted. O'Fallon, whom Wilkinson labeled a "vain blockhead," engaged in a discordant correspondence with the Spanish Governor Miró while the "Doctor" prepared for an invasion of Louisiana from Kentucky. These developments frightened President Washington who viewed the South Carolina project as a serious threat to peaceful relationships with Spain in the Southwest.

The cunning O'Fallon had hoped to take advantage of tensions between Spain and England which he assumed would render Louisiana vulnerable. Spanish seizure in 1789 of a British vessel in Nootka Sound off the coast of British Columbia had provoked a serious confrontation. With France, her perennial enemy, weakened by revolution, Great Britain saw little danger in challenging Spain in both North and South America, and for a brief time Spain and England teetered on the brink of war. Rumors of a possible British expedition from Canada down the Mississippi to attack Louisiana circulated in the Upper Mississippi Valley. O'Fallon viewed it as a propitious time to encroach upon Spanish territory and her Indian trade. Much to his chagrin, however, Spain settled the Nootka Crisis to

England's complete satisfaction. This rapprochement doomed O'Fallon's dreams and removed a source of no minor concern to the Washington Administration.

Indeed, the saga of Dr. O'Fallon is one of the most intriguing in the annals of the Old Southwest. Until they parted company, he and James Wilkinson had a mutually exploitive relationship. Each tried to manipulate the Spanish authorities in Louisiana as he kept a watchful eye on the other, waiting for an opportunity for betrayal. After Wilkinson's correspondence to Miró implicated O'Fallon as a prospective filibuster, George Rogers Clark, whose name was often connected with a planned British invasion of Louisiana, replaced Wilkinson as O'Fallon's chief advisor and deputy. O'Fallon further cemented his relationship with Clark when at the age of fifty he married Clark's fifteen-year-old sister. Wilkinson judged this marriage to be "additional proof of his [O'Fallon's] circumspection and good sense."[8] O'Fallon eventually came to blows with Clark, his teenage wife left him, and he died early in 1794—a passing barely noted and little mourned.

Of the three companies chartered in 1789, The Tennessee Yazoo Company had received the smallest grant of land. Its activities under the leadership of the energetic Zachariah Cox caused little concern among the Spanish, but his efforts to establish a colony at the Muscle Shoals of the Tennessee River met resistance from the Creeks as well as the Cherokee. Cox, who in 1784 had attempted to colonize the Shoals as part of the Houston County scheme authorized by the Georgia legislature, led a group of settlers from Tennessee to the Shoals in the spring of 1791. Though William Blount for some time had dreamed of a speculative venture at Muscle Shoals, he was now Governor of the Southwest Territory, and despite his connection with the Tennessee Company, Blount would have been obliged to enforce Washington's order to prevent settlements by the Yazoo companies. The Cherokee, who now realized that they had the support of Federal authorities, forced the abandonment of Cox's tiny Muscle Shoals settlement early in 1792.[9]

Easily the most recognizable historic figure involved in the 1789 speculations was Patrick Henry. He was the moving force behind the Virginia Company, the least active of the three grantees. The Company's acreage lay to the north of Walnut Hills, between the thirty-third parallel and the Tennessee line. Henry, who sought stock in the Tennessee Company as well, kept a constant eye on developments which led to the formation of Southwest Territory after North Carolina in 1789 ceded its western lands to the Federal government. He hoped to participate with his fellow Virginians in land deals in the vicinity of Chickasaw Bluffs where Memphis was later to be built.

George Washingon's selection of Blount as governor of the Southwest Territory—and the subsequent appointment of Sevier and Robertson as generals in its militia—was a stroke of genius. Now they were obligated to enforce the Administration's policy of no encroachment on Indian lands. These appointments, along with concessions made to the Creek chief Alexander McGillivray in the 1790 Treaty of New York, doomed to failure the 1789 Yazoo companies which technically ceased to exist when proper remittance of payment to the Georgia treasury was not made. Unlike the South Carolina group, neither the Tennessee nor the Virgina Company, however, had planned to establish a government separate from the United States.[10]

The speculative spirit seems to have been in the hearts of many Americans when they arrived on the Atlantic seaboard. Before long the best parcels of land in the tidelands and along the river valleys were occupied, and soon the covetous eyes of the speculator gazed in the direction of the Ohio Valley and Great Lakes. Indeed, frontier lands had always been a seductive factor in the lines of easterners, many of whom now turned their attention to Georgia's vast western domain. In this sense, the first wave of Yazoo ventures was merely a prelude to the drama that unfolded in 1795.

While the four companies chartered that year were granted basically the same Georgia lands sought by the former groups, the ventures differed in two primary ways: first, with few exceptions, the new financiers were from the North, New England, or Europe; secondly, in terms of acreages sought by individual investors, the schemes were the most grandiose in the annals of American land speculation. *Stupendous* is hardly an adequate word to describe either the colossal size of the claims or the amplitude of the fraud.

The assemblage of the Georgia legislature at Augusta in November of 1794 attracted land speculators as honey does flies. Enterprising frontiersmen understood the implications of Eli Whitney's cotton gin, invented the previous year. Kentuckians and other westerners still seethed over Spanish interference with the flow of Mississippi River trade, and speculators, probably more than the angry farmers, confidently anticipated the success of Thomas Pinckney, who had been dispatched to Spain to resolve conflicts with that nation in the Southwest. Memories of the earlier Yazoo ventures remained fresh and the fraudulent excesses of the "Pine Barren" speculation in southern Georgia also heightened the already epidemic speculative fever. In sum, conditions were ideal for the fomentation of the most shameful land fraud ever concocted in America.[11]

By every account, the primary leavening agent in the batter was James Gunn, an unprincipled opportunistic Virginian who marched to Georgia during the Revolutionary War with the forces of General Nathanael Greene. One could no more ignore Gunn's role in this event, according to one colorful observer, than one could "snub Satan in giving an account of Pandemonium."[12] To put it mildly, Gunn had covered himself with less than glory through an assortment of sordid deeds ranging from theft of a famous Virginia stallion Romulus, to an impudent challenge of General Greene to a duel. In a large sense, his was an appropriate pedigree for the unsavory role as chief agent of corruption in Augusta. The ironic ingredients in the recipe were the many prominent Federal officials from every corner of the nation. They were the ultimate corruptors.

It does not speak well for post-Revolutionary Georgia that James Gunn was an incumbent United States Senator whose first order of business was the machination of his re-election by the legislature in 1794 when it met in Augusta. This having been accomplished, Gunn set about achieving his ultimate goal—promotion of the new Yazoo ventures. Or, in the words of an earlier chronicler, he cranked up "the grosser engines of bribery and corruption."[13] Senator Gunn was such an effective engineer that he steamed the locomotive of venality right through the Georgia legislature. Only one member resisted bribery.

The action of that body was as swift as it was corrupt. Passed by the House on January 2 and the Senate on the 3rd, the law was signed on the 7th by Governor George Mathews. For $500,000, or a cent and a half an acre, four companies received 35 million acres. In the process, the Georgia authorities had spurned better offers. Philadelphians Albert Gallatin and Alexander J. Dallas, both of whom later became Secretaries of the Treasury, were among the prospective investors whose offers were rejected. All but one of the solons held at least a few shares; quite a few speculators claimed tracts measured by the hundreds of thousands of acres. Supreme Court Associate Justice James Wilson involved himself to the tune of a million acres! According to one account, Wilson was an "active lobbyist, present in the Senate and the House with bribe money in his hands."[14] As Caesar Rodney, Delaware Republican, later said on the House floor, the legislature was "assailed by every possible artifice of seduction."[15]

Of the former Yazoo companies, only the Tennessee Company was revived. Though the tenacious Zachariah Cox remained is figurehead, a mysterious Charleston merchant named William Maher provided most of the cash. As might be expected, however, William Blount and John Sevier had their names in the pot as well. The Upper Mississippi Company obtained the northern portion of the grant formerly held by the Virginia Yazoo Company—a strip just south of Tennessee, bounded on the east by land of the Tennessee Company. Most of the land was granted to the Georgia and the Georgia Mississippi Companies. The bounds of the former roughly coincided with the upper portion of the old South Carolina territory, while those of the latter contained the Natchez District. The Georgia Mississippi Company's tract ran from the Tombigbee on the east to the Mississippi on the west and from just above the thirty-first parallel northward to just above the Yazoo River mouth so as to include Fort Nogales, recently built by the Spanish. Though most of the investors in the other three organizations hailed from out of state, Georgians dominated the Georgia Mississippi Company. The enabling act prohibited the sale of shares to foreign governments, but one did not have to be a United States citizen to hold stock. In fact, Maher forthwith headed for Europe where he remained for three years!

It did not take long for the citizenry of Georgia to perceive that January 7, 1795, was a day of ignominy. A venal legislature had sold their birthrights; not only veterans, but every family could have enjoyed a slice of such a domain. Senator James Jackson protested the confiscation of the rights of their children and of "unborn generations" to "supply the rapacious grasp of a few sharks."[16] His colleague, Senator Gunn, was burned in effigy. Reactions ranged from presentments by grand juries to the organizing of lynch mobs, though none of the latter got a knot around the neck of a villainous lawmaker. These protests gave rise to the public career of one of Georgia's most esteemed public figures, William H. Crawford, who was then a young schoolteacher.

Revulsion rapidly spread across the nation and the Atlantic Ocean as well. President Washington forwarded a copy of the repugnant act to Congress, which adopted a resolution of condemnation; and concern was expressed in many circles that the action of the Georgia legislature might impede the negotiations of Pinckney in Spain. Meanwhile, Spanish officials in Florida moved to protect their interests with the Indians, particularly the Choctaw. They dispatched troops to build a new post, Fort San Fernando de las Barrancas, near Chickasaw Bluffs, and convinced the licensed trading firm of Panton, Leslie, and Company to ship in a stock of trade goods at the new site.

As the Georgia Constitution of 1789 provided, another constitutional convention was called in 1795 to consider amendments to the original document. When this body met in May of 1795 it received numerous grand jury presentments and individual protests. Since members of this body were elected at the same time as the "Yazoo" legislature, they merely took note of the protests and passed them on the next meeting of the legislature. But the furor would not subside. In July, Senator Jackson returned home from the capital at Philadelphia and entered the fray. Bribe offers ranging up to a half million acres of land failed to quiet his voice of protest. That fall he resigned his Sentate seat to lead the anti-Yazoo fight and won election to the Georgia House of Representatives as part of a protest landslide.

Though its actions were not quite as swift as those of its predecessor, the 1796 legislature assembled in January, and by February 13 it had declared the Yazoo sale null and void. With a flair perhaps unmatched in the annals of United States legislative history, that body symbolically purged itself in a fascinating rite of purification. Two days after passage of the Rescinding Act, its members marched in a procession to the front of the capitol where they ripped the repugnant pages out of the journal, and ceremoniously burned them in a "fire from heaven" drawn down by a sunglass.[17]

Though this heavenly fire may have cauterized the wounds of many Georgians, it could not vaporize the financial and political manifestations of the Yazoo sale. The ink from Governor Mathews' quill had hardly dried on the notorious 1795 bill before many of the Yazoo grantees sold their interests for handsome profits. The size of some of the transactions staggers the imagination. James Greenleaf, most likely the all-time champion land speculator in the United States, quickly bought nearly fourteen million acres from the Georgia Company. Within three months, he had disposed of nine million acres to New York and Boston speculators who, in turn, resold the land at an average price of 14¢ per acre. Though the speculative fever infected the entire eastern seaboard, it was epidemic in New England, where, in the words of one historian, "Every class of men, even watch-makers, hair-dressers, and mechanics of all descriptions, eagerly ran after this deception."[18] Bostonians, it was estimated, invested two million dollars.

News of the Rescinding Act stunned investors in Boston and other eastern financial centers where for years the status of the Yazoo claims would dominate conversation. Obviously, the entanglement caused considerable financial distress among the purchasers, who had to organize and prepare to defend their claims. Georgia was insistent that the sale was invalid, and the stage was set for lengthy litigation and an acrimonious congressional battle.

Meanwhile, on October 27, 1795, Thomas Pinckney concluded in the Spanish town of San Lorenzo a highly popular treaty which established the northern boundary of Florida at the thirty-first parallel and which resolved other issues including the free navigation of the Mississippi. Finally, Federal governance was established in a large segment of the Old Southwest when President Adams affixed his signature on April 7, 1798, to the enabling act creating Mississippi Territory.[19] When Governor Winthrop Sargent, a New England Puritan, arrived in the territory, he encountered a host of extremely anxious settlers who expected him to create order out of the labyrinth of land claims based on British, Spanish, and Georgia grants. His actions, however, seemed hardly adequate. Though he unequivocally denied any valid claim by Yazoo companies to land within the Mississippi Territory and advocated an accommodating Federal land policy, Sargent disappointed many citizens when he failed to repudiate the antedated Spanish grants.

Because several of the Governor's closest associates held these antedated Spanish claims, this soon became one of the issues contributing to the emerging factionalism in the territory. As might have been expected, many of those not favored by the Spanish with antedated grants gravitated toward the Republican Party, and after the election of President Thomas Jefferson, they lobbied for replacement of Sargent. Party affiliation aside, the entanglement of land titles cast a pall over the territory. Suspense over land titles, in the word of petitioners to Congress, "deminishes [sic] the actual value of our properties—interrupts in some measure our peace and tranquility of mind and checks the Spirit of democracy."[20]

By no means did Jefferson's appointment of William Charles Cole Claiborne of Tennessee to replace Sargent prove a panacea for landowners in Mississippi Territory, but he became a catalyst in the process of disentanglement. The act creating Mississippi Territory also instructed the President to appoint a commission to negotiate with Georgia the cession of her western lands to the Federal government, and on April 24, 1802, Georgia finally relinquished all claims to her lands lying within the Mississippi Terrritory.[21] Though the 1802 cession confirmed British and Spanish grants "fully executed" prior to Pinckney's Treaty as well as claims under the Bourbon County Act, widespread unrest persisted because so many claims were not validated. Consequently, President Jefferson requested of Claiborne a complete report on the status of land grants in the territory.

Governor Claiborne concluded his meticulous summation of land claims with a warning: The government must clarify titles and sell vacant land reasonably. If not, "this most distant and infant settlement of the United States . . . would be rendered more weak and defenseless by the banishment of the poorer Class of White Citizens and the introduction of a few wealthy characters, with a large increase of negroes, a discription [*sic*] of inhabitants, already formidable to our present population."[22]

Congress responded in a generous and constructive manner with passage of the Land Act of 1803.[23] It confirmed titles to British and Spanish grants which were under cultivation on October 27, 1795; it awarded tracts of up to 640 acres to heads of households cultivating other lands at the time of Spanish evacuation in 1797; and to persons in neither of these categories, it gave pre-emption rights to parcels which were under cultivation on the date of the Act and which were no larger than 640 acres. In addition, this Act created two land offices in the territory, established two commissions to resolve conflicting claims, and outlined procedures for resurveying the claims. The Pearl River separated the two land office and commission districts. Though the 1803 Act established a mechanism for coping with land problems in the Old Southwest, their resolution would still take years.

Meanwhile Yazoo speculators continued efforts in the halls of Congress and in the Federal courts to recoup losses following Georgia's rescinding legislation. Congress in 1800 empowered the same commission that negotiated the Georgia Cession of 1802 to recommend a compromise for Federal reimbursement of losses suffered by Yazoo claimants.[24] The debate over the proposed settlements, led by the eccentric Virginia congressman, John Randolph, was as rancorous as it was prolonged, and it evolved into an open revolt within Jeffersons's Republican Party. Randolph and his fellow insurgents became known as the "Tertium Quids" (Latin for "third somethings").[25]

So determined was Randolph to defeat the compromise that he declared "I can never desert or relinquish, till I have exercised every energy of mind, and faculty of body I possess, in refuting so nefarious a project."[26] On another occasion, he attacked Federalists in the manner of a barefisted fighter:

> What is the spirit against which we are now struggling, and which we have vainly endeavored to stifle? A monster generated by fraud, nursed in corruption, that in a grim silence awaits his prey. It is the spirit of Federalism! . . . Say what you will,

the marrow and pith of this business will be found in the character of the great majority of its friends, who stand, as they have
before on this floor, the unblushing advocates of unblushing
corruption.[27]

Randolph then called the Yazoo frauds a "many-headed dog of Hell."[28]

Nor did the Virginia congressman spare those northern Republicans
who sympathized with the Yazoo claimants. Jefferson's Postmaster General, Gideon Granger, particularly felt Randolph's barbs for Granger's
open lobbying in behalf of the New England Mississippi Land Company,
an organization of Yazoo claimants. Administration friends and officials
came to the aid of the Postmaster General, and Randolph found himself
the recipient of some retaliatory remarks in the House, including cruel
references to his simian facial structure.[29] Randolph, however, did not
wither under this fire.

Realizing just how formidable the resistance in Congress was to reimbursement for their losses, the claimants—labeled more recently as "Yazooists"—took their cause simultaneously to the courts in the patently
collusive case of Fletcher v. Peck. Both the plaintiff, the seasoned speculator Robert Fletcher, and defendant John Peck, who claimed 600,000 acres
of Yazoo land, were acting on behalf of the New England Mississippi
Land Company. Fletcher sued Peck for a "covenant broken" when Peck
sold him land which he did not rightfully possess—15,000 acres from the
Georgia sale of 1795. The contract used by Peck when he sold the land to
Fletcher was specifically designed to test the questions being raised by
the New England Mississippi Land Company. Peck was a director of the
company and Fletcher was a sympathizer with Peck and his fellow claimants. Both parties would benefit should the court rule in Peck's favor as
they anticipated. Peck's sale would be legal, Fletcher's title valuable. Above
all, Congress might be influenced to compensate all Yazooists! Eventually the suit filed by these friendly adversaries in June of 1803 reached
the Supreme Court where Chief Justice John Marshall ruled in favor of
the speculators in March of 1810. A legislative grant was a contract which
a subsequent legislature could not violate, he wrote, regardless of the
motivation of either assembly. Because only Congress could provide financial relief for the claimants, the decision merely added moral support to
their cause. It is ironic, nevertheless, that this contrived case led to a landmark constitutional decision affirming the sanctity of contracts and bol-
stering the position of nationalists.[30]

Marshall's decision further infuriated Randolph and his followers, and the vituperative exchanges continued on the floor of the House of Representatives. In 1813, John Wales Eppes, Jefferson's son-in-law, defeated Randolph, whose anti-Yazoo mantle fell upon George M. Troup, another Georgia congressman. Almost as a final thunderclap in the congressional debate, Congressman Troup in March of 1814 addressed the House in bitter Randolphian style.

> This measure flows from corruption, as a stream flows from its source; it flows from the corrupt act of the Legislature of Georgia. . . . The Yazoo Legislature sold for five hundred thousand dollars—Georgia sold to the United States for one million two hundred and fifty thousand dollars only, and now you propose to give five millions to the claimants to compromise their claim. . . . Posterity will say that these claimants, like the gods of Milton, carried the mountains in their hands, and wielding fifty millions of acres under the decision of the Supreme Court, have carried everything before them.[31]

Troup declared, in conclusion, that the proposed compromise was repugnant to the laws of God and nature.

Though the Republican insurgency previously led by Randolph did not subside in his absence, the new Congress quickly enacted the compromise he had so abhorred. Signed on March 31, 1814, the settlement provided that $5 million of the proceeds from land sales in Mississippi Territory should be distributed among the four original companies and several groups of subsequent claimants.[32] The commission created by the Act immediately began adjudicating the claims, and with the final payments by the U.S. Treasury in 1818 the story of the most fantastic land speculation in American history was finally concluded.

Meanwhile, back in Mississippi Territory where most of the unclaimed land in the Old Southwest was situated, uneasiness over land titles persisted for a number of reasons. Only part of the confusion stemmed from the Yazoo frauds or from disputed Spanish and English claims. Most of the unrest was caused by disgruntled credit purchasers and pre-emptioners, who were extremely vociferous. However, the flood of petitions to Congress and the executive branch hardly disguised the fact that only free land would satisfy westerners. At least this reality was clear to Jefferson's Secretary of the Treasury, Albert Gallatin, who convinced the President in 1809 to open land offices in Mississippi Territory in order to sell profitable unclaimed parcels before Congress acquiesced to the land-hungry frontiersmen.

Based upon gross statistics, which indicate that a high percentage of the purchasers allowed their entries to revert back to the government, historians have assumed that the credit system was a "failure," but a recent micro-study of 190 entries in Mississippi Territory east of the Pearl proves that the credit system was quite successful from the point of view of the frontiersmen. Historians were deceived by the total number of reversions. A detailed analysis of the individual records of the 190 entrymen reveals that many of the original purchasers reclaimed land which they had intentionally allowed to revert to the government. In other words, shrewd frontier farmers used their capital to buy slaves and make improvements on their properties instead of making timely payment to the government. A shrewd businessman himself, Gallatin may have caught on to this trick early in the game by carefully studying land office records.[33]

As they had ever since King George III issued his notorious Proclamation of 1763, squatters constantly posed a serious problem. Federal and territorial officials, however, persisted in their efforts to discourage and remove squatters from their illegal habitations on Federal and Indian lands. In a few cases, Federal troops forcibly removed squatters and burned their cabins, but ultimately the tide of public opinion assured them of victory. On occasion, these illegal settlers closed down public sales by threats and intimidation. Governor David Holmes caved in to their pressure when, in 1815, with approval of the territorial assembly he established Monroe County in the northeastern portion of Mississippi Territory out of the recently acquired Creek lands and began taxing the people prior to official Federal sale of the land.[34]

In addition to the antedated Spanish claims, another source of controversy was titles based on Spanish warrants of survey. Since Spain had considered these claims valid, the territorial claimants were incensed at the reluctance of Federal authorities to view them as such. Consequently, for years these landholders bombarded Washington officials with petitions demanding their validation until Congress gave them relief in 1811 in a bill which also vacated lands held on antedated claims which the register judged to be fraudulent.[35]

Of the various land controversies, however, none were more bitterly contested than those relating to unconfirmed British grants in the hands of nonresidents—many of whom claimed extensive tracts in excess of 20,000 acres. In the eyes of local Anglophobes, Federal authorities unduly protected these British claimants, and as Anglo-American relations deteriorated during the Administrations of Jefferson and Madison, this issue became intensely emotional. In the Bigbee settlements, residents were particularly alarmed. Judge Harry Toulmin believed that titles to all land adjacent to the Tombigbee River were clouded by British grants—an opinion shared by Thomas Rodney.[36] Though there was need for establishing a Federal district court in the vicinity of the port of Mobile, especially to hear maritime cases, numerous citizens opposed creation of such a court for fear that it would work to the advantage of absentee British claimants. Likewise, because statehood would afford these British claimants access to the Federal courts, this issue retarded movements for admission as a state. Though unsettled British claims plagued Mississippians long after statehood, cotton profits assured that virtually no fertile land remained uncultivated.

The web of conflicting land claims in the Old Southwest was so entangled that it defies all attempts at brief summation or clarification. Its impact was felt locally in matters pertaining to statehood and immigration, and nationally on the growth of sectionalism and the entrance into the War of 1812. Of its many threads, however, the one most visible and enduring was the one labeled *Yazoo*.

The Yazoo debate was a disturbing distraction in a crucial moment of American history. Despite John Marshall's famous decision and the congressional compromise of 1814, it left in the national annals a distinct sense of undying guilt and anger. It befogged national land policies in an era and area when the public mind should have been clear and committed. Long after the last echo of angry debates had died away in the halls of Congress there still came petitioners seeking assistance in establishing their claims to Mississippi lands. Like the ghostly raven of history, Yazoo came knocking evermore in the chronicles of the Old Southwest. That now-familiar Indian word took on a far more sinister meaning than just the name of a lazy river which flowed turgidly through miles of alluvial lands and which seasonally bore thousands of bales of cotton southward to market. How different might have been the course of American history had Georgia ceded her western lands to the Federal government twenty years earlier than she did!

5

Wilderness Artery

Winthrop Sargent, the newly arrived governor of the Mississippi Territory, wrote Secretary of State Timothy Pickering on April 20, 1799, that he had just received the latter's "Public and private Favours of December 10th."[1] Pickering's letters had made the long and uncertain journey by trail and flatboat from Philadelphia to the dot of civilization in the southwestern corner of the republic at Natchez. Sargent at that moment sat in the midst of a possible international crisis. Daily there arrived at the foot of the Natchez bluffs an almost continuous procession of flatboats from the expanding trans-Appalachian frontier. The rivermen often departed for New Orleans in a disputatious mood, and it would have taken little to start a fracas that might have turned into a serious incident in the Spanish domain downstream. These were ticklish years when the right of deposit guaranteed in Pinckney's Treaty of 1795 dangled at the end of hempen flatboat lines, and any sort of incident could be turned into a Spanish excuse to abrogate this crucial right.

Communication was the very essence of safety for the American Southwest, yet it took as long to get a dispatch to the national capital as it did to send one from London to Philadelphia. Pickering emphasized this fact: "The passage of letters from Natchez," he wrote Sargent, "is as tedious as from Europe, when westerly winds prevail."[2]. Since the mail often took three months, the Secretary understated his case.

Governor Sargent must have felt an uneasy loneliness, sandwiched between Spanish Louisiana on the west and several formidable Indian tribes to the north and east. The time was ripe to open a post road between Natchez and Tennessee. Specifically, he outlined a route northward from the town of Natchez to Grindstone Ford on Bayou Pierre near the extremity of the Natchez District, then northeastward through the Choctaw and Chickasaw Nations, to the Muscle Shoals on the Tennessee River, and from thence across the Duck River to Nashville and on eastward by the Tellico Blockhouse to Knoxville. Sargent had little difficulty in convincing the Administration of the strategic importance of the proposed road which would follow an ancient Indian path long known as the Chickasaw Trace.[3]

Undoubtedly the Secretary of State wished to open a direct line of communication with Natchez for reasons in addition to those relating to national security. Commercial pressures were growing phenomenally in the lower Mississippi Valley. How early the river trade developed is not precisely known, but evidence indicates that flatboats descended the Mississippi in the 1780s. In 1787 James Wilkinson relied on this western trade artery when he went downstream from Kentucky with a flotilla of flatboats laden with tobacco and flour. In addition to agricultural produce, this colorful scoundrel carried with him dreams of riding the crest of western dissatisfaction to profitable leadership of a Mississippi Valley republic, dreams that failed to materialize despite Spanish encouragement. With each season the fleets of heavily loaded boats increased in size and frequency. By 1801, Mississippi Territorial Governor W. C. C. Claiborne—a loyal Jeffersonian and a prolific correspondent—could inform Secretary of State James Madison that nearly 600 vessels had been counted at Natchez en route to the Crescent City. The total included 514 flatboats, 50 keelboats, 19 pirogues, one brig, and one schooner. Kentucky alone had sent $1,182,864 worth of produce in 1802, and the year before the whole Ohio Valley had shipped cargoes valued at $3,649,322 to the port of New Orleans. Traffic increased so rapidly that in 1807 more than 1800 vessels carried to New Orleans cargoes worth a total of $5,000,000. The next year one tourist counted 83 rivercraft docked at Natchez Under-the-Hill at one time. Though the War of 1812 temporarily slowed the growth of trade throughout the Old Southwest, traffic on the Mississippi River after the war increased at a phenomenal rate.[4]

In addition to the clamor of western farmers and brokers for an improved route back to Tennessee and Kentucky, national security considerations also influenced the rapid decision to accept Sargent's recommendation. Clearly, the great inflow of American commerce into the port of New Orleans would strain, if not entirely rupture, Spanish–American relations. Rowdy flatboatmen hellbent on the disposition of their produce and a drunken celebration before returning upstream were hardly the most tactful and felicitous of diplomats. A suspicion, bordering on paranoia, of Spanish and British interference in Indian affairs in the Old Southwest also explains how Natchez assumed a national importance out of all proportion to its size and population.

Administration officials quickly realized the necessity of linking Natchez with Tennessee, it was another matter to convince the Choctaw, Chickasaw, and Cherokee of the wisdom of opening a Federal road through their territory. Already tribal leaders, particularly the Cherokee, were complaining of a stream of intruders onto their land; with the opening of the road, the stream would become a torrent.

In accordance with Congressional acts of 1799 and 1801, President Jefferson appointed General James Wilkinson, Benjamin Hawkins of North Carolina, and Andrew Pickens of South Carolina as commissioners to conduct the delicate negotiations which began in the summer of 1801. First they met with a Cherokee delegation at Kingston on the Tennessee River some thirty miles southwest of Knoxville where Wilkinson served as the principal spokesman for the commissioners. Forewarned of Cherokee unhappiness over white intruders, the general attempted to disarm them in an oily manner befitting his later reputation. "You have been alarmed by songs of lying birds and the talks of forked tongues. You have heard that your father would press you for further concessions of land, and, it has been said by some, even as far as the Big river. You will know, hereafter, how to listen to such thieves, liars, and mischief-makers, and will treat them as they deserve."[5]

Wilkinson referred to treaty violators, land speculators, and squatters from Tennessee who were held in great contempt by the powerful Cherokee spokesman, Chief Doublehead, who replied that the whites had sufficient roads. Besides, the Cherokee looked with much disfavor upon all sorts of people traveling through their country; already fifty squatter families trespassed on his people's land. No! The Cherokee would not grant permission to improve the road from Knoxville to Nashville.

Fresh on the heels of their failure to extract a concession from the Cherokee, the commissioners met with the Chickasaw at Chickasaw Bluffs on the Mississippi—site of present-day Memphis. Alarmed and somewhat truculent, the Chickasaw expressed fear that passage of the Natchez to Nashville road through their Nation would lead to white invasion and a disruption of their way of life. Though they were "not so far advanced in the habits of civilization as their neighbors, the Cherokee," the headman expressed pride that they had "never spilt blood of a white man," a reference to the loyalty which the tribe transferred from the British to the Americans after the Revolution.[6]

After a delay of several days, George Colbert, the influential mixed blood, took an interesting stand. Since the Americans had requested no cession of land, he could support the government proposal provided that the Chickasaw retained the ownership of the ferries and houses of accommodation. The other chieftains concurred with Colbert's clever maneuver, and on October 24, 1801, they signed the treaty. Two months later downstream at Fort Adams, the commissioners just a week before Christmas extracted permission from the Choctaw for the road to cross their Nations.[7] By then Wilkinson, Hawkins, and Pickens had traveled together for six months.

The failure of the Cherokee to give permission to cross their lands caused Nashville, rather than Knoxville, to become the northeastern terminus of the newly authorized post road. From Nashville it ran southwestward for 100 miles through Tennessee and northern Alabama along a stretch of poor ridge ground between the Duck and Tennessee Rivers. The distance from Natchez to Nashville was variously estimated to be from 500 to 550 miles along a route that crossed the swamps of the Big Black, the Pearl, the Tennessee, and Duck Rivers as well as dozens of lesser bottomlands.[8] In what is now central Mississippi it followed rather closely the watershed line between the Pearl and the Big Black Rivers. The existing path amounted to a combination of narrow Indian trails which ran along the high ground from one tribal village to another and which may have originated as animal trails. Until improved, its width necessitated that man or beast travel single file.

Because of its diverse origins, the trace over the years bore a number of titles—Chickasaw Trace, Path to the Choctaw Nation, Path of Peace, Notchey Trace, Columbian Highway, Military Road (not to be confused with Jackson's Military Road), or the Government Road—until it widely became known as the Natchez Trace a decade or so after it was surveyed and opened. Indeed, the word *trace* is a derivation from an old French word meaning "a line of footprints or animal tracks." Since many segments of the road probably began as buffalo or deer trails, its most enduring name is appropriate. The least fitting designation, however, is the "Notchey Trace", though it was long known as such in some areas. While some of its segments may have been blazed in that manner for the convenience of the white men, it is ludicrous to suggest that Indians resorted to such a practice.

General James Wilkinson directed the preliminary survey of the trace in 1801, and in the following year Edmund Pendleton Gaines, who later distinguished himself as an army general, marked the path through the Indian Nations. It was to be at least five years, however, before the completion of any meaningful improvements. The unexpected suspension of the right of deposit in New Orleans in 1802 caused Postmaster General Gideon Granger to request the Army to widen the trace to sixteen feet, causeway the swamps, bridge smaller streams, and at least fell trees across others so that mail riders could keep dry. Though the bridges and causeways were not actually constructed, the troops did widen the route through the Natchez District, for some forty miles beyond, and over the last 150 miles leading into Nashville. In 1806 Congress did appropriate $6000 for improvement of the trace, but over the years the portions through the Indian Nations largely remained unimproved.[9]

The Natchez Trace was a pioneer Federal internal improvement project which officially had a highly anomalous status. Ostensibly the opening of the Natchez Trace was to facilitate delivery of the mail to the distant southwest outpost. In addition to the considerations of rapid communication to such a troubled spot, however, the route clearly had strategic military implications. At times the trace was referred to as the military road, even by President Jefferson. He may have called the trace a military road because it was first surveyed by Army officers and cleared by troops. Post and military roads unquestionably were constitutional. At this time, however, the President's strict interpretation of the Constitution caused him to be uncomfortable with Federal construction of other types of roads. Nevertheless, for thousands of years rulers have understood that while roads benefit all sectors of society their strategic military advantage is paramount.[10]

As important as were these strategic considerations, the road soon figured more prominently in the facilitation of the rapidly rising western river commerce. By 1801, the rich lands of bluegrass Kentucky, central Tennessee, and southern and eastern Ohio were annually sending mounting tonnages of country produce downstream to the New Orleans port. Grain mills had been perfected, streams dammed, and the necessary power made available to turn rich wheat harvests into highly marketable flour. Cornmeal, hempen goods, tobacco, whiskey, and cured meats also were often listed on the cargo manifests.[11]

Regardless of its condition, the Natchez Trace quickly became heavily traveled by boatmen returning to Tennessee, Kentucky, and points beyond after having sold their cargoes downriver at Natchez or New Orleans. As a rule, the wide variety of river craft were dismantled and sold for lumber or firewood by their owners at their destinations. Only a few keelboats and barges returned upstream. Though mail riders galloped up and down the trace, and on occasion American troops marched over it in both directions, most of the traffic was northbound. A few preachers, peddlers, slave traders, government officials, and tourists rode south from Nashville, but the Natchez Trace was never a major route of immigra-

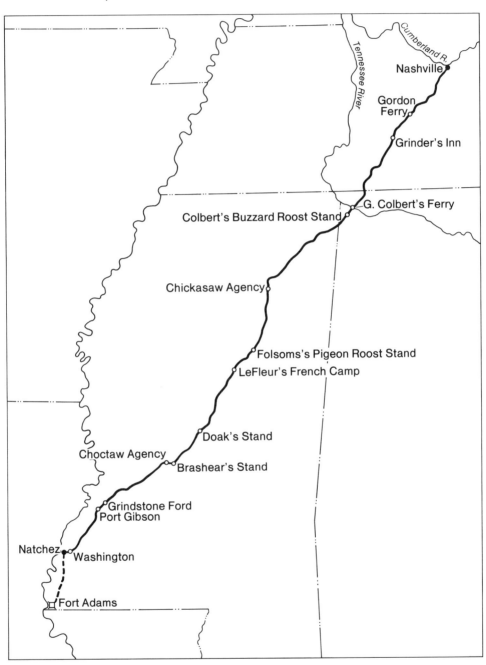

tion into the Old Southwest. Travel was expensive, so virtually everyone carried a fair amount of money; some a great deal. Indeed, it was not unusual for the saddlebags of returning farmer-boatmen to be bulging with Spanish and French coins—silver as well as gold. As the port of New Orleans steadily became more vital to the economy of the West, the number of gold-laden travelers up the trace increased. Some traveled afoot, but most rode "Opelousas"—ponies purchased in Louisiana or the Natchez District. To complete the round trip from Kentucky to New Orleans or Natchez and back took three months, give or take a few days.

Unfortunately, few of the returning boatmen have recorded their experiences in journals, but a number of travelers—mainly tourists, clergymen, or businessmen—did provide for posterity a glimpse of life on the trace. Perhaps the most celebrated veteran of the early years of the Natchez Trace was Englishman Francis Baily who left New Orleans on June 21, 1797, arriving in Natchez six days later. Baily eventually reached Nashville on July 31 after departing from Natchez on July 5 in the company of a party of Kentucky flatboatmen. Though his journey took place before the road was designated as a post road, his experience typifies that of the early users of the trace. En route, the party met Indians, struggled with poorly defined trails, braved stream crossings, rounded up strayed horses, and in general coped with all the adversities of the trail.[12]

While there were few accommodations on the trace in 1801, the number of inns or taverns, generally known as "stands," kept pace with the flow of traffic. During the decade following the War of 1812, one had a choice of rest stops even in the Indians Nations. When the trace was first improved as a post road it ran for 205 miles through the Chickasaw domain. In 1797, Baily found only one stand in that stretch, but by 1821 there were seventeen. Similarly, in 1800 there was only one place for the traveler along the 160-mile segment in the Choctaw Nation to resupply—a trip that averaged four to seven days. By 1806, there were three stands; by 1812, six, and by 1820, nineteen. When the trace was officially opened, it ran for seventy-two miles through the reasonably well populated Natchez District. So accommodations were never extremely difficult to find there. Nevertheless, the number of way stations increased within the Natchez District at a surprising rate.[13]

Some of the proprietors of the stands were white men who had resided for years among the Indians and who had taken Indian wives. Others were mixed bloods.[14] In most instances, these establishments were on a farm or plantation where food for man and beast was produced. And it was not unusual for them to be men of substantial means with many African slaves. Though most were reputed to be congenial hosts, their services and commodities were often costly. Whatever the price, the fare was plain or even rough, and the sleeping facilities were primitive. Most wayfarers, nevertheless, commented favorably on their treatment.

Parson William Winans, who rode over the trace in 1810, noted: "We were always treated respectfully, and sometimes in their rude manner with cordial hospitality and kindness by the Indians with whom we had intercourse. The greatest rudeness we witnessed was in the white men we met at the taverns or stands." As to be expected, some establishments gained a wide reputation for their hospitality. Such was the case with the stand kept by Turner Brashears about forty miles inside the line separating the Choctaw Nation from the Natchez District. A native of Maryland, Brashears moved among the Choctaw in the late eighteenth century. Because he soon mastered their tongue, the Spanish sought his service as an interpreter. Evidently his fluency in Choctaw explains, at least in part, why Brashears soon became a person of consequence. A Methodist preacher, Jacob Young, took note of his "fine public house." Then he added: "Although he had an Indian wife, he was himself a gentleman. He had a good many colored people, and appeared to be a man of considerable wealth. He treated us very well but knew how to make a high bill."[15]

Not all the facilities received praise, however. Some had dirt floors and virtually no accoutrements of civilization. "You feel blank and disappointed when you walk in and find a cold dirt floor, naked walls, and no fire," complained one 1815 sojourner. "Camping out is far better than such an accommodation."[16] Many travelers took his advice. It was not unusual for returning boatmen and others to band together in parties as large as a dozen—sometimes larger. With safety and company in numbers, these groups often camped out. In the spring of 1805, Samuel P. Hildreth and his brother Charles went up the trace with a party of fifteen Kentucky boatmen. Well mounted and provisioned, they traveled approximately thirty-five miles a day. At night they bedded down near a spring or creek. The regimen was spartan, arising before sun-up and riding all day. Horses were hobbled at night and fed fresh-cut grass and green bark when the corn supply was exhausted. Trail food was coarse, hurriedly prepared, and washed down with brandy or whiskey as long as it lasted.[17]

Hildreth expressed no fear of robbers or trail bandits. Was this because he was traveling in the company of such a large group? Partially but not entirely. Despite the myth of crime and violence that is so prevalently associated with the Natchez Trace, relatively few travelers met with serious misfortune along its route. Yes, pirates, particularly around the turn of the nineteenth century, did menace travelers as they floated down the Mississippi with their valuable cargos and as they rode homeward up the Natchez Trace. The amazing fact, however, is how few lives and fortunes were lost on the trace after it became well defined and traveled, considering the number of people and the amount of gold in their possession. In the some twenty-five years of documented history of the trace, no more than three authenticated cases of murder are recorded.

At first, however, a couple of ruthless outlaw bands—the Masons and the Harpes—terrorized travelers on the road to and from Nashville. Governor Claiborne reacted vigorously. On April 27, 1802, Claiborne wrote Colonel Daniel Burnet—a regimental commander of the territorial militia—that a set of pirates alternately infested the Mississippi River and the road leading from Natchez to Tennessee. The bandits operated in the vicinity of Walnut Hills (Vicksburg) where they had access to both river and road.[18]

These "Pirates and Robbers" had attempted to board the boat of Colonel Joshua Baker, a Kentucky merchant en route south with several flatboats loaded with horses and farm products. Later, on the Natchez Trace, Mason and three of his men robbed Colonel Baker's party, and when the robbery was reported, Claiborne was incensed. "These Men must be arrested; the honor of our Country, the Interest of Society, & the feelings of humanity, proclaim that it is time to stop their Career," the governor emphasized to Burnet. Though he doubted that Colonel Burnet could legally "execute (strictly) a Military Order," Claiborne urged him to mount a posse of fifteen or twenty volunteers to arrest the thieves. And, finally, the governor assured Burnet that he hoped "the honor of taking these men will be conferred on the citizens of your neighborhood" and that "should they succeed I promise them generous reward."[19]

Added insult and injury to those already committed on the trace was perpetrated by some Indians shortly after the Baker incident when a band of Choctaw robbed Andrew Bracken, a recent immigrant, of several horses and some other property. Governor Claiborne wasted no time in communicating with Agent John McKee whom he instructed to convey the seriousness of the crime to the Choctaw chiefs. "This is the first outrage since the Treaty at Fort Adams," he pointed out to McKee, "and if the chiefs should cause the offenders to be severely punished; it will probably be the last." Bracken's property was returned to him, and Indian molestation of the trace henceforth remained more of a fear than a reality.[20]

The demise of two of the most notorious land pirates was as gruesome and swift as had been their felonious assaults. One of the Harpe brothers, Micajah, who was generally known as "Big Harpe," was beheaded in an act of criminal retribution. Reportedly, his assassin worked so slowly that Harpe cursed with his last breath, "You are a God Damned rough butcher, but cut on and be damned!" Whether Mason's decapitation was swifter is a matter of conjecture, but his head ended up in the possession of Wiley ("Little Harpe") and James May who encased it in clay for preservation until they could exchange it for a $2,000 reward in Natchez. As they placed their exhibit before the magistrate, their identity was made known by a passerby who recognized their horses as stolen property. Whereupon the pair made good their escape only to be captured immediately in Greenville. After a trial and conviction, they were hanged in February of 1804. [21]

The legend of violence, however, rested heavily upon the history of the Natchez Trace and colored it out of all proportion to its actual past. The road was remarkably safe, especially in view of the fact that almost every party that traveled it carried a considerable amount of money. Among travelers there seems to have existed the same neighborliness and co-operation that characterized travel on other American frontier trails and roads. From the outset it was discovered that a party of no more than fifteen members was the most efficient unit. Larger groups wasted time making and breaking camp and at stream crossings. Too, a larger number of animals caused much confusion and strayed too far at night in search of forage. Though no one kept statistics on the number of travelers who passed over the trace annually, the number was relatively large. A good basis for substantiating this is the huge number of flatboats reaching downriver markets as mentioned above. [22]

One of the first historians to place violence along the trace in its proper perspective was William Baskerville Hamilton, who truly mastered the sources relating to the Mississippi Territory, especially those pertaining to its social and intellectual history. [23] His criticism of the romanticists who perpetrated the myth of crime and violence along the trace has been borne out by the most recent scholarship. "Lawlessness along the Trace (and everywhere else in the country) there certainly was, . . . but the evidence seems to be that the most thrilling and general type of skullduggery along the trace was the temporary theft of horses by the Indians, in order that they might reap a small reward for "finding" them." [24] This humorous reference to the temporary theft of horses is supported by the files of the State and War Departments. While there was a great deal of crudeness and roughness on the frontier, statistical analyses of court records indicates no higher incidence of felonious crimes in rural than in urban areas of the antebellum South. Impressionistic evidence extracted from local contemporary publications, as contrasted to the notations of tourists who often arrived with set opinions, confirms the findings of cliometricians. Michael F. Beard, who has exhaustively studied newspapers published in Mississippi Territory, finds reports of very few homicides, even in the notorious Natchez Under-the-Hill.[25]

Though Hamilton's point is well taken and has been supported by research over the past half century, it is likely that most travelers embarked upon a ride over the trace with some apprehension. Surely, Mississippi's premier historian of the nineteenth century, J. F. H. Claiborne, romanticized when he declared that the road "became perfectly secure" after the demise of Mason and the Harpes and when he stated that "the Choctaws never robbed nor permitted robbers to live among them."[26] On the other hand, Claiborne justly credited the countrymen and mixed bloods who operated stands along the route with preserving the peace, a condition that was as profitable to them financially as it was beneficial to the tribesmen among whom they resided. As pointed out in preceding chapters, many of the tribal leaders correctly perceived that perpetration of atrocities by their people would have dire consequences over the long run. Not only did the chiefs urge restraint, but in a number of cases they ordered the apprehension and punishment of serious offenders.

The wild and bawdy reputation of Natchez Under-the-Hill undoubtedly accounts for much of the myth of the violence attributed to the Natchez Trace. No other port on the Mississippi had a reputation for licentiousness, dissipation, and debauchery that exceeded that of the port of Natchez, which in the 1790s extended some 800 yards from the base of the cliffs out into the river. Insofar as possible, residents of the stately mansions atop the bluff dissociated themselves from the prostitution, gambling, and violence in the shantytown below. Undeniably these were there. After all, Natchez Under-the-Hill was the second leading port on the river from 1800 to 1840. As such it contributed substantially to the economy of the Old Southwest. Here arrived the manufactured products from Europe and the American Atlantic Seaboard that were to be distributed throughout the Natchez District. At these docks agricultural staples grown in the upper Mississippi Valley and livestock from Louisiana and Texas also were unloaded.

The image of the Natchez Under-the-Hill as a cesspool of sin, however, totally overshadowed its tremendous economic significance. Who remembers the name of the leading merchants of the port? But who has not heard of Mike Fink, king of the keelboatmen, who loved to brag of his animalistic parentage? "I'm half wild-horse, and half cock-eyed alligator, an' the rest o'me is crooked snags an' red-hot snappin' turtle." Everyone who has read tales about the frontier has encountered some variant of this boast. Indeed, Mike Fink and Natchez Under-the-Hill symbolized the myth of the wild and savage West, a myth created largely by the pens of traveler-journalists who indelibly fixed the wild and savage image of Natchez Under-the-Hill in the minds of Americans.[27] Even today, it is a rare article in either popular or scholarly periodicals that does not emphasize the criminal element.[28]

Other than Federal officials, no group had more of a vested interest in the opening and maintenance of the trace than did the merchants of Natchez. Perhaps no merchant had a greater personal stake in the trace than Abijah Hunt, who possessed extensive holdings in Natchez. A native of New Jersey, Hunt accumulated a small fortune as a sutler in General Anthony Wayne's army in the Old Northwest before settling in Natchez where he developed a chain of stores and cotton gins. Like Governor Sargent, Hunt was a Federalist. He was also a man of action. When authorities failed to act quickly on Sargent's request for the opening of a road to Nashville, Hunt traveled through the wilderness to Philadelphia to personally lobby for the project. Sargent's interests were not the only ones he pressed. For the enterprising Hunt received the appointment as the first postmaster in Natchez as well as a contract to carry the mail over the lower half of the trace—even before improvement to the road! It was politics and not the quest for wealth, that led to his demise. Words between Hunt, the Federalist, and George Poindexter, the Jeffersonian territorial delegate to Congress, resulted in a duel in 1811. Across the river just above present-day Vidalia, Louisiana, Hunt took a ball in his stomach from Poindexter's pistol and died a few hours later. The wealthy bachelor left his tremendous fortune to his nephew David Hunt who, along with his descendants, continued to play an important role in Natchez. No other individual merchant had such a direct interest in the trace, but others, such as James Wilkins, Samuel Postlewaite, and Alexander Moore, undoubtedly understood the economic impact which the Natchez Trace had on their community.[29]

Also resting in the shadow of the land pirates are a host of other individuals who used the trace. Among the most fascinating is John Lee Swaney who for at least a half dozen years carried mail up and down the trace as a rider of the woodland pony express. Sometimes riding alone and at other times in the company of a fast-moving party of returning boatmen and officials, Swaney braved all kinds of weather. Mounted on a sturdy horse with a half bushel of shelled corn and his well-oiled deerskin mail pouch strapped to his saddle, Swaney traversed the 500 miles of the trace in ten to fifteen days. Few men experienced the range of adventures that befell Swaney, who encountered some of the trail's most notorious figures during his service. In addition to Samuel Mason, Wiley

Harpe, and Micajah Harpe, Swaney claims to have been acquainted with many other thieves and murderers. He first met the Harpes when he was a jockey at a race track in Knoxville. It was there, according to Swaney, that the Harpes began their criminal escapades after losing everything in a bet on one of their race horses. Of course, Swaney also rode the trace with lonely and frightened pilgrims who simply sought the safety of his presence. Regardless of the company he kept, Swaney provided the slender line of direct communication between the outer fringe of American civilization in the Old Southwest and the national capital during the crucial years when the United States and Spain maintained delicately strained relations in Louisiana and along the Gulf Coast. No doubt Swaney carried in his pouch many of the governmental communications which determined the destiny of the young republic.[30]

The Natchez Trace cut through the heart of a region today often called the "Bible Belt," and it is probable that more preachers trod or rode its paths than robbers and murderers. Exactly when the first clergyman ventured down the trace is not known. It is known, however, that as early as 1800 three Presbyterian missionaries, prevented by low water from proceeding by boat, ventured down the path from Nashville to Natchez. Few of the so-called "soul merchants" were as colorful, however, as the eccentric Lorenzo Dow, a Methodist evangelist from Connecticut. Because of the range and speed of his travels, Dow called himself the "Cosmopolite," but others preferred the appellation of "Crazy Dow." Dow's trademark was a long black cloak, he wore an untrimmed beard, and his uncut hair was as wild as the look in his eyes. Dow loved to provoke confrontations and he resorted to all manner of tricks and trumpeting to stir up emotions at camp meetings. He was but one of a host of preachers and missionaries who rode into the Old Southwest to conduct emotional revivals for the isolated frontiersmen and to minister to the Native Americans. Two other early Methodists were Jacob Young and Tobias Gibson. Joseph Bullen and Cyrus Kingsbury were among the first Presbyterian missionaries to travel the trace. Of course there were many other individuals representing any number of religious denominations. To these men of the cloth, more than to any other single group, we are indebted for written accounts of conditions along the trace.[31]

Thus for the first two decades of the nineteenth century the muddy and boggy Natchez Trace was a somewhat treacherous but tremendously significant economic, political, and cultural line of communication to the southwest corner of the republic. Despite what Postmaster General Gideon Granger had called the "badness of the road," it was in fact an all-weather route over which travelers could make their way, though often with some difficulty, during any month of the year. Only on three occasions during the War of 1812 did significant numbers of American troops march over the trace. Nevertheless, the availability of this strategic artery of communication provided national leaders with a greater confidence in the security of the Mississippi Valley and Gulf Coast.

More important, in retrospect, were the descriptions of the new land that quickly spread up the trace. Significant is the fact that through this wilderness artery pumped a mythology best described as a potpourri of dreams or attractions. The images were as varied as the types responding to them. As a route of immigration, however, the trace was of secondary importance. While a few families used it as a way to the Old Southwest, much larger numbers poured in after the War of 1812 from Georgia and the Carolinas.

Among the most important of the new roads was the Federal Road, which ran from Athens in Georgia to the Tombigbee settlements and from thence across the lower Mississippi Territory to New Orleans. A lateral trail connected Fort Stephens and Natchez. Actually, the Athens road was the final segment of a shorter route from Washington, D.C., via Virginia, the Carolinas, and Georgia which cut some 500 miles off the trip. Though Congress had studied the proposed route immediately after the Louisiana Purchase and had authorized its survey as early as 1804, it was not until 1811 that the Army improved the link with Athens into a route approximating a useful wagon road. After expending considerable effort and enduring a great deal of aggravation, the Postmaster General established an express mail service along the horsepath from Athens in 1806. His seventeen-day schedule for riders to cover the distance between Washington and New Orleans represented a bit of bureaucratic optimism, however. The significance of the Federal Road as an artery of immigration is discussed in Chapter 9.

Also of major importance was the trace opened by Edmund P. Gaines which connected the Tennessee River with the Tombigbee at Cotton Gin Port where there was a gin as early as 1801. Almost immediately this route became well traveled by emigrants from the Carolinas who had made their way down the Tennessee River and its tributaries. It also became commercially significant. After Gaines trace was later extended to connect with the headwaters of the Big Black River, even more traffic was diverted from the Natchez Trace.[32] Delivery of the mail and government dispatches over these wilderness roads was important, of course, but the real significance of the opening of the central and eastern traces was that they facilitated immigration. These one-way travelers recorded their own stories of advances into the Old Southwest.

By the 1820's the Natchez Trace fell into a state of disuse and disrepair as the spirit of the once colorful and important road moved across the Mississippi where the buffalo had already gone. In just a few decades the Indians would follow, and after the Civil War, so would the restless cowpunchers—sons of Southerners, both black and white, who earlier had herded cattle in the Old South and Old Southwest. Meanwhile, Robert Fulton and Robert R. Livingston had proved that steam-powered craft could buck the swift current of the mighty Mississippi in a magical fashion. Soon the river was full of steamboats and the Natchez Trace was empty of its rollicking rivermen. Now they could ride all the way to Pittsburgh for a few dollars aboard boats that could carry the mail along with them. Just as a multiplicity of forces had given life to the best-known trace of the trans-Appalachian West, new forces had caused its death. How appropriate that the deadliest of them all was the clanking steam engine which for over a century—in boats and on rails—would dominate the nation's frontiers on both sides of the Mississippi.

In a sense, one could view the Natchez Trace as a Bunyanesque ribbon binding together the package known as the Old Southwest. The history of the trace is the story of the flow of humanity into the farthest reaches of the frontier of the young republic. Collectively, this cast of frontier characters contributed to the nascent manifest destiny which cemented the Old Southwest to the nation and foretold American transcontinental expansion. Thus it is highly fitting that the Federal government has memorialized this road through the construction of a unique parkway that follows in many instances the precise path of the old Natchez Trace and that seldom meanders far from it. Since the name of James Wilkinson generally is associated with deception, it is not often that one would select his words as a text for a discourse on American history. General Wilkinson in 1802 was responsible for the defense of the exposed frontier of the Old Southwest. When he transmitted the preliminary survey of the route of the proposed road from Nashville to Natchez, he offered an observation that at the moment must have been viewed as a gross exaggeration. "This Road being compleated I shall consider our Southern extremity assured, the Indians in that quarter at our feet & the adjacent Province laid open to us." In retrospect, his were prophetic words![33]

6

Rough Riders in the Old Southwest

"Thousands of cattle are grazed here for market" reported historian J. F. H. Claiborne in 1841 on his return to Natchez from a tour of the Piney Woods of southeastern Mississippi. His colorful description of the pastoral life there was punctuated with references to numerous herds of cattle grazing on the carpet of grass "three feet high" beneath the forest of longleaf pine "rolling like waves in the middle of the great ocean." He registered surprise at the "valuable trade in cattle" which "enriched" many people of the region who commonly owned between 500 and 1000 head. Claiborne wrote of drama as well as dollars; his depictions of the round-ups have the ring of a classic western.[1]

For over a century, historians ignored the herdsmen whom Claiborne, a gentleman of the Natchez District, had found as intriguing as they were ubiquitous. Finally in 1949, Frank L. Owsley, with his controversial *Plain Folk of the Old South*, briefly directed attention to these pastoral frontiersmen before they faded back into obscurity. Because the herders had been relegated to historiographical oblivion so long, Owsley liked to compare his study as "akin to archaeology." And in the same breath he accurately predicted that they were "still in danger of being reinterred."[2] The debate which Owsley stirred up was short-lived; a third of a century would elapse before scholars redirected their attention to the significance of cattle and swine raising in the antebellum South.[3]

Considering the size of the livestock population its value, and the relatively small amount of land under cultivation in the region, it is remarkable that so few historians have mentioned the herdsmen. In the lower South, for example, there were 3,436,352 cattle in 1840, 5,396,460 in 1850, and 8,024,307 in 1860; the number of swine increased from 5,570,327 in 1840 to 9,056,897 in 1850 and to 9,732,413 in 1860.[4] According to some estimates, the value of Southern livestock in 1860 was twice that of the same year's cotton crop and roughly equal to the combined value of all Southern crops. In the census of 1850, the reported value of livestock on farms in Alabama and Mississippi was over a third of the value of the farms—a truly impressive figure if we keep in mind that probably only a small percentage of range animals were counted. On the other hand, less than 10 percent of the total acreage in the South was listed as improved at mid-century.[5] It is puzzling that figures of such magnitude did not stimulate greater interest among scholars. Such is especially the case in view of strong impressionistic evidence of the presence of huge numbers of cattle and swine on the Southern frontier throughout the colonial and early national periods.

Most explanations of this academic myopia refer to the Civil War, which completely distracted historians of the South. Since that conflict was the pivotal event in the history of that section, this reaction is not difficult to understand. Nevertheless, the extent to which it has dominated historical research for a century is surprising. Scholars north of the Mason-Dixon line displayed similar proclivities, concentrating their attention on King Cotton, sectionalism, the resulting conflict, its aftermath, and minority history.

The paucity of sources also explains the reluctance of scholars to write about the intrepid frontiersmen who tended the herds in the trans-Appalachian West. They left few written accounts of either their social or business lives. Nor did the early entrepreneurs who dealt in meat, hides, tallow, hooves, and horns or the myriad items manufactured from them. While census reports, tax rolls, and estate inventories contain much data pertinent to the livestock industry, the manipulation of that information was extremely tedious prior to the computer revolution. It is hoped, however, cliometricians soon will apply their formulae to these sources as well as to the mountains of trading records in foreign repositories. Meanwhile, past researchers can hardly be blamed for preferring to work in the abundant plantation records, particularly when the information contained therein held so great an appeal. So pervasive has been the myth of the plantation South that even scholars could not escape its impact.

Historians of the South are not alone in their failure to give serious credence to Owsley, who insisted that "the South was a great livestock region." This advocate of the "plain folk" admitted that statistics prior to 1840 were sorely inadequate, but he insisted that "grazing . . . was of greater relative importance to the antebellum South than in any other part of the United States." He did, however, have data which proved that "the South produced a larger number of mules, swine, and beef cattle in proportion to population than in any [other] section until 1860."[6]

It is curious that frontier historians were not driven to a re-examination of the Southern frontier by Owsley's work. They continued to ignore cattle raisers and other herders in the South despite Frederick Jackson Turner's inclusion of them in his constantly quoted description of the "procession of civilization" from Cumberland Gap to South Pass. Turnerians seemed to have forgotten that the father of Western History, in the same essay, asserted that "the experiences of the Carolina cowpens guided the ranchers of Texas."[7] In recent years, however, several scholars have turned their attention to herding in the Old Southwest and have suggested reasons why stock raisers have been neglected.[8]

Colonial records indicate that stock raising, if not the very earliest, was among the earliest successful economic pursuits from Virginia all the way to Florida. From the time of the settlement of Saint Augustine in 1565, residents complained that Indians rustled their cattle.[9] However, the ubiquity of stock raising is of far greater significance than its chronology. Because livestock flourished in all the colonies of the American Southeast—Spanish, English, and French—the movement of Old World cattle from the Atlantic Seaboard into the Mississippi Valley was multi-directional and continuous throughout the colonial and early national periods. Though Spanish cattle bloodlines were clearly predominant by the end of the colonial period, colonists from numerous European nations introduced a variety of breeds. The same applies to the pedigrees of horses and hogs.

It was the intentions of the proprietors of South Carolina "to introduce planters, not graziers," but the settlers soon recognized the peculiar suitability of the land for stock raising. As one observer explained in 1682, an ox could be raised "at almost as little expence in Carolina, as a Hen is in England." He must not have exaggerated, for by the early eighteenth century vast herds were reported. Some folk owned a thousand while frequently men ran several hundred each. Hogs, foraging easily on the mast, abounded as well.[10] From Virginia to Florida this unanticipated industry flourished during the colonial era, though not everywhere as extensively as in South Carolina.

The same can be said of the Old Southwest. Because the French did not immediately attempt to settle agricultural colonies along the Gulf Coast and in the Mississippi Valley, several decades passed before sizable herds developed there. Accounts of the 1729 Natchez Indian destruction of the French settlement adjacent to their town mention the slaughter of livestock by the attacking natives. As did all European immigrants, the first Louisianians raised a small number of farm animals. Soon, however, herding became a commercial enterprise. Reports indicate that in 1746 a "cattle ranch" was operating on Deer Island, separated by a narrow channel from the colony at Biloxi, and that settlers there owned a sixty-ton vessel "manned by a crew of five or six sailors."[11] It is assumed that the boat carried cattle to New Orleans and to neighboring islands in the Gulf for transfer to ships bound for the West Indies. Cattle raising on the coastal islands and on the adjacent mainland continued well into the twentieth century.

The suitability of the Old Southwest for stock raising was readily apparent to representatives of the powers competing for its dominion—France, Spain, and England—as was the potential of the West Indies as a market for meat and related products. Though the degree to which that potential was realized still remains unknown, stock raising increased with each passing decade. By mid-century a nascent cattle industry had developed on the luxuriant prairies to the northwest of New Orleans in the Opelousas region. By 1770 large herds ranged from Opelousas to Natchitoches, and by the end of the century stock raising had become the most prevalent use of the land from one extreme of the Old Southwest to the other.

From the banks of the Mississippi to the coastal plains of West Florida travelers frequently sighted cattle, and had their reports not so consistently referred to huge herds, some accounts may have lacked credibility. By 1791, so many cattle roamed in the environs of Natchez that Ezekiel Forman complained to Spanish officials that hundreds of cattle daily ravaged the land where he wanted to settle.[12] In light of the thousands of head reported grazing not too distant from the west bank of the river in the vicinity of Opelousas and Atakapa by this time, Forman's complaint seems realistic. And in just a few years, the oft-cited tourist Estwick Evans wrote of seeing "vast herds" of cattle grazing along the Mississippi in 1818.[13] On another occasion he wrote of seeing "thousands" along the river banks. A noted authority of Mississippi Territory, William B. Hamilton, suggests that even larger herds may have been kept along the Tombigbee above Mobile where more of the land was suited for pastoral use and where more immigrants may have brought with them a herding life style. According to an 1809 letter written from Fort Stoddert, one individual in the Tombigbee region owned 10,000 cattle! In 1766 a British engineer named an individual who owned 1000 head near Mobile. While this figure seems extraordinary, herds of up to a thousand were often observed on the rolling plains of South Alabama.[14]

Decades prior to the founding of the English colonies in North America, Spanish officials expressed great enthusiasm for the establishment of an important livestock industry in Florida. Little did they suspect in the sixteenth century that British raids—along with Indian interference—would prevent fulfillment of this ranching potential. After the conclusion of the French and Indian War in 1763, however, the cattle industry in Florida—especially in the panhandle extending into the Old Southwest—boomed.[15] Throughout the last third of the eighteenth century many glowing reports of the cattle herds in the environs of the Perdido River were recorded. British surveyor Bernard Romans, for instance, in 1772 praised the pastures between the Perdido and the Tensaw as "incomparable" and surpassed by "no Country on Earth . . . either in Quantity or Quality or Variety." Then he estimated that the ranges between the two rivers maintained "above Ten Thousand Cattle and Horses."[16] Doubtless, Florida played an important role in the multi-directional diffusion process emphasized by Jordan and others, but the extent to which the Spanish black cattle were related to those in other Southern colonies and states probably will always remain subject to conjecture.[17]

Since even experienced cattlemen find it difficult to estimate accurately the size of grazing herds, the number of animals reported by the observers cited above remains somewhat suspect. However, it must be kept in mind that travelers relied on conversations with local residents as well as on their own visual inspection of the herds. In the absence of widespread statistical data prior to 1840, the only alternative is reliance upon the observations of contemporaries and attempt to objectively use them. Fortunately, however, sufficient Spanish census figures and territorial tax lists are available to confirm conclusively the extensiveness of cattle raising in the Old Southwest.

For example, in the Natchez district, Spanish officials listed the following totals for cattle: 1784—3,100 to 3,400; 1787—4,476; 1788—6,966; 1792—15,181; 1794—18,302. Converted into ratios of people (slaves included) to cattle, the figures are: 1:2.07 in 1784; 1:2.32 in 1787; 1:3.02 in 1788; 1:3:49 in 1792 and 1:4.12 in 1794. A 1788 census listed 17,351 cattle west of the river in the "Post du Oppeloussais" owned by 316 family units comprising 1,983 people, slaves included, for a ratio of 1:8.75.[18] One stockman there reported 1,000 head, six others owned 500 or more, and thirty-eight possessed between 100 and 450. In Nueva Feliciana, just south of the Natchez district, in 1789, 109 families owned 4,481 head, a ratio of 1:4.21.[19]

Captains Eduardo Nugent and Juan Kelly, who were Irishmen in Spanish service, discovered considerable cattle herds during their 1770 tour of Louisiana on orders from the governor. They began their circular route at Atakapas, moved northward to Opelousas, then struck out to the northwest to Natchitoches on the Red River, and returned through Rapido. In these four regions, they recorded a total population, slaves included, of 1,296 persons and 5,752 cattle for a combined ratio of 1:4.44.

Opelousas with 1:7.75 and Atakapas with 1:6.65 had the highest, and as would be expected, those districts were described as having the most favorable terrain.[20]

Consul Daniel Clark of New Orleans enclosed an 1803 census of the district of Atakapas in a letter to James Madison that revealed continued growth of the herds there. The census disclosed a total population of 3,746 people, 7,315 horses, and 58,871 cattle—a person-to-cattle ratio of 1:15.72. Consul Clark emphasized to Madison that the totals of horses and cattle were "particularly defective" for fear of impending taxation, estimating that a more accurate figure would be 75,000 cattle and 13,000 horses.[21] Clark's point is well taken; from time immemorial, property owners have minimized taxable possessions.

Mississippi territorial tax lists provide another convincing index of the cattle economy. Some of the most complete figures include:[22]

Washington County	1804	9,071 head
Claiborne County	1804	4,744 head
Jefferson County	1805	5,088 head
Adams County	1805	11,199 head
Washington County	1805	9,532 head
Wilkinson County	1805	5,816 head

In the files of the late William B. Hamilton of Duke University is a card showing an 1805 total of 35,041 horned cattle for the counties of Adams, Claiborne, Jefferson, Washington, and Wilkinson.[23] His totals vary but little from those above; both sets of data indicate the largest concentrations were near Natchez and along the Tombigbee and Chickasawhay Rivers, which are north and northwest of Mobile. Herds ranging from 200 to 1,000 head accounted for most of the stock. It is reasonable, keeping in mind Daniel Clark's warning above, that livestock in those areas far exceeded figures on the tax rolls. Besides, since the stock generally roamed at large, it was virtually impossible to arrive at an accurate count.

The presence of such large numbers of cattle in the Old Southwest raises questions for students of cultural as well as economic history. The greatest of all American myths is that of the cowboy. Indeed, most of the world views Americans as cowboys, and we often see ourselves in the same manner. No greater evidence exists than the recent craze, now cooling down, for western garb; pickup trucks (high-tech horses) are the latest means of a vicarious "western" experience. That the Old Southwest was also a land of cowboys has too long been ignored. As the southern herdsmen ranged westward through the Carolinas, Floridas, Georgia,

Alabama, Mississippi, and Louisiana, they developed techniques which were more comparable than dissimilar to those associated with the post-Civil War cattle kingdom.[24]

Though in some locations the cattlemen cracked whips instead of twirling lariats, horsemen had tended livestock for generations before significant numbers of Anglos took lessons from Spaniards in the Nueces Valley of Texas.[25] Not only were mounted herdsmen of various nationalities more common in the lower Mississippi valley than is generally acknowledged but also Indians rounded up their stock on horseback, as did black slaves who tended their masters' cattle. Though some aspects of the "Iberian ranching system" probably were introduced first from the West, many Americans were exposed to and practiced Spanish ranching techniques on the cis-Mississippi frontier.[26]

Open ranges, roundups, branding, long drives, and stock regulations concerning such matters as fencing and strays were not restricted to the trans-Mississippi ranching experience. Admittedly, neither the roundups nor the drives in the Old Southwest were on a Texas scale, but the mood and tone would make readers of Zane Grey or Louis L'Amour feel at home. Aficionados of the roundup are invited to read in its entirety Claiborne's colorful description of cowboying Piney Woods style, partially excerpted here. The men, "mounted on low built, shaggy, but muscular and hardy horses . . . and armed with raw hide whips of prodigious size, and sometimes with a catching rope or lasso," scoured the woods "in gallant style, followed by a dozen fierce looking dogs . . . sometimes driving a herd of a thousand heads to the pen." After describing their "dexterity" as horsemen, Claiborne continues, "In this way, cheering each other with loud shouts and making the woods ring with the crack of their long whips and the trampling of the flying cattle, they gallop thirty or forty miles a day and rendezvous at night at the *stamping ground.*" (Italics are Claiborne's) The account concludes with a campfire scene—complete with jugs of "old corn"—seemingly too familiar to have been written in the Old Southwest in 1841—a quarter of a century before Joseph G. McCoy bought his first herd of cattle in Abilene![27]

As interesting as these implications are to cultural historians, they may prove to be of even greater significance to students of economic history. In light of the well documented failures to discover profitable staple crops in the Mississippi Valley during the colonial period, strong evidence supports the argument that cattle raising constituted the first really profitable and lasting agricultural industry in the Southwest. True, in Louisiana, sugar, and in Alabama and Mississippi, cotton would eventually predominate. Nevertheless, until cotton became king—and perhaps throughout the antebellum period—more free persons probably sustained themselves by herding than by any other commercial means.[28]

Earliest accounts of the cattle industry in the colonial South indicate that stock raising quickly was viewed as a profit-making endeavor, with the West Indies providing the most lucrative market.[29] Though little has been written about the extent and steadiness of this market, shipment of meat and animal byproducts to the West Indies continued throughout the eighteenth century and probably into the nineteenth. Just as occurred earlier along the Atlantic seaboard, in the Old Southwest primary domestic markets soon appeared at New Orleans, Mobile, and Pensacola; later, shipping points of less significance developed along the Gulf Coast and on the banks of the navigable streams emptying into the Gulf. As was the case on every frontier, military posts and naval bases in the Old Southwest also purchased meat and other products.

Though New Orleans and Mobile are often mentioned as cattle markets, insufficient data exist to analyze how much of the beef was consumed locally and how much was shipped to the West Indies or to the growing urban centers on the eastern seaboard. John G. Clark, in his economic history of New Orleans, leaves many unanswered questions concerning this trade.[30] Domestic consumption of meat has been considerable if the tax on butchers together with the tax on flour constituted, as Clark reports, substantial support of services at the turn of the nineteenth century. Another unanswered question is the relationship between Mobile and New Orleans as markets for beef and other cattle-related products. Ample evidence indicates that shipments were made from Mobile to New Orleans periodically in both the eighteenth and nineteenth centuries—a curious fact considering the size of the herds northwest of New Orleans and in the Natchez District, and in light of the occasional drives from East Texas.[31] Until more records are uncovered and analyzed, we can only speculate on the size and nature of Gulf Coast trade in cattle, beef, hides, horns, and tallow.[32] The importation of beef and pork from inland areas in varying amounts of virtually all river and sea ports greatly complicates efforts to understand the nature of these markets.

So the cattle raisers had beeves aplenty and markets for them. But what were they worth? Evidently a good bit. A lad along the Leaf River in southeastern Mississippi bragged of the success of his father's first drive in about 1803. "When my father was eighteen years of age he went with a drove of beef cattle to New Orleans. He first went to Baton Rouge, thence down the river. He soon sold out advantageously; for he came home with a young Negro man and his wife, some money, and my mother, whom he had met and married on the route."[33] Obviously, to this family the value was high; but in terms of cash, what were cattle worth?

On the hoof, cattle brought a surprisingly high price. A variety of factors such as age, sex, size, weight, and potential for breeding determined their value. Planter John Ellis contracted for the delivery of 107 head to White Cliffs south of Natchez in 1786 for an average price of $16.82 per head, including five two-year old bulls.[34] While the adjutant at the Natchez fort in 1788 paid approximately $14.31 a head for 300 head, two years later the estate of Frederick Calvert sold 200 head in lots varying from twelve to thirty for prices ranging from $3.57 to $8.70 each, averaging $4.98.[35] Even if we assume that the government paid a prime price, it is impossible with existing data to explain such an abrupt fluctuation, though it might be explained by its being sold hurriedly to close the estate. In one of the largest, if not the largest, sales recorded in the Natchez area around 1804, 2,019 head were sold in one transaction at thirteen dollars each.[36] Though fattening was probably limited in scope, records suggest some feeding out of beef; for, in 1803, a Samuel Kelly of Sandy Creek paid $36 for two cattle specifically designated as "Fat Beeves."[37] Since the cattle raisers themselves rarely kept records of their affairs, we can only assume from this fragmented evidence that herders were not an impoverished class.

Fresh beef was also marketable. Over a six-year period from 1785 through 1790, for instance, Spanish officials annually purchased in Natchez an average of 77,916 pounds of fresh beef at 6¼ cents per pound, with the greatest purchase being 90,960 pounds in 1788. We can only conjecture at the number of cattle these figures represent, considering waste, cuts bought, and carcass sizes.[38] Because certificates for the meat were redeemable in cash only in New Orleans, they served as a form of currency, frequently converted to dollars by area merchants rather than individual vendors.

Probate files, especially wills and estate inventories, reveal considerable information on the value of animals as well as their importance generally in a frontier society.[39] Not only do estate inventories frequently provide sale prices, but perhaps more importantly they indicate the relative value of property. In 1811, for example, an appraisal listed ordinary cattle at $7 each and fat steers at $25. Of particular interest, however, is the data these documents provide on the worth of cattle relative to slaves, the most valuable of all property other than real estate. In the estate of Isaac Guion, 55 cattle equaled in total dollars the value of a prime field hand.[40] Another shows that in 1808, 300 head of black cattle equaled the value of six of the highest-priced male slaves—a ratio of 50 cattle per slave. The ratio in Mobile during the 1780s generally was 40 to one.[41] Clearly these drives to market were worthwhile. If we just knew how often they occurred!

Spanish correspondence reveals that the price of beef in Natchez and Mobile not only soared during the American Revolution, but that at times beef was hardly available. It sold in 1781 for $25 per barrel in Natchez; so inflated were the prices that officers at Fort Panmure which was located there found it extremely difficult to supply meat for the garrison.[42] The wartime situation at Mobile provides an excellent index to the economic importance of cattle there as well as an example of the British efforts to impede Spain's military capabilities by encouraging the Indians to drive off the sorely needed livestock. Spanish officials countered by appointing *vaqueros* at handsome salaries. Profiteering cattlemen, who supplied both the British and Spanish forces, drove the price as high as $12 per head by 1780.[43]

During the War of 1812, hostile Red Stick Creek Indians not only massacred a number of settlers—many of them mixed bloods—at Fort Mims but also drove off or slaughtered considerable livestock. One of the most informative sources of the status of the cattle industry north of Mobile is the lengthy, detailed petition to Congress from residents of the Fort Mims area in 1816 demanding reparations for property destroyed or stolen by the Indians and even, in some cases, by United States troops. Seventy-six claimants attached detailed affidavits of their losses, which totaled $121,020.[44]

Item	Number	Average $ Value	Total $ Value	Percent of Total Claims
Cattle	5,447	7.03	38,284	31.6
Horses	305	58.06	17,710	14.6
Oxen	6	20.00	120	00.0
Hogs	2,474	3.00	7,416	6.1
Sheep	465	3.98	1,853	1.5
Goats	32	2.62	84	00.0
Corn	8,039 bushels	.72/bushel	5,765	4.7
Slaves	55	430.82	23,695	19.5

Cattle accounted for nearly one-third of the dollar value claimed, and slaves one-fifth. The ratio of slaves to cattle in terms of dollars was 1 to 61.28, a figure deviating but little from those found in the above-mentioned probate records, especially considering the increasing importance of cotton.[45] Some claimants designated their horses as "used at cow pens for riding horses," an additional substantiation of the tending of stock by horsemen. The quantities of corn suggest its use, at least in part, as animal feed. Considering the soil there, it is not surprising that cotton accounted for a small number of claims, but industrial equipment and inventories of timber products and brick point toward the use of slaves as craftsmen and herders as well as field hands.[46]

One of the most fascinating implications of this document is the involvement in cattle of claimants who, on the basis of other losses, are clearly enterpreneurs—persons not generally attracted to unprofitable activities.[47] Actually, this evidence merely affirms a practice dating back to the earliest colonial investments in livestock—investments which constitute prima-facie evidence of stock raising as a business. Both historian Peter Wood and geographer Gary S. Dunbar take note of absentee ownership of cattle herds by businessmen in colonial South Carolina; Wood particularly notes the use of African slaves to tend such herds.[48] Jacob R. Marcus finds that Jewish investors in Georgia towns "engaged in ranching systematically and on a relatively large scale" in order to take advantage of the West Indian market. Mordecai Sheftall, for example, was "a farmer, rancher, tanner, shipper, storekeeper, and sawmill owner" who owned slaves and who gave his sons land stocked "with black horned cattle that grazed on free range."[49] In his important book mentioned above, Jordan points out the absentee ownership characterized cattle raising throughout the South.[50]

From the earliest colonial experiences in the South, livestock—particularly cattle—was of considerable value. By the late eighteenth and nineteenth centuries the worth of cattle had become so universally accepted that the animals served as a form of currency. This fact is substantiated in the observations of Major Howell Tatum, a North Carolinian who fought in the American Revolution and who later served as a topographical engineer to General Andrew Jackson in 1814. In his revealing journal, Tatum referred to the excellent range for cattle along the entire Gulf Coast and noted that ownership of the animals had "become an object of primary Importance with the settlers." Then he explained that cattle were "considered as a species of circulating medium in most of their contracts. In fact," he continued, "this currency circulates pretty generally from hence [Louisiana] to, and on, the waters of Tombigby & Mobile rivers."[51]

Most of the historians who have written about cattle raising fail to emphasize that many planters also ran considerable herds of livestock. Indeed, "plantation" may be a misnomer for some of the eighteenth-century operations. "Ranch" may be more accurate, yet Marcus is one of the few historians, if not the only one, who employs this term.[52] Though Gray avoided this appellation, he did point out that planters in the Carolinas commonly ran as many as a thousand head of cattle specifically to market in the West Indies. Perhaps for a different market, but such was also the case in the Old Southwest. Natchez planter Anthony Hutchins, for instance, owned 1,000 head in 1792; by 1801 his herd was considerably larger, probably over 1,500.[53] Traveler Estwick Evans, who noted in 1818 that "some of the planters yearly mark thousands of calves, and send them to the prairie to feed," is only one of numerous observers of plantation herds.[54] A 1775 map of Mobile Bay and the Tombigbee River shows cow pens on plantations, which indicates that cattle raising by planters was not confined to the Mississippi River area.[55]

Spanish census figures confirm such reports. Of the forty-four largest tobacco producers in Natchez in 1789, all but eight appear on the 1792 census as owners of significant numbers of cattle. Since Spain severely regulated the tobacco market in 1790, it is probable that these eight emigrated prior to 1792.[56] The papers of planter John Bisland contain evidence of his involvement in every aspect of the cattle industry—grazing, branding, breeding, feeding, veterinary study, and sales of animals and their by-products.[57] Planters' wills and the inventories of their estates further substantiate the economic importance of cattle in their overall agricultural operations. Other strong evidence includes the findings of cliometricians Robert W. Fogel and Stanley L. Engerman who calculated that "the rearing of livestock (including the raising of feed) took . . . about 25 percent" of the labor time of slaves on large cotton plantation.[58] Cattle not only contributed to the self-sufficiency of the plantations, but sales of the animals also provided badly needed cash.

Though it has historiographical as well as economic significance and though it towered anatomically over the lowly pig with whom it often shared the range, the cow by the end of the antebellum era straggled far behind the more numerous porker in terms of total value. So heavily was pork relied upon as a food source in the nation that an outspoken Georgia physician, Dr. John S. Wilson, in 1860 expressed his concern with a bit of humor.

> The United States of America might properly be called the great Hog-eating Confederacy, or the Republic of Porkdom. At any rate should the South and West . . . be named dietetically, the above appellation would be peculiarly appropriate; for in many parts

of this region, so far as meat is concerned, it is fat bacon and pork, fat bacon and pork only, and that continually morning, noon, and night . . . the meat is generally fried, and thus supersaturated with grease in the form of hogs' lard . . . hogs' lard is the very oil that moves the machinery of life, and they would as soon think of dispensing with tea, coffee, or tobacco . . . as with the essence of hog.[59]

In 1972, Sam B. Hilliard confirmed the substance of Dr. Wilson's observation by juxtaposing animals and plants: "If the 'king' of the antebellum southern economy was cotton," he wrote, "the title of 'queen' must go to the pig."[60] *Queen!* What a nice cognomen, compared to the late eighteenth century portrait in these words by Richard Parkinson, an English traveler.

The real American hog is what is termed the wood hog; they are long in the leg, narrow on the back, short in the body, flat on the sides, with a long snout, very rough in their hair, in make more like the fish called a perch than anything I can describe. You may as well think of stopping a crow as those hogs. They will go to a distance from a fence, take a run, and leap through the rails three or four feet from the ground, turning themselves sidewise. These hogs suffer such hardships as no other animal could endure.[61]

Though the bacon and ham which the hogs produced was the principal source of meat in colonial and antebellum South, it nevertheless often has been denigrated. For instance, an early Virginian observed, "Hogs swarm like Vermine upon the Earth, and are often accounted such."[62]

Vermine, perch, or *queens*—take your pick! The point is that hogs were raised virtually everywhere in the South in tremendous numbers, and they became of increasing value with the passing of each decade in the antebellum period. Though all cattle raisers did not also tend herds of swine for commercial purposes, many did—especially those whose animals ranged in the woods. Stockmen who lived on the prairies scattered throughout the Old Southwest primarily raised cattle.

Both Hilliard and the McDonald-McWhiney team have so thoroughly expounded on pigs and pork that their work hardly needs replication here. Hilliard was correct. In terms of taste, pork was "the South's first choice." While McDonald and McWhiney praise Hilliard for counting so many hogs, they disagree with where he locates them. Rather than in the hands of plant growers, the research team insists that the pigs were primarily raised by herders "as their principal occupation and who did so out of both tradition and choice."[63]

The people of the Old Southwest who herded the multiplying thousands of pigs were more often than not Scotch-Irish frontiersmen, descendants of Celts who for countless centuries have preferred a pastoral lifestyle. McDonald and McWhiney admit that these frontiersmen were "contemptuous of work and did as little as possible," but they were not so poor as contemporaries misinterpreted. "In the literal sense of the phrase, they lived 'high off the hog.' " They lived so high that McDonald and McWhiney contend that "in most of the Old South the hog was king."[64]

Surely these two historians would admit that cotton really was king in the minds and pocketbooks of the political spokesman of the South— the antebellum planters. But statistically McDonald and McWhiney have a point; maybe cotton was a pretender to the throne. As was mentioned earlier, McDonald and McWhiney call attention to the fact that the value of southern livestock in 1860 was double that of the cotton crop and nearly equal to the value of all crops combined. To further emphasize the magnitude of the southern herding industry, they compare the 67,026,000 hogs marketed in the South during the last decade and a half before the Civil War to the 4,223,497 Texas cattle which Webb states were driven to market from 1866 to 1880. The ratio, in round figures, is sixteen to one, but any Texan knows that one of their steers equaled at least sixteen wood hogs![65]

Though the exact size and nature of the cattle market in the Old Southwest in the early nineteenth century may never be determined, census data after 1840 indicates that it was substantial. In the early decades, the cow and the pig may have taken turns on the throne or even shared it at times. As imperfect as census data may be, it reveals the following numbers of cattle: *(in the entire South)* 1840—7,401,292; 1850—9,733,810; 1860— 12,843,411; *(in the lower South)* 1840—3,436,352; 1850—5,396,450; 1860— 8,024,397. For the same years, the ratios of pigs to cattle in the lower South were: 1.65 to 1.0; 1.67 to 1.0; 1.21 to 1.0.[66] Of course, it was virtually impossible to accurately count animals on an unfenced range, and most livestock owners probably gave census enumerators low figures just as they did to the tax assessors. Hence, these ratios represent rather rough estimates. Nevertheless, it would be surprising if the hogs were not far more numerous than these figures indicate.

Cattle were worth three to five times more than hogs, keeping in mind that in many areas the two types of animals shared a common range and were the property of the same owner. Just how prevalent cattle were in the Old Southwest is indicated by a report of a Mississippian from Marion County in 1850 to the U.S. Commissioner of Patents. Ebenezer Ford reported that for the past twenty years or longer over "one million head of cattle yearly" had been raised in an area of "about 200 miles" square. "The Beef is sold at 3 to 4 years old," wrote Ford, "from $10 to $12 per head."[67]

In measuring the economic impact of cattle raising, we must bear in mind the numerous related or subsidiary industries. When one considers the vastness of today's plastics industries, one can imagine the extensiveness of leather and horn consumption of yesteryear. In 1812, for instance, the value of leather tanned in Mississippi Territory was second to cotton cloth among manufactured items.[68] Who knows the number of saddleries, shoe, boot, coach, and harness makers in operation in the Old Southwest at the turn of the nineteenth century? And they must have multiplied along with the cotton boom. Tanners, saddlers, cobblers, and other leather workers appear in the earliest censuses, often in larger numbers than might be anticipated.[69] Indeed, many questions must be posed and answered about the domestic markets for hides, tanned leather, tallow, and horns before we can ascertain the full significance of cattle during the colonial and early national periods.

Now that attention has been directed to the widespread ownership of cattle by planters in the Old Southwest, historians must reassess their role as stockmen, and at the same time, re-examine the interrelationship among planters, farmers, and herdsmen throughout the antebellum period. Until after the War of 1812, planters raised stock for sale. According to the Mississippi territorial tax roles for 1805, the largest numbers of cattle were in the regions where the most cotton also was produced. Hence, William B. Hamilton wrote, "It is wrong to attempt to apply the terms of any cattle stage frontier to the Natchez region, because cattle became an increasing and integral part of the economy of that staple crop district."[70] Many planters actually were ranchers. Hamilton may have been correct with respect to the immediate environs of the town of Natchez, but even in the outer regions of the Natchez District there was a "cattle stage." In this statement, Hamilton exposed his anti-Turnerian bias.

Phillips, Owsley, and even such recent scholars as Hilliard have overlooked the nuances of agrarian life in the Old Southwest. McDonald and McWhiney, regardless of the merits of their Celtic thesis, have virtually forced scholars to reevaluate previous economic and social models of life in the antebellum South. The activities of herdsmen, farmers, and planters probably were more complementary, more interrelated than previously recognized.

It is fun to speculate on how earlier scholars would have reacted to such discoveries. Owsley, whose study of the plain folk was far from complete when his life ended, would likely derive a great sense of affirmation from the spotlight now focused on the herder. Similarly, Turner would smile at how rigidly and/or blindly his followers have viewed as textual his oft-cited "procession" quote. Armed with data now available, even Phillips—who held a deep affection for Turner—might find some merit in the insistence of McDonald and McWhiney that society in the antebellum South "was organized around symbiotic and functional relationships."[71]

As scholars probe more deeply into various aspects of stock raising east of the Mississippi, they inevitably will bring to light considerable information concerning the role of blacks, particularly in the tending of cattle. Indeed, had historians paid more attention to the cattle industry of the cis-Mississippi West, significant contributions to the history of blacks would have been made simultaneously.

Mounted slaves, in their roles as "cattle hunters," displayed considerable skill as horsemen on the Carolina frontier. Peter H. Wood, in his study of blacks in colonial Carolina, traces the origins of their equestrian and herding skills to the Gambia River valley of Africa where many of the first Carolina slaves had gained experience in tending stock.[72] Generations of their descendants watched over cattle and other animals as the culture of their masters spread across the South into Texas and eventually on to the Great Plains.[73] Travelers often described the pastoral activities of African slaves, one asserting that they "are among the best horsemen in the world."[74] A 1770 regulation concerning land grants in Louisiana leaves little doubt concerning the use of slaves as cowboys. In order to become a grantee, applicants had to be "the possessor of one hundred head of tame cattle, some horses and sheep, and two slaves to look after them."[75] It is interesting that Phillip Durham and Everett L. Jones, in their pioneer study, ignored the deeper antecedents of black cowboys, simply attributing their vocational origins to "Texas and the Indian Nations."[76]

One of the most telling arguments in support of the westward diffusion of the cattle industry involves the Native Americans. Indians of the

Southeast, experiencing some of their earliest and most persistent contact with stockmen, quickly emulated open-range herding, an economic orientation which intensified after removal to the Indian Territory.[77] John R. Swanton, in his studies for the Bureau of American Ethnology, discussed the role of cattle and horses in the economies of the Five Civilized Tribes, a point also stressed by Arrell Gibson in his excellent study of the Chickasaw. How soon they began the practice is a matter of speculation, but the Indians tended stock on horseback by the eighteenth century. Particularly the Chickasaw and Seminole gained reputations for the quality of the horses bred by them.[78]

When agent Benjamin Hawkins toured the Creek country in 1798–99, he particularly noted the "valuable" herds of cattle in virtually every town he visited. Often he cited the owners' names as well as the exact numbers possessed. Not only did he refer also to horses and other stock, but Hawkins recorded that a number of persons had "fenced their fields . . . for the benefit of their stock," pointing to one old chief who had "with his own labor made a good worm fence."[79] Hawkins' reference to so many Scotch-Irish clearly points toward their influence on the Creeks, but this is not to suggest an absence of influence of the Spanish. The Indians engaged in controlled burning to enrich the foraging beneath the fire-tolerant pines, a practice emulated by herders and perfected by modern foresters.

With each passing decade, many Native Americans intensified their herding activities. An 1821 inventory of the property at the Choctaw Mission station at Elliot indicates the value of their cattle as well as the continuing interest of the Indians in raising them. The list sent to the Secretary of War included 285 head of "neat cattle" at $8 each, seven horses at $60 per head, six oxen at $37.50 per head, and seventy acres of improved land at $10 per acre. The value of cattle exceeded any other category of property except the twenty-two buildings listed for a total of $4000 and exceeded the value of the stock of merchandise in the store. It is particularly significant that one steer was worth 80 percent of the value of an acre of improved land in 1821 at this station of the Choctaw Mission founded by the nondenominational American Board of Commissioners for Foreign Missions. Cattle evidently constituted a stable and powerful medium of exchange within the Choctaw Nations as well as in other regions of the Old Southwest.[80]

As is so often the case, an intense re-examination of the herders of the Old Southwest will force us into many related avenues of research. And if we follow them, we will enrich our knowledge of topics too numerous to list completely. To name just a few: black cowboys and cattlemen; native American livestock; West Indian and other international trade; markets for hide, leather, tallow, and horns; the extent and chronology of Hispanic cultural diffusion from Florida and the Mississippi Valley; crop-stock relationships; and herder–farmer–planter interdependency. The process will require the skills of geographers, sociologists, demographers, and genealogists working in cooperation with social, economic, and family historians. And when their labor is finished, they may prove the Owsley's student Herbert Weaver was right: "Perhaps no region has been more misrepresented than the antebellum South."[81]

7

Dance of the Prophets

The news that the United States was at war with England stirred excitement throughout the Old Southwest. In New Orleans many Americans welcomed the dispatch which arrived from Washingon, D.C. on July 9, 1812.[1] The planters, farmers and merchants blamed the hard times on British interference with American shipping. Adventurers and speculators believed that victory over Great Britain would cement United States control over the part of West Florida already occupied. Many of them also coveted the balance of West Florida as well as East Florida for its suitability for growing cotton and grazing stock. Control of the navigable streams flowing through the Floridas into the Gulf of Mexico also enticed them. In addition, the majority of the settlers in the Old Southwest suspected that Englishmen based in Pensacola were inciting and arming the Indians.

To the territorial governors, however, the timing of the news could scarcely have been worse! The Old Southwest, politically and organizationally, was still in a formative stage. William C. C. Claiborne had served as Mississippi Territory's second governor until President Jefferson had appointed him the first governor of Orleans Territory. He and James Wilkinson had formally accepted possession of Louisiana on December 20, 1803 in behalf of the United States and Claiborne had protected American interests there since 1804 as the only governor of Orleans Territory. Now Louisiana was in the union, and Claiborne was waiting for the General Assembly to confirm his election as the first governor of the new state when he received Secretary of State James Monroe's message that the War of 1812 had begun. Since the 1810 annexation of West Florida as part of Orleans Territory, its defense had been uppermost in Claiborne's mind. More than ever, he fretted over the vulnerability of the Gulf Coast.[2]

117

Addition of the segment of West Florida between the Pearl and the Perdido Rivers to the jurisdiction of Mississippi Territory in May of 1812 caught its governor, David Holmes, unprepared to exercise immediate and effective control of the region, despite the fact he was in office during the 1810 West Florida rebellion. After passage of the enabling act in May, Congress continued to debate the conditions under which American forces could occupy West Florida as far west as the Perdido. Consequently, as late as the following October, Holmes remained uncertain of his authority to occupy Mobile which was still garrisoned by Spanish forces.[3]

Like Claiborne, Governor Holmes advocated the occupation of Mobile, but, as he noted to General James Wilkinson, he had reservations about sending the entire militia out of Mississippi Territory. "Remonstrances and petitions have been presented to me stating the danger to be apprehended from the Negroes and Indians should the Militia be marched out of the Territory."[4] Holmes then asked Wilkinson to assign a cavalry unit for defense of the territory and for 200 muskets to arm the militiamen remaining at home. After repeating the need to guard against a slave insurrection, the governor closed with a statement that reveals how unprepared his militia was for action. "I have been compelled to purchase for the use of the Troops two hundred and fifty blankets. They have been delivered to them upon the condition that if the Government requires it, the Cost shall be deducted out of their pay. Many of them are without shoes, and in other respects badly clad. Can this be remedied?"[5]

The anxiety of Governors Claiborne and Holmes was in good measure justified. Both Spain and Great Britain held a long-standing interest in control of the Indians of the Southwest for commercial as well as strategic purposes. Geographically, Mobile was one of the most inviting points along the Gulf coastal waters to a foreign navy and an invading army. Both in Washington and New Orleans the fact was known that not too far away the British were using Pensacola as anchorage for American prize ships and as a base for repairing their own damaged vessels. From ships anchored along the coast, they were trading goods and ammunition to the Creek and Seminole Indians. Even more upsetting, however, was the persistent rumor that the British had landed black troops at Pensacola with a design to incite slave uprisings. An additional concern was the smugglers who were running coffee and other contraband from Pensacola to Mobile.[6]

On February 13, 1813, General John Armstrong, the newly appointed Secretary of War, ordered General Wilkinson to prepare for occupation of Fort Charlotte in Mobile.[7] This order was issued following congres-

sional action permitting United States forces to occupy the Spanish territory west of the Perdido.[8] Armstrong authorized the assembling and
preparation of the regular military forces then in Mississippi Territory
and Louisiana as well as the recruiting of local militia companies. Commodore John Shaw's naval command was at the moment in no condition
to expose itself too freely in the Gulf.[9]

In March of 1813, General Wilkinson and his men set out in barges
from New Orleans for Mobile by way of Lake Pontchartrain and the Mississippi Sound. When his personal barge swept into a deep backwash of
the sound, it capsized and all hands barely escaped a highly unheroic
death by drowning. Finally, in stormy weather on April 10, 1813, Wilkinson's task force of some 600 men and five gunboats reached Mobile
Bay. However much hardship they had endured during the rough passage, they were considerably overmanned for the task at hand. Only a
mere handful of Spanish troops occupied the outpost on Dauphin Island
near the entrance of Mobile Bay, and the garrison at Fort Charlotte under
the command of Captain Cayetano Pérez consisted of just sixty men with
inadequate cannon and no provisions. Once considered impregnable if
properly manned and armed, Fort Charlotte in its present condition posed
little threat to the invading Americans.[10]

Wilkinson assured Pérez that the American forces came not as enemies, but to relieve the Spanish garrison from occupying a post within
the "legitimate limits" of the United States. After an exchange of flowery
and stilted notes between the commanders, Pérez had no choice other
than to sign the rather elaborate Articles of Surrender drafted by Wilkinson and abandon the fort. On April 15, 1813, Pérez departed with his
troops for Pensacola, leaving West Florida from the Pearl to the Perdido
in American hands, but not in peace.[11]

The dislodging of the last Spanish foothold at Mobile often overshad-
ows one of the high ironies of the struggle to defend the Old Southwest:
the failure to give Major General Andrew Jackson of the Tennessee militia at the outset of the War of 1812 a challenging military assignment.
Months before war was formally declared in June of 1812, Jackson had
expressed a vigorous willingness to lead volunteer militiamen into battle.[12]
However, the proffer of his services along the Canadian border was
rebuffed in Washington where the Administration remembered his friendship with Aaron Burr. In addition, Jackson's hospitality to Burr precluded
any support for an appointment from James Wilkinson, the military commander in New Orleans. Surely, Wilkinson—who had turned on Burr,

his fellow plotter—had learned of the denigrating letters that Jackson had written about him and was waiting for an opportunity to retaliate.[13]

In October of 1812, the War Department requested Governor Willie Blount of Tennessee to raise a militia force of 1500 volunteers for service in the Southwest where they would be available either for the defense of New Orleans or to seize eastern Florida. Though the Administration did not instruct Blount to overlook Jackson, his old political ally, for command of the Tennessee militia, it did hint that he might name someone else to the post. Blount simply could not pass over his old political ally and he commissioned Jackson a major general of the United States volunteers with a stroke of his pen. Now Jackson finally had a chance to display his military genius, but as a subordinate to the villainous Wilkinson! What a bitter pill to swallow. Service in that capacity, Jackson admitted, was "a sting to my feelings," but nevertheless he served because it was "the duty of every citizen to do something for his country."[14]

Tennesseans responded to the service call in droves; instead of 1,500, nearly 2,500 men proved ready to go south to fight Spaniards, British, Indians, or anybody else who resisted them. But Jackson raised the martial spirit of the volunteers assembled in Nashville to new heights with his rhetorical reminders of the perpetual western frustration:

> Every man of the western Country turns his eyes intuitively upon the mouth of the Mississippi. He there beholds the only outlet by which his produce can reach the markets of foreign and of the atlantic States: Blocked up, all the fruits of his industry rots upon his land—open, and he carries on a trade with all the nations of the earth. To the people of Western Country is then peculiarly committed by nature herself the defense of the lower Mississippi and the city of New Orleans.[15]

To the Tennessee farmers and flatboatmen who recalled the troubles with Spanish authorities, Jackson's words were reason enough to go to war.

In the midst of a fierce winter, General Jackson dispatched cavalry troops under the command of General John Coffee down the trace to Natchez on December 31, 1812.[16] Then, on January 7, Jackson led the infantry troops aboard flatboats to negotiate the frozen Cumberland, the Ohio, and the Mississippi. For thirty-nine days Jackson and his men braved the wind-swept rivers and the tremors of earthquakes before they disembarked at Natchez to await orders from New Orleans. During the thousand-mile voyage three men and one boat were lost.[17]

Awaiting Jackson at Natchez were several communiqués from Wilkinson in New Orleans, each with clear instructions for the Tennesseans to encamp at Natchez until further notice. Wilkinson offered several explanations for his order to halt at Natchez: He had received no further instructions from Washington; there were inadequate provisions in New Orleans for additional troops and animals; a march on Mobile or Pensacola could best be initiated from upriver. In reality, Wilkinson could ill afford to have such a strong-willed officer as Jackson on his doorstep. But whatever the reason, his orders were clear: Stay in Natchez.[18]

On the day he took the oath of office in Washington, Secretary of War John Armstrong countermanded the call-up of the Tennessee militia. His curt order arrived on March 15: Jackson and his men were dismissed! The outraged Jackson viewed such a seemingly insane action as a plot of the "publick villain" Wilkinson and an imbecilic Armstrong. Over 2,000 men dismissed 500 miles from home, amidst Indian country, and without pay, food, supplies, or medicine. Dismissed with a mere presidential thank-you. The only official expression of concern for the troops were implications from Wilkinson that Jackson's men could best serve their country and themselves through enlistment in his army.

At this point Jackson and his men were, to a large extent, victims of policy changes and international forces totally unknown to them. Actions viewed at the time by Jackson as vitriolic retribution from New Orleans and Washington actually were prompted by the Administration response to the division in Congress over support of an invasion of East Florida and to Russian efforts to patch up differences between the United States and England. Even had the Secretary of War informed Jackson of these developments, it is not likely that Jackson would have given credibility to the reports. Indeed, Armstrong's brief message did state that the causes for the mobilization and deployment of his militia had "ceased to exist."[19]

Nor was Jackson going to abandon his men or encourage them to enlist in Wilkinson's army. Instead, he would lead them back to Nashville even if he had to personally provide for their subsistence. Lead them he did, and in such a manner that the myth of "Old Hickory" was born. During the march back up the trace, Jackson exhibited all of the traits of leadership which endeared him to his men and ultimately the nation. He and the other officers walked so as to provide mounts for the infirm. As he led his starving and weary troops home, Jackson showed both the sternness and gentleness required of a great leader. But above all he was viewed as tough—tough as hickory. In January, it was Andrew Jackson who had boarded the flatboats, but it was "Old Hickory" who arrived back in Nashville in April.

The War Department's dismissal of Jackson's militia also mystified Louisiana's Governor Claiborne. Because he perceived no lessening of impending dangers in the Old Southwest, Claiborne wondered if some unpublicized treaty had been negotiated, particularly one with Spain regarding Mobile. The diastrous failures in 1812 of American attempts to invade Canada made Secretary of War Armstrong's action even more difficult to understand. In a letter the governor emphasized to Jackson his continuing concern for the defense of the lower Mississippi: "At this perilous crisis so respectable a reinforcement of men whose patriotism and valour are so well established would have given security to this exposed Section of the Union, from all attacks from without, & commanded from the savages in our vicinity an adherence to the most pacific course."[20]

Regardless of whether or not the answers to Claiborne's question were to be found in the commanding general's headquarters in New Orleans, Wilkinson's tour of duty in the Old Southwest ended in June when he was ordered to the Canadian frontier. Shortly after occupying Mobile, Wilkinson surrendered his command to Brigadier General Thomas Flournoy, who proved to be almost as much of an enigma as the man whom he had replaced.[21]

One of the last official acts of General James Wilkinson as commanding officer of the United States armed forces in the Old Southwest was to boast that Mobile had been taken "without the effusion of a drop of blood."[22] Unfortunately, however, an absence of bloodshed would not be characteristic of the area surrounding the old Spanish domain. By 1813 there was a disturbing restlessness among the Choctaw, Creeks, and Seminole. So concerned was Governor Claiborne over the hostile posture of some of the Choctaw from the Lower Towns that he dispatched a representative into the Nation to verify the incitement by British and Spanish agents.[23] It was not among the Choctaw, however, that the most serious trouble was brewing.

Among the Creeks a deep dissatisfaction stemming from numerous and diffuse sources was seething. In part, the roots of Creek uneasiness related to the opening and expansion of so many roads and trails—activities viewed by many of their leaders as an evil omen. Immigrants were already taking advantage of the widening of the Federal Road from the Chattahoochee River to Mims' Ferry on the Alabama, and the Secretary of War had ordered General Wade Hampton to open a wagon road from Muscle Shoals to Fort Stoddert along a route surveyed by Edmund P.

Gaines. Of course, the United States President assured the Indians of American amity toward them and compensated them for passage through their nations. Even the friendly chiefs, however, despaired at the slowness of the annuity payments and the increased traffic.[24]

It was not only the sight of immigrant wagons in ever-increasing numbers that disturbed the Creeks. Equally as threatening was the opening of the rivers to free passage across the Creek country. The Alabama system, plus the Tombigbee, formed natural conduits between the Tennessee Valley and Mobile Bay, and when Agent Benjamin Hawkins informed the Creek leaders that Federal officials demanded safe passage along these arteries, they reacted unfavorably.[25] The Creeks well understood that the rivers through their country were more than a route for traders; in this free and unrestricted use, they perceived a threat to their hold on the land itself.

An immediate source of animosity between white frontiersmen and the Creeks involved the murder of settlers along the Duck River in Tennessee and near the mouth of the Ohio. A party of Creeks led by Little Warrior, leader of the Creek war faction, had journeyed to the Northwest as far as Canada in the spring of 1812. By the time they headed back south, Tecumseh—and possibly the British as well—had heightened their hostility toward Americans. En route home Little Warrior's band attacked a settlement near the mouth of the Duck River, killing a man, a woman and five children. They also took a Mrs. Martha Crawley captive, but she eventually escaped. These murders plus the circulation of Mrs. Crawley's explicit account of her abuses caused such a reaction among settlers that friendly Creeks, after a stern protest and admonishment by Hawkins, tracked down the guilty Indians and executed Little Warrior and the other murderers.[26] It was well that they did so, for Governor Blount had advised the Secretary of War that Tennesseans "probably cannot be restrained, if satisfaction is not given in reasonable time, from taking it."[27]

In February of 1813, other Creeks participated in the slaughter of seven families near the mouth of the Ohio. It was a ghastly atrocity in which bodies of the victims were brutally mutilated. In one instance they cut open a woman, ripped out her unborn child, and left the fetus impaled upon a stake.[28] The Indian cause in the Old Southwest could scarcely have suffered a harsher blow than this, especially following on the Duck River attack. These brutal acts created panic among the settlers and aroused them—especially the Tennesseans—against the Creeks.

As damaging as such incidents were to Creek-white relations, far more destructive was the schism within the Creek Nation following the celebrated visit of the Shawnee leader Tecumseh in October of 1811. Earlier, en route from the Northwest, Tecumseh and his followers had passed through the Chickasaw and Choctaw Nations, where their anti-white tirades fell upon deaf ears. So they proceeded on to Florida where the Seminole provided a more receptive audience for Tecumseh's hostile rhetoric. It was among the closely related Creeks, however, that Tecumseh found his most enthusiastic and numerous converts.

In his campaign to arouse the Creeks against their white neighbors, the Shawnee chieftain spoke with as much eloquence as contempt against Jefferson's civilization policy. Tecumseh was the guest of Big Warrior at the annual council of the Creek Nation, and it was there that his campaign for converts peaked. He and his band performed a shamanistic ritual well designed to transport their hosts into a state of hypnotized unreality. Then, to his highly receptive audience, Tecumseh delivered an hour-long oration, exhorting his brethren to cast aside the ways of the white man and annihilate his race.

Though no transcript was made of what is presumed to be Tecumseh's dramatic appeal to the Creeks, the revered frontiersmen Sam Dale was present. Historian J. F. H. Claiborne, relying upon Dale's report, preserved the essence of Tecumseh's oratory. First the Shawnee orator shamed his listeners: "But now your blood has become white; your tomahawks have no edge; your bows and arrows were buried with your fathers."[29] Then Tecumseh urged the Creeks to retaliate.

> Brethren of my mother! Brush from your eyelids the sleep of slavery, and strike for vengeance and your country. . . . Their bones bleach on the hills of Georgia. Will no son of those brave men strike the paleface and quiet these complaining ghosts? Let the white race perish! They seize your land; they corrupt your women; they trample on the bones of your dead! Back whence they came, upon a trail of blood, they must be driven! Back—aye, back into the great water whose accursed waves brought them to our shores! Burn their dwellings—destroy their stock—slay their wives and children, that the very breed may perish. War now! War always! War on the living! War on the dead! Dig their very corpses from their graves. The redman's land must give no shelter to a white man's bones.[30]

Tecumseh concluded with promises of British arms and assurances that his prophets would accompany them into battle in order to "catch the bullets of their enemies." As proof of the power of his medicine, the Shawnee leader accurately predicted the appearance of a comet and earthquakes!

No doubt there was latent in much of the Creek population a smoldering distrust and hatred of the ever-encroaching Americans. For, after the departure of Tecumseh and his brother the Prophet, there surfaced among some factions highly emotional and mystical dances and incantations. Utilizing the force of this anti-white hysteria, prophets—Creeks trained by the Shawnee—stomped through the villages jangling war beads, waving red war sticks, exhibiting hairy talismans, and preaching wholesale destruction of all signs of Jefferson's carefully nurtured "civilization." These prophets had convinced themselves and their converts of their supernatural powers with their dances which must have been as frightening as they were convincing and which often ended with convulsions. A dancer witnessed by Samuel Manac, a mixed-blood Creek, "began to tremble and jerk in every part of his frame, and the very calves of his legs would be convulsed and he would get entirely out of breath with agitation."[31]

How it must have pained Benjamin Hawkins to report that "the Prophet's party have destroyed, in several places of the Upper towns, all the cattle, hogs, and fowls" and that they had "moved out of their towns into the woods, where they are dancing 'the dance of the Indians of the Lakes.' " Hawkins further explained that the goal of the hostile faction was "to destroy everything received from the Americans; all the chiefs and their adherents who are friendly to the customs and ways of the white people; to put to death every man who will not join them."[32]

Amidst the numerous tribes comprising the Creek Nation, a general state of alarm and confusion was created by the excesses of the prophets whom many of their brethren feared as conjurers, wizards, or witches. Their boasts of magical powers at times paralyzed even the tribesmen who actually opposed their tactics and goals. The incidents along the Duck and Ohio Rivers further contributed to the forces of division, which ultimately proved to be uncontrollable. Soon the Creeks found themselves embroiled in a civil war as complex as it was bloody. [33] The faction lead by the prophets called themselves the "Red Sticks," an appellation derived from their vermilion war clubs and the red-dyed sticks prepared by Tecumseh as a device to reckon the timing of his national rebellion. The goal of the Red Sticks was the elimination of all vestiges of white culture. Opposing them were those Creeks who argued that it was folly to abandon the road to civilization. Among the most formidable leaders of the opposition was Big Warrior, head of all the Creeks and a giant of a man. Red Stick sentiment was strongest among the upper Creek tribes while the lower tribes generally supported Big Warrior's pro-white point of view.

Benjamin Hawkins' agency was essentially geared to peace, and he was wholly unprepared to arm the friendly Indians. He did, however, expend considerable energy attempting to counteract the rampant fanaticism generated by the Shawnee and the British agents. The seasoned old Indian agent cajoled, scolded, and propagandized the chiefs in letters and council meetings. In clear and prophetic logic he told the Creeks of the fatal dangers of associating themselves with the British, of the strength of the expanded United States, and of the certain tragedy which would befall them if they followed the fanatics. Unlike the Shawnee, he sternly warned, the Creeks had no open frontier into which they could retreat.

For the belligerent Creeks, however, 1813 and 1814 were not years of rationality. Already the armies were gathering; the war of devastation was upon them. The Red Sticks continued their destructive raids on their unsympathetic Creek neighbors while they chanted their incantations and performed the "Dance of the Lakes." The rebels wreaked havoc on their kinsmen in an effort to eradicate all evidences of white civilization—animate or inanimate. A prime example was the destruction of mixed-blood Samuel Manac's plantation near Fort Stoddert. The Red Sticks destroyed livestock valued at $5,300 (700 cattle, 48 goats and sheep, and 200 hogs), a fully equipped cotton gin, his home, and scores of other items. Manac's total claim against the United States Government amounted to $12,595.25—a figure approximating a quarter of a million 1987 dollars.[34] It was only a matter of time before they would victimize whites as well.

Early in June of 1813, a party of Creeks set upon a United States post-rider on the Federal Road between the Escambia and Burnt Corn creeks, beat him severely, then took his horse and abandoned him afoot in the insect-infested swamp. Then the Indians delivered the stolen pouch to Pensacola where Spanish officials rifled its contents before forwarding the mail to New Orleans. On other occasions the Creeks turned over stolen mail bags to the Spaniards.[35]

The next month, mixed-blood chief Peter McQueen led a delegation of some 250 to 300 upper Creeks to Pensacola in quest of arms and ammunition. Enroute they attacked a settlement in the Tensaw area and took some of the captured slaves to Pensacola to be sold.[36] Settlers as well as officials such as Benjamin Hawkins kept abreast of British and Spanish activity in Florida through Indian spies. Hence, it is likely that Americans quickly learned that the Spanish officials had given McQueen's party a sizable quantity of powder and shot. News of these events stirred the Tombigbee–Alabama settlers to action.[37]

Colonel James Caller, senior officer of the Mississippi Territorial Militia in Washington County, mustered a force of approximately 180 men to cut off McQueen's party as it returned from Pensacola. The militiamen crossed over the Tombigbee and Alabama swamps and through the pine barren fringe to the Burnt Corn fork of the Escambia River where a small number of warriors had camped with most of McQueen's pack animals. On the morning of July 27, Caller's troops fell upon the surprised Creeks, who abandoned most of the recently obtained munitions and fled into the swamp.

Unfortunately, Caller's poorly disciplined and greedy men failed to administer the *coup de grâce*. Instead, they proceeded to loot the camp. Meanwhile, the Indians, with reinforcements from the main party, mounted from the cover of the swamp such an effective counterattack that the militiamen retreated in utter panic with as much of the booty as they could carry. So complete was the disarray that the command never reassembled; its elements made their separate ways home as best they could. Though some heroes, such as Sam Dale, gave a good account of themselves during the disaster, the Battle of Burnt Corn was far from a day of glory for the southwestern frontiersmen.

In one sense, Burnt Corn was no more than a bush skirmish. Two Americans lost their lives and fifteen were wounded; no one knows what casualties the Indians suffered. The significance of that encounter, however, was to be measured in far more ominous terms. Henceforth the Creeks would fight back, however erring their aim with firearms. For the whites after July 27, 1813, the challenge was a bitter one. Defense of the Old Southwest would require sudden and drastic changes in the enlistment, training, disciplining, and equipping of the raw backwoods militiamen. Clearly, Burnt Corn was but a prelude to much fiercer encounters with the Creeks and maybe with the British and Spanish as well.

Indeed, the mounting of a defense force on the Spanish-Indian frontier of the Old Southwest in the summer of 1813 was a herculean task. The Mississippi Territory stretched some 400 miles from the Mississippi to the Chattahoochee at the thirty-first parallel, and by 1813 it ran from the Tennessee line to the Gulf of Mexico. Although Governor Claiborne diligently labored to unite the various nationalities in Louisiana, support for the United States in that new state was far from consolidated. Fortifications along the Mississippi River and the Gulf Coast were minimal, and the entire region suffered from inadequate overland communications. The Natchez Trace passed through three Indian Nations, and although they were friendly, fears of lurking Red Stick sympathizers preyed on the minds of everyone who traveled along that important route. Above the Tombigbee settlements hovered the divided and often hostile Creek tribes. To the east was an exposed front of approximately 200 miles with only the Federal Road penetrating this wilderness, and it was subject to ambush and attack.

According to Judge Harry Toulmin, residents north of Mobile faced a danger that "no human prudence could guard against."[38]

> On two sides we have the Indian tribes and the Spaniards who are fomenting a spirit of hostility:—on a third side we have an extensive wilderness, detaching us from the settlements on the Mississippi: and on the fourth side,—we have the ocean. The wealth of many of our citizens consists in extensive herds ranging at large in the woods.[39]

This part of the Southwest, concluded Toulmin, had "no adequate protection from the nation at large."

So weak was the American military arm in this quarter that it was unable to keep the Spanish from burning two American blockhouses east of Mobile along the Perdido just after General Thomas Flournoy succeeded Wilkinson as commander of the Seventh Military Division. What an inauspicious initiation for Flournoy—an aged attorney from Augusta, Georgia, with little military experience—who assumed command under the most superficial orders pertaining to relations along the border. Just a month prior to Burnt Corn, Flournoy reminded the Secretary of War that he was "without any sort of instructions on the Subject of Spanish affairs," and then requested either "discretionary powers" or instructions "explicit on every subject Connected with the present Service."[40]

The Burnt Corn incident came as no surprise to the remote settlers, and it should not have caught territorial officials unaware. On the day of this skirmish (July 27, 1813), Governor David Holmes wrote Secretary John Armstrong that he believed "the Creek Indians are now engaged in active hostilities against the United States."[41] The situation on the eastern frontier of Mississippi Territory above Mobile had become so intense, wrote Holmes, that Creek agent Benjamin Hawkins "has been obliged to retire to Georgia." In this letter, written in the relative safety of the town of Washington near Natchez, Holmes informed Armstrong that he intended to muster six militia companies of infantry and two troops of cavalry under the command of General Ferdinand L. Claiborne for protection of the settlements north of Mobile, but that he was unable to do so because of a lack of arms and supplies.[42]

Little wonder that Judge Toulmin and his neighbors felt so neglected "by the nation at large." In addition to a multiplicity of external dangers and threats, they now had to cope with internal dissension in the form of a bitter and ridiculous controversy between General Flournoy and Governor Holmes. Correspondence between the two reads more like the lines of a farce than a record of national defense. Flournoy was more interested in protocol and regulations than in exercising judgment and facing reality, and under his command the historic jealousies and frictions between regular forces and militias were exacerbated. Flournoy questioned his right under existing federal statutes to command units of the Mississippi Territorial Militia. So what if the law does not authorize you to call out the militia? responded Holmes. The governor of Mississippi Territory can order the militia to report to you. You can accept them for the duration of the emergency; then pay and subsist them in a manner similar to any Federal Troops.[43]

Both the Creek Nation and the white settlements were thrown into pandemonium after Burnt Corn. Frontiersmen rushed their families with as many possessions as they could carry to places of safety. In the fall of 1813, there were some twenty stockades either in existence or under construction in the Tombigbee region of Mississippi Territory. While these could sustain attack by bow and arrow or poorly primed rifles, they could not withstand a more effective British-supported attack. The occupants of these strongholds were forced to leave their livestock and growing crops unprotected in the open country. Facing a war with the Creeks—and possibly one with British invaders—the Old Southwest from the Perdido to the Mississippi stood nakedly exposed and highly vulnerable.

Among the fortifications scatttered along the sprawling Tombigbee–Alabama frontier was the hurriedly constructed Fort Mims, a palisaded homestead on the east bank of the Alabama River virtually at its juncture with the Tombigbee. Strategically, the Fort stood on the easternmost rim of the white settlement line directly in the path of a movement of over 1,000 fanatical Creek warriors toward Mobile. In addition to the residence of Samuel Mims, enclosed within the stockade were a blockhouse, several dwellings, various outhouses, and a militia guardhouse. Hastily fortified in midsummer of 1813, Fort Mims was in no sense properly defensible. Indian spies had warned its residents and its garrison of 120 militiamen of the massive Creek presence more than a week prior to the attack. If there was ever an occasion when American pioneer settlers should have been prepared and alert beyond all excuses for certain attack, it was at Fort Mims in August of 1813.[44] Instead, the lack of alertness and precaution by Major Daniel Beasley was reprehensible. Chosen by General Claiborne to command the defense of Fort Mims, Beasley was a lawyer from Jefferson County, Mississippi Territory. Perhaps a lack of military experience explains his apparent recklessness; whatever the reason, discipline was lax. Many of the militiamen, as well as their commander, indulged too frequently in the stock of liquor recently delivered to the fort. Along with Beasley, blame for the disaster must also be shared to some extent by the settlers who had congregated at the Mims plantation and by General Claiborne who was headquartered only a few miles down the Tombigbee at Fort Stoddert.

In addition to intelligence from Claiborne and reports of friendly Indians, the contingent at Fort Mims received other warnings which also were ignored. When a slave returning from an errand to a neighboring plantation reported large numbers of Red Sticks in the nearby swamps, he was denounced as a liar and threatened with punishment. Only the day before the attack, two slave cowboys dashed in from the herds to warn of painted warriors among the grazing cattle, and when a patrol did not confirm their report, the slaves were flogged. On the very morning of the disaster, a well-known mixed-blood settler, Jim Cornells, also brought word of stalking Indians. Why was Beasley so skeptical of these reports when only two days earlier General Claiborne had informed him that as many as 1200 Creeks had amassed in the general vicinity of the Tombigbee settlement? Even more incredible is the fact that the eastern gate to the fort remained blocked open by drifted sand! According to some accounts, Beasley was incompetent; according to others he had been drinking.

Jim Cornells had indeed seen Creeks. Under the leadership of the well-known mixed-blood chiefs William Weatherford and Peter McQueen and the fanatical Prophet Josiah Francis approximately 700 Creeks were preparing for the assault. The remainder of the large Creek force had continued northward to harass other settlements. Inside the stockade on the morning of August 30, 1813, were some 300 whites, mixed bloods, and friendly Indians along with at least 150 slaves. They were oblivious to the Red Sticks who had crept within four-hundred yards of the palisade.[45] As the assembled victims reveled in the sylvan beauty of a lazy summer day, the Indians patiently waited for the appointed hour of attack—high noon, the same hour chosen by the whites for the assault at Burnt Corn.

At the drum roll that called the troops to their noon meal the Red Sticks struck with deadly suddenness, wielding rifles, knives, bows and arrows, clubs, hatchets, and torches. Among the first to be cut down was Major Beasley as he futilely attempted—sword in hand—to shut the neglected eastern gate. William Weatherford's shouts for mercy for the women and children seemed to further infuriate the crazed attackers. Though confusion overcame the leaderless garrison, most of the militiamen and settlers gave a good account of themselves from the cover of the various structures within the compound. In the end, however, most of them suffered horrible deaths—many by smoke or flames. Alabama historian Albert James Pickett writes that the final defenders, in quarters too cramped for rifle fire, met their demise like "beeves in the the slaughter-pen of the butcher."[46] Ironically, the blood spilled in those pens was as much Indian as white, for mixed bloods on both sides were the main participants.

Often in exaggerated form, news of the carnage spread across the nation even before an official body count was taken. Nearly three weeks after the Red Sticks had departed from the smoldering ruins of Fort Mims, General Claiborne with heavy heart dispatched Major Joseph P. Kennedy to bury the dead. After driving buzzards and ferocious dogs away from the mangled remains, Kennedy's detail counted 247 bodies at the site. Obviously many more perished; how many more will forever remain unknown. Indian casualties also ran high. Captain Kennedy reported at least one hundred dead Red Sticks in the area, and an equal number may have died elsewhere of their wounds. It is impossible to ascertain how many of the slaves, women and children were spared, but many were later recaptured. Some of the blacks may have preferred and secured asylum among the Indians.

For the Red Sticks, Fort Mims was a bitter and Pyrrhic victory which produced short-term disillusionment and long-term calamity. The belief that supernatural powers would stop bullets proved to be a delusion; the retribution which they paid for Fort Mims—the loss of their ancestral homeland after the costly Creek War—was the ultimate calamity. For the Spanish, who had supplied munitions and supplies, if not arms, Fort Mims signaled the need for a cautious policy for fear of a full-scale invasion of Florida east of the Perdido. For the British, it meant the intensified animosity of the Southwesterners.

The horror of Fort Mims threw the population of Mississippi Territory into a state of hysteria as frontiersmen flocked to the stockades. At first, they waited in fear for what seemed to be almost certain doom. Soon, however, they unleashed a white force equally as bloodthirsty as that of the Red Sticks—a force driven by a determination for retribution and a fear of slave rebellions spinning off from the Creek civil war. For years residents of the Old Southwest had considered Florida a refuge for escaped slaves. To make matters worse, Governor Holmes believed that the British were raising a force of West Indian Negro troops for an invasion on the Gulf Coast in order to encourage slave insurrections above the thirty-first parallel. Now the Spanish and British were suspected of inciting slave revolts as well as Indian uprisings! The holocaust at Fort Mims also accentuated the serious questions about the leadership of General Thomas Flournoy, the lack of discipline of the untrained and under-supplied militia, the locus of the command of and the financial responsibility for the militia, and the judgment of Agent Benjamin Hawkins.[47]

The bloody massacre at Fort Mims was the catalyst that speeded up revolutionary forces in the Old Southwest. Deafened by the roar of the "Lake Dance" and deluded by the northwestern prophet craze, the Red Sticks left unheeded the council of their truest friend, Benjamin Hawkins, who sensed that theirs was a dance of doom. The United States had grown sufficiently strong to defend itself against foreign powers and their Indian allies, and the Creek Nation had no great wilderness into which it could retreat. Within a year the holocaust of August 30, 1813, was to be repeated in reverse; for the Creeks this was the year of Armageddon.

8

"Unnerve the Arm that Draws the Bow and Raises the Tommyhawk"

In 1813, a year of near hysterical national turmoil, the military and Indian situation in the Old Southwest was one of bafflement and confusion. In many respects it was also an enigmatic one. At no time during their internal struggles did the Creeks in any numbers attack their white neighbors. Border incidents like those on Duck River and the Ohio, and later in Burnt Corn and Fort Mims, were either acts of zealots out to avenge perceived injuries to their people or feuds between Creeks and mixed bloods.[1] Jim Cornells, Daniel Beasley, Samuel Mims, and most of the people involved in the early fights along the Alabama were mixed-blood descendants of white traders. Though the attack on Fort Mims was a retaliation by Red Stick chiefs, mostly mixed bloods, for the surpise skirmish at Burnt Corn, that incident may have well been an extension of the civil war.[2] After all, many of the persons on both sides of the stockade walls were mixed-blood kinsmen.

Equally as confusing in 1813 were the roles of the Spanish and British, both of whom were held accountable for arming and inciting the Indians to a greater extent that they did.[3] Spain's position in Europe and South America had deteriorated, and since Florida was only peripherally important to her as a line of defense for Cuba and Central America, her interests would best be served by avoiding war with the United States. Though the British trading firms, which stood only to lose by an Indian war, called for peace, Britain's sea power clearly posed a threat to the Gulf Coast.

As for the Creeks, it was a tragedy that their vision was so badly blurred at this critical moment in southern Indian history. The Red Sticks, who had fallen under the spell of the prophetic blandishments of their northwestern cousins, lost perspective of the actual condition of their people. Their wilderness domain had become a less dependable source for sustaining the scattered Nation. There was left to the Creeks after 1800 little choice but to accept Jefferson's civilization policy so effectively presented and demonstrated by the shrewd old agent Benjamin Hawkins.

By 1810, several intangible pressures were being exerted in the Old Southwest which neither the Creeks nor their white neighbors comprehended. Tucked away in Washington, and comfortably isolated from the raw backwoods of the region, were government officials densely ignorant of the realities of the Indian problems. They were incapable of a sensitive understanding of conditions and hence of finding an amicable solution to attendant issues.

From a humane standpoint, doubtless no greater administrative mistake could have been made than placing the management of Indian affairs largely in the hands of the Departments of Treasury and of War. The former was too penurious to act promptly, even if it had had a full commitment to treaty agreements. The latter was too feebly led to even attend to its own central responsibilities of defense. Under the parsimonious administration of the Swiss-born Secretary of the Treasury Albert Gallatin, annuity payments were slow of delivery if not deliberately withheld. The delays and evasions in the distribution of payments weakened the credibility of the United State Government with its Indian wards.[4] Indeed, the broad pyramid of territorial and national officials precluded amicable Indian relations and hastened dissolution of native culture.[5] Blended in with these many ingredients, of course, were the pressures of migration, which were sufficiently intense to color the white perspective and increase the anxieties of the tribesmen.

For the Creeks in 1813 it was a tragedy that their Nation had become so torn by internal strife at a moment when the United States had become involved in a major international struggle. At first, the Indians had no direct concern with the War of 1812; they were drawn into it as pawns, first by the Shawnee, then by the Spanish and British, and finally by the United States. Friend or foe, their cause was lost from the outset!

The massacre at Fort Mims was an inflammatory incident which released cataclysmic frontier forces in the Old Southwest. One of these was the stormy personal force of Andrew Jackson fomenting furiously in the eye of the martial storm with no early chance to vent itself. The Jackson record prior to the Creek War reveals at least two overweening personal facets— his obsession with the need to obliterate the Indian presence and his frustration over his unfulfilled military aspirations.

Perhaps the combination of circumstances which hardened Jackson's attitude toward the southern Indians will never be fully understood, but certainly his experiences as an immigrant on the Tennessee frontier account for his antipathy toward Indian occupation of so much virgin land. In no part of the Old Southwest were clashes between intruders and tribesmen more bloody than among the Cumberland sites.[6] Jackson became almost as bitter toward Congress and those officials administering Indian policy as he was toward the wards themselves. Indian agents especially were the recipients of his wrath, particularly Choctaw agent Silas Dinsmoor, who infuriated Jackson by the enforcement of the requirement of passports for slaves traveling up or down the Natchez Trace. Dinsmoor, a New Englander who was rather fastidious in requiring proof of ownership of slaves who passed by his agency, did not win many friends with his strict application of the law. On one occasion he detained slaves belonging to Jackson who reclaimed them in a show of bravado intended to intimidate Dinsmoor who happened to be absent from the agency when Jackson called.[7]

In terms of his military career, Andrew Jackson in the prewar years was a thwarted man. A major general in the Tennessee militia since 1806, Jackson had become convinced that he was a well-nigh invincible military leader. Though he had neither military training nor battlefield experience against a worthy foe, he was vigorous in his martial orations and orders.[8] The War Department went out of its way to refuse Jackson's offers of personal service on either the Canadian or the Southwestern frontier.[9] The aborted expedition downriver to Natchez during the frigid winter of 1812–13 was enough to break the spirit of a less determined commanding officer. Indeed, by late summer of 1813, Jackson's military future was clouded. It seemed that he would have no opportunity to serve on any front no matter what fortune or misfortune befell the Americans.[10] At that low ebb in his life he sorely needed a cause in which he and his Tennessee Volunteers could serve basically on their own terms. In the Duck River and Fort Mims massacres, the Creek Indians gave him just such a cause!

Some six weeks prior to Fort Mims, Secretary John Armstrong had requested the governors of Tennessee, Georgia, and the Mississippi Territory to march militia into Creek country to suppress the Red Sticks.[11] His letter reached Nashville in time to coincide with the arrival of the news of the Fort Mims massacre. Though the Secretary had instructed Governor Willie Blount to raise 1500 volunteers, fresh memories of the unhappy experience of the past spring led Governor Blount to call up 5000 men—half from the state's western section, half from the eastern. Political considerations also influenced the decision of Blount who ordered

Jackson to recruit the westerners and Major General John Cocke the easterners. The two forces were to merge under Jackson's command and march toward the confluence of the Coosa and Tallapoosa Rivers as were the armies from Georgia and Mississippi Territory. Tennesseans enthusi-astically answered the call, firmly believing that their enlistment was for only three months—a persistent notion that soon would test the leader-ship of their officers to the breaking point.[12] Jackson contended that as federalized militiamen their tour was for six months; however, Jackson, facing a mutinous army, agreed to abide by Governor Blount's opinion that they were state militiamen called up for three months.

For Jackson personally, the call for troops came at one of the most unfor-tunate moments of his life. On September 1, he and Colonel John Coffee had become involved in a gunfight with Thomas Hart Benton and his brother Jesse in Nashville's City Hotel—a fracas resulting from Jackson's service as a second in a duel in which Jesse Benton received an embar-rassing and painful wound in the derriere.[13] One of Jesse's pistol shots shattered Jackson's left shoulder and another pierced his arm. After nearly bleeding to death and barely escaping amputation of the arm, Jackson remained bedridden for three weeks.

Lying abed wracked by pain from the injured shoulder, Old Hickory issued a stirring call for his troops to heed the tap of the adjutant's drum. In his general orders, he urged them to stand ready to avenge the bloody savagery of Fort Mims and to throw a protective military cordon about Mobile. The slaughter of "upward of three hundred" without even spar-ing "women and helpless children" called for a "retaliatory vengeance." Jackson spoke in behalf of "those distressed citizens of that frontier who have yet escaped the tomahawk" and expressed confidence that they had not in vain implored the brave Tennesseans for aid.[14]

In East Tennessee, Major General John Cocke was busily raising a com-mand of comparable size and having supplies transported to Ditto's Land-ing on the Tennessee River. Remarkably, there seemed to be only a minimum amount of communication or co-ordination between the two Tennessee commands, although the little correspondence that took place among Jackson, Cocke, and Blount reflected the sectional conditions of Tennessee politics.

The dominant personality of Andrew Jackson was revealed in the strong-est possible light during this period. Psychologically he created the image that the Creek campaign would be short and furious; to a man, his "brave Tennesseans" would emerge as heroes and would be home in time to hang their fresh laurels over humble hearthsides for Christmas. The volunteers who gathered and marched south to the ringing echoes of anti-Creek oratory seemed oblivious to the shriller overtones of battle with the British and possibly the Spanish. They had heard of Pensacola and Mobile, but were ignorant of the wilderness-shrouded distances separating the Gulf Coast from their homeland. After the ruffle of the enlistment drums had died away, the volunteers' ardor was cooled by the realities of battle march and stark encampments. The Jacksonian oratory had skipped blithely over the important matters of military logistics![15]

Meanwhile, in the Mississippi Territory, General Ferdinand L. Claiborne had moved his Third Infantry Regiment eastward from Baton Rouge to the Tombigbee frontier, and in the territorial capital, Governor David B. Holmes was recruiting more militia companies.[16] At this unpropitious moment a rancorous dispute erupted between Claiborne and his commander, General Thomas Flournoy, who had dismissed Major Thomas Hinds' Mississippi Dragoons from Federal service. Hinds's cavalrymen, who represented the aristocracy of the Natchez District, had left their comfortable homes expecting a quick battle and glory. Instead, Flournoy assigned them to guard the isolated corn fields and log cabins against Red Stick attacks. Regardless of its importance, Hinds's troops considered this patrol duty demeaning, and they expressed their objections in a remonstrance sent through General Claiborne to General Flournoy. The stern Flournoy, who viewed the communication as an act of insubordination, ordered the dragoons returned to the territorial governor as unfit for United States service. Many of the dismissed troops were neighbors of Claiborne, who was related by marriage to Hinds and who was the brother of William C. C. Claiborne. Probably because he, too, actively attempted to reconcile matters, General Flournoy reprimanded Claiborne over a week after he ordered the return of the dragoons to the command of Governor Holmes.[17]

Flournoy's reprimand was not a measure of his lack of confidence in Claiborne, for he ordered Claiborne to destroy Holy Ground, the fortified town on the Alabama River occupied by William Weatherford—also known as Red Eagle—and the Red Sticks after the attack on Fort Mims. However, Flournoy soon received word that General Thomas Pinckney of South Carolina, commander of the Sixth Military District, was in command of the entire Creek War and that he should relinquish the Third Regiment to Pinckney. So Flournoy marched with his remaining troops back to New Orleans, leaving Claiborne's forces considerably weakened.[18]

Undaunted and bolstered in spirit by the support of friendly Choctaw under Chief Pushmataha, on November 13, 1813, Claiborne led his troops out of encampment at Pine Level, ten miles above Fort St. Stephens, destined for Holy Ground. The Mississippians constructed Fort Claiborne some 20 miles from the town where the Creeks had barricaded themselves behind a breastwork of pickets and fallen trees. According to the prophet Josiah Francis, Holy Ground was also protected by an invisible barrier fatal to any white who passed through it. On December 23, 1813, Claiborne's forces attacked, and when the magic destruction of the whites failed to materialize, prophet Francis fled the scene with many of his followers. Weatherford and a small band of his warriors did, however, put up a spirited defense. When the odds became hopeless, Weatherford leaped astride his gray charger and made a dramatic escape by jumping his mount off a high bank into the river, a feat made legendary by exaggerated reports that he had plunged off a sixty foot cliff.[19]

Claiborne's men captured or destroyed considerable supplies and provisions stored in the some 200 houses in Holy Ground before advancing upriver a few miles to demolish a smaller village containing sixty dwellings. Though most of the Creeks in these two towns had escaped death, they realized now that their prophets had spoken falsely: Red Sticks were not invincible. The ability of the Creeks to communicate between the heart of their Nation and Pensacola was now disrupted. With this accomplished, General Claiborne led his troops back to the fort named in his honor and discharged them because their enlistment terms had expired. Colonel Gilbert Russell's Third Regiment remained in garrison at Fort Claiborne.

In Georgia, Governor David B. Mitchell had also earlier responded to Secretary Armstrong's instructions to raise a militia force of 1500 men for service against the Creeks. By August 21—a week before the Fort Mims massacre—over 2,000 Georgians had answered the governor's call.[20] For a variety of reasons, however, the size of the Georgia forces under the command of Major General John Floyd, including friendly Indians, probably never exceeded 1,500 in the campaign. Plagued constantly by a shortage of rations, Floyd's men in November reached the Chattahoochee where they constructed Fort Mitchell on the west bank at the site of the present town of Fort Mitchell, Alabama.

After destroying the hostile Creek town of Autosse on the Tallapoosa in late November, the Georgians built Fort Hull forty-one miles west of the Chattahoochee. Nearly two months later, the Creeks inflicted a beating upon Floyd's army on nearby Calabee Creek. Late in February, with his militiamen half starved and counting the days until the end of their enlistments, Floyd left the frontier in the hands of a small force of regulars, complemented by a few volunteers, under Colonel Gilbert Russell and led his disheartened Georgians home. The capable and energetic Russell constructed Fort Bainbridge midway between Forts Mitchell and Hull while he awaited reinforcements from South and North Carolina. By the end of March of 1814, the reinforced Georgia army had erected Fort Decatur on the Tallapoosa, and thus a chain of posts now connected western Georgia with the middle of the Creek country. General Pinckney planned for them to stockpile supplies for Jackson's Tennessee army.

Thus in late 1813 the Creeks were surrounded by the floundering volunteer armies that soon would crush their nation. From a historical perspective, the approximately 8000 regulars and militiamen called into service against an entire population of only twice that number appears as overkill. Despite the frightening rumors of British and Spanish arms, the Creeks still fought primarily with bows and arrows, clubs, tomahawks, and knives.[21] Like their white adversaries, they were woefully short of provisions because the rebels had destroyed farms and cattle ranges in their frantic assaults on the transplantation of Anglo-American culture.

Far from the Old Southwest on the nation's northern border, the Creeks suffered a harsh blow to their morale when Tecumseh was slain and the Shawnee all but annihilated in the Battle of the Thames in Canada on October 5, 1813. This source of false prophecy and mysticism that had inspired large numbers of Creeks to rebellion vanished, and there is little doubt that American successes about Lake Erie and along the Thames stiffened Andrew Jackson's determination to crush the Creeks.[22]

Still weak from his gunfight wounds and with his arm in a sling, Andrew Jackson led his volunteer army from Fayetteville early in October of 1813. After a hasty mobilization, it was headed on a long wilderness march into the Creek Nation with little planning and woefully inadequate logistical support. No advance deposits of supplies had been made along the route, which led through unmarked and uncleared woods. A thoroughly inefficient private commissary, or contractor system, was entrusted with the vital task of supplying and transporting goods.[23] There prevailed in the eloquent call to arms of the Tennessee leaders the notion that the Creek part of the war would be over before the end of the ninety-day terms of enlistment. But once the poorly clad Volunteers had set foot on the trail, slept in biting autumn air, and felt the pangs of hunger, heroism became a more remote goal.

Until they crossed the Tennessee River at Ditto's Landing, the Volunteers moved rapidly, but at this point their march slowed down. For the next four months, the Tennessee army dealt with natural forces almost as fierce as the Creek warriors promised to be. After scrambling across the Raccoon and Lookout Mountains, the troops encountered forests where movement became little more than a step-by-step advance. Added to the woes of the rugged terrain and lack of supplies was the unusually cold and wet winter of 1813–14.

Old Hickory was tested as well. Late in October, his suppliers—Read Mitchell, and Company—informed him of their inability to fulfill their contract for provisions, and almost at the same time he learned that six volunteers under Captain James Paulson's command had refused to cross the Tennessee River because their three-month enlistment term was almost expired.[24] The throbbing pain of his shoulder injury and the debilitating effects of diarrhea compounded his misery.[25] But Jackson was undeterred. "I am determined to push forward," he wrote to his trusted friend and quartermaster, William B. Lewis, "if I have to live on acorns."[26] Then he sent Lewis back to Nashville in quest of supplies and ordered John Coffee to forage among Indian villages.

The same day Jackson showered his troops with another stirring campaign address. "You will hail their [the Indians'] bellowing approach by a substantial salute with the bayonet," he assured his men, and asked, "What Indian ever stood the charge of the bayonet. . . ?"[27] Oratory was a poor substitute for food and shelter. However warm and fervent it was, it did not blanch the chill of approaching winter in the lower Appalachian highlands. What had begun in August as a conquering horde of fierce Tennesseans led gallantly into battle against the elusive Red Sticks now had become a demoralized body of countrymen entrapped in the fogs of a dismal wooded mountainous area, wondering about their next meal and looking forward to the expiration of their enlistments. From Fort Strother on the Coosa River their leader lamented to Governor Blount: "It is with extreme pain I inform you that a turbulent mutinous disposition has manifested itself in my Camp. . . ."[28]

On the very eve of being in position to confront the warring Creeks, Jackson's army was almost out of supplies, and his hopes were dim that more would be delivered in time to check wholesale desertion or starvation. The only bit of heartening news was that of the successful raid by General Coffee's command on a couple of well-stocked Creek corncribs.[29] So desperate had the situation become that Jackson appealed to General Thomas Flournoy in Mobile for aid. He also solicited meat and bread from the farmers in Madison County, Mississippi Territory, explaining that he feared "monster famine" more than hostile Creeks.[30] At the same time,

Old Hickory reassured them of his determination to destroy the rebel villages on the Coosa.

During the first week of November the West Tennesseans engaged in their first battle with the Creeks. On November 2, Jackson ordered General Coffee to destroy an Indian town defended by 200 hostile warriors thirteen miles away at Tallushatchee, and at daybreak the next morning Coffee attacked. It was a slaughter. With losses of only five dead and forty-one wounded, the 1,000 mounted troops killed 186 warriors and took eighty-four women and children captive. This was first blood, and Jackson boasted to Governor Blount, "We have retaliated for the destruction of Fort Mims."[31]

One of the villages which switched allegiance to Jackson after Tallushatchee was Talladega, thirty miles south of Fort Strother. Soon after, learning that 1,000 Red Stick warriors led by William Weatherford were besieging the town, Jackson on the morning of November 9 deployed 1200 infantrymen and 800 cavalrymen in a sweeping semicircle attack a half mile from Weatherford's braves. Using the tactic of fire, retreat, and fire again, the volunteers drew the Indians into a death trap, but a number escaped when the American communications broke down. Even so, nearly a third of the Red Sticks were killed, and over half of the warriors who escaped were wounded. This was the first time that Major General Andrew Jackson had commanded troops in a formal battle, and thus it was in a bouyant sense of victory that he reported to Governor Blount, "The friendly Creeks from Talladega tell me that the enemy consider themselves already completely beaten."[32]

The buoyancy was short-lived, however. In the hurried march on Talladega, Jackson had had to leave behind his sick and wounded in an unguarded and unnourished situation, trusting that General James White, a long-time friend of Governor Blount would arrive to protect them with the advance of General Cocke's army. White's failure to do so opened a rift between the West and East Tennessee commands. Had he not been forced to return to Fort Strother, Jackson felt he could "have broken down the Creek force and made them fully sensible that they have heretofore been indebted for their safety to our forbearance alone."[33]

Realizing that Jackson had insufficient provisions even for his own forces, Cocke ordered White to bypass Fort Strother and head south. He had other reasons too. "Let us then take a direction," he wrote White, "in which we can share some of the dangers and glories of the field."[34] Though Governor Blount attempted to placate Jackson, hard feelings per-

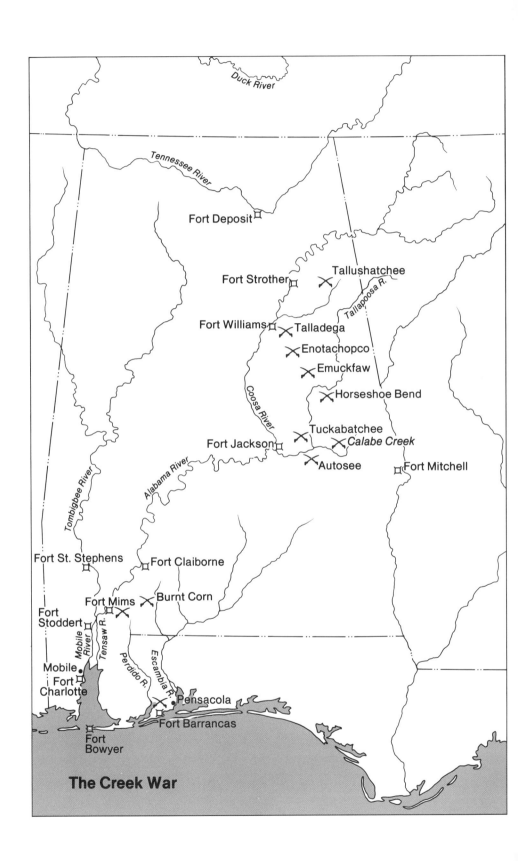

The Creek War

sisted, and in the end, Cocke would have to answer to Jackson's charges of insubordination.[35]

In mid-November General Thomas Pinckney advised Jackson to penetrate to the heart of the Creek Nation at the confluence of the Coosa and Tallapoosa Rivers, protecting at all times the rear of his advance.[36] From that date until the following April, however, the major problems of the Tennessee commands were logistical, not Red Stick warriors. In monotonous refrains, Jackson and Cocke pleaded for provisions. Patriotism was fading rapidly in the face of hunger.

One sifts through all the general orders and pronouncements without detecting a sense of the importance of prior preparation for supplying troops in so difficult a field of action. The persuasive pleas of Blount, Jackson, and Cocke for enlistment were not matched by planning and organization—a serious deficiency in face of the extremely short terms of enlistment. The Creek campaign on all fronts proved to be an almost insurmountable logistical challenge. There were no interior roads, no interconnecting channels between the rivers, and in most cases the rivers were blocked by rocky shoals. The campaign was mounted at the beginning of a difficult winter by ill clad and poorly sheltered troops. The only redeeming factor was that they faced an enemy who was even more inadequately prepared to fight.

Himself fending off chronic dysentery, cold, and gnawing hunger, Old Hickory as a commander at Fort Strother faced equal measures of famine and desertion. On December 9, 1813, Jackson learned that his entire first brigade planned to desert during the night. Immediately he ordered the mutinous unit to parade on the west side of the fort. As the brigade assembled, artillarymen posted themselves in front of and behind the formation and trained two small fieldpieces on the rebellious troops. Meanwhile loyal militiamen commanded the eminences above the road back to Tennessee. From astride his horse Old Hickory addressed the brigade. When the men did not respond to his praises and his appeal to their sense of honor, Jackson announced that they would leave only over his dead body. He interrupted their silence with orders for the gunners to light their matches. Jackson was not bluffing and the troops knew it. Out stepped the rebellious officers with vows of renewed loyalty. Old Hickory had made his point.[37]

But had he? Attempted desertions seemed to crop up like woods fires as the end of the three-month enlistments approached. Though Jackson held firm and put out the fires, decisions by the Secretary of War and Governor Blount nearly stopped the invasion and ended his career. The

Secretary agreed with the militiamen that their terms began at muster rather than departure from Tennessee; the governor urged him to bring his army home. Men made of stuff other than hickory would have bent or broken. Not Jackson. He fired off to Governor Blount one of the most powerful and moving letters of his career—a letter that reflected his indomitable spirit and immeasurable patriotism.

After warning his friend Blount that the Creeks had not been conquered, Jackson posed a barbed question. "And are you my Dear friend sitting with yr. arms folded . . . recommending me to retrograde to please the whims of the populace and waiting for further orders from the Secy. war."[38] Jackson then denigrated the "fireside patriots, those fawning sycophants or cowardly poltroons" who supported withdrawal of his army. Jackson's strong words to the governor continued: "Arouse from yr. lethargey—despise the fawning smiles or the snarling frowns of such miscreants—with energy exercise yr. function—the campaign must rapidly progress, or you are forever damed and yr country ruined."

When Jackson gave his men the choice of pressing ahead with him or heading back to Tennessee, most of them left. He stayed and his luck changed with the new year. But not before another brush with disaster. After 800 raw recruits marched into Fort Strother in mid-January of 1814, the undaunted Jackson moved his forces southward toward the center of the confluence of the Coosa and the Tallapoosa Rivers with the most tenuous of logistical support. At dawn on January 21, the Red Sticks launched a skillfully designed attack upon his camp at Emuckfaw Creek. His brother-in-law, Major Alexander Donelson, was killed, and though Jackson's men inflicted heavy casualties upon the attackers, he wisely headed back toward Fort Strother. At Enotachopco Creek, however, the Red Sticks surprised his troops as they crossed the stream. Much to Jackson's "mortification," the undisciplined recruits scattered in a "disastrous retreat."[39] Utter disaster was prevented by one of Jackson's most memorable displays of personal courage and inspiration. Because twenty-five of his men held their ground across the creek, Jackson had time to rally his troops. Standing in the midst of a shower of musket balls, he provided a sufficient example and leadership. His re-formed columns counterattacked and drove off the Indians after a brief but intense battle. When the firing ceased, 200 dead Indians littered the banks while his casualties amounted to 20 dead and 75 wounded. The clashes at Emuckfaw and Enotachopco, though by no means victories, had a number of salutary effects: the Red Sticks suffered such severe casualties that they withdrew into defensive positions; excellent reconnaissance resulted; enlistments surged in Tennessee; Jackson's confidence and stature grew; and spirits in Washington soared.[40]

Intelligence reports indicated that the major rebel stronghold was located at the Horseshoe Bend of the Tallapoosa River. By March Jackson commanded a combined force of 5,000 men, including regulars, volunteers, and Indian allies. It was time to attack. Before leading them to Horseshoe Bend, however, Old Hickory knew he must thoroughly discipline them. Enotachopco had proved that. When Generals Cocke and Isaac Roberts dissented, Jackson sent them home under arrest, and he ordered a court-martial for a young private who had momentarily gone berserk and threatened an officer with his gun. The general turned a deaf ear to pleas for clemency, and a firing squad shot Private John Woods, barely eighteen years old, with every man on the post a witness.[41]

On March 14, the day of the execution, Jackson headed downriver, leaving 450 men behind to guard Fort Strother. Traveling by boat ahead of him was Colonel John Williams, whose regiment would build Fort Williams thirty miles to the south. With assurances from General Pinckney that supplies were forthcoming from Mobile, Jackson struck out due east from Fort Williams toward the enemy fortress with upward of 4,000 men in his command, including friendly Indians. Sixty miles distant awaited 1,000 Red Stick warriors together with some 300 women and children protected by a brilliantly designed fortification across the narrow neck of a hundred-acre peninsula. The five- to eight-foot-high breastwork of horizontally laid logs and timbers zig-zagged much in the fashion of a rail fence along a slightly concaved line, and it was heavily dotted with portholes from which the defenders could train a deadly crossfire on the attackers. Indeed, the sophistication of its design astonished Jackson on his arrival there at mid-morning on March 27.

Astonishment was no deterrent to Old Hickory. He stationed General Coffee's troops along with friendly Creeks and Cherokee across the river from the bend in order to deny the rebels an escape route. Though Jackson's bombardment of the breastwork did not endanger the defenders, it distracted them while Coffee's men cut loose the fleet of canoes tied at the inner bank as a precaution by the Red Sticks. Then other men crossed the river and fired some huts well behind the barricade to provide a diversion for the frontal assault. In truly heroic fashion, the Tennesseans charged through withering fire, jammed their weapons into the port holes, fired for a while muzzle-to-muzzle amidst the stunned Red Sticks, and then, on a second attempt, scrambled over the wall. The defenders continued to fight from the concealment of the brush inside the compound before attempting every possible avenue of escape. All exits were sealed. A few Red Sticks leaped from the river bluffs only to be trapped in the debris below.

As Jackson later described it to his wife Rachel, "The *carnage* was *dreadful*."[42] The slaughter did not stop until darkness covered the peninsula, and when the bodies were counted the next day, the tally of dead Indians reached 900. Obviously, few warriors had escaped—all but four of the 300 captives were women and children. Amazingly, only forty-seven of Jackson's men were killed; 159 were wounded. In addition, 23 friendly Creek and Cherokee braves died and 47 were wounded.

Lesser men would have been completely satisfied with this victory. Jackson was not. He grieved at the loss of his friend Major Lemuel P. Montgomery, who had died leading the first assault over the breastwork. Besides, William Weatherford, or Chief Red Eagle to the Creeks, who had been one of the leaders of the Fort Mims massacre happened to be away from the stronghold that day. Regardless of Jackson's momentary displeasure, Horseshoe Bend stands as one of the key victories of the War of 1812. Had Old Hickory not totally broken the Red Stick capacity and will to fight, the course of the war in the Old Southwest might well have been different.

Surely Jackson realized this by the time he thanked his troops on return to Fort Williams for their magnificent victory, and accurately predicted: "Their midnight flambeaux will no more illumine their Council houses, or shine upon the victims of their infernal orgies. They have disappeared from the face of the Earth. In this Place generations will arise who will know their duties. The weapons of warfare will be exchanged for the utensils of husbandry; and the wilderness which now withers with sterility and seems to mourn the dislocation which overspreads it, will blossom as a rose, and become the nursery of the arts."[43]

Jackson did not savor the victory for long, however. Still short of provisions and buffeted by March winds, the Tennesseans resumed their southerly advance, on April 5, intent on smashing any vestiges of Red Stick resistance.[44] But there was really no great significance to the post-Horseshoe Bend raids. The Creeks were a broken, frightened people suffering mightily from hunger and exposure.[45] Their manpower was greatly reduced, and the system which Benjamin Hawkins had worked so diligently to establish was now in ruins. Many of the vanquished fled south to Florida, but hundreds came into Jackson's camp to surrender, further draining his perilously low provisions. As quickly as they appeared, Jackson ordered them to settle north of Fort Williams where they would be isolated from Florida—and British or Spanish assistance. On April 18, the victors arrived at the Hickory Grounds just above the confluence of the Coosa and the Tallapoosa where they reconstructed old French Fort Toulouse and renamed it Fort Jackson after their leader.[46]

The one chief who had not come into camp, however, was William Weatherford, but when it became apparent that his absence placed the other leaders in a most uncomfortable position, he appeared before Old Hickory in a display of courage befitting a noble legend. Unattended, Weatherford strode into Fort Jackson and dumbfounded Jackson by claiming the same protection granted to his fellow chiefs. His complete lack of fear and his eloquent admission of his rebellious activities moved Jackson, who played the role of a wise conqueror. Weatherford agreed to convince the remaining holdouts to join him in surrender, whereupon he left camp and made good his word. His role as a warrior had ended. After the war he settled down to the life of a respected planter and from time to time paid his respects to Old Hickory at the Hermitage. Weatherford, in his ancestry and actions, personified the complexities of the frontier of the Old Southwest. One-eighth Creek and seven-eighths French, Scotch, and English, his familial influence provided an avenue to tribal power. Weatherford seemed proud that his white blood was European, not American. Once he boasted that "not a drop of Yankee blood" flowed in his veins.[47]

Within a few days after Weatherford's appearance, General Thomas Pinckney with his South Carolina militia arrived at Fort Jackson full of praise for the Tennessee army and its commander. After an appropriate round of celebrations, Pinckney ordered Old Hickory to lead his victorious troops back home for their long-awaited release from duty. Within hours they had departed.[48]

No Tennessean needed a furlough more than Andrew Jackson. The pain from his wounded arm and the debilitating effects of chronic dysentery had taken their toll. His body needed a rest, and personal affairs at the Hermitage awaited his attention. In addition, Old Hickory wanted to sound out public reaction to his feud with Cocke and especially to the Administration's plans for a peace treaty with the Creeks.

In anticipation of Jackson's success, the Secretary of War had appointed General Pinckney and Agent Hawkins as commissioners assigned to negotiate a peace treaty with the Creeks even before their destruction at Horseshoe Bend.[49] Pinckney received extremely broad instructions, with the only firm stipulation requiring that the Creeks indemnify the United States for the cost of the war. Otherwise he had the widest latitude. On April

23, 1814, General Pinckney sent Hawkins, who was viewed more as an advisor than a principal negotiator, an outline for a prospective treaty. The Creeks must cede sufficient land to cover the cost of the war, grant rights to build forts, trading houses, and roads, and guarantee free navigation of streams. In addition, they must surrender all prophets and other instigators of the war and desist from trade with foreign powers.[50]

The responsibility of peacemaking with the Creeks called for the utmost justice and humanity so that a line might be drawn between the rebellious Red Sticks and their peaceful brethren. After all, internal conflicts within the Creek Nation had brought on the war. In the beginning, the well-being of neighboring white settlers was not an issue and only isolated attacks occurred upon travelers through the Creek Nation. Too, in 1814 little proof existed of foreigners providing arms to the rebels. Indeed, the future of Indian affairs in the Old Southwest would rest in the hands of the negotiators. Benjamin Hawkins and Thomas Pinckney, from the perspective of the Creeks, represented wise selections.

From the moment of their appointment, however, Pinckney and Hawkins were viewed by many westerners, especially Tennesseans, as too soft on the Indians, and a howl of protest went up on news of the terms proposed by Pinckney. General Jackson's voice was among the loudest; he had stern notions of sacrifices to be demanded of the Creeks. Indemnification was not enough. They must be separated from Florida by a band of Anglo-American settlement connecting Georgia to the Mississippi Territory, a strategy he felt could easily be realized in view of the fertility of the land.[51] Now, according to Jackson, was also the appropriate moment to extinguish Cherokee and Chickasaw claims within Tennessee. This protective cordon of white farmers he justified in terms of the enhancement of national security and of southern political strength in Congress.[52]

The outcry from the Tennesseans was effective; indeed, they would control the treaty-making. On June 8, Jackson accepted a commission as a brigadier general in the Regular Army with brevet rank of major general, whereupon he replaced Pinckney as commander of the Seventh Military District. A year and a half earlier, his services had been spurned; now he occupied the position formerly held by his old nemesis James Wilkinson and commanded military actions along the broad front of the Old Southwest.

When Armstrong assigned Jackson to relieve Pinckney, he also ordered him to return to Fort Jackson and finally conclude the treaty with the Creeks. Theoretically, Jackson's instructions were the same as those given earlier by Pinckney to Hawkins.[53] In reality, however, his appointment represented a fundamental shift in the approach to the administration of Indian affairs in the Old Southwest—one which had a dramatic, long-ranged bearing on future policy. The attitudes of Hawkins and Jackson toward Indians were poles apart. The former sought the reinstitution of Jefferson's civilization policy within a geographically reduced Nation; the latter envisioned the dismantlement of the Creek Nation! Or did he already foresee removal of all Indian tribes from the Southwest?

A heavy heart must have pounded in the chest of Benjamin Hawkins when he discerned the punitive mood of Andrew Jackson upon his arrival at the fort on July 10, 1814. Immediately, the general ordered Hawkins to call an assembly of *all* Creek chiefs—friendly and hostile—on August 1 and to deliver with the invitation a warning that their failure to appear would initiate a destructive retaliatory strike. The Tennessee militia still was at his command and would remain on station throughout the negotiations.[54] Since virtually all the chiefs who answered his call on the appointed day had allied themselves with Old Hickory in the campaign, they were stunned beyond belief at the terms he demanded.[55]

The price of the indemnity, as calculated by Jackson, was one-half of the Creek domain—23 million acres of land or three-fifths of Alabama plus one-fifth of Georgia. His allies were to pay as dearly as his enemies! The other demands seemed irrelevant: cessation of all intercourse with the British and the Spanish; the right to construct roads, forts, and trading posts; and delivery of all instigators of the war. Rather than the terms of the Administration in Washington, these clearly were the terms of Jackson and his constituents. His latest biographer, Robert Remini, explains, "Actually he was less the government's agent than the agent of westerners, all of whom wished the treaty to both punish the Indian and reward the white man."[56] More specifically, policy in this particular instance was made in Nashville, not Washington.

After futilely and repeatedly objecting with vehemence, eloquence, and cunning, the Creeks capitulated on August 9, 1814, when thirty-five chiefs, only *one* of whom was a Red Stick, affixed their signatures to the document. A good measure of the pathetic irony of the scene was the face-saving gesture of awarding three square miles of land each to Jackson and Hawkins and a square mile each to the two interpreters.[57] Jackson's ultimate humiliation of his former allies was his curt announcement that the proceeds from the sale of his land, if conveyed to him, would go to needy Creeks. His word, however, was never tested; conveyance was never made to Jackson, who was now known as "Sharp Knife" among the Indians.

Fort Jackson marked a pivotal point in the history of the Native Americans. It left the Jeffersonian Indian policy a shambles and destroyed the fruits of Benjamin Hawkins's years of faithful labors. For Hawkins personally, the treaty was a devastating blow from which he never recovered, and which no doubt hastened his death in 1816.[58] Compared, however, to its long-range impact, these immediate results were insignificant. American Indian policy—no longer really in the hands of Washington officials—had turned onto an irreversible path toward obliteration of sovereign tribes and the total confiscation of their ancestral domains—a policy soon to be known as "removal."

Before General Jackson could retrace his steps from Nashville to Fort Jackson to impose his destructive treaty upon the Creeks, it was clear that the closing campaign of the War of 1812 in the Old Southwest would move onto a broader field. Rumors already were flying through the lower Alabama country that Peter McQueen and other rebellious Creeks had found haven in Pensacola and were preparing for new raids along the border. The desperate plight of all Creeks led Jackson to urge Washington officials to act expeditiously in delivering food and clothing to the region for strategic as well as humanitarian reasons. "The whole Creek Nation is in a most wretched State," wrote Jackson to Armstrong the day after the signing of the treaty, "and I repeat, that they *must* be *fed* and *clothed* or necessity will compel them to embrace the proffered friendship of the British."[59]

Fear of British and Spanish activities gave Jackson's troops light feet. He moved his army some 400 miles down the Coosa and Alabama Rivers to Mobile in only eleven days, arriving in Mobile on August 22. His fears had been well founded. With the cooperation of the local Spanish officials, the British had already assumed command of Pensacola. Jackson instantly ordered the renovation and refortification of Fort Bowyer, located at the westernmost tip of a long, narrow peninsula jutting out from the eastern shore at the mouth of Mobile Bay. Meanwhile, trails between the two coastal cities were crowded with messengers whose reports stirred Jackson into action. Not only were the British arming the Indians, but they had recruited a black regiment as well.[60]

Surely, the British planned an invasion of the Gulf Coast. But where? The answer to that question could wait, but first large numbers of troops must be mustered. Without delay another army of volunteers was being assembled in Georgia, Louisiana, Mississippi Territory, and Tennessee.[61] Meanwhile, Old Hickory deployed the troops already under his command.

Jackson reported the successful defense of Fort Bowyer "with lively emotions of satisfaction." On September 15, only 158 men in the fort had repulsed an attack by four ships aided by 258 marines and Indians who had marched overland from Pensacola. To Secretary of War James Monroe he boasted of the defense as "An achievement glorious in itself, and so important in its consequences [that it] should be appreciated by the Government."[62] And well it should have been. The capture of Mobile would have enhanced the British relationships with the Indians and widened considerably their options for invading the Gulf Coast and Mississippi Valley.

On the distant Gulf Coast frontier, Andrew Jackson assumed broad military and diplomatic authority. His truculent letters to Governor Mateo González Manrique at Pensacola, for instance, bristled with provocations.[63] In fact, they were so militant that Secretary Monroe wrote in October that President Madison was concerned that Jackson leave diplomacy to other officials and take no action that would lead to war with Spain.[64] Instead, Monroe implied, the American commander should concern himself with defensive preparations for the widely discussed expedition en route from England.

Jackson acted before he received this letter—not that it would have deterred him. In his mind, the most effective move to blunt the pending British invasion was the removal of the British presence at Pensacola, which would greatly reduce the perimeter of his defense. Luck was with him. His faithful friend and fellow Indian fighter, General Coffee, was at the very moment leading 2,000 sorely needed cavalry down from Tennessee, and in late October Jackson departed from Mobile to rendezvous with Coffee for an attack on Pensacola despite the presence of British warships anchored in the harbor there. As much to the dismay of the British as to the surprise of the Tennesseans, Spanish resistance at Pensacola on November 7, 1814, was virtually nonexistent. The British ships were not positioned to fire effectively on the invaders: so rather than attract artillery fire from the Americans, naval officers chose to keep their guns quiet. Disgusted, the British ships destroyed Forts Barrancas and Santa Rosa as they sailed out of a now defenseless Pensacola harbor.

Jackson's decision to take Pensacola without government orders proved to be a fortuitous one. For there he learned that a change in British plans called for a full-scale assault directly on New Orleans. Prior to his march on Pensacola, the general had been informed that their overall strategy involved the isolation of New Orleans by preliminary expeditions, including one against Mobile. Their plans also called for occupation of Pensacola with or without Spanish approval. The source of this information was James Innerarity, a native of Scotland and nephew of William Panton of Panton, Leslie and Company. Innerarity, who headed the Mobile office of Panton, Leslie, had received his infomation from an American merchant in Havana, Vincent Gray, who attributed it to Lt. Col. Edward Nicolls of the British Marines. In Pensacola, however, Jackson learned of a change in the British plans. An armada of sixty ships and 14,000 troops would depart momentarily from Jamaica for an invasion of New Orleans. Jackson promptly returned to Mobile so that he could provide for its defense before departing for New Orleans.[65]

On November 22, 1814, Old Hickory lead his army westward out of Mobile along the Federal post road which ran just north of the thirty-first parallel.[66] After crossing the Pearl River, Jackson turned south to the northern shore of Lake Pontchartrain. On November 30, he and his men sailed across the lake and camped overnight on the outskirts of the town. On the morning of December 1, Jackson entered New Orleans where he found, as expected, a frightened and divided citizenry. After Governor Claiborne welcomed the general, Jackson responded with a call for unity and a promise to save their city. His indomitable spirit was contagious. Almost as if by magic, the Tennessean unified the town's widely disparate communities. Dividing lines of wealth, nationality, race, language, religion, morality, and civility disappeared under the spell of Jackson, who understood human nature as well as military tactics. He masterfully orchestrated their common disdain for the British. After a personal interview with pirate leader Jean Lafitte, who had the same character traits which Jackson admired in William Weatherford, the general accepted Lafitte's offer of men and munitions. While most New Orleanians praised Jackson's alliance with Lafitte, many were unhappy with his enthusiastic acceptance of two battalions of free blacks.

New Orleans lies on the east bank of the Mississippi River nearly 150 miles from its mouth.[67] Because the wide river forms an unfordable crescent around the town, it was invulnerable to a western assault. Invasion up the river, though possible, would be quite costly. Thirty miles above the mouth of the Mississippi stood the heavily fortified Fort St. Philip and twenty-five miles below New Orleans Fort St. Leon overlooked English Turn, the long bend in the river that was unnavigable by sailing vessels without a change in wind direction. Geography, then, dictated that an attack on New Orleans would come from the east—through Mobile and then overland, or through Lake Borgne which lies east of New Orleans and which blends into the Gulf of Mexico. With the knowledge that the British expedition was headed for New Orleans, not Mobile, the most likely avenue of attack would be through Lake Borgne. A narrow strait, known as the Rigolets, connected Lake Pontchartrain and Lake Borgne. Indeed, the commonly used water route from New Orleans to Mobile via Lake Pontchartrain ran through the Rigolets, through Lake Borgne, into the Gulf, and eastward over to Mobile Bay. There were three likely routes into New Orleans from Lake Borgne. The British could take the Chef Menteur road from that lake to the Plain of Gentilly, the only stretch of dry land leading to New Orleans from the east. Another British option was to ascend one of the bayous running from Lake Borgne toward the Mississippi River. Or they could go through the Rigolets and across Lake Pontchartrain to Bayou St. Jean which extended to the outskirts of New Orleans. The St Jean route probably was the best approach, but the British decided against it because they lacked sufficient numbers of light-draft boats and because they had been misled into believing that the fort guarding the entrance into Lake Pontchartrain was heavily fortified.

Barely two weeks after Jackson arrived, the British armada was sighted among the islands at the entrance of Lake Borgne, and on December 14 the British captured the squadron of American gunboats which were outnumbered and outgunned. Since he no longer had a watch on Lake Borgne, Jackson guarded the routes from Lake Borgne. Despite their confidence in Jackson, the inhabitants of New Orleans panicked. In this atmosphere relations between Governor Claiborne and the state legislature grew tense. Old Hickory, who had little patience with the legislature, declared martial law in effect on December 16. To offset the unpopularity of this measure, Jackson ordered a review of the city militia on Sunday, December 18. The review created a carnival-like atmosphere and gave the general an opportunity to have widely respected Edward Livingston read Jackson's moving call for heroism and sacrifice. Livingston, the town's most celebrated legal figure and an old friend of Jackson, played his role perfectly and the pageant was a great success.

Meanwhile, the British had chosen as their staging area the sandy, insect- and reptile-ridden Pea Island, just east of the Rigolets in Lake Borgne near the mouth of the Pearl River. Disembarkation was a back-breaking task. Boats carrying the men to Pea Island had to be rowed, often against wind and tide. Nevertheless the British completed this operation on December 20. Two days later, Major General John Keane ordered the movement of British troops across Lake Borgne and up Bayou Bienvenue toward New Orleans. On the morning of December 23, Colonel William Thornton with 1,800 redcoats reached the plantation of General Jacques Villeré—just 1,000 yards from the Mississippi. General Villeré's

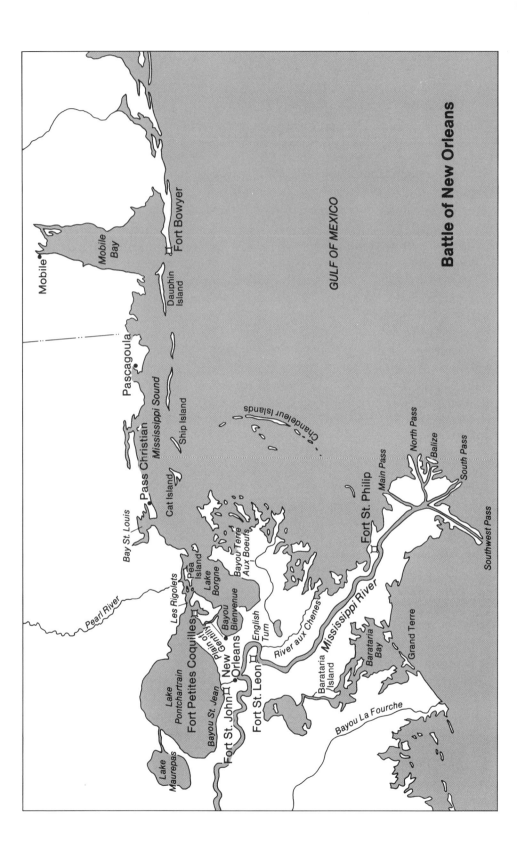

Battle of New Orleans

son escaped from the British and reached Jackson's headquarters by early afternoon. Old Hickory was furious. Who had failed to follow his orders to obstruct Bayou Bienvenue? Even in his fury Jackson remained gracious, serving a glass of wine to the young Villeré while he gathered his staff to prepare for a fight that night.

General Keane, who had joined the British column, overruled Colonel Thornton's request to press forward—a display of timidity which probably saved New Orleans. Jackson, who had no more troops than Keane at that precise moment, was totally off guard. Prisoners held by the British had misled Keane into believing that Jackson had as many as 20,000 troops. What luck for Jackson!

Fearing that Keane's presence may have been designed to distract Jackson's attention away from a much larger troop movement up Chef Menteur, Jackson stationed forces to guard that entrance into New Orleans. Then he planned a pincer tactic, directing his Tennessee friend General John Coffee to move along the cypress swamp on the left while Jackson's main forces headed down the edge of the Mississippi River in search of the British who, by nightfall, had camped along its banks. In addition, Jackson, ordered the *Carolina*, an armed schooner carrying a crew of ninety, to sail downriver and to begin a bombardment of the British camp at half past seven. At first the weather cooperated. The bright moonlight made it easy for gunners aboard the *Carolina* to spot their targets. As Jackson had hoped, the cannon fire caused a tremendous confusion among the British. As soon as the bombardment ended, Jackson ordered a frontal attack. The fighting was furious and often hand-to-hand. Neither side gave way. Then the weather stopped cooperating and a heavy fog added to the confusion. Jackson disengaged his troops and waited for daylight. His decision was wise, for fresh, disciplined troops were joining Keane's forces. Records show that both sides suffered a casualty rate of 10 percent—a rather high figure.

The next day was December 24. On that day across the Atlantic in Ghent, Belgium, ministers representing England and the United States signed a peace treaty ending the War of 1812. In New Orleans, where two months would pass before news of the treaty would arrive, Jackson began construction of his first line of defense along an abandoned millrace known as Rodriguez Canal. The ten-foot-wide ditch ran inland from the river for about three-quarters of a mile. Eventually he ordered a second and a third line of defense built. Jackson intended to have two rallying points should the redcoats overrun Rodriquez Canal.

On Christmas Day the British celebrated with cannon fire the arrival of Sir Edward Pakenham, commander of the invasion and brother-in-law of the Duke of Wellington. He immediately sensed that his command was in an unenviable position—squeezed between a swamp and the Mississippi River from which the enemy could shell his troops. On December 27, Pakenham attempted to clear American warships from the river. Though his artillery destroyed the *Carolina*, a larger armed vessel— the *Louisiana*— escaped. The next day at daylight Pakenham ordered two columns to advance on Jackson's position, one close to the river and another close to the swamp, but he called off the attack when the *Louisiana* caught his soldiers in a deadly cross fire. After this failure, Pakenham ordered his heaviest guns trained on the Rodriguez Canal fortification in the hope of knocking out the American artillery and breaching the fortification. This activity convinced Jackson that Pakenham's forces indeed represented the major British thrust, so Jackson took Jean Lafitte's advice to extend his line well into the swamps. By a superhuman effort the British troops transported additional guns taken from their fleet through Lake Borgne and up Bayou Bienvenue and trained them on Jackson's fortification. They completed this task on New Year's Eve. Now Pakenham's guns could pour 300 pounds of lead per salvo into Jackson's line.

When the fog cleared on New Year's morning of 1815, Pakenham could not believe his eyes. Jackson's forces were massed for a dress parade, a good antidote for the loss of confidence that many New Orleanians were demonstrating after the British attack on December 27. Again the Jackson luck held. Pakenham's units were not in position to charge and his cannon were loaded with demolition ammunition instead of antipersonnel shot. The British had little choice but to begin the barrage as planned. Of course, confusion reigned momentarily among the Americans who scampered to their positions. Jackson's headquarters took a number of hits, but he and his staff amazingly avoided injury. Within minutes, Old Hickory was on the line inspiring and instructing his troops. For two hours, the opposing forces pounded each other with artillery, but by three in the afternoon all was quiet. Pakenham's tactics had failed and his gun placements had suffered considerable damage. Sugar from the barrels stacked around the guns in lieu of sandbags had disabled a number of pieces, others had sunk into the mud, and American fire had destroyed some.

The bright and determined Pakenham, a veteran of the Napoleonic Wars, did not dispair. Although battle fatigue and bayonet-like dampness took their toll on the morale of his troops, Pakenham now placed his hope on a diversionary movement on the west side of the Mississippi. The only problem with this rather clever move was that he lacked boats to ferry the 1,500 troops that he wanted to deploy across the wide and deep river. Not to be deterred, Pakenham ordered the canal leading from the Mississippi to the Villeré plantation be dug deep and wide enough to accommodate the barges that had transported the troops up Bayou Bienvenue. Completion of this herculean task provided a lull that Old Hickory used to good advantage. He deepened Rodriguez Canal, lengthened it, and raised the height of the rampart. Jackson also extended his line into the swamp and angled it back toward the town.

On January 7 the British ferried men and cannon across the river as planned, but they landed so far downstream that they could not move up the west bank fast enough to send a cross fire over on Jackson's line by the appointed hour. This was another piece of horrible luck for the British, especially since the American units on the west bank were greatly outnumbered.

If so much blood had not been spilled, it would be appropriate to call the British attack on January 8 a comedy of errors. Not the only one, but the biggest error was committed by the Forty-Fourth Regiment. Its members were assigned to carry the fascines—bundles of sugar cane—designed to fill up the canal in front of Jackson's line and the ladders needed to scale the rampart. Just as the soldiers of the Forty-Fourth neared their position for the attack, they realized that they had forgotten the fascines and ladders! Unbelievably the commander of the Forty-Fourth had allowed his men to advance 500 yards beyond the British redoubt before they realized the fatal mistake. Even though they dashed back to pick up the critical equipment, the battle had begun before they could regain their position in the line of attack. Some of the men threw down the heavy fascines in the face of the withering fire; Jackson's men shot others. The sight of their desperate comrades at the ramparts without the fascines and ladders caused the entire British advance to halt. Their bravest efforts to regain momentum were futile.

This mistake would have been fatal even if the Americans had not been shooting their cannon and firing their rifles like soldiers possessed. Jackson had positioned his men three or four to the yard along the exposed fortification, and about one per yard in the woods and swamp. The extent of the slaughter defies description. Redcoats and red blood literally covered the battle field. Contemporary accounts of the stacked bodies and strewn body parts range from the grotesque to the almost humorous.

The main charge lasted only a half hour, the entire battle only two hours. Generals Samuel Gibbs and Pakenham had been killed. Fortunately, many of the bodies inside the redcoats were not dead; some were unscarred because they belonged to soldiers who had feigned death—not such a cowardly act in this situation.

As the British retreated, Jackson turned his eyes apprehensively to the west bank of the Mississippi. He could hear the guns, but he did not know that they actually signaled disaster. Across the river, Colonel William Thornton had completely routed the American units. Though not many of Jackson's men were killed, most of them had tucked their tails and run in the face of a superior enemy force. Commodore Daniel T. Patterson, naval commander at New Orleans, had ordered the heavy guns spiked, but his men were so anxious to retreat that they failed to complete the job. Consequently, Thornton's men quickly restored a number of the guns to service and were ready to enfilade Jackson's line when they received news of the devastation on the east bank along with orders to rejoin the main British force.

Jackson considered an attack on the retreating redcoats, but decided it was not wise to abandon his rampart. After all, General John Lambert, who now commanded the British contingent, had some 6,000 soldiers with which to mount a counterattack. Jackson agreed to Lambert's request for a truce so that the British could bury their dead and tend to their wounded—adding the proviso that neither commander would move forces to the west bank. Old Hickory waited with much caution and patience as Lambert slowly evacuated his men. The last of the British troops crossed Lake Borgne on January 27, but the last battle of the War of 1812 remained to be fought. Instead of sailing for home, the British expedition charted a course for Mobile. Since Fort Bowyer guarded the only deep-water channel into Mobile Bay, Lambert insisted on capturing it before launching an invasion of Mobile. Located on the western tip of a long, narrow peninsula, Fort Bowyer was vulnerable to an amphibious assault in the absence of naval support. On February 8, 1815, Lambert landed 600 men east of the fort and disembarked the remainder of his army on Dauphin Island just across the channel to the west. Initially the Americans resisted. However, with British cannon trained on them from land and sea, and with vast numbers of redcoats poised for an assault, the Americans capitulated on February 11. Because news of the peace treaty signed at Ghent arrived before the British attacked Mobile, the last battle of the War of 1812 was fought on this sandspit which separated Mobile Bay from the Gulf of Mexico.[68]

Fort Bowyer may be an interesting footnote, but in the scope of American history, New Orleans is synonymous with the War of 1812 and its two most important results: the emergence of Andrew Jackson as America's postrevolutionary hero and the validation of America's independence from England. There is a beautiful irony in Jackson's defeat of the British, whom he despised as a result of their abuse of him as a teen-aged prisoner of war during the Revolution.[69] Not only did his victory symbolize his personal revenge, but it accented the two biggest miscalculations of the British at New Orleans—that the American soldiers would not fight and that the Louisianians would not remain loyal to the United States. Expressed in another way, the British had miscalculated Andrew Jackson, who was the source of the courage and loyalty of the Anglo-American frontiersmen.

The War of 1812 had a number of other ironies. The signing of the Treaty of Ghent before the Battle of New Orleans is judged by many as the greatest irony of the war. To some Anglo-American frontiersmen, maybe it was. Certainly it was not for the thirty-four *friendly* chiefs who had with broken hearts affixed their signatures to the treaty forced upon them at Fort Jackson on August 9, 1814. And certainly it was not for the Indian warriors who fought with Jackson against the British. In later years, historians might wax eloquently about the irony of the biggest battle of the war being fought after the ceremonies at Ghent, but for Jackson's Indian allies in both the Creek War and the Battle of New Orleans, the highest— and bitterest—irony was that they contributed, through these victories, to the demise of their Indian nations.

Ironic or not, the Creek War and the War of 1812 spelled doom for the Indians and changed the Old Southwest drastically.[70] Anglo-Americans, often with their African slaves, rushed into the lands opened by Jackson; nor would they be satisfied until the Indian domain was all theirs. The forces of Manifest Destiny were mounting, and the West, with Andrew Jackson as its new hero, would soon play a leading role in the conversion of the new republic into a democracy.

9

"Where smiling Fortune beckoned them"

In a large sense, the history of man is the history of migration. What nation exemplifies this more than the United States, and within it, what section more than the Old Southwest? It seems as if the first Europeans had hardly placed foot on America's Atlantic shores before "smiling Fortune beckoned" them ever westward into the bountiful continent. In few regions did her smile prove more alluring than in the Old Southwest.[1]

When Thomas Jefferson and the Republicans wrested the presidency from the Federalists in 1800, the only new states west of the Appalachians were Kentucky and Tennessee. By 1820, however, the Great Migration had swelled the total to eight, and Missouri Territory was clamoring for statehood. During these two decades the population of the West skyrocketed from a total of 386,000 to 2,216,000; of these westerners, 220,000 lived in Mississippi and Alabama.[2]

Historians still debate the relative impact of the different forces behind this flood tide of immigration. No one can discount the importance of economic developments such as soil exhaustion, post-Revolutionary changes in the staple markets, private and public sale of lands, and the growth of the cotton culture after Eli Whitney's invention of the cotton gin. Security of the borders from foreign intervention and the defeat of the Indians played significant roles too. As important as these factors, perhaps, was the myth of the West—a myth so appealing to a people with such a strong Puritanical bent. West of the mountains lay a veritable Garden of Eden or a latter-day Canaan, and a patch of it could be had for the taking. Of the Old Southwest, a typical immigrant wrote, "The crops [here] are certain, and want of the necessaries of life never for a moment causes the heart to ache—abundance spreads the table of the poor man, and contentment smiles on every countenance."[3] The stories of the fertility, abundance, and sweetness of this Utopia—from which the Indians surely would be driven—so intoxicated residents of the original southern states that they poured into the Old Southwest after the conclusion of the Creek War and the War of 1812.

Only a handful of Frenchmen populated the Gulf Coast and lower Mississippi Valley prior to the end of the French and Indian War in 1763 when Britain obtained the Floridas and Spain received Louisiana. As pointed out in Chapter 4, land grants attracted a few Englishmen to the Old Southwest in the era of British dominion, and during the Revolution some Tories moved into the Natchez District. While a few British migrants also resided near Mobile and Pensacola, most of the early settlers in the Tombigbee region were hearty frontiersmen from the southern colonies.

It was not until after the Treaty of San Lorenzo in 1795 and the resulting creation of Mississippi Territory in 1798 that the first wave of migration began—a wave which lasted until the outbreak of the War of 1812. During this decade, migration into the Natchez District and the Tennessee Bend was steady, but the movement of settlers into the Tombigbee area was not of a similar magnitude. The flow into the Old Southwest from 1798 to 1812, however, was insignificant in comparison to the postwar flood of settlers which began in 1815 and which subsided in 1820 with the impact of the Panic of 1819. Later migrational peaks coincided with the various Indian cession treaties.

Prior to the War of 1812, settlers had clustered in three regions of Mississippi Territory—the Natchez District, the lower Tombigbee basin, and the Tennessee Valley.[4] During this period the Natchez District attracted the most immigrants. According to Spanish records, some 4,500 people resided there in 1798, but the 1800 Census lists 3,600 whites, 2,987 slaves and 159 free people of color—an increase of 50 percent. By 1810 the population of the Natchez District had risen to a total of 28,787.[5]

Considering their isolation, the proximity to the Indian towns, and the Spanish presence below the thirty-first parallel, it is not surprising that in 1800 only some 1,250 Americans lived in the Tombigbee settlements. By 1810, however, slightly over 3,000 people were enumerated as living there—nearly one-third of them slaves.[6] Meanwhile, some two hundred and fifty miles to the north in the Tennessee Valley, immigration had increased at a more rapid pace during the prewar decade, and after the Georgia Cession in 1802 the boundary of the Mississippi Territory was extended from the Yazoo River line to the Tennessee border in 1804. At that time the trickle of settlers into the Huntsville area turned into such a stream that the new county of Madison was organized in 1808. Within

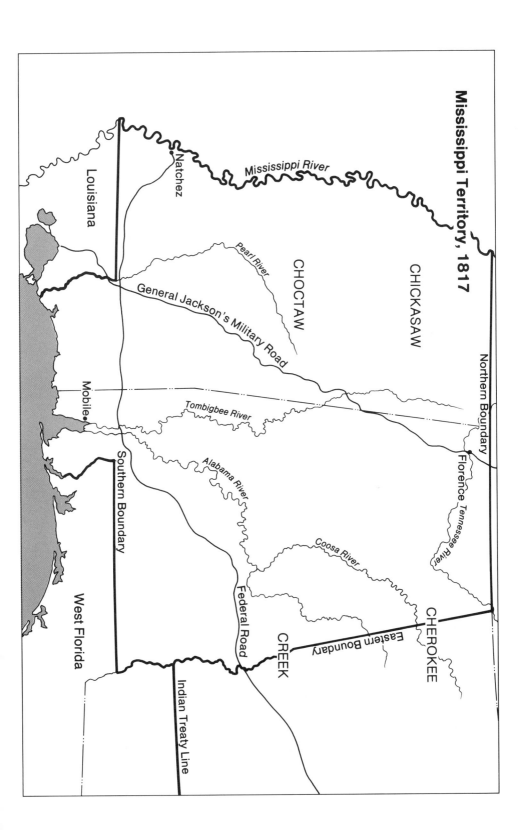

Mississippi Territory, 1817

two years, its population approached 5,000 people, one-fifth of whom were slaves.[7]

By 1810, Mississippi Territory boasted a population of 15,826 white inhabitants and 13,984 slaves, and its governmental structure had also grown considerably.[8] In 1800 Congress allowed the election of a two-house assembly which selected a nonvoting territorial delegate to Congress. Because counties multiplied in proportion to settlement, by the end of the War of 1812 the number of counties had increased from the original three to fourteen.

The final shot in the Battle of New Orleans signaled the beginning of a race into the Old Southwest known as the "Great Migration." The danger of British intervention had vanished; Jackson had pacified the Indians and begun the process of their removal. With the acquisition of West Florida from the Pearl River to the Perdido, numerous waterways had become available for unrestricted shipment of cotton, timber, and naval stores to the seacoast. In addition, Eli Whitney's remarkably simple cotton gin proved easy to replicate. Though the reasons for migration might be debatable and the modes of transportation varied, the stream of pilgrims into the Old Southwest remains a well-documented historical episode. By land and water the people came: sometimes atop fine horses or in fancy carriages, but more often on shank's mare or in the sturdy farm wagons. Down the rivers they floated in flatboats and rafts; a few made their way tediously upstream after sailing from the Eastern Seaboard to the coastal ports. Later, or course, steamboats speeded the journey.

When smiling fortune beckoned American pioneers into the Old Southwest after the War of 1812, they responded with alacrity. As Thomas Abernethy so aptly wrote, "Seldom in history has an area been settled so rapidly."[9] Graphic are the census figures which show that the population of the area that later became Mississippi doubled in the decade between 1810 and 1820. During the same period the population of the future state of Alabama increased more than sixteenfold. Living in 1810 in the counties that later became Mississippi were 31,306 people, including 14,523 slaves; enumerators listed 9,046 in the Alabama counties of whom 2,565 were bondsmen. Ten years later 75,448 pioneers lived in Mississippi and 144,317 in Alabama. The 1820 figures represent more than a tenfold increase in Mississippi and more than a hundredfold in Alabama.[10] Little wonder that contemporaries spoke of the Great Migration into the Old Southwest as the "Alabama fever."

As phenomenal as the growth of the entire state of Alabama may have been, the population of no other specific region increased at such a spectacular pace as did the Tennessee Valley. For example, there were less than

5,000 people in the two-year-old county of Madison in 1810, but during the next decade six new northern counties were organized. In the 1820 Census, enumerators counted 58,540 persons, including 18,618 slaves, in the seven Alabama counties which bordered the Tennessee River. With statehood imminent, the population of a few central Alabama settlements also exploded. Between 1818 and 1820, for instance, Tuscaloosa County increased seventeenfold and Montgomery grew nearly as fast. While no region in Mississippi grew so astronomically as that, immigrants had been entering the Natchez District steadily ever since the organization of the Mississippi Territory in 1798. Consequently, in 1820 the five counties bordering the Mississippi River boasted a total population of 33,148.

As will be discussed in Chapter 12, title to Indian lands in Alabama was extinguished through cession treaties earlier than in Mississippi. Undoubtedly, even though Alabama lay more in proximity to the older southern states, had the Indian lands of Mississippi opened up earlier than those in Alabama, the massive migration into the Old Southwest might have been known as "Mississippi fever." Immigrants settling in Mississippi during the years 1815–1819 could legally settle only in three areas: (1) on a strip of land in the southern part of the state, (2) east of the Tombigbee along the Alabama line, and (3) in the Natchez District. In Alabama, however, they could select a site from a gigantic area of choice lands previously claimed by the Creeks, Choctaw, Cherokee, and Chickasaw. Hence the population explosion in Alabama in the decade 1810–1820.

From whence did the pioneers of the Old Southwest come in response to Dame Fortune's smile? In the jargon of the academician, they migrated along isothermal lines. More simply put by a lawyer and jurist of the Old Southwest, "They usually came due west from their former homes, and were surely to select, as nearly as possible, a new one in the same parallel, and with surroundings as nearly like those they had left as possible."[11] William H. Sparks illustrated his dictum further: "With the North Carolinian, good spring water, and pine knots for his fire, were the *sine qua non*." While the isothermal axiom largely holds true for the pilgrims caught in the post War of 1812 epidemic of "Alabama fever" and even applies generally to the settlers of the Natchez District, there were obvious exceptions among the early immigrants. As will be discussed in Chapter 10, a small remnant French population dotted the Gulf Coast, a few British land grantees had settled in West Florida after 1763, and some American Loyalist families had moved to the area during the Revolution. In addition, some hardy souls came down from the Middle Colonies and New England in the early territorial period.[12] These non-southern pilgrims, however, were the exception.

Historian Frank L. Owsley, Sr., in his now classic 1945 article entitled "The Pattern of Migration and Settlement on the Southern Frontier," develops the social and scientific explanations of why immigrants into the Old Southwest followed isothermal lines when they sought new homes.[13] Owsley describes the familiarity of the earth in a new location along with its crops and creatures as the migrant's "mental furniture." These two words tell much of the story. The planting of familiar crops filled a psychological need; in addition, tried and proven methods of cultivation made production and marketing of produce more practical. The relocated farmer knew how to use his present implements which worked effectively in a soil that differed but little, if at all, from that on his previous farm.[14]

Thus, it was no accident that pilgrims into the Old Southwest settled on land similar in most respects to that of their home region. "Like the children of Israel," Owsley explains, "they sent their Calebs and Joshuas ahead to spy out the land and prepare the way."[15] Narratives of the migrations contain frequent references to this practice. For families, communities, and church congregations—rich or poor—the practice of scouting the public domain for the right location was common. One wonders, nevertheless, if many patriarchs gave as detailed instructions to the advance parties as did Judge Charles Tait whose family emigrated from Georgia to Alabama. The judge's instructions to his son James A. Tait were explicit. The chosen tract must include:

> . . . a stream near at hand for a mill and machinery—a never failing spring at the foot of a hillock, on the summit of which a mansion house can be build in due time; that it have an extensive back range where our cattle and hogs can graze and fatten without the aid of corn houses, that on the right and left there is an extensive body of good land where will settle a number of good neighbors and from whom the pleasure and benefits of society will soon be realized.[16]

Those who could not afford the luxury of scouting parties were guided to lands of their liking by letters from courageous and adventurous relatives or friends who sent word back home of the bounty and beauty of a new-found land. Brave the precursors were, but the majority of the pioneers who moved into the Old Southwest did so with the assurance that familiar soil and climate awaited their arrival.

Though many of the settlers may have resided temporarily in one place or another en route to their ultimate homesites, their roots extended back to one of the original southern states. Owsley capsuled the process beautifully: "The Carolinas settled Georgia, and, with considerable aid from Virginia, settled Tennessee. The remainder of the states of the Lower South were the children and grandchildren of the Carolinas, Georgia, and Tennessee."[17] Owsley's prose reveals his understanding of the familial nature of the migration process. Though his use of statistics may appear crude to today's cliometricians, Owsley substantiated with census figures the conclusions garnered from narrative sources.

Because the Census of 1850 was the first one in which the birthplaces of free families were recorded, the 1850 population figures are used to track patterns of migrations. Of course, those totals provide only a rough approximation of sources of immigration because there is no way of calculating the number of natives of various states who died prior to 1850. Similarly, it cannot be assumed that the rate of emigration from a particular state was constant over the decades. Regardless of these caveats, the 1850 figures permit historians to trace the directional flow of population into the Old Southwest—or for that matter, into any section of the nation. In 1943, Professor William O. Lynch presented an extremely useful analysis of the 1850 data in a seminal article that should be studied simultaneously with Owsley's. Because Lynch found that roughly 400,000 persons of Virginia birth, exclusive of slaves, lived outside their native state in 1850, he concluded that "Virginia easily held first place as a breeding ground for colonists for several decades after 1783." Lynch viewed slavery as only one of many factors which controlled migration. He concluded, therefore, "that most migrating southerners, and northerners likewise, would have sought homes and opportunities just about where they did had slavery not existed between 1783 and 1861."[18]

Origins of Free Migrants into the Old Southwest

COLONIZING STATES	RECIPIENT STATES			
	Georgia	*Alabama*	*Mississippi*	*Louisiana*
Georgia	——	59,000	17,500	5,900
South Carolina	52,200	48,700	27,900	4,600
North Carolina	37,500	28,500	21,500	2,900
Tennessee	8,200	22,600	27,400	3,400
Virginia	7,300	10,400	8,400	3,200

Source: Census of 1850, rounded to nearest 100.

Clearly the Old Southwest—western Georgia, Alabama, and Mississippi—was peopled by Georgia, South Carolina, North Carolina, Tennessee and Virginia. Though the story of Mississippi differs little from that of Alabama, there is one interesting contrast: Alabama was the primary colonizer of Mississippi. On the other hand, relatively few Mississippians moved eastward into Alabama. While Georgia was one of the original states, her population in 1790 was only 82,548. By 1800 this figure had increased by 96 percent; in 1810 the percentage of increase dropped to 56 percent, and by 1850 it was 31 percent with a total population of 906,185. The aggregate 1850 population for Alabama was 771,623 and for Mississippi 606,326.[19]

Natchez contained by far the most heterogeneous residents in terms of their origins. During both the Spanish and British dominions, it had attracted some immigrants from the original states as well as a few from Great Britain and her West Indian colonies. After 1798, however, most families arriving in the Natchez District hailed from the southern states, though there was a sprinkle from the states north of Maryland.[20] From the earliest days, however, the majority of the early settlers east of the Pearl came from the Carolinas and Georgia. As was emphasized in Chapter 6, a large percentage of this vanguard raised cattle as had their ancestors in Georgia and South Carolina. Judge Harry Toulmin in one of his innumerable letters mentions the Georgia origin of settlers above Mobile.[21] Until this day, herds of cattle graze on the lush grasses of the coastal plains and in the pine barrens.

Predictably, Tennesseans—many of whom were recently transplanted Carolinians—comprised much of the river of humanity which spilled over into northern Alabama. As the Tennessee Valley became crowded, other Tennesseans filtered down the central river valleys of Alabama. A significant number of Virginians, after they found the choicest tracts along the Tennessee and Alabama Rivers already occupied, moved into the basins of the Tombigbee and Black Warrior Rivers as well as into the fertile prairie known as the "black belt"—an appellation derived from its rich, dark soil. Everybody with "Alabama fever", however, did not unpack east of the Tombigbee River; thousands crossed over into the Piney Woods of South Mississippi, into the Natchez District, and, after the 1820 Treaty of Doak's Stand, into the rich Mississippi Delta. In both Alabama and Mississippi the Virginians had an impact far in excess of their numbers because so many of them were persons of substance who contributed immediately to the rapid rise of the plantation culture, often bringing with them large numbers of slaves.

The Great Migration was not just an American affair. "Alabama fever" had spread across the Atlantic to the Britisn Isles and on across the English Channel to western Europe. The significance of the foreign contingent lay in the international impact of the myth of the American garden rather than in their numbers. In *The South in the New Nation 1789–1819*, Thomas P. Abernethy refers to the alarm expressed in British newspapers at the tide of emigrants from Europe. An Edinburgh editorialist ranted that "it is impossible to look at the vast multitudes, of all conditions and professions, crowding to the land of promise, without a sensation of wonder."[22] Now we can smile at the Scotsman's overreaction when he concluded, "It is a spectacle without a parallel since the time of the crusades." In London, another observer blamed the exodus on high taxes and commented that "The *Times* is not angry, only very, very sorry that such things should be."[23] Alarmed as these and other Europeans may have been, not as many of their brethren unpacked in the Old Southwest as they did in more significant numbers in cooler climates of America.[24] Those foreigners who did migrate to the Old Southwest, however, tended to congregate in the urban centers such as Natchez, New Orleans, Mobile and Pensacola.

Surely one of the most romantic chapters in the history of the settlement of the Old Southwest involved a contingent of French refugees after the fall of Napoleon.[25] The U.S. Congress in March of 1817 granted some of the Bonapartists exiled by the restored Bourbons four townships provided they cultivate the vine and olive. Early that summer the French advance party arrived in Mobile. At Fort Stoddert they consulted with Judge Harry Toulmin and other leading figures before engaging a barge to tow them up the Tombigbee. On the advice of Choctaw Factor George S. Gaines, they laid out a town they named Demopolis at the "White Bluffs" near the juncture of the Tombigbee and Black Warrior Rivers. Tragedy, however, had followed them across the Atlantic; Demopolis was not on the lands allotted to them. Regretfully, they abandoned their improvements and planted a new town about a mile to the east that they called Aigleville in commemmoration of the eagle on the summit of Napoleon's standard.

It seemed, however, as if the Bonapartists were bedeviled. A number of them had moved to plots which also were not allotted. Greedy, land-hungry Anglo-Americans soon discovered this error and pushed many of the exiles farther into a wilderness of dense forests and canebrakes suitable neither for viticulture nor olive groves. Indeed, the Choctaw west of the Tombigbee proved better neighbors then the unprincipled squatters on their own flanks. To make matters worse, receding flood waters left stagnant pools as breeding ponds for disease-carrying mosquitoes. In the history of the American West, there may never have been pioneers less suited for the vicissitudes of the frontier than these Bonapartists. Nevertheless, the Frenchmen displayed the kind of courage and determination befitting their station, and their silk stockings soon gave way to deerskin leggings. Even so, the grave was the only reward that many reaped. Despite a valiant effort, the colony failed. A small number of these gentlefolk managed to return to France, while some melted into Mobile's business community, and others started anew in Texas; a few even endured as frontier farmers. It is unfortunate that neither photographer's plate nor painter's brush captured the striking contrasts provided by the "vine and olive" experiment.

As interesting as their story is, the Bonapartists represent an anomaly—granted, one that illustrates the international spread of "Alabama fever." Most of the frontiersmen were recognizable types. Indeed, Frederick Jackson Turner's oft-cited "procession of civilization" marched through the Old Southwest just as it did the Old Northwest. In Chapter 6 considerable emphasis was placed on the cattle raiser, who, as Turner pointed out, "guided the ranchers of Texas."[26] Though Turner did not include the planters in his most famous essay, he was quite aware that in the Old Southwest planters formed part of the procession too. According to the Turner model, the farmers—and planters—were the least transitory of the frontiersmen. In effect, theirs was the permanent frontier. In one sense, such was the case; in another it was not. For the farmers fell into two categories: permanent and nonpermanent.

A large number of the "smaller" or "poorer" farmers fell into the latter category. More often than not, they arrived in the agricultural vanguard and seemed intent on staying put. Many of them comprised the category known as "squatters," but others acquired title to their land only to sell for a profit, sometimes before the ink had fully dried. Were these restless souls in reality a special class of speculator? Or did these men simply have "the West in their eyes" as New England schoolmaster Timothy Flint believed? According to Flint, they never ended their hunt for the American Canaan.[27] The wife of one itinerant farmer had her own philosophy which was not as sophisticated as Flint's. "It is all for the mere love of moving," she explained—or complained. "We have been doing so all our lives—just moving from place to place—never resting—as soon as ever we get comfortably settled, then it is time to be off to something new." The woman was then asked why she did not put her foot down.

"Oh, my dear," sighed the lady, "you don't know what it is to be married to a gadding husband."[28]

The odyssey of Gideon Lincecum demonstrates that "smiling Fortune" also nodded frequently to families of substance.[29] Seldom did the early pioneers who came overland from older eastern settlements record their experiences, but Gideon Lincecum did. And one can assume that most migrants shared the kinds of joys and tribulations that he describes so vividly. The Lincecums first moved from South Carolina down to the Georgia frontier where they relocated several times. After the War of 1812, Gideon, now married and with a family of his own, caught "Alabama fever" and finally moved into the rich cotton lands in the Mississippi "black belt" on the upper Tombigbee.

Though he was twelve years old when he learned to read, write, and cipher, Gideon Lincecum was a precocious chap who read medicine when he was not toiling in the fields or hunting. While still a youth in the wilds of west Georgia along the Ocmulgee, he contracted to teach forty-five rambunctious students for nine months at ten dollars each. Later he wrote:

> These children had been born and raised to the age I found them among the cows and drunken cowdrivers on the outer borders of the State, and they were positively the coursest specimens of the human family I had ever seen. I saw very distinctly that no civil or ordinary means would be applicable to their conditions.[30]

By the end of the term, however, they had all become "tame and quite polite," and the school committee offered Lincecum $1,000 to teach another session—an offer which he spurned to "take to the road again."[31]

In March of 1818, the Lincecum caravan of about twenty-five persons— his parents, siblings, wife, brother-in-law, and slaves—began the final 500-mile leg of their migration. After six weeks on the trail they stopped briefly in Tuscaloosa on the Black Warrior River before making the final twelve-day trip through an "unhacked forest" to better lands on the Tombigbee. They chose a spot just above present-day Columbus, Mississippi, only a few miles from some Choctaw. Along the trail a wide variety of wild nuts and fruits abounded, and the menfolk had little difficulty shooting deer, turkeys, ducks, and pigeons. Some of these Gideon stalked with his bow and arrow. Evidently, the "music of great gangs of wolves around the camp every night" did not unduly frighten them because he recalled that "the entire trip was delightful beyond description."[32] In 1848, Dr. Lincecum moved to Long Point, Texas, where he acquired another plantation and continued to practice medicine. By the time of his death in 1873, the eighty-two-year-old pioneer had established a national reputation as a naturalist.

It was not unusual for families—once they reached the newly opened land—to try out several homesteads before putting down their roots for any length of time. Owsley reflected his rural heritage with this description of the process. "Like a great drove of blackbirds lighting in a grain field, with each bird milling about, making short flights within the field in search of a more satisfactory location, the agricultural immigrant after reaching the region of his choice often moved about several times within the same general community before making a permanent settlement."[33] Though genealogists—using land records, tax roles, and other sources— have often found evidence to support Owsley's blackbird analogy, the migrants themselves seldom left written records of their "short flights." One of the few who did was a schoolteacher and Methodist circuit rider named Abiezer Clark Ramsey.[34]

A. C. Ramsey was still a toddler during the winter of 1807–08, when his father William packed the household possessions on two horses and left Jackson County, Georgia, for newly opened lands to the west of the Tombigbee in the Mississippi Territory. Astride a third horse rode William's wife, Elizabeth, holding tiny Abiezer in front of her while two-year-old Andrew sat behind his mother. William and their Negro girl walked and tended the pack horses. William had been born in 1770 in North Carolina. There he had buried his childless first wife before moving to Georgia where he had married Elizabeth, a native of Ireland seventeen years his junior. As did most emigrants, the Ramseys began the long trip through the Creek country with considerable trepidation. Swollen creeks and rivers, however, proved more dangerous than the Indians, who were more helpful than harmful. In February of 1808, William Ramsey and his family arrived in what is now Wayne County, Mississippi, with twenty-one dollars in cash. They had little time to fret, however, even though the only available corn for sale was fifty miles distant at Saint Stephens on the Tombigbee River at four dollars per bushel.

The activities of the Ramsey household during the next few months beautifully portrayed the life of a Turnerian frontier family: raising a cabin, burning canebrakes, clearing forests, planting crops, crafting furniture, spinning yarn, weaving cloth, and tending to the endless chores. The yield of the rich loam soil allowed the marketing of a surplus from the first crop. So plentiful were pumpkins, for instance, that A. C. recalled his father's boast that he "could nearly walk all over his field stepping on pumpkins."[35] And so diligent was the mother that she wove sufficient cloth to sell at two and a half dollars a yard in Mobile! But all was not idyllic. Indians stole one horse, another fell off a bluff to its watery death, and the third was bartered for cattle.

William Ramsey had chosen a site on the road between the lower Choctaw towns and Mobile where they traded regularly. En route home, intoxicated Choctaw sometimes camped near by, and at first the "fighting, scratching, and yelling" caused alarm, particularly to Mrs. Ramsey.[36] Soon it was learned, however, that these Choctaw "had a system . . . in their drunken sprees." When the debauchery began, one of the Indians always remained sober and served as a sentinel to "keep the drunken ones out of the fire and prevent them from killing each other." Protection of the white settlers—especially the women—from harassment by his drunken brethren was an important responsibility of the guard Indian. In this way, the Ramsey encounters with Indians may have been more fortunate than those of some frontier families. On the other hand, their religious, educational, social, and economic experiences typified life in the Old Southwest before the War of 1812.

More importantly, however, the Ramsey family demonstrates the tendency of migrants to move several times after their arrival in the Old Southwest. Indeed, William Ramsey made more than several moves. He relocated his family eight times in a dozen years![37] A year after his arrival in the valley of the Chickasawhay, Ramsey had moved further down the river. After "one or two crops" he sold out again. Next he moved to Greene County to the settlement near present-day Leakesville. The many friends whom he enjoyed there consisted largely of Scots, formerly Presbyterians who had converted to Methodism.

Shortly afterward, Ramsey disposed of this place and rented another parcel of land along the Chickasawhay which proved so unhealthy that within months the family decided to "seek a less dangerous place" back from the river bank "in the same neighborhood."[38] The fifth relocation took them to the eastern side of the river for about a year. Then, still on the east bank, they shifted downstream about five miles south to the Bethel Church. The year of 1818 found them relocated on the Pascagoula River in Jackson County where the boys were introduced to the concept that education must be beaten into the pupils with a hickory stick. This dictum, however, proved less radical than other pedagogical experiments soon encountered such as classroom "jury trials" and mock hangings.

The Ramsey family had hardly settled down on the Pascagoula before William bought land farther west along the Pearl River in Lawrence County. But his failing health after a half century of frontier toil caused him to soon sell the newly acquired property. With the capital from this sale he bought livestock and some land about twenty miles to the west along Red Creek, a tributary of the Pascagoula. Years later, William's son clearly expressed disapproval of his father's disposition to continually acquire, improve, and sell farms. "I think Father made a mistake on moving so often," wrote A. C. Ramsey, who concluded that the "severe exposure and hard labour . . . no doubt contributed greatly in laying the foundation of the disease which finally terminated his life."[39] Undoubtedly it did. Even so, his father probably delighted in the sylvan beauty of their isolated farm. After a dozen of "short flights," as Owsley called these restless relocations, Ramsey grazed his stock in private contentment. His dog-trot home stood on a picturesque hill four miles from his only neighbor and near an excellent spring. His family offered no complaints that canoes provided their easiest communication with the nearest large settlement and closest mill twenty miles away. Only predators such as panthers, wildcats, wolves and foxes interrupted their peace by "depredations on sheep, lambs, hogs, and cattle." Apparently the numerous bears posed few problems.[40]

Rich and poor alike enjoyed few options in the routes available for travel into the Old Southwest. Those in the vanguard found themselves staying very close to nature; streams and Indian trails—paths worn by animals searching for food and water—stood as their only choices. Undeniably, the mighty Mississippi River dominantly influenced the initial settlement of its lower valley. In conjunction with the Ohio, Tennessee, and Cumberland Rivers and their tributaries, the Mississippi carried the earliest familes into the Natchez District.[41] Similarly, the streams of the eastern half of the Mississippi Territory served as the first conduits of immigration. Within just a few years, however, individuals and families braved the trails easily recognizable by the Indians but followed by Anglo-Americans only with great difficulty at first. With the passage of a very few decades, however, the Federal government, after treaties smiliar to those discussed in Chapter 5, improved the trails into traces and roads. By the time "Alabama fever" raged, primitive traces had evolved into true roads, and soon steam engines renewed the importance of the countless streams flowing through the Old Southwest.[42]

Though the perfecting of the steam engine eventually led to the abandonment of some sections of the Natchez Trace and the diminished importance of other roads, traces remained important avenues of migration into the Old Southwest during the decades following the War of 1812. One of the most important of these was the Federal Road which connected St. Stephens on the Tombigbee River with Milledgeville, Georgia, where it connected with other highways leading eventually to Washington and Philadelphia.

As in the case of the Natchez Trace, the genesis of the Federal Road lay in the urgency to establish better mail service between the nation's capital and New Orleans. After a frightening failure of communication between those cities in 1805, Secretary of War Henry Dearborn struck an agreement with the Creek Indians which authorized the United States to clear "a horse path" from the Ocmulgee to the Tombigbee and to fell logs across streams. In response to a plea from the Postmaster General, Congress quickly appropriated $6,400 to survey the route, improve a four-foot path, construct bridges, and build causeways. Though much is made of the passage of the Cumberland Road Act in 1806, seldom do historians mention this bill that was enacted almost simultaneously.[43]

Appropriating money for the road proved far easier than completing it. Inexperienced and inadequately equipped soldiers made such slow progress over the harsh terrain that Congress had to appropriate additional funds in 1809. Though this road between Saint Stephens and Fort Hawkins near the Ocmulgee was not officially finished until January of 1812, postal service over it began in the spring of 1807 and continued until its interruption by the Creek War. Evidently publicity emanating from the treaty and congressional action explains why traffic through southern Georgia quickened until the outbreak of the War of 1812. The increasing number of whites heading westward via this route in the prewar years despite the delays in its completion provided fuel for the dissident Creek faction.

Peggy Dow, wife of famed Methodist evangelist Lorenzo Dow, noticed recent improvements to the road when they traveled from Natchez to Milledgeville, Georgia, via Fort St. Stephens in 1811. She noted that after crossing the Alabama at Ft. Mims, the couple "struck the road that had been cut out by order of the President."[44] "This made it more pleasant travelling," Peggy Dow commented in her journal, "and then we frequently met people removing from the States to the Tombigbee, and other parts of the Mississippi territory."[45] At this point evidently the path was reasonably well improved; the first day beyond the Alabama they made between thirty and forty miles. Peggy Dow observed that the road was "newly cut out" and that "the fresh marked trees served for a guide."[46]

Though she was fatigued when they reached Benjamin Hawkins's agency and still sore from falling off her horse two days earlier, Mrs. Dow recorded no disparaging observations on the nature of the improvements.[47]

In many regions, westerners applied the appellation "Federal" when they associated a road with the Federal government for whatever reason. Hence readers must keep in mind the residence and era of writers or speakers when they encounter this term. Also known as the Federal Road, for instance, was the trail across Cherokee lands which connected Nashville and Chattanooga, Tennessee, with Athens, Georgia. Since the Chattanooga–Willistown road ran southwestward out of Chattanooga, undoubtedly some migrants into northern Alabama traveled the network.[48] Another ancient trail, the Great Indian War Path, ran to Chattanooga from Kingsport and Blountville up in northeastern Tennessee on the Kentucky border. As spokes from the hub of a wheel, a number of roads emanated in all directions from Chattanooga. Nevertheless, the route through this mountain community did not rival the Federal Road from the Ocmulgee to the Tombigbee as an artery of migration into the Old Southwest.

First used to transport supplies by way of the Tennessee River to Fort Stoddert, Gaines Trace eventually became an important route of immigration into the northern Tombigbee Valley. It ran southwestward from Colbert's Ferry below the Muscle Shoals of the Tennessee to Cotton Gin Port, the highest point of navigation on the Tombigbee, two miles southwest of present-day Amory, Mississippi. So named because the government constructed a gin there for the Chickasaw during the Washington Administration, Cotton Gin Port was founded in an area already steeped in history. It may have been the site where de Soto crossed the Tombigbee in the sixteenth century, and near it the Chickasaw handed the French several defeats two centuries later.[49]

To avoid payment of Spanish duties, Choctaw Factor George Strothers Gaines shipped goods down the Tombigbee after packing them some eighty miles from the Tennessee River. Local historians may never agree for whom the road was named—George S. or his older brother Edmund Pendleton Gaines—or the exact route it followed. Because of his two decades of honorable service as factor to the Choctaw, his assistance during the Creek War, and his role in treaty negotiations, George clearly is the sentimental favorite as the trail's namesake. Evidence indicates that E. P. Gaines, then a young Army lieutenant, officially surveyed it as part of the Natchez Trace in 1805—a section that was later abandoned as too circuitous. G. S. Gaines through his influence with the Indians, however, opened it in 1810 to general use and popularized it through his reliance on the Tennessee–Tombigbee route as a supply line.[50] In recognizing the potential of connecting these two important river systems, George was one of several early eighteenth-century frontiersmen who presaged the recently completed Tennessee–Tombigbee Waterway.

Whatever the outcome of this namesake debate it will not alter the fact that Gaines Trace eventually became heavily trafficked by immigrants into the northern regions of Mississippi Territory and that eventually stagecoach lines operated over it. From Cotton Gin Port, the road extended ten miles to the west to a way station owned by the mixed-blood Chickasaw chief Levi Colbert. From Colbert's stand, one branch ran southwest to the Natchez Trace and another branch veered southeast into the Tombigbee prairie region.

No path in the Old Southwest is as surrounded by unfounded myth as Jackson's Military Road. Its only connection with the War of 1812—not an insignificant one—is the fact that experiences during that struggle reinforced Jackson's deep concern for the military security of the West. Many Americans mistakenly believe that Old Hickory led his troops over this route during the war despite the fact that its construction did not begin until June of 1817—two and a half years after the end of hostilities[51]

Secretary of War William H. Crawford, who agreed that population of the Southwest would assure its security, gave Andrew Jackson carte blanche in the construction of a road linking New Orleans with Tennessee and the upper South. So the general chose as its termini a spot on the Tennessee River twenty miles south of Muscle Shoals and Madisonville, Louisiana, across Lake Pontchartrain from New Orleans. Then he designed a road that ran virtually in a straight line between those points. Over half of the route, which reduced the total distance between Nashville and New Orleans by 208 miles, fell within the bounds of the new state of Mississippi. Jackson's construction strategy called for one company of soldiers to work northward from Madisonville while another cut southward from the Tennessee River. In August of 1820, after the soldiers had labored for just over three years, officials proclaimed the project completed.

At first, travel on the newly opened road was heavy, but the traffic did not remain sufficient so to prevent the steady encroachment of nature. Within a few years, some sections became impassable, particularly in south Mississippi. Completion of the Robinson Road from Columbus, Mississippi, on the Tombigbee, to the new state capital at Jackson, siphoned off much of the traffic. For south Mississippi, nevertheless, Jackson's Military Road was not a total disappointment. After the project had begun, Congress appropriated funds for a branch connecting Madisonville with Mobile, and early in 1819 it was completed as far as Bay St. Louis on the Mississippi Gulf Coast. Rather than being important for migration, coastal routes served a greater purpose for communication and commerce. Until construction of a railroad, however, most coastal travelers relied primarily on schooners and steamers.

By the time that "Alabama fever" became epidemic after the War of 1812 potential migrants into Alabama from the Piedmont region of Georgia had two options. They could take the Federal Road into the Alabama–Tombigbee basin and to points beyond. Or they could gain access to the fertile Tennessee Valley by heading northwestward on the road to Nashville until it intersected near present-day Chattanooga with a trail down to the Huntsville settlement. As was mentioned earlier, in response to a population boom there Madison County was organized in 1808. Eventually a road connected Madison County to the Tuscaloosa at the head of navigation on the Black Warrior River which flows into the Tombigbee.

Though some Georgians settled early in the Great Bend region (Madison County), far more of them moved down from Tennessee, Kentucky, and North Carolina. Obviously, a jump down from Kentucky and especially from Tennessee was more expedient. From North Carolina, some pioneers followed the French Broad to Knoxville from whence, as mentioned above, a well-traveled trail led to Huntsville via the Chattanooga hub. To avoid this mountainous route, others circled down through Georgia or headed for lands in more southerly parts of the Old Southwest.

Migration into the Great Bend of the Tennessee illustrates an oft-overlooked factor—the impact of the American Revolution on subsequent movement to the frontier. Numerous heads of families which settled Madison County soldiered during the Revolution and/or during expeditions against the Cherokee and Creeks. The beauty and fertility of this country had so impressed them that many made good their vows someday to return.[52] Undoubtedly, studies of the military records of pioneers would show that service in various western regions often was a determining factor in the selection of future home sites.

The history of settlement in the Great Bend also indicates that generally the squatters there were men of small to moderate means who intruded into Indian lands and unsurveyed Federal tracts with the fullest intent of bettering their lot in life through the purchase of real estate. Admittedly, there were some unsavory, rapacious freeloaders with greedy hearts and hands, but the records indicate that these characters were in the minority. An 1809 census listed 353 heads of squatter families in Madison County, 23 percent of whom owned one or more slaves. Of them, 30 percent had only one, 17 percent two, and 13 percent three; 91 percent owned from one to ten. Over 300 of these 353 applied for the purchase of Federal land when it was offered for sale. Surveyor Thomas Freeman, in an 1808 report to the Secretary of the Treasury, painted a picture of these intruders as substantial citizens. "In justice to these people," Freeman emphasized,

> I must remark that contrary to the general character of those who have hitherto intruded on public land, they are quiet, peaceable, *extremely industrious*, and fully sensible to their situation with respect to their government. Each [is] anxious to be prepared against the day of sale, to purchase, if possible, the spot he has selected, and at all events—disposed and ready to obey the laws of their country, or will of the Executive.[53]

Obviously, the characteristics of squatters varied from one locale to another, but it would be interesting to determine just how typical the Great Bend squatters were in terms of their intentions and efforts to buy land.

As was pointed out in Chapter 4, the Great Bend country had been wrapped in the cloak of speculation since the Bourbon County debacle. So it should come as no surprise that when the government placed the Madison County lands on the auction block, the heaviest bidders included speculators from Georgia, Tennessee, South Carolina, and Virginia. Nor should it shock students of the frontier to learn that Thomas Freeman, who surveyed the county, purchased nearly 8,500 acres at a total cost of $18,181.70.[54]

While Freeman did obtain a number of tracts for some of the squatters, he bought most of the acreage as a speculative venture.[55] His acquisitions, of course, were public and apparently aboveboard. Nevertheless, Freeman's involvement points out the need for studies of the roles played by surveyors on the frontier. To what extent did they participate overtly or covertly in speculation? After all, their field notes contained information that would have been invaluable in the hands of speculators. One wonders, for example, how many surveyors kept two sets of notes—one for the Federal government and one for their own use. Even without a written record, most of them probably could have retained in their memories considerable topographical information. With reference to the initial land sale in Madison County, it is interesting to note that the squatters held their own. Yes, speculators snapped up nearly half of the land offered, but 85 percent of the individual purchasers were settlers who bought farms ranging in size from 160 to 960 acres.[56] This fact seems to substantiate surveyor Freeman's contention that the Great Bend squatters generally were well intentioned, responsible settlers.

Too often traditional historical interpretations place importance on personal difficulties as motivations for emigration. Accordingly, literature on the West abounds in references to the number of debtors, lawbreakers, henpecked husbands, deserted wives, and other unlucky souls who fled to the fringes of the frontier. While these personal reasons for migration were valid in some instances, genealogical investigations suggest that these escape motives were seldom major factors in decisions to migrate. Instead, family histories often point to specific conditions in localities from which migrants removed.[57]

Mention is often made of wornout soil, for instance, but in some situations this factor is questionable when the migrants move to areas where the soil is described as sterile and barren. In other cases, the quest for unbroken soil is not valid for the immigrant wishing simply to tend livestock—which was obviously the desire of many who migrated to the Mississippi Territory. Perhaps more important than the soil, for them, were the local laws regarding livestock in their former place of residence?

Numerous writers have concluded that migrants moved to the public domain to acquire title to newly opened Federal lands. Unquestionably, ownership of land was the goal of many, if not most, settlers. But that is not the question. Were the laws governing Federal disposal of land more favorable in the West than prevailing laws in their former places of residence? Or were private purchases so expensive for the migrant as to make Federal lands more attractive? Were titles defective in their former places of residence? The answers to these and other questions may well alter conclusions regardng the attraction of western lands.

The study of individual family histories often points to unfavorable social and political conditions in the older areas as factors motivating emigration. Did control by old-line families diminish political and economic opportunities for the potential migrants in the older, established communities back east? What impact did pivotal or traumatic family events have on migration? Genealogical evidence indicates, for instance, that men who married girls from families with more local influence than their own often migrated. Young men tended to leave home with a close relative—an older brother or sister—upon the remarriage of a parent. Similarly, younger sons sometimes headed for the frontier upon the death and estate settlement of their fathers.

As some of the examples cited earlier in this chapter indicate, children from families with a history of migration tended to migrate more frequently than those of parents who stayed put. In other words, the person who migrated with his nuclear family as a child was more likely to migrate as an adult than was the adult who had never moved from his place of birth. And as is also mentioned earlier, military service led a number of individuals into the Old Southwest, although the Revolutionary War and the War of 1812 temporarily retarded migration.

To prove such contentions, however, the researcher must identify individual migrants and then learn all the exact places of former residence. And, most importantly, the researcher must view the migrant in the context of his extended family and their associates rather than as a lone individual. By no means is this an easy task.

The study of individual families also will indicate the prevalence of sending out relatives to scout for desirable home sites. Rarely did an individual or family, after a decision to emigrate, simply travel until they found a place they liked. Genealogists suggest that in many regions an overwhelming majority knew their exact destination before they packed for the move. Most early residents of the Mississippi portion of the region east of the Pearl, for instance, could probably trace their selection of the Chickasawhay River, the Pearl River, or the Leaf River as their new home directly to the earlier actions of a relative.

The importance of extended family connections and relationships, while not entirely ignored, has not been emphasized sufficiently as the key factor in migrational decisions. There are numerous examples of settlements which demonstrate the impact of family relationships on site selection. An excellent illustration is the family of William Powe, who settled on the Chickasawhay River in present-day Wayne County, Mississippi, circa 1811.[58] By 1816 the Powe family had reconstructed an Old Cheraw District, upper Pee Dee River, South Carolina society along the Chickasawhay. Proof of extensive family connections with William Powe convincingly demonstrates that the migration of so many related families was not a coincidence, especially when there is no evidence of land speculation in that vicinity. Furthermore, such close relationships raises a question regarding the impact of an extensive kinship pattern on decisions of nonrelated neighbors to emigrate to another locality. This, of course, is a question that would be extremely difficult to answer, even by historians who are also competent genealogists. Colleagues who have observed social and political forces at work in isolated rural communities might be inclined to agree that nonrelated settlers would be inclined to move on. Whether or not such was the case, it is probable that kinship was a major factor in the migrational decisions of most residents of Mississippi east of the Pearl River at the time of statehood. Obviously, the availability of suitable land also heavily influenced their actions regardless of their state of prior residency.

In the final analysis, however, there were probably almost as many reasons for migrating as there were migrants. It is the task of historians to sort them out into identifiable groups. Overlaid on top of the myriad social, economic, and political forces were the unmeasurable influences of government policy and speculative propaganda. With the aid of computer programmers and genealogists, however, family historians of the future likely will be able to solve the mysteries of migration.[59] And when they do, they surely will uncover a multiplicity of reasons. While some pioneers viewed the West as a refuge from badgering creditors, intolerable spouses, wornout land, a streak of horrible luck, or even the hangman's noose, others followed the alluring smile of Dame Fortune westward for positive reasons. The majority probably saw land behind her smile— land where they could prosper among family and friends. Real land or mythical land? Maybe some of each. Historians can only conjecture. But that smiling Fortune beckoned thousands and thousands of migrants into the Old Southwest is an undisputed fact.

10

Nabobs and Nobodies

From the outset of Anglo-American settlement, the southwestern frontier developed a distinct regional individuality in social and economic organization. There was a mixture of frontier farmers and landed planters, the latter bringing with them from the Atlantic seaboard an aristocratic heritage which included ownership of slaves.[1] Numerically, however, the predominant element in the social structure were the subsistence farmers who more often than not were really herders of the type discussed in Chapter 6. Present in much smaller numbers were yeoman farmers in the English tradition whose agricultural practices differed considerably from those of the far more numerous Celtic herders.

A heterogeneous lot, the peoples of the Old Southwest formed a diverse and evolving society. More often than not, however, this society has been described in simplistic, even mythological, terms when it actually was characterized by complexity and fluidity. Life among the nobodies along the interior river valleys, for instance, could hardly have differed more from the life of the nabobs whose plantation homes stood high on the bluffs of the Mississippi River and on its broad, fertile delta. Because the social structure was not static, "nobodies" sometimes became "somebodies," especially in the Natchez District where several patterns of life existed.

The relationship between the planter nabobs and the other freemen remains a puzzle and stands as a major challenge to future historians. The presence of Afro-American slaves adds to the complexity of this unresolved question. While planters counted their slaves in larger numbers, many small farmers owned slaves also. So did the Indians. The existence of slavery tempts historians to describe the Old Southwest as more South than West. But in fact, it was more West than South if we equate the "West" with the "frontier."

183

Unquestionably, the Natchez District was the most cosmopolitan and heterogeneous region within the Old Southwest. Virtually all contemporary chroniclers and subsequent generations of historians agree on this point. William B. Hamilton, the most knowledgeable of all students of early Natchez society, described the district as "a lodestone which drew young and ambitious men from all parts of the United States, and from other regions of the world, in the manner of New York City."[2]

Though the metaphor may sound overpowering, Hamilton's point is well taken. Land and commercial profits attracted to Natchez speculators of a variety of national and ethnic origins. They represented most western European nations as well as their colonies, and of course they lived beside Africans, mulattos, and Indians of various tribes and blends of blood mixtures.[3] While the population of Natchez did not boom as explosively as that of a mining community, its cosmopolitan nature made it comparable. Indeed, in both instances, the immigrants were seeking a bonanza. Despite the heterogeneity of its populace and the years of Spanish rule over this district, the culture which developed in Natchez was fundamentally English, a condition reflecting the preponderance of Anglo settlers.[4] A number of English families congregated there after the Peace of Paris of 1763 and during the American Revolution. The absence of any significant residue of Spanish culture also illustrates the difference in Spain's philosophy of colonization which, unlike that of England's, emphasized bureaucratic control rather than the migration and settlement of agrarian colonists. The few Spaniards who remained in Natchez, including several former officials, engaged primarily in commerce.[5]

Fluidity also characterized territorial society. Not only did migrants freely move in and out, but its structure was loose. Even in Natchez and its environs, the white population was not divided into fixed social classes, but had an openness explained by the materialistic goals of the settlers as Hamilton so aptly observed. "Enjoyment of prestige was based on wealth, and not blood, and the pursuit of the former engaged the devotion of the people."[6] While it is unlikely that social classes, in the strict sense, existed in the Old Southwest until well after the War of 1812, it is probable that earlier a status hierarchy developed that was based on length of residency, ownership of land, family ties, and, among planters, number of slaves.[7]

Because of the extreme variations within the social milieu of the territory, many of its residents did not fit the stereotype of an axe and log-cabin frontiersman.[8] Midway through the territorial period, Natchez emerged as an urban commercial center. Though a number of minor inland villages or settlements appeared on the streams flowing through the Natchez District, only one truly urban center thrived. Natchez, designed by the Spanish atop a two-hundred-foot bluff, remained the financial and commercial capital of Mississippi Territory until statehood. As such, it never actually relinquished its role as the social capital also, despite the pretensions of Washington, the center of territorial government a few miles distant. After becoming the territorial capital, the town of Washington briefly rivaled Natchez as the focus of culture and power. Even with its pre-eminence, however, Natchez only enjoyed a population of 1500 in 1810.[9]

The city proper, always distinguished from its disreputable port, Natchez Under-the-Hill, grew from an estimated 100 houses in 1797 to nearly four times that number twenty years later. By then, many homes were of brick and were adorned with balconies and iron grillwork. This led the oft-quoted traveler Fortescue Cuming to compare its appearance to West Indian towns. In 1812, the flourishing port city supported artisans in twenty-four trades, eight attorneys, and an equal number of physicians. The fifty-six commercial establishments included twenty-four mercantile houses, a bank, and three weekly papers.[10]

Another measure of the complexity of the economy was the organization of those skilled in the "mechanical arts" into the Natchez Mechanical Society.[11] Its members, who represented a wide range of occupations, were rising entrepreneurs who sought leverage through unity against the wealthy merchants, planters, and other established professional men. After its incorporation in 1803, the city of Natchez boasted of a highly structured city government that was empowered to regulate the lives and businesses of its citizenry to an extent that would surprise today's urban resident. Perhaps the most imaginative action of the city fathers involved the maintenance of trees on the commons as well as a nursery for the growth of the Pride of China trees, which shaded the town's streets.[12]

Though depictions of the territorial capital six miles northeast of Natchez vary widely, Washington nevertheless was second only to Natchez as an urban center. As the seat of territorial government—and thus Federal largess—it attracted those wielding and seeking influence. In addition, the presence of healthful mineral springs, as well as Fort Dearborn and Jefferson College also cast a distinctiveness on the town as did the numerous planters who resided near by. Admittedly, Washington represented an oasis of punctilio and ceremony which reached a peak population of nearly a thousand in 1815, but J. F. H. Claiborne's oft-cited description of it as a lively cultural and social center is no doubt romanticized.[13]

Whatever the similarities and differences between Washington and Natchez may have been, life in those rival towns offered a stark contrast to that of settlers many miles from the Mississippi, particularly those in the river valleys above Mobile. Squatters along the Tombigbee, who lived equidistant from Georgia and Natchez, more closely resembled the Turnerian frontiersman, and they were viewed as such by the more pretentious residents of the bluffs of the Mississippi, who often traced their roots to Maryland, Virginia, or the Carolinas. Though sectional antipathies were strong, it is doubtful that Bigbee pioneers were as depraved, vicious, illiterate and lawless as some Federal officials and travelers—often from patrician stock—painted them.[14]

Sprinkled along the Gulf Coast between the Pearl and Pascagoula Rivers were occasional settlements of Frenchmen among whom also resided a surprising number of free blacks. While the freedmen had more recently migrated from New Orleans, the French *inhabitantes* were descendants of the Mississippi Valley's first European settlers. These Catholics mainly were subsistence farmers who kept considerable herds of cattle and hogs, and some of them also manufactured naval stores—spars, masts, pitch, and tar.[15] Though their homes were not officially incorporated into Mississippi Territory until 1811, their presence further illustrates the lack of homogeneity within the population of the Old Southwest.

These coastal folk, whom Ephraim Kirby a land commissioner and territorial judge accurately described as "generally peaceful, honest well-disposed citizens," had enjoyed their isolation under Spanish rule.[16] Following the transfer of Louisiana to American dominion in 1804, however, they experienced a flurry of violent encounters. The shifting international frontier placed them at the forefront of Anglo-Spanish confrontation. Prior to Jefferson's 1808 Embargo, English and American privateers and corsairs played havoc with the coastal trade to the extent of provoking several pitched battles. To enforce the Embargo, American gunboats appeared and their crews also engendered much ill will by rustling livestock. Little wonder that these peace-loving coastians—French and freedmen—sought Spanish protection from overzealous conventionalists such as Sterling Dupree whose brigandlike raids in 1810 were discussed in Chapter 3.[17]

Representative of the enterprising free blacks who often became artisans or entrepreneurs on the Gulf Coast was Carlos Asmer. A resident of Bay St. Louis, he began a coastal taxi service between Pensacola and New Orleans in a small sailboat. By the close of the Spanish period in

1810, Asmer was the proud captain of his own schooner on which he transported freight and passengers, often in the employ of Spanish officials. In addition, Asmer owned livestock and real estate.[18]

If thus far historians have been unable to sort out the complexities of relationships among the Caucasians in the territory who at least shared a common racial heritage, how long will it take scholars to understand the even more complicated interrelationships among Caucasians, Africans, Indians, and mixed-bloods?[19] By 1816, the percentage of blacks in the total population of the Natchez District had risen to 52, again up 10 percent since 1801. Though the growth of the cotton economy precluded any meaningful drive for abolition, interesting manifestations of social liberalism regarding blacks arose without serious repercussions. Manumissions were common, and undoubtedly many of the recipients were participants in or products of miscegenation.[20]

One of the most fascinating instances of miscegenation and manumission involves a William Barland who educated, bestowed considerable property upon, and freed, the twelve children whom he sired in a union with a Negro slave, Elizabeth, purchased in 1789. Thus he established in Natchez through a single family a lineage of wealthy educated blacks who were, in Barland's words, "brought up in the practice of industry and the morality of the Christian religion."[21]

Hamilton characterized miscegenation with Indians as "considerable" and that with Africans as "extensive." While his point is well taken, he may have been more accurate had he reversed the adjectives.[22] Impressionistic sources such as travel accounts and correspondence abound with references to unions between whites and Indians. Indeed, the more familiar one becomes with accounts of frontier life in the Old Southwest, the more one concludes that mixed-bloods constituted a far larger segment of society than historians have previously suggested. Though the Natchez District obviously was the home of numerous mixed-bloods, they were still more numerous in settlements adjoining the tribal lands, and of course within the Indian Nations themselves.

In his perceptive study of the Indians of the Old South, J. Leitch Wright, Jr. makes the point that "substantial" numbers of Indians "passed unnoticed into white society."[23] Such was also the case in the Old Southwest, particularly if the designation "Indian" includes persons of mixed European and Native American ancestry. Indeed, the odds are extremely high that members of any family in the deep South which traces its roots back to the territorial days have some Indian blood in their veins. Between the Euro-American and the Native Americans of the Old Southwest there was a compatibility that bordered on affinity, especially among the Celts and the French Canadians. Whites moved with ease into Indian society from the first contact of the two peoples, at least prior to the Creek War. And the converse was true if the mixed-blood behaved, spoke, and dressed like a white. The prevalence of white-Indian miscegenation leads one to suspect strongly that many of the squatters who moved into the Old Southwest were themselves mixed bloods who were welcomed into the Nations, and in some cases the loudest voices raised in complaint against so-called intruders were those of mixed-blood chiefs. In other words, most of the intruders were welcomed by at least some factions.

It must be kept in mind, however, that there was a wide spectrum of mixed-bloods who differed in their religious, political, economic, and social behavior to the same extent as did the Anglo-Americans who surrounded them. Some mixed-bloods modeled themselves upon the white nabobs; others upon the nobodies.[24] Still others emulated various tribal models. And in the Old Southwest—as in the Old South—the genes of Afro-Americans, Native Americans, and Anglo-Americans mixed in every conceivable combination. Until proven otherwise, mixed-bloods more nearly resembling the African slaves owned by Native Americans as well as whites fell victim to the racial prejudices of certain groups of whites and Indians. As was pointed out above, until very recent times mixed-bloods have received but scant attention from historians. Perhaps in due time, genealogists and family historians will attribute some of the distinctive characteristics of society in the deep South to this seldom recognized heritage.

Little wonder, in view of the conglomeration of humanity within the Old Southwest, that travelers so often commented on the varied and colorful types of persons they encountered. Considering the possible combinations of ethnic backgrounds, blood lines, and life styles, the range from the most archetypical nabob to the lowliest nobody must have been intriguing.

To many observers, however, the average "squatter" was more worthy of disdain than found intriguing—particularly to Northerners or Englishman. A case in point are the denigrating comments of land commissioner Ephraim Kirby who responded in 1804 to Jefferson's questions concerning the quality of the land, encroachment upon Indian territory, and the character of the people above Mobile. It is clear that Kirby found few redeeming qualities in these early settlers. According to him, the

Tombigbee region was an "asylum" for criminals and loyalists from the Carolinas and Georgia who were "attainted and proscribed for treasonable practices during the Revolution." This latter class, he explained, hated the American government and had lived so long beyond formal political restraints that they were "hostile to all law and every government." He did not equivocate in his outspoken opinion of the residents of Washington County.

> The present inhabitants (with few exceptions) are illiterate, wild and savage, of depraved morals, unworthy of public confidence or private esteem; litigious, disunited, and, knowing each other, universally distrustful of each other. The magistrates without dignity, respect, probity, influence or authority. The administration of justice, imbecile and corrupt. The militia, without discipline or competent officers.[25]

Jefferson no doubt concluded that this was a shaky human foundation on which to build the strategic population barrier that he had in mind.

Though he did not refer to his neighbors as criminals and savages, a year later Judge Harry Toulmin did emphasize to the territorial delegate, William Lattimore, that "neither youth nor age has any instruction or consolation here. They are born," he continued, "amidst the clouds of ignorance—and die without having the heart gladdened with the cheering light of revelation." The schools were "few and ill supported" and houses of worship "utterly unknown among us as among our Chactaw [*sic*] neighbors."[26]

Pine barrens constituted much of the land lying west of the Tombigbee, and it was here that the omnipresent cattle grazier found a pleasant, undisturbed haven. Toulmin, probably to a greater degree than Kirby, understood these unlettered, ancestral "crackers" who considered as squatter domain any range into which their wayward herds roamed. Ownership meant little or nothing to these progenitors of the latter trans-Mississippi cattle kings; they asked only that the ground be solid and the grass green. For the United States Government in the strategic first decade of the new century, these herdsmen were possibly as much a threat as a buffer amidst the delicate international and Indian negotiations.[27]

The adjectives "rough," "coarse," "honest," and even "poor" may have described with considerable accuracy many of the early settlers in the Old Southwest, but by no means were all of them poor and ignorant.

Among them were families of some wealth who only briefly endured a plebeian life style before enjoying the patrician comforts to which they were accustomed. This particularly applied to a number of the immigrants who arrived after the War of 1812. Until well into the antebellum period, however, even planter families occupied log cabins while their mansions were constructed and furnished—often a long-drawn-out process.

Along with their other cultural baggage, the southwestern frontiersmen brought with them a strong sense of a personal God and a faith in fundamental Protestantism. Their religious philosophy was that of poor people constantly struggling against overwhelming economic odds set by the will of God, and as John B. Boles points out, revivalists quickly realized that "poverty was congenial to religious commitment." Most church-goers, according to Boles, were of the "common sort" who were "habituated to work and poverty." Consequently, "the clergy ministered to their acceptance of a less than comfortable life by minimizing the importance of affluence in the long run."[28] So, from the outset of American settlement, the frontier of the Old Southwest was a promising one for the evangelist in search of souls and congregations.

At first the Baptists, Methodists, and Presbyterians competed for converts on fairly even terms, and all three promoted a theology of individualism. "Each," Boles concludes, "contributed to the peculiarly non-abstract religious frame of mind that prevailed in the South: a personal, provincial, pietistic emphasis on the work of God in the hearts of individuals." Within several decades, the Presbyterians lost ground. Though the Baptists with their system of "farmer-preachers" eventually prevailed, throughout much of the nineteenth century the Methodist circuit riders enjoyed an advantage as they patrolled the very fringes of the frontier. Eager to "break the first bush," these hardy itinerants at times followed wagon tracks so fresh that they encountered prospective converts before they had unpacked their possessions. When Richmond Nolley identified himself as a Methodist minister on one such occasion, the settler complained of their ubiquitous presence.

> I quit Virginia to get out of the way of them, and went to a new settlement in Georgia, where I thought I should be quite beyond their reach, but they got my wife and daughter into the church. Then in the late purchase—Choctaw Corner—I found a piece of good land, and was sure that I would have some peace of preachers; but here is one of them before my wagon is unloaded.[29]

Methodist lore is replete with stories of the dangers faced by sad-dle-weary itinerants. Among the most fearsome story characters were the wild panthers in the trees overhead, the wolves trotting behind the horses, the bears that unexpectedly blocked the path, and the snakes that curled in the blankets of circuit riders who were too worn out to ride any longer.[30]

Perhaps the most courageous of the militant servants of the Lord to enter the Mississippi Territory in the early days was the indomit-able Lorenzo Dow who sustained himself during his treks through the wilderness by killing turkeys and who protected himself from bears and wolves with roaring night fires.[31] Dow's eloquence brought many an old backslider to tearfully come forward and fall on his knees in re-pentance.

The Reverend Jacob Young, himself a sturdy crusader, described Lor-enzo Dow as a mighty preacher who faced down Calvinists and back-woods rowdies with equal courage and defiance. Another Methodist itinerant, Brother James Axley, was just as forceful in his condemnation of all forms of debauchery—especially whiskey drinking and tobacco chewing. The folly of pride and vainglory was also one of his favorite themes. Though some of the frontier parsons were well educated, many styled themselves as "unlarnt." Like Brother Axley, however, they "knew well how to divide the words of God, and give every man his portion." And theirs was a wrathful God of tremendous force who "toted thunder in his fist and flung lightning [sic] from his fingers."[32]

One of the most picturesque scenes in American backwoods history was a revival campground with its fire pots in full blaze, a congregation singing in thunderous tones, and a stern-looking minister beseeching the very embers of Hell to consume unrepentant sinners. Adding to this boisterous scene were hysterical shrieks for God's mercy and the sight of a variety of contagious bodily agitations which overcame the enraptured worshipers. The most frequently mentioned physical manifestation of the spirit was the "jerks." This exercise usually began with a jerking movement of the forearms which quickly affected every muscle of the body. Some women jerked their heads to and fro with sufficient violence to cause their long hair "to lash and crack like a whip," producing sounds clearly audible at twenty feet. And at times these convulsions spread like wildfire. Tradition has it that at one meeting twenty thousand frantic frontiersmen "tossed to and fro like tumultuous waves of a sea in a storm" and that some of the jerkers clutched saplings for support while their uncontrollable feet "kicked up the earth as a horse stamping flies." In some instances, even the dogs became afflicted![33] Meanwhile, on the fringes of the encampment all manner of wickedness prevailed, some at the hands of hardened criminals and prostitutes, and others at the momentary loss of propriety in the arms of love-hungry worshipers. Thus the old quip that at some revivals more souls were made than saved.

John Milton himself could have described no wilder scene. Indeed, many suggest that he wrote the script. For *Paradise Lost*, along with the Bible and a hymnal, comprised the "trinity of the circuit," which most of the itinerant Methodist preachers carried in their battered saddlebags.[34] Of course, preachers from several other denominations frequented camp meetings, especially Baptists and Presbyterians. Exactly who started this movement in the Old Southwest may never be known, but the Presbyterians must be credited with assembling the first ones in Kentucky and Tennessee. Nevertheless, their ultimate source was the Great Awakening of the 1730s and 1740s, and the lingering effects are clearly visible in the deep South today.[35]

Whether annual camp meetings—sometimes called "holy fairs" or "religious holidays"—were emotionally prolonged social gatherings or a season of genuine spiritual rejuvenation is a question that troubled contemporary religious leaders just as it does church historians today. Frontier evangelists nevertheless understood the efficacy of camp meetings, though few expressed their thoughts as clearly as Parson Winans. Winans, a circuit rider in territorial Mississippi, observed that prospective converts were "much more effectively operated upon in large masses than either singly or in small parties. Sympathy and examples," he explained, "have great influence, whether for good or evil, in moving the minds of men."[36]

Whether fairs or holidays or true holy days, the camp meetings should not detract from the important role of the pioneer preacher who shared the hard and grinding poverty of life with frontiersmen as he ministered to their spiritual needs. Regardless of their denominational affiliation, these men of the cloth rank high among the unsung frontier heroes of the Old Southwest. In a large sense, the Methodist circuit riders may have paid the highest price of all the clergymen. With a monetary renumeration not large enough to be dignified with the term *salary*, they were expected to continually cover a circuit generally 500 miles in circumference while depending on the generosity of their constituents for food and shelter. Though they took no formal vows of poverty and chastity, they might as well have. For riding circuit precluded the possibility of being either a provider or a companion. And celibacy, privation, and loneliness were not their only challenges; it was not unusual for preachers to double as instruments of the law. At camp meetings and services, they often dealt personally and physically with rowdies, and on occasion they were expected to play the role of peace officer in the community. Though many frontier clergymen were barely literate, they did promote education. As they had from the earliest colonial days, Presbyterians excelled in this role.[37]

On this frontier, there were as many different life styles as there were varieties of ethnic and economic backgrounds—ranging from the gentility of the plantation mansion to the crudeness of the roughest log cabin. This reality, however, generally has been obscured by the myth of the wild and savage frontier created and perpetrated by accounts of outsiders, many of whom were as biased as they were uninformed. Obviously, life in the manor often was not as genteel as it appeared; neither was it always so crude in the hut.

This reality did not escape the discerning eye—and mind—of naturalist James Audubon who, ironically enough, may have revealed a bias of his own in this description of them:

> Although every European traveller who has glided down the Mississippi, at the rate of ten miles an hour, has told his tale of the Squatters, yet none has given any other account of them than that they are "a sallow, sickly-looking sort of miserable being," living in swamps, and subsisting on pignuts, Indian corn and bear's flesh. It is obvious, however, that none but a person acquainted with their history, manners, and condition, can give any real information respecting them.[38]

Often American sojourners were as guilty as the Europeans of misjudging the settlers whether they resided along river banks or deep in the forest. While travelers afoot or atop a horse seldom moved at such a speed as "ten miles an hour," Audubon's point about the superficiality of their observations is well taken. And sad though it may be, the squatters rarely recorded their condition and thoughts, and if they did it is unlikely that their records would survive.

The Reverend Hamilton W. Pierson, long-time agent for the American Bible Society in the Old Southwest and at one time President of Cumberland College in Kentucky, echoed Audubon. Writing in 1881, Pierson lamented that "comparatively little has been written which is the result of extended personal contact with, and intimate personal knowledge of, the people." Southwesterners, Pierson insisted, had been "largely the subjects of exaggeration and caricature."[39]

Historian J. F. H. Claiborne commented extensively on the multifarious nature of society on the southwestern frontier in the early antebellum period in the oft-cited journal of his trip through the Mississippi Piney Woods. His may be the best extant account of patterns of life in the interior of the Old Southwest in the decade or so after the War of 1812, and it deserves to be studied with care, for it reveals that graciousness and hospitality were not found only on the estates of the lordly class. The account also indicates that though an unhealthy climate hovered over much of the Old Southwest, there were pockets in the Piney Woods that were "remarkable for the almost universal exemption of disease" where "the men are robust, active and long-lived; the women beautiful, and the children lively as crickets and ruddy as rosebuds." Claiborne, himself a child of the Natchez District, poked fun at the affluent "river planters" who survived the fevers by swallowing "some filthy potion three times a day throughout the year."[40]

As noted in Chapter 6, Claiborne does refer to the prevalence in the Piney Woods of the Celtic herder about whom Grady McWhiney and Forrest McDonald have commented so extensively—a class of folk generally denigrated by Northern and English visitors for their poverty and coarseness. In his recent book, *Cracker Culture: Celtic Ways in the Old South*, McWhiney postulates that the ubiquitous "cracker" in the antebellum South really was a Celt whom the English Northerners naturally found as strange as they did repugnant. *Cracker*, a Scottish term denoting a boastful person, has been used for at least two centuries in the South to denote the settlers on the bottom rung of the social ladder—nearly always applied in a disparaging way. Because "deep cultural contrarities" separated Celtic crackers from Northern or English visitors, the latter generally described the former either with great curiosity or disdain or both.[41]

According to McWhiney, "a wide range of observers generally characterized Southerners as more hospitable, generous, frank, courteous, spontaneous, lazy, lawless, militaristic, wasteful, impractical, and reckless than Northerners." On the other hand, Northerners were "more reserved, shrewd, disciplined, gauche, enterprising, acquisitive, careful, frugal, ambitious, pacific, and practical than Southerners."[42] Though McWhiney's study relates to the entire antebellum South, his summary matches perfectly the descriptions by outsiders of the common folk of the Old Southwest. Ephraim Kirby's correspondence, for instance, illustrates both sets of these characteristics.

Those observers who spent considerable time among the "crackers" in the Old Southwest understood that their culture was leisure oriented. They lived, so to speak, off the fat of the land while their herds went untended, devoting all their time to hunting, fishing, dancing, smoking, drinking, fighting, and visiting—not to mention the pleasurable activity of conceiving large flocks of little crackers. In a haphazard way, invariably noted by outsiders, these frontiersmen planted some corn, peas, sweet potatoes, and greens to eat and maybe some cotton and tobacco to trade. Wild fruit, in season, added a bit of variety to their table which was generally set in a ill-kept cabin. One Yankee noted that he observed a Southerner who planted his crops on a hillside so that "when his pumpkins are ripe and his potatoes dug, all he had to do is start them and they roll right down into his kitchen."[43]

A delightful episode experienced by Claiborne in the Piney Woods illustrates how heavily some families depended on the sweet potato. Though pork, beef, and turkey graced the table of one particular home, virtually every other dish or drink was derived from this single farinaceous vegetable. There was baked, fried, and boiled sweet potato, bread and pie of the same origin, and even "coffee" and beer made from potatoes. After supper Claiborne slept on a mattress of potato vines, but only fitfully. He dreamed "that we had *turned into a big potato*, and that some one was *digging us up*.[44] Feeling ill the next day, he was treated effectively with potato poultices and potions. And when he was recovered, he was sent on his way with a packet of potato chips. The nonculinary usefulness of the crop was extolled by Claiborne, who calculated that one acre "will yield from three to five hundred bushels" and that "with little culture" it will "grow on soils too thin to produce corn."[45]

Itinerant preacher Hamilton W. Pierson was in and out of the primitive homes of western Tennessee, which were characteristic of the humble pioneer domiciles throughout the Southwest. He described a log house of less than fifteen feet square which contained a loom in one corner, a long narrow table, a couple of chairs, two benches, and the traditional corner bed. In the front of the room there was a broad fireplace that threatened to consume the room, its contents, and the human occupants.[46]

The size of a house, of course, varied, but sixteen feet square seemed to be the standard. Chimneys were made of logs backed with clay and, when it was available, covered with mortar, and the floors were of unplaned planks. Generally a single window without glass provided air and illumination. As the family grew, so did the domicile by adding an identical cabin just a few feet to one side with a covered "dog trot" in between. A shed was often attached to the rear. Methodist clergyman William Winans, who erected such a home in 1815 on a quarter section of land and who owned seven slaves, considered himself as well housed as 90 percent of the citizens of Mississippi Territory.[47] Even fairly wealthy frontiersmen resided in similar homes, though some eventually encased them with painted planks. By the turn of the nineteenth century, a few planters and merchants in the Natchez District had erected mansions resembling those associated most often with the antebellum era, but they were in an extreme minority.

Even the more commodious log cabins in the Old Southwest offered few luxuries, and most were rather primitive. Many had no windows and those which did rarely had glass panes. Ventilation posed no problem as a traveler noted as late as 1850 just one night out of Mobile. "Our bed-room was ventilated on an entirely new principle; that is to say, by wide cracks in the floor, broad spaces between the logs that composed the wall, huge openings in the roof, and a window with a shutter that could not be closed." Indeed, many a visitor fell asleep while watching the twinkling stars through gaps in the roof only to awake with his blanket covered with snow. Guest beds were a rare luxury and visitors often sprawled on the floor with their feet to the fire or slept in a loft. Particularly among the herders, some of the cabins were hardly habitable—a tendency which McWhiney of course attributes to their Celtic origins. Others, however, such as the one described by Audubon as so "beautifully clean" that even the slab floor looked "newly washed and dried," reflected considerable domesticity and pride.[48]

Except in Natchez, which boasted of as many as six inns in 1808, and a few other emerging towns, public accommodations were seldom available. And when the weary wayfarer did happen upon a stand, tavern, or inn, he often had to deal with bedbugs, fleas, and other vermin. In the absence of inns, travelers were grateful for accommodations in a home however clean or unclean it might be. This custom gave rise to a genre of funny stories of squalid lodgings; many of which involved preachers. These itinerants doubtless became experts on the subject of "vermin, filth, hog, and hominy."[49]

The Old Southwest was a hospitable frontier. Whether he visited a mansion on the banks of the Mississippi or a cabin beside the Chickasawhay, a traveler was made to feel at home. In the one, food may have been served more graciously, but certainly no more generously than in the other. Often outsiders complained of the kind of food served, but not of how freely it was offered. Among the planters, visitors may have found more familiar fare, but universally the tastes of the settlers in the Old Southwest varied from those of Northern and English tourists who generally complained of the absence of wheat bread, fresh milk, butter, cheese, mutton, and even Irish potatoes.

Milk and butter may have been more available on the plantations where domestic help abounded, but surprisingly enough, seldom was it at hand in the cabins of the herders. Their cattle ran on the open range and only on the most special occasions would they take the trouble to feed, water, and milk cows. Another frequent complaint of visitors related to the scarcity of beer or cider. In the Old Southwest—indeed, as was true in Tennessee and Kentucky—the alcoholic drink of preference was whiskey. And of course McWhiney attributes most of these dietary preferences to the dominance of the Celtic heritage in the South. Not only did travelers notice that their hosts preferred whiskey, but they also noticed how much was consumed.

The Celtic herder, however, was not alone in his enjoyment of excessive libation. As Hamilton points out, "drunkenness" was "characteristic of the region as a whole" and "not confined to any class."[50] He refers to the fact that both nabobs and nobodies partook readily, but he might have included members of the military and government bureaucracy who also found considerable comfort in spirits. The venerable Silas Dinsmoor, who so strongly opposed the use of firewater by traders, explained to the Secretary of War that "Wine and Brandy are as necessary to my health in this climate as beef and bread to my subsistence. . . . I use both with temperance," he assured his superior, "and suffer none under my authority to use them to excess."[51] At Fort Stoddert in 1799, the commander defended his requisition of fifteen gallons of brandy and thirty gallons of wine as not extravagant in light of the scarcity of medicine at his post. On the very next page of the letterbook, however, is his report that his doctor had died "by a fall on a bottle full of Rum." Then the commander added that the medical man had "expired almost instantaneously" and that he would give his superior the "particulars" during his next visit.[52]

According to some accounts, clergymen of varying denominations sold as well as consumed spirituous drink. An "eminent Methodist preacher" for years brought down "twice a year" a flatboat load of whiskey from

Ohio for sale in Natchez, at which time he preached there and at Washington nearby "with great fervor and unction" before heading back upriver.[53] Whether it was a mint julep delicately served in crystal on the veranda of a mansion or a hefty draft from an old clay jug in a log cabin, it is clear that few frontiersmen missed an opportunity to imbibe. This fact is borne out by a claim that there were twenty-five licensed taverns in Natchez in 1803[54]

Gambling also was a universal pastime on the southwestern frontier. Though it is most often mentioned in reference to the barrooms and bawdy houses in Natchez Under-the-Hill and the race track and taverns in the more genteel city above, gambling was no stranger in the remote areas also. Horse racing and card playing were the two most popular ways of generating wagers, but any game of chance would do. Indeed, gambling was so widespread that many men adopted it as a profession. Though professional gamblers are most often associated with Mississippi River steamboats and with the port cities of Vicksburg, Natchez, and New Orleans, those shady figures were ubiquitous in the Old Southwest also. They boarded steamers wherever they paddled and also had a way of appearing amidst any crowd where money might be circulating. And from time to time they drew the wrath of reformers who periodically ran them out of town and, once in a while, dangled one of the unlucky sharks in a hangman's noose.[55]

Perhaps a more universal source of pleasure on the frontier of the Old Southwest was the use of tobacco in virtually every known form. Most men and many women smoked, chewed, or dipped, and frequently they did all three. In a sense, it is highly appropriate that every July the National Tobacco Spitting Contest is held in Smith County, Mississippi, on the fringes of Sullivan's Hollow—in myth, if not in fact, the toughest settlement in the Piney Woods of Mississippi.

In their accounts of the frontier, visitors generally made note of these "nasty" and "dirty looking" habits; particularly chewing, which one visitor described as a "detestable universality." It is not difficult to understand the uneasiness of uninitiated outsiders at sharing close quarters with tobacco chewers. One Englishman, for instance, complained of being "crammed" into a stagecoach with eight other passengers, five of whom chewed. "During the night," he wrote, "they aimed at the windows with great accuracy, and didn't *splash* me," but his luck did not hold out. By the next afternoon, "tobacco-chewing became universal, and the spitting was sometimes a little wild."[56] While the use of tobacco in its various forms was not confined to the backwoodsmen, in the more commodious homes and public buildings considerable efforts were made by the men-folk to be genteel and considerate, and cuspidors were conspicuous in all well appointed settings. This legacy is still readily found in most rural courthouses today in the deep South.

Another universal pastime in the Old Southwest was dancing. In the music rooms of the more stately homes in Natchez or Mobile it was the minuet; in the barns and taverns of the interior it was a jig or a reel. But rich or poor, white or black, everybody on the frontier welcomed a chance to listen and dance to music, generally produced by the fiddle or the banjo. As the cotton culture of the antebellum period evolved, pianos were found more frequently, especially on the plantations and in the urban areas. They were extremely rare, however, in the cabins scattered through the forests and along the isolated river valleys. The sight of a piano, accord-ing to one observer, caused "great wonderment to the denizens of the surrounding pine woods. One man, when he first saw it, thought it an ironing table; another took the pedals for pistols, and another mistook it for a fancy chest for keeping nice clothes."[57] The Celtic frontiersmen of the Old Southwest knew more of bagpipes than of pianos, and their music remained similar to that of their ancestors.

As it did in so many sides of life, Natchez provided a marked contrast in the realm of entertainment or amusement. Indeed, in the entire his-tory of the American frontier, it is doubtful that another example can be found of such urbanity amidst such a small urban population. The anom-aly is explained by the presence of so many wealthy and cultured fami-lies who lived within a fifteen- to twenty-mile radius of the town and who nourished a wide range of cultural activities in the frontier town.

As did residents of all urban centers of its era, Natchez dwellers of all classes flocked to an assortment of traveling attractions that stopped en route to or from New Orleans. These included circuses, menageries, fire-works displays, wax figures, acrobats, and even a balloon ascension. Though visiting was a favorite pastime of the well-to-do, planters and merchants spent many hours supporting the arts and enriching their minds through an appreciation of literature. They patronized itinerant perfor-mances as well as those of a vigorous theatrical association not unlike the "little theatres" found in so many communities today.

As early as 1806, a traveling dramatist performed in a local tavern, and in 1808 patrons organized the Natchez Theatrical Association, which flour-ished for at least two generations. Its repertoire and published newspa-per criticism both indicate that its audience was far more sophisticated than one would expect to find at the most distant outpost of the American southwestern frontier, though devotees of the theater in the East might have found the programs somewhat pedestrian.[58]

Though the sources reveal less about the status of painting in Natchez, they do indicate that the community was not devoid of an appreciation of that form of the arts. In the opening decades of the nineteenth century several artists solicited students for instruction in oil, water, and transparent painting, and the region produced in this period at least one good painter, James Tooley. John J. Audubon taught briefly in both Natchez and Washington, and it is believed that he learned to paint in oils during his tenure in Natchez. Newspaper advertisements for the sale of copies of the old masters also indicate that residents of this Natchez District prized the visual arts.[59]

It is unlikely that the reading tastes in the Natchez District varied significantly from those in any enlightened community in the East or perhaps even in the British Isles. No other scholar was better acquainted with the intellectual life of Natchez than William B. Hamilton, who emphasized that Natchez was "no frontier community totally isolated from the printed heritage of English literature." Hamilton further asserted that "the citizenry read, and read early, about the same standard books one would expect any literate community . . . to read."[60]

As early as 1795 there were small but well-selected private libraries, and by 1802 book dealers advertised. Not only did that trade persist, but at times it even flourished; in 1808 a shipment of 3,500 books was auctioned. The titles are as impressive as the numbers. In addition to the time-honored classics and contemporary best sellers, also in demand were medical treatises, cookbooks, Biblical concordances, dictionaries, and other useful reference works. Literary societies maintained reading rooms in Natchez and Washington. Among the more interesting of them was the Mississippi Society for the Acquirement and Dissemination of Useful Knowledge, incorporated in 1803. Though some were transitory and others were politically motivated, similar societies were organized in each of the counties along the Mississippi River.[61]

Though the list of the founders of the Mississippi Society for the Acquirement and Dissemination of Useful Knowledge reads like a "Who's Who" of the Natchez District, its most distinguished charter member was the noted scientist William Dunbar. Charles S. Sydnor, the mentor of Hamilton, who undoubtedly stimulated the latter's keen interest in the intellectual history of antebellum Mississippi, connects the unusual assemblage of mathematically and scientifically trained men in Mississippi Territory to the importance of surveying. Not only did international boundaries have to be run, but both public and private boundaries of extremely valuable parcels of land had to be surveyed. Andrew Ellicott, Isaac Briggs, Seth Pease, Thomas Freeman, Garrett Elliot Pendergrast, Silas Dinsmoor, and Gideon Fitz were some of the interesting collection of scientifically trained men who walked the streets of Natchez and Washington from time to time.[62]

William Dunbar, clearly the foremost scientist in the Old Southwest, was educated in Glasgow and London before arriving in West Florida in 1773. After settling in the Natchez District in 1785, Dunbar made a fortune as a cotton planter and gained a wide reputation as an inventor, astronomer, and explorer. Recommended by Thomas Jefferson for membership in the American Philosophical Society, Dunbar contributed fifteen papers to its publications.[63] In 1804 Jefferson commissioned Dunbar with Dr. George Hunter to explore the Red and Ouachita Rivers, and Dunbar's report is one of the first official descriptions of the trans-Mississippi West. His interest ranged into medicine as well, and Dunbar spearheaded the vaccination of half the population of the Mississippi Territory in 1802, which may have prevented a disastrous epidemic.[64]

To a large extent, Natchez remained for decades an enclave of "civilization" or "culture" amidst the extensive frontier of the Old Southwest. Many immigrants discovered this fact for themselves. Methodist minister Winans, for instance, was terrified at his assignment there in 1810, for he believed that Natchez was inhabited by "a mongrel race compounded of French, Spanish, and Negro, with a slight sprinkling of Anglo-Saxon ruffians and outlaws" who were "illiterate and profligate." After his arrival, however, Winans conceded that, instead, he had found a preponderance of refinement.[65] One indication of that quality was the emphasis placed in the Natchez District on education. It is not known just how many early private tutors resided with some of the wealthy families, but shortly after the turn of the century a rash of small private academies appeared. The most notable effort to foster education, however, was the founding of Jefferson College by the territorial assembly in 1802. Outside of the Natchez District, little emphasis was placed on education, and some suggest that the Celtic herders generally looked upon "larnin' " with disdain.[66]

Historian Charles S. Sydnor was probably accurate when he concluded that "the intellectual level of this settlement in the wilderness was much higher than the level to which its material civilization had advanced by the close of the eighteenth century."[67] Students of intellectual and urban history as well as the frontier would do well to further analyze Natchez as a community and compare it to other frontier cities such as Denver and San Francisco. The nuances of Natchez's economic and family history remain a mystery. Consider its diverse origins: it was founded by the French who shortly thereafter decimated the Natchez Indians, governed for decades by the Spanish, and settled by the English. Wealthy merchants as well as aristocratic planters lived there, and a rowdy port sullied its reputation. In addition, it was the terminus of a major road—the Natchez Trace. Yet in the eyes of most Americans, Natchez is seen primarily as the symbolic capital of the antebellum cotton kingdom. Hardly ever is it viewed in the context of a frontier town. But it was—no less than Abilene, Denver, or San Francisco. Admittedly, it was also quite different, and that is precisely why it deserves a closer examination.

For both the nabobs and nobodies, the military was an important social ingredient in their lives. Its role in the Creek War, the War of 1812, and in controlling the Indians has been discussed in earlier chapters. In another sense, however, the Army was an important factor in economic development and in acculturation. Purchases and payrolls stimulated local economies, and the presence of the military generally enhanced frontier life. Soldiers built roads and fortifications and in an emergency provided medical care and sustenance. The military post provided buildings for a wide range of community services and public meetings.

While the presence of the Regular Army was important—of greater significance socially was the militia. Because the rank and file chose their leaders, participation gave everyone a sense of service and of belonging, even though the officers generally were men of property. This role provided an outlet for the energies of the younger sons of the landed class and gave them important opportunities for leadership. For all classes, however, the militia was a social bonus. The musters provided a welcome break from the arduous frontier life and were important occasions for everyone in the county. In this respect they were not unlike a fair. There were political speeches, feats of skill, contests, and of course drills by the militia. In Adams County a crack infantry company and cavalry troop developed, which evolved into social organizations that prided themselves on their dances and incredibly elaborate uniforms. Though not as pretentious in the other counties, universally the militia played a multiplicity of important roles, and it was commonplace to hear men identified by their rank within the local militia.[68]

On a bright Saturday afternoon in 1826, Anthony Campbell, a sixty-two-year-old former magistrate, rode along the road leading to the Natchez landing with his mind probably on business with one of its merchants. Or he might have been just enjoying a break in a streak of bad weather. Without warning, a stranger knocked the upright citizen from his horse by repeated blows from his whip, and after the stunned victim fell to the ground, pounced upon him and bit off his left ear, chewed it up, and swallowed it. Campbell survived to report the assault and thus added another incident to support the contention that violence was characteristic of the frontier of the Old Southwest. It so happened that the stranger, who later identified himself as John Irvin, was extracting retribution from Campbell for driving him along with his fellow gamblers, pimps, and prostitutes from Natchez Under-the-Hill in 1816.[69] But was the entire Old Southwest really as violent as this barbarous attack would lead us to believe? The answer has to be that it probably was not.

As was pointed out in Chapter 5, Natchez Under-the-Hill was a busy port that afforded the boatmen every pleasure they wished to buy. There, was, however, only one such port above New Orleans, and it was hardly typical of the entire frontier. Nevertheless, the Old Southwest in some respects was a rough, tough, and even crude frontier. This fact, for instance, explains why Mike Fink, king of the keelboatmen who climaxed his career as a mountain man, became a legendary hero in own time. The pioneers, according to his biographers, "could respect a hero even stronger then they, a man who could roar like a bull and fight like a wildcat."[70] On the other hand, one can question the prevalence of violence as a characteristic of society in the Old Southwest without denying the legend of Mike Fink.[71]

Students of frontier violence have recently offered significant evidence to refute the myth of lawlessness in the antebellum South. As pointed out in the discussion of the Natchez Trace in Chapter 5, serious questions regarding the myth of violence on the trace were raised as early as 1937 by Hamilton. More recently, Michael Beard, after a meticulous study of extant Natchez newspapers of the first quarter of the nineteenth century, finds reports of very few homicides, even in notorious Natchez Under-the-Hill, and he argues persuasively that the myth of the wild and savage West was created by the pens of the traveler-journalist who arrived with preconceived notions not dissimilar to those of Parson Winans.[72]

Studies of the Mississippi territorial statutes reveal a strong "law and order" sentiment, and statistical analyses of court records in Georgia indicate that crimes against persons in the antebellum South were no more prevalent than in the states carved out of the Old Northwest.[73] Much more work needs to be done, however, before definitive statements can be made on the extent of violence in the Old Southwest. Indeed, observers of the rural South today would be hard pressed to deny that it is easy to find an altercation on a Friday or Saturday night in a country bar or at a local athletic contest—evidence that tends to support those historians who emphasize the violent side of frontier life. It is doubtful that cliometricians will quickly refute Everett Dick's contention that the Dixie Frontier was pretty rough and crude.[74]

How did the women fare on the rough and crude frontier of the Old Southwest? What did they do? What did they think? Were they all as content as the wife of Gideon Lincecum who migrated with him from South Carolina across Georgia and Alabama Territory to a spot just above present-day Columbus, Mississippi? When at last the hardy emigrants reached the fertile Tombigbee bottoms, Gideon's wife—"with one of her sweetest and most satisfied looking smiles"—expressed her contentment with their new homesite. She assured him of her happiness and exclaimed, "Who could look at this fat game, so easily obtained, this beautiful river with its handsome dry bluff, and gushing spring water and be otherwise?"[75]

Apparently, Gideon Lincecum was as stouthearted and strong backed as he was nimble of mind; so perhaps his wife was as happy as he remembered her. This is a dangerous assumption, however, for little is really known about the feelings and well-being of the typical frontierswoman of the Old Southwest. It is tempting to assume that her lot differed but little from those of her counterparts who later trekked across the plains and mountains to the Pacific Coast and points in between.

Over the past decade scholars such as Glenda Riley, Sandra Myres, and John Mack Faragher have taught us much about women who braved the trans-Mississippi West. But how similar and how different they were from the southern women who moved into the Old Southwest remains to be discovered. Apparently more of the women who moved west of the ninety-eighth meridian were literate. At least, they left more easily followed autobiographical tracks, so to speak.

While a considerable amount is known about the wives of the southern planters, who displayed a greater literacy, very few diaries, journals, or letters of the "plain womenfolk," to coin a phrase, seem to have survived. In other words, wives of the nabobs probably varied considerably from those of the nobodies, but just how they did remains largely a matter of conjecture. Prior to the late antebellum period, all women of the Old Southwest most likely endured common hardships of the trail and hearth. Obviously, the women who had slaves to perform many chores were relieved of much tedium and backaches, but they still may have shared similar stresses and joys of frontier life with their less affluent sisters.

One of the latest studies of women on the frontier indicates that Gideon's wife spoke the truth—that she was deeply pleased by the abundance of the fertile land, by the freshness of the air, and by the purity of the streams. Annette Kolodny in her book the *Land Before Her* hypothesizes that pioneer women dreamed of the wilderness as a garden to be cultivated, using these terms in their fullest meaning. Kolodny contrasts this dream with the perception of the frontiersmen of the wilderness as a virgin land, an unspoiled Eve, to be taken.[76] Hopefully, before too long the validity of her thesis in relation to the Old Southwest will be tested, and in the process perhaps we will learn more about the lives of their children as well.[77]

Whatever her dreams, the reality of the pioneer woman generally was constant and never-ending work both in and outside the cabin. Inhabitants of late-twentieth-century America who enjoy every conceivable kind of labor-saving device probably cannot conceive of the extent of their toils while frequently being with child and facing the dangers of confinement. One wonders how they had time to cook on an open hearth, do dishes, wash clothes, clean the cabin, and run after a wild brood of offspring when cloth diapers were a luxury and disposable ones had not even been dreamed of. Many days they had to tote their own water from the creek or well and split firewood and kindling. When did they find time to dip candles, render lard, boil soap, spin cotton and wool, weave cloth, sew new garments, mend old ones, hoe the garden, feed the chickens?

A few privileged wives of planters were relieved of these burdensome chores and enjoyed enough leisure to read good books, keep diaries, write letters (maybe even poems and prose), play music, dance, spend considerable time in conversation, entertain guests, and visit with neighbors. At the other extreme were the cracker women who were often criticized as awful cooks, bad housekeepers, and just as lazy as their menfolk. Whether they were or not, these Celtic women withstood considerable drudgery and, unfortunately for historians, left little record of what they really thought of their lot.[78]

Just as it is impossible to depict the typical physical terrain of the Old Southwest, it is impossible to portray the typical frontiersman living upon it. The human threads woven across the warp of the social tapestry of the southwestern frontier were as varicolored as the features of its typography. Until recently historians paid attention mainly to the nabobs and generally ignored the nobodies. The work of Frank L. Owsley, however, called attention to the plain folk, and the recent emphasis on minority history scattered the historiographic clouds that had covered several frontier types. Now scholars are focusing on the entire array of humanity that populated the Old Southwest: planters, cattle raisers, African slaves, free Africans, Indians, mixed-bloods (who were found in every category listed except pure-blood Africans and pure-blood Indians), countrymen, traders, soldiers, bureaucrats, scientists, and others, mindful that both sexes were represented in most roles. The varicolored mosaic of different races, cultures, and classes that comprised the Old Southwest suggests that the frontier was far from the homogenizing influence that Frederick Jackson Turner theorized it was.

11

State-Making

If the historian examines only demographic factors in the period from 1795 to 1820, the political fortunes of the Old Southwest (the Orleans and Mississippi Territories in this instance) appear relatively static. The population was surprisingly stable until the end of the War of 1812, and economic growth in the Southwest lagged behind that of other regions to the north and east. These statistics, however, reveal less than the whole story. Political divisions based upon personalities, kinship ties, sectional differences, class distinctions, and national and ethnic origins appeared early and persisted throughout the period. With reference to territorial politics Thomas Jefferson in 1807 observed, "It seems that the smaller the society, the bitterer the dissensions into which it breaks."[1]

Furthermore, the Old Southwest, like most frontier regions, was blessed or cursed (depending upon one's point of view) with ambitious and volatile personalities who both colored and obscured territorial developments. In the Mississippi Territory, these included Andrew Ellicott, Winthrop Sargent, Anthony Hutchins, W. C. C. and Ferdinand Claiborne, Cato West, Andrew Marschalk, Robert Williams, Cowles Meade, Harry Toulmin, James and John Caller, David Holmes, and George Poindexter. Their counterparts in the Orleans Territory included, besides W. C. C. Claiborne who served as governor of both territories, Daniel Clark, Jr., Edward Livingston, and James Wilkinson, not to mention an array of "ancient Louisianians," or Creoles, who deeply resented American control of the region, which prevented them from dominating the offices of influence. In the background appeared men of lesser stature who were no less vocal or outspoken, however, in expressing strong opinions on every topic of importance as well as on some of lesser significance. They delighted in circulating petitions, spreading rumors, indulging in innuendo, and signing memorials and remonstrances of both complaint and supplication to Congress as they sought redress from wrongs, both actual and imagined, as well as personal favors for themselves and their relatives and friends.

In the social and political milieu of the first two decades of the nineteenth century, the road to statehood in the Old Southwest was strewn with obstructions. The Orleans Territory was the first to test the murky waters of national politics on the question of statehood. These efforts immediately ran into opposition from within as well as from beyond its territorial boundaries. In Congress eastern anti-expansionists doggedly opposed the admission of new states to the Union, basing their objection on several grounds, including in the case of the Southwest that of slavery expansion. Even in the face of this powerful opposition, the future state of Louisiana enjoyed certain advantages over neighboring Mississippi Territory. Geographically its area was relatively small, ultimately embracing only 44,930 square miles, as compared with Mississippi Territory's 98,408 square miles. Much of the latter was still controlled by three Indian tribes, a fact that created "islands" of settlement, which confused outsiders. The Louisiana population, on the other hand, was concentrated largely along both banks of the lower Mississippi River and in New Orleans. Though the prospective new state had public land problems aplenty, they were not as extensive or confused as were those in Mississippi Territory.

From the outset of American occupation, the governing body of the Mississippi Territory faced the insurmountable task of trying to draw widely separated settlements into a semblance of unity and harmony. Not only did distances between communities create social and political isolation, but unevenness and diversity of topography were further divisive forces. The extensive domains claimed by the Choctaw, Chickasaw, and Creek Nations constituted another major obstruction to rapid settlement.

By 1810, three areas of territorial settlements had developed; these were on the lower Mississippi, the lower Tombigbee River, and in the elbow of the Tennessee River. Separated as they were geographically, these settlements contained within themselves marked social and economic differences. Over the years no feasible means of controlling internal sectional rivalries and contentions among the settlements was developed. Few historical facts pertaining to the Old Southwest are so well documented as this. Scores of petitions and resolutions originating in the three separate areas reflected the deep feeling of neglect and discrimination felt by the inhabitants of each. At one time or another they questioned the suitability and administration of laws, the applicability of gubernatorial proclamation, judicial inattention, and the apportionment of legislative representation. Even the belabored and overburdened postal system was frequently called to account for its failures and incapabiltities of serving these remote settlements.

Unrest and a nagging feeling of insecurity were disquieting elements in the collective lives of the frontiersmen on the southwestern border. From the creation of the Mississippi Territory in 1798 until the conclusion of the War of 1812, the region was involved in a succession of political crises, none of which was more unsettling than that pertaining to Spanish influence in West Florida and at the mouth of the Mississippi. Even the purchase of Louisiana in 1803 failed to resolve most of the political concerns and uncertainties along the Gulf that had existed since the birth of the republic. President James Madison's West Florida Proclamation of October 27, 1810 generated as much uncertainty as it resolved. Would this acquisition be merged with the Orleans Territory and subsequently with the state of Louisiana, or would it be added to the already unwieldy Mississippi Territory? The anxiety that ruffled the minds of the inhabitants of West Florida was not only the drawing of territorial or state boundaries. Of greater concern to them was the compassionate resolution of a variety of land claims. In many instances it took more than two decades for West Florida claimants to secure an unassailable title to their land.

No political issue in this part of the republic created deeper concern than the adjudication of conflicting land claims. Officially, land matters were under the control of the Federal Government; nevertheless they were basic in the making of almost every local political decision. All political acts and changes in some way reflected this issue, since they invariably raised sectional suspicions and angers. The vast majority of settlers who came to the region before 1795 claimed their lands under British or Spanish grants, and they brought forward their tangled web of indefinable claims to be validated or repudiated. Even after public land sales began in 1809, a small army of squatters or pre-emptioners annually pushed settlement lines beyond those established by government surveyors and then prayerfully sought compassionate recognition of their "hardship" claims. No area of the Old Southwest escaped the chaos of this class of settler. These tenacious settlers quickly classified themselves as oppressed and suffering pioneers who, because of demonstrated hardihood and fortitude, deserved special privilege in the sale of public lands.

Land and its distribution became a central theme for most political actions. It conditioned the advancing cause for statehood perhaps even more than the desire to apply locally the great principles of republican government. Most pioneers clearly understood the legal implications of questionable land claims; comparatively speaking, they viewed the abstract principles of democracy as more remote to their immediate welfare.

The Mississippi Territory embraced one of the largest political units in any part of the Union. But in this case, size was a deterrent to the advancement of statehood. Remoteness of the settlements east of the Pearl River— concentrated above Mobile and to the north near the Tennessee River— aroused intense sectional jealousy toward the more mature counties along the Mississippi River. In May of 1809, petitioners from the Tombigbee country informed the Congress that already 5,000 people were living in their section.[2] Because of their isolation near the lower center of the hundred-thousand square-mile territory, they lamented that they were "but mere cyphers in the Territorial Government." These Tombigbee petitioners acknowledged that the Federal Government bore the "leading expenses" of territorial administration. Even so, their communication stated, the "petitioners are Subjected to enormous taxes for the support of the same Government, while enjoying scarcely any advantages from the expenditure of the public money."[3]

Though nature had long since decreed that their trading area was to be different, settlers along the lower Tombigbee contended that they were as patriotic as those living about Natchez. Since the number of courts in this area was inadequate, there existed the danger that the eastern settlements would become an asylum for derelict social elements, which would menace both life and property. Finally, the people of this area felt a closer bond with the small farmers to the north in Madison County than to the rising aristocracy to the west along the Mississippi. They went so far as to request the division of the Mississippi Territory and the creation of a new territory bounded by the Pearl River of the west, the Tennessee border on the north, Georgia on the east, and Spanish West Florida on the south. These generous boundaries would have enclosed three-fourths of the established territory.[4]

When this petition containing such bold suggestions reached the House of Representatives it was referred to a committee containing such influential representatives as John Breckinridge and George Bibb of Kentucky and Josiah Quincy of Massachussetts. The moment, however, was not propitious for considering either a revision of territorial boundaries or the admission of a new state. Congress was engrossed in issues leading to the War of 1812, and more immediately with the debate over the admission of Louisiana.[5] This in no way, however, dampened the ardor of the determined Mississippi petitioners. Forthcoming supplications sought relief in several other areas.

With perpetual and annoying consistency, the Tombigbee settlers raised the public land question almost monthly. Disturbed by the fact that the Federal Government refused to commence land sales or grant pre-emption rights to intruders on public lands until the confused web of conflicting land claims in the Natchez District had been untangled, they looked to division of the territory as the most practical answer.

The petitions also revealed that these "easterners" suffered from a step-child complex: they simply felt sorely neglected by the territorial administration ensconced so far away on the bank of the Mississippi. In a memorial of this tone, settlers clustered east of the Pearl River cried in anguish:

> Representatives of the American People! We have Petitioned for a Government.—At present we have only the name of one. We know nothing of our Executive Officers:—We know nothing of our Delegates in Congress.—They know nothing of us. We covet not the honor of being part of a State on the Mississippi.—A change of names will not bring us nearer the seat of Government;—it will not give to the Mississippi Legislature any greater knowledge of us,—any greater sympathy with us,—any greater zeal for our security, for our interests, or for our rights.[6]

Clearly, they perceived that statehood without division would not improve the governance of their area.

Led by John Johnston, John Caller, William McGrew, and William D. Felps, the Tombigbee settlers were eloquent in enumerating their handicaps and in cataloging the advantages of independent territorial status for their section. They believed that a territorial division such as they had described would improve land sales, stimulate public spirit among the people, help civilize the Indians, and promote and protect local trade. Once again their petitions were assigned to a special congressional committee, which in turn consigned them to the oblivion of the clerk's holding files.[7]

While settlers east of the Pearl River indulged themselves fulsomely in the right of petition, legislators in the territorial capital on the Mississippi pursued a different strategy. They opposed division of the territory and sought ways of overcoming the disunity. In their minds the Mississippi Territory could not be drawn into a unified state so long as Indians occupied large and divisive blocks of land within its borders. In late 1809, they requested President James Madison to institute proceedings to procure from the Indians by treaty and purchase the tract of country lying on the Yazoo River in order to draw the isolated settlement into a more compact political unit.[8] Again the bone of divisionary separation was laid bare.

Even though the population numbered only 50,352, two years later the territorial legislature requested statehood "with its present limits" in language that leads one to suspect that it sought to take advantage of the fear of war and concern for national security. Curiously, the petitioners referred once to the populace as "purely American" and again as "truly American." Statehood, they argued, would "operate as a strong inducement of Emigration to this County" and would strengthen "the frontier of the United States." Moreover, it would "add to the prospect of discharging the debt due to the State of Georgia." Although the territorial legislature considered the prospects for an early accumulation of the necessary 60,000 people for admission promising, Congress was skeptical. It was even suggested that Congress consider revising the Northwest Ordinance to reduced the population requirement for the creation of a new state.[9]

The President and Congress were well aware of the contractual stipulation of the 1802 Georgia Compact. In surrendering its western lands Georgia had been assured that no new state would be formed from them until there was the requisite 60,000 population. Too, the Federal Government agreed to pay Georgia the sum of $1,250,000 at the time of the admission of a new state as reimbursement for its cession.[10] Between 1811 and 1817 constant reference was made to the Georgia Compact, and it constituted a significant stumbling block to Mississippi's efforts to attain statehood while short of the prescribed population.

During the entire territorial period there prevailed in Mississippi a bizarre psychological sense that the people suffered oppression by the national government because of its repugnance toward territorial subjects and governments. This feeling was stimulated largely by the fact that the governors, judges, territorial secretaries, and all other Federal administrative officials were appointed by the President. For the most part the appointees were outsiders. In order to boost the population and hasten the transition from territory to state, Congress was requested on December 27, 1811, to add the newly annexed West Florida Territory to Mississippi. In support of this request, an impressive list of petitioners argued a commonality of interests and a geographical continuity of streams and land forms to prove that nature itself had outlined clearly defined boundaries for the proposed enlarged territory. Congress responded on May 14, 1812 to this request by adding the area between the Pearl and Perdido Rivers to the Mississippi Territory, thereby settling its raging dispute with the new state of Louisiana.[11]

Nonetheless the question of Mississippi statehood had to await the passage of time. Unless Congress wished to rewrite the Ordinance of 1787 and revise the Georgia Compact, there was no legal excuse for considering the cause of statehood before 1816. In the meantime the territorial legislature asked Congress on November 9, 1812 to maintain the unity of the region and to ignore the territorial congressional delegate's request for division of the territory. Before this latter petition arrived in Congress, the House of Representatives had already prepared an enabling act which looked toward the granting of statehood to Mississippi.[12]

Earlier George Poindexter had reported to the House of Representatives on December 17, 1811, the findings of the special committee regarding independent statehood for the Mississippi Territory, but the report left the boundaries of the new state largely undefined. In the intervening years, advocates of statehood introduced other issues. Some of the petitions that reached Washington from the South contained criticism of the "regal prerogatives" exercised by the territorial governor under the terms of the Northwest Ordinance. It was said he was accountable only to the President for acts of malfeasance and corruption in office. Too, it was said frequently, the governor "felt the power and forgot the right" of the people. The special congressional committee in its report echoed the complaints of various disgruntled territorial groups, but it was unable to overlook a lack of population in the region or to satisfy the terms of both the Northwest Ordinance and the Georgia Compact. Nevertheless, it proposed that new territorial boundaries and a reorganization be undertaken. It suggested that a line be drawn from the mouth of the Iberville River on the Mississippi upriver to the mouth of the Yazoo River, thence eastward to the Georgia border, southward along that border to the East Florida line, thence to the Gulf and around Lakes Pontchartrain and Maurepas (just north of New Orleans) to the beginning point on the Mississippi. At best, these were generalized boundaries that outlined a pancake-like coastal state embracing the strategic river mouths and Gulf Coast, but more particularly it left political control still concentrated in the Natchez area and contemplated robbing Louisiana of a part of its population. The committee guessed this revised territory would contain at least 80,000 souls.[13]

This and other proposals to divide Mississippi Territory brought immediate protest from territorial legislators. However restrictive the terms of the Georgia cession might seem to others, they advocated adhering stoutly to the principle that only one state could be created from the cession. In the eyes of the legislators, since the people of the Mississippi Territory were parties to the 1802 compact equal to Georgia and the Federal Government, any modification of boundaries would require their consent. Thus the legislators disavowed any instructions to the territorial representative to seek Georgia's prior consent to a division, and they pleaded with Congress to enact no legislation authorizing such a condition.[14]

The slowness and inefficiencies of communication added further complications. There was a constant overlapping in time sequences of actions in Washington and the Mississippi Terrritory that caused additional confusion. Nine days after the territorial legislature prepared its memorial, and obviously before it could have reached Washington, Congress passed an enabling act on November 18, 1812. This bill left the original boundaries intact, but only for the time being. It provided that when the population between the Tombigbee River and the Georgia border reached 60,000 free inhabitants a second state would be created there with the assent of the Georgia legislature. Accordingly, in June of 1812, Congress requested the Georgia legislature to approve the formation of two states from the Mississippi Territory under the prescribed conditions.[15] Georgia responded with its official sanction to the creation of one or more states from its ceded western lands.

From 1809 through 1817, there must have been moments when congressmen wondered whether or not they were hopelessly ensnarled in an endless maze of actions and counteractions relating to the creation of a state or states from the Mississippi Territory. Throughout there were differences of opinions and sectional attitudes, and no doubt motives as to the proper time for action. A group of territorial legislators from the southwestern Mississippi River counties sent up a petition in mid-December of 1812 asking that statehood be further delayed. The points at issue were purely pragmatic ones of public land, population, and geographical separation.[16]

This "southern junta" wanted statehood delayed because of lack of funds, inability of land purchasers to pay their debts, the need for a moratorium on debts and foreclosures of land purchases, disruption of the cotton trade due to wartime conditions, and the absence of the legally requisite population. These petitioners were rising cotton planters or their representatives, speaking realistically in terms of what they conceived to be their immediate sectional needs. For them, this was not the right time for statehood.

In Congress, this "Beasley Petition," so named after its first signatory, was held over in the House of Representatives until February 26, 1813, when consideration of it was postponed indefinitely.[17] On the same date the Sentate also discussed the document and concluded that the territorial supplicants had failed to formulate their communication "in sufficiently and unexceptional form" which "a bill of that importance requires." The Senate postponed consideration of Mississippi statehood because of "the embarrassed situation of land titles in that territory" and insufficient population. A second request from Mississippi urged Congress to come to grips with the problem of adjudicating both British and Yazoo land titles before admission "so as forever hereafter, to save the present holders from risks of litigation, expense and ruin."[18] Since the Jay Treaty of 1794 confirmed British land grants issued before the Revolution, these petitioners wanted this issue resolved before statehood. Admission would lead, of course, to the establishment of Federal courts, and, as was pointed out in Chapter 4, many settlers, especially lawyers, feared that British claimants might win lawsuits in Federal courts. In no other territory did land tangles retard statehood to the extent that they did in Mississippi.

The smoke had hardly lifted from the battlefields of the War of 1812 before Mississippi territorial petitioners again busied themselves composing eloquently worded requests to have the eastern part of the territory declared a war ravaged area.[19] The territorial legislature claimed that by 1815 enough immigrants had arrived in the Old Southwest to justify beginning the process of state-making; if there was a lack of population, the rush of new settlers would quickly overcome the deficiency. The legislators believed that the people of the territory were ready to assume the necessary tax burden and that Mississippians should be allowed to make good their wartime pledge to share this burden equally with the central government. In their words, they were "not of that class of political economists who worship at the shrine of a calculating avarice." The Mississippians, however, preferred to undertake this obligation within the context of an independent people. In return, they would "contribute an equitable proportion of the means required to meet the exegencies [sic] of the Nation." As territorialists, they claimed, they were not allowed any more freedom than their forebears had received as subjects of British rule in North America.[20]

Congress assigned this latter petition on January 31, 1815 to the committee on new states, which reported it to the full House a month later with the recommendation that Mississippi Territory be formed into a state as soon as it could be determined there were 60,000 inhabitants within its borders. The statehood committee expressed the opinion that should there not be sufficient population by spring of 1815, postwar immigration would raise the numbers to the required level by the actual date of admission.[21]

The only remaining question about the formation and admission of the new state was whether or not Congress would agree to an enabling law at that date as a favor to the Mississippi Territory, or would it persist on waiting until there was the legal number of inhabitants?[22] Actually the precedent for such action had already been established when Congress admitted Ohio before that state actually had the necessary 60,000 population. The Committee on New States reported to the House of Representatives that it was not certain if the territorial inhabitants were actually ready to assume the political and financial responsibilities of statehood. The committee was aware, however, that the territory had anticipated statehood longer than any other thus far admitted to the Union. It acknowledged that Ohio had not been required to wait until it had the necessary population. Fortunately, by 1815 the nagging question of the Yazoo grants had been extinguished by Congress in 1814 when it had voted to compensate the remaining claimants, and no other feverish issue had arisen to plague the region. Thus the way seemed clear for passage of an enabling law, and the making of necessary preparations for framing a constitution. When the enabling act was submitted to the House in February of 1815, however, the House voted to table it due to disagreement over boundaries.[23]

Despite the apparent willingness of the Committee on New States to promote Mississippi statehood, the same harmony did not prevail in the Old Southwest by this date. Inhabitants east of the Pearl River were even more convinced that they were being discriminated against by settlers along the Mississippi and by the governor and legislators. They were also aware that the bulk of the new immigrants coming into the territory after the War of 1812 had settled in the eastern section, especially in Madison County just below the Tennessee River. Meanwhile the cotton planters and slaveholders on the western river border were gaining a firmer grip on territorial political affairs. There consequently arose a rancorous dispute over a division of the huge territory. Sectional arguments centered around dissatisfactions with legislative apportionment, distances and difficulties of travel and communication, a feeling that the eastern courts were insufficient for the area's needs, and belief that territorial legislation was generally inadequate for all the people. Meanwhile, as residents of the Mississippi River counties saw the same population pattern developing, their doubts about the desirability of unified admission increased. Once they realized that they would be unable to retain political control, leaders west of the Pearl soon viewed separation more favorably.

In a petition to the United States House of Representatives, December 14, 1815, the eastern settlers protested that the "principle of republican government" were being violated "to a most flagrant degree" in the Mississippi Territory, citing the inequitable representation in the Territorial Legislature. Only eight members resided east of the Pearl where the "majority" of the population by 1815 lived, while sixteen members represented the "minority" west of the Pearl. The petitioners expressed outrage at the location of the "seat of our government within six miles of its western limits" in a territory which stretched "three hundred and fifty miles from East to West." After enumerating other discriminations, real and imagined, they declared that they "would tremble at the idea" of statehood without an alteration of "this extraordinary" and "unjust power" in the hands of the politicians of the Natchez District.[24]

Exactly two months later, legislative representatives from east of the Pearl petitioned Congress, requesting that apportionment of members to the prospective constitutional convention should be based upon the free white population only and not upon the whole population, as the slave counties along the Mississippi River preferred. The petitioners contended that the white population east of the Pearl outnumbered that of the other half of the territory, and consequently, they feared that the Territorial Legislature, given the opportunity, would perpetuate this historic sectional imbalance.[25]

Partly in reaction to the various eastern petitions that were sent off to Washington, a convention of representatives from fifteen western counties was held on October 29, 1816, at John Ford's house on the Pearl River just above the thirty-first parallel. After selecting former territorial secretary Cowles Meade as president of the convention, it memorialized Congress not to divide the territory, which only slightly exceeded the size of Virginia or New York but had less capacity "for sustaining a *population* or commanding a *resource.*" The delegates believed that three-fourths of the inhabitants were opposed to division, and that the resources of the more prosperous area of the prospective new state would enable the people to develop institutions worthy of the nation. They also pleaded that Mississippi Territory had a strong claim on the central government for support because of its major role in the late war.[26]

A formal message was prepared to inform the citizens of the five counties not represented in the meeting of the convention's resolutions. Judge Harry Toulmin was instructed to act as a special delegate in the national capital to inform the territorial delegate Dr. William Lattimore as to the desires of the people in the territory. The address was distributed to the members of the Territorial Legislature in a further attempt to maintain the integrity of the territory.[27]

Within a month after the Pearl River convention adjourned, a local census count confirmed that there were nearly 75,000 inhabitants in the twenty territorial counties, with Madison County on the Tennessee accounting for more than 10,000 of this number.[28] The sudden growth of population in the Tennessee bend area convinced the inhabitants of that region that their politcal fortunes were better in a single state. As a result, they switched position. Instead of supporting a division of the territory by drawing an east-west line along the thirty-second parallel, they favored unified admission.

Judge Toulmin, a recent convert to the idea of a single state, arrived in Washington just in time to become involved in a debate with Dr. William Lattimore on the subject of division. When the petition of the Legislative Council of the Territorial Legislature was delivered in the United States House of Representatives on December 9, 1816, it was referred to a special committee. A week later William Lattimore reported for the special committee, which now favored the creation of two states. After reviewing conditions in the wide-ranging territory, it had divided the territory by a north and south line in order to create two states. After recognizing that the people of Mississippi were hopelessly divided on the question, the committee proceeded to explain: "This is, probably, a question on which these people would never agree among themselves; and hence the necessity of the parental interposition of the General Government to decide it for them in such a way as may be best directed to their local interests, and not incompatible with the interest of the United States." The committee emphasized that it did not wish to "retard the admission of either part."[29]

In the opinion of the congressional committee, the formation of a single state from the territory would place an unmanageable problem on a single executive officer to suppress internal disorders, to prevent external invasion, and otherwise to administer the affairs of such a diverse state. There was no continuity of settlements or reciprocity of local interests of the various parts, in the committee's opinion, and there was the distinct probability that both the Congress and the people of the territory could easily find themselves on a collision course because of local interests and jealousies.[30] In addition, the committee doubted if commercial intercourse would ever develop between the Mississippi settlements and those along the Tombigbee or Tennessee until Indian claims were extinguished and the navigable streams cleared and deepened.

When in 1816 the people realized that there were more than 75,000 inhabitants in the Mississippi Territory, the Territorial Legislature memorialized the Congress, December 6, 1816, to enact necessary enabling legislation to permit the formation of an independent state government.[31] On the same date representatives from the eastern counties asked that the territory be divided into two parts, arguing, "It would seem evident that [there] ever will be two great and distinct interests in this Territory . . . Nature never intended the present limits of this Territory to be embraced in one state," they declared, "and if it were effected, that the Interests and welfare of each portion would be jeopardized, and the seeds sown of enduring dissension and animosity." The longer the pen stayed on the paper, the more graphic their words. "In truth, the Western Section of Country [the Mississippi counties], whilst it would endure a Severe Taxation, would loose [*sic*] all the Advantages and blessings of Self Government." Indeed, this truth was now apparent to most Mississippians as was the prospect of inevitable discord within one gigantic state. "The most rancorous jealousies and animosities would spring up," the petitioners reiterated, "The local prejudices of Detached Communities, unfitly brought together, are strong and unconquerable." Thus creation of two states was the only reasonable solution.[32]

At few times and places in the westward movement of the American frontier did so many local, national, sectional, and political forces work in such diverse directions. Not only did the normal sectional rivalry between western and eastern counties prevail (in this case the east was the frontier), but also there were partisan factions within each group. There were those who pretended to favor union with Louisiana; holders of uncertain British land titles feared statehood would lead to their displacement; and certain tax-conscious property holders opposed the formation of an independent state on any condition. Those who favored retention of the original territorial boundaries contended that immigrants who settled in the eastern counties did so with ample knowledge that the nation, through the Georgia Compact, was contractually committed to the creation of a single state.[33]

Aligning with the Mississippi advocates of two states were congressional forces which favored division not to placate its Mississippi proponents but to bolster the waning political strength of the South. Southerners recognized that the population of Eastern and Midwestern states was growing faster than it was in their section of the country. If this trend continued, slavery and its expansion might be threatened by future restrictive legislation. Two new states promised materially to strengthen the South's influence in the Senate, if not in the House of Representatives.[34]

After an almost interminable amount of debating, memorializing and petitioning, the Congress and President James Madison brought the issue of statehood to a head on March 1, 1817. On that date Congress passed and the President signed the act enabling the people of the western part of Mississippi Territory to write a constitution in preparation for admission as a state. Two days later Congress organized the eastern counties into Alabama Territory.[35] Dr. William Lattimore, the territorial delegate, had agreed to a boundary compromise that placed the Mobile district, the Tombigbee settlements, and Madison County in the Alabama Territory. Congress linked the Pascagoula and Pearl River settlements with the Natchez District counties to form the State of Mississippi. As with all compromises, there were ironies and disappointments. The greatest irony is that the faster-growing eastern half of the territory was denied statehood until two years after the admission of the less populous western half, a reality viewed more as an outrage than an irony by the easterners, who were furious beyond words. A lesser irony was the attachment of the Gulf Coastal residents in the environs of the Pascagoula to the State of Mississippi when they identified themselves more closely with Mobile. Conversely, the political leaders west of the Pearl denigrated Dr. Lattimore for awarding Mobile to Alabama Territory. Lattimore retorted that he represented all the former Mississippi Territory; besides he reminded his critics, Mobile was tied to Savannah, Georgia, as closely as it was to Natchez.[36]

The enabling law directed the process by which Mississippi's founding fathers would write the state's fundamental laws. A constitutional convention was to be convened in the territorial capital of Washington on the first Monday in July with delegates elected by county according to a prescribed formula. All qualified white males twenty-one years of age or older were to participate in the elections. The constitution drafted by the delegates had to guarantee Federal control of public lands, but the new state was to receive 5 percent of the net profits from Federal land sales within the state to finance roads and canals after Georgia had received $1,250,000. The enabling act mandated a republican form of government not in any way repugnant to the Federal constitution.

The constitutional convention which assembled in the Methodist meetinghouse on the Jefferson College campus in Washington on Monday, July 7, 1817, was controlled by conservative men. But liberal voices were not totally absent. The matter of statehood had been discussed for such a long time—in fact the longest period of any prospective state, even including Kentucky—that no one was ignorant of the issues to be resolved. Among the forty-seven delegates who took their seats and elected former territorial governor David Holmes as president of the convention were such prominent territorial leaders as George Poindexter, Dr. William Lattimore, Daniel Burnet, Cowles Meade, Walter Leake, Louis Winston, Cato West, John Ford, and Gerard C. Brandon.[37] Seventeen were lawyers, fourteen planters, three farmers, two physicians, two merchants, and one a surveyor. Though most of the delegates had lived in Mississippi for at least ten years, only one, Gerard C. Brandon, had been born in the territory; John McRae of Green County in the Piney Woods area to the east had been there only two years. A majority of the delegates, however, had held public office in the territory and five of them would later serve as governor of the State of Mississippi. Surprisingly, six natives of Pennsylvania were present, but, as might be expected, the others hailed primarily from Virginia, the Carolinas, and Georgia.[38]

The delegates at the constitutional convention had at their disposal copies of the Second Kentucky constitution, along with the Tennessee and Louisiana constitutions. Obviously the assemblage was not composed of crude frontiersmen fresh from backwoods trails and isolated settlements. The convention journal shows that the delegates adopted an elaborate set of procedural rules before getting to substantive issues. At the same time, the delegates left little evidence that they were creative political theorists or sophisticated constitutionalists. The strong vein of conservatism which characterized much of the debate, however, reflected the expanding prosperity of a growing planter-slaveholding society.[39]

After a few of the delegates vented their unhappiness over the boundaries inflicted upon them by the Congress, the convention drafted a preamble which set forth those boundaries and which declared the name of the state to be *Mississippi*. Within its revised boundaries, the new state contained approximately 46,865 square miles of surface area and approximately 29,000,000 acres of land.[40] In 1817, however, no one could make even an educated guess as to how many square miles of the state's territory were either settled or open to settlement. Great blocks of Indian and public lands remained unsurveyed and beyond the immediate reach of settlers. The new constitution, under Federal mandate, reserved these tax free. Also reserved for education was the sixteenth section of each township, which the delegates instructed should be managed in the future without waste or damage. Though public and Indian lands were placed beyond the state's reach, their ultimate sale to private owners was of major concern. The Mississippi River, its navigable laterals, and the Gulf of Mexico were declared free and open channels of local and interstate commerce.

It would be difficult to identify all the influences that bore upon the Mississippi Constitutional Convention or to list the various documents that guided it. The structure of organization, phraseology, and emphases that appear in the finished document, however, reflect a heavy dependence upon the first and second Kentucky constitutions, sometimes as they were translated through those of Tennessee and Louisiana. For example, as a cardinal reason for adopting a constitution, the Mississippi delegates repeated "the rights of life, liberty, and property" statements contained in the Kentucky and Louisiana constitutions. There were only occasional traces of originality involving either fundamental ideology or organization in the Mississippi document. Nor did the delegates reveal in Washington that July any zeal for constitutional debate comparable to that in the Indiana convention, despite the fact that most of the delegates held or had held some kind of public office.

Like many of the American state constitutions framed in the nineteenth century, Mississippi's constitution reflected a high degree of adaptation of older and tested principles to local needs and personal whims. Some of the more interesting adaptations and amplifications occurred in the provisions for granting of suffrage. The document awarded the franchise to every "free white male person of twenty-one years or upward" who either paid a state or county tax or who was enrolled in the militia. Since military service was compulsory, it is doubtful that any real restriction on the franchise existed. Votes on this section indicate that some delegates favored either a property qualification or a meaningful tax requirement.[41]

There were proscriptions placed upon state officials. Members of the House of Representatives were to be twenty-two years of age, two years a resident of the state, and owner of 150 acres of land in Mississippi or of real estate valued at $500. Senators were to be thirty-six years of age, four years a resident, and possessors of 300 acres of state lands or $1,000 worth of real estate. Governors were to be chosen by a direct vote of the people, but the votes were to be delivered to the speaker of the House of Representatives who counted them and announced the results in the presence of the General Assembly. This official was to be thirty years of age, twenty years an American citizen, five years a state resident, and the owner of 600 acres of land or $2,000 worth of real estate.[42]

Because a major issue in the administration of Mississippi Territory had been the maintenance of adequate courts, the delegates paid considerable attention to the establishment of an effective and independent court system. Thus a portion of the judicial article was an original contribution, even though it bore traces of transfer from other state provisions. Unusual was the restriction that no judge was to be appointed or continued on the bench who had reached the age of sixty-five years. The judicial article outlined a somewhat complicated system of courts. Though the same judges sat individually in their home districts as Superior Courts of original jurisdiction and collectively as a Supreme Court with final appellate jurisdiction, the judge whose decision was on appeal to the Supreme Court could not "constitute one of the court to determine the question of such decision." No doubt delegates were deeply conscious of the bitter discontent expressed in petitions from the southeastern part of the territory in the first decade of the century. An effort to create an entirely separate Supreme Court failed, however. The constitution gave the legislature latitude to establish chancery courts, probate courts, and justices of the peace.[43]

In formulating the general provisions, delegates had ample opportunity to assert their views as to the management of the state's internal affairs. In this area they asserted an extremely conservative philosophy of government and society. Paradoxically the right to hold office was denied persons who did not profess a belief in God, but ministers and priests were barred from holding public office. In this postwar era of inflation and excessive organization of banks, the constitutional delegates reserved to the state the right to subscribe one fourth of the stock of any bank granted a public charter.[44]

Reflective of the prevailing social attitudes, divorces were to be granted only after suits in chancery were tried and the award of a divorce was sanctioned by a two-thirds vote of the General Assembly. Wisely, the constitution prevented the organization of any new county unless it contained 576 square miles or more. In keeping with the doctrine embodied in the Northwest Ordinance, it proclaimed that education "shall forever be encouraged" and that the sixteenth section of each township should be leased in strict conformity with the basic objective of the Federal grant.[45]

When it came to dealing with the vital area of slavery, the constitutional delegates relied heavily upon the constitution of Kentucky, which protected the rights of both the slave owner and the slave. This article guaranteed the right to import slaves, provided that no owner should permit his chattels to become public charges, prohibited the importation of African slaves, required owners to treat slaves with humanity, and reserved to the General Assembly the authority to develop a slave code, including permission for owners to manumit slaves. In cases when the slave had "rendered to the state some distinguished service," the state could emancipate the slave provided it fully compensated the owner. The document prohibited the introduction of slaves who had committed high crimes. While slaves were denied an inquest by a grand jury, their trials were regulated by law, and in capital cases the General Assembly could not deprive them of an impartial trial by a petit jury.[46]

The Mississippi constitutional delegates turned to older and tested sources for definitions of human rights. With modest editorial changes, they set forth in the twenty-ninth section of Article I, entitled "Declaration of Rights," all the essential elements of individual and social freedoms guaranteed in the United States Constitution and later transcribed in the Kentucky, Tennessee, and Louisiana documents.[47] On the whole, the Mississippi constitutionalists produced a document that contained little of either original political philosophy or what could be defined as a distinct frontier contribution. Rather it reflected what was to become an enduring fact in state-making along the American frontier—an adaptation of the classical American political and federal forms to the needs of the new state. This fact inspired a New England newspaper editor to observe it as "so similar to the constitutions of many of the other states, that its perusal does not excite much interest."[48]

Basically the leadership of the Mississippi Constitutional Convention had been schooled in the older and settled states long before they reached the frontier of the Old Southwest. The generally conservative document produced by them was not, however, without some liberal tinges. As mentioned above, there was virtually no restriction on the suffrage for free adult males, the people directly elected both the governor and the lieutenant governor as well as the sheriffs and coroners. In addition, the section on slaves contained some liberal provisions. Contrary to what one might expect, men from the western counties such as Dr. William Lattimore and Cato West provided the liberal leadership that emerged. The convention journal indicates that George Poindexter, subsequently Mississippi's first congressman and second governor, was its leading member. Had he prevailed completely, however, the document would have been even more conservative.[49]

Poindexter, who had become attorney general for the district west of the Pearl shortly after his 1802 arrival in Mississippi Territory, later served as a territorial judge and delegate to Congress. His political career, punctuated by episodes in a continuous vitriolic feud with *Washington Republican* editor Andrew Marschalk, was one of the most colorful and tempestuous in the territory. After his term as Mississippi's second governor, he became a United States Senator. But he fell into disfavor with the majority of his constituents by opposing President Jackson's successful effort to kill the Second National Bank and because of his haughty and irascible manner.[50]

At noon on August 15, 1817 the delegates signed the completed constitution, an event "immediately announced by a federal salute from a six pounder, stationed near the hall of the Convention." After the celebration, Mississippians wasted little time implementing the long-awaited document. In September state and congressional elections were held. Meanwhile on August 28, David Holmes, in one of his last actions as governor of Mississippi Territory, forwarded an authenticated copy of the new constitution to Secretary of State John Quincy Adams together with an account of the measures taken to implement it. The electorate expressed its appreciation to Holmes in September by choosing him to be the state's first governor, and in October the General Assembly elected Walter Leake and Thomas H. Williams as Mississippi's two Senators. On December 10, 1817 the painfully divisive road to statehood ended when President James Monroe affixed his signature to the congressional resolution that admitted Mississippi into the union "on an equal footing with the original states, in all respects whatever."[51] The nation now had twenty states.

The strokes of President Monroe's pen opened an era of population and political expansion in the southwestern cotton-slave kingdom and eventually gave rise to a significant sectional force in the republic. On that December day of 1817, approximately half of Mississippi's total area was still in the hands of the Chickasaw and Choctaw tribes, and the overwhelming portion of the land was virgin forest yet to be surveyed and offered for sale. While it would be nearly a century before the forests were decimated, the same was not true for the Indian Nations.[52]

In this era of political fermentation and change, no historic force stood more clearly revealed in the interminable arguments and counter-arguments over Mississippi statehood and boundaries than emergent sectionalism. If any event in the history of the Old Southwest was inevitable or preordained, it was the division of Mississippi Territory. On February 4, 1817, Congressman Charles Tait of Georgia, a friend of John W. Walker of Madison County, reported from a special house committee a bill to create the Alabama Territory. Basically, the Tait bill outlined boundaries already established with the creation of Mississippi, directed appointment of a governor, secretary, and judges, and declared that territorial legislatures presently serving from the counties now comprising the Alabama territory shall constitute the territorial assembly. The Tait bill became law on March 3, 1817. Until the Alabama territorial government—to be located in St. Stephens—was established, Mississippi territorial officials remained in authority. Likewise, laws of the Mississippi Territory applied until superseded by new statutes enacted in St. Stephens. Many officials at the local level remained in office under new commissions. Funds which remained in the territorial treasury in March of 1817 were divided between Mississippi and Alabama.[53]

President James Monroe appointed as territorial governor Georgia planter William Wyatt Bibb, a former physician, congressman, and United States Senator. Bibb's two-year term was a quiet one, compared with the administration of David Holmes, last governor of Mississippi Territory. However, border difficulties with the Seminoles, rivalries between Tennessee Valley settlers and those along the Tombigbee, the emotional tensions over land sales and titles, and the inrush of new settlers generated excitement if not serious problems.[54]

Perhaps the most controversial issue involved the final and permanent location of the newly designated boundary between Mississippi and the Alabama Territory. Settlers on both sides of the Tombigbee were equally aroused. Rumors that the border might actually be shifted to annex the Tombigbee channel and the port of Mobile to Mississippi provoked a rash of petitions to Congress which were extremely emotional. The petition of a group of Tombigbee and Alabama River settlers who vigorously protested rumored annexation to Mississippi was typical of the response. Their section, they sarcastically reminded Congress, had not fallen victim in an imperial conquest to be transferred "like the vassals of European potentates, from one sovereignty to another." As free Americans, their rights to form their own government were inherent. Passionately they argued that the divisional line along the Tombigbee formed "the most inconvenient & unnatural boundary imaginable." They explained why:

Such a boundary separates neighbors. It places under different governments those who are in the habit of daily intercourse. It facilitates the invasion of both civil & criminal process, & multiplies the means of rendering the laws a laughing stock to the lawless. . . . It will frequently separate one part of a family from the other, & leave the plantation of a citizen in one state & his mansion house in another.[55]

The rivers that flow into the Gulf through the Mobile Bay, the Alabamians exhorted, "ought to be subject to the regulation of a single sovereignty."[56]

Since the newly-formed Alabama Territory lacked congressional representation at the moment, the inhabitants regarded the right to petition as their only means of making themselves heard in the national capital. Supplementing the former petition, territorial legislators in March of 1818 protested reduction of their territory by moving the border eastward to the course of the Tombigbee. "The interest of this Territory in all the rivers flowing into the Bay of Mobile is obvious, permanent, and nearly exclusive," they explained. These "kindred streams . . . naturally belong to the Territory of Alabama." Furthermore, they waxed poetically, "They have their sources in her bosom. They run through the very heart of the Country." The legislators closed by beseeching Congress to postpone any decision until the admission of Alabama as a state when "the two parties shall be placed on a footing of equality."[57] Though a bill was introduced in Congress on April 1, 1818 to slightly move the southernmost line between Mississippi and Alabama eastward and to clearly mark the entire boundary, no action was taken on it after the first reading. The boundary remained as originally drawn in the March 1, 1817 Mississippi enabling act.[58]

The fermentation which agitated other territories along the American frontier stimulated the public mind of Alabama. With Mississippi and Indiana already admitted to the Union, and the Illinois Territory in the process of seeking admission, Alabamians looked forward to changing their own status. Territorial legislators reminded Congress that actually Mississippi had only 47,000 inhabitants in 1817, and that neither Indiana nor Illinois had more population than Alabama Territory. They requested immediate enactment of an enabling law. In 1818 a local census indicated the territory had 45,871 whites, 21,384 slaves, and 339 free people of color—a total population of 67,594.[59]

On March 2, 1819, Congress passed an act enabling the people of Alabama Territory to write a constitution and form a state government. As in the case of Mississippi, the law prescribed the process for the election of delegates, defined the state's borders, dictated public land policies, and outlined the incorporation of republican principles. Even if there were not the necessary 60,000 then actually in the territory, the rapid inflow of immigrants assured that this number would be there by the time the constitution could be framed and ratified.[60]

The Alabama constitutional convention assembled in Huntsville on July 5, 1819. It had perhaps the best precedential background for the making of a constitution of any convention to date. Although the Alabama Territory was scarcely more than a year old, it had behind it territorial experiences extending almost a quarter of a century. The trials and tribulations of the Mississippi Territory were also a part of the Alabama heritage. Delegates who gathered in the convention were experienced in matters of local government and were sectionally sensitive to the needs of their area. Indeed, many of them had prepared and signed the vehement petitions cited above. The scholarly Huntsville attorney and planter John W. Walker who had married into a prominent family in his native Georgia was elected president of the convention. Walker rivaled Judge Harry Toulmin in political prominence. Among the delegates were such famous old Tombigbee–Alabama–Black Warrior pioneers as Sam Dale, the Indian fighter, Toulmin, and others. The apportionment of delegates had been meticulously made, and the southern Tombigbee communities were well represented as reflected by their influence in the convention.[61]

Original contributions of a frontier nature and origin written into the document prepared in Huntsville must be considered subtle. Immediately available to the delegates were the four more recently drafted constitutions of Louisiana, Mississippi, Indiana, and Illinois.[62] Besides these, there were at hand the old standbys of Kentucky and Tennessee. While a comparison of the Mississippi and Alabama constitutions reveals a remarkable similarity in general structure, some fundamental differences appear. The Alabama Constitution reflected the rising influence of the tide of yeoman farmers and the long-standing grievances in the older, isolated settlements. The Huntsville statesmen took care to introduce their instrument directly in the name of the people while the Mississippians had written, "We, the representatives of the people."

In their declaration of rights the Mississippi constitutionalists had guaranteed religious freedom as a general principle, but later in enumerating the general powers of government declared those persons "who denied the existence of a God" ineligible to hold office. Alabamians had a strong guarantee of religious freedom, but officers of the state were required to take an oath that enlisted God's help in the performance of their duties. Otherwise a man could hold office without making further profession of belief of God.[63]

A more liberal feature of the Alabama Constitution was the removal of property qualifications for voting and office holding. Residential requirements for office holding ranged from two to four years; legislators had to be white males, twenty-one years of age or older. The document required the governor, who served for two years, to be thirty years of age, a native American, and four years a resident of Alabama. It extended the right to vote to "every white male, twenty-one or older, who was a citizen of the United States and who had resided in Alabama at least a year prior to an election." Except for persons accused of "treason, felony or breach of the peace," voters were "privileged from arrest" while traveling to and from the polls or while casting their ballots. Representatives in the state legislature served for one year, senators for three years. No provision was made for a lieutenant governor, and the matter of succession was left in the hands of the legislature. In this case the delegates failed to profit by the error Kentucky made in its 1792 constitution, a fact which Harry Toulmin well knew.[64]

In 1819, with the explosive situation along the southern border of East Florida from which sprang the Seminole raiders, Alabama delegates made fairly elaborate provision for a state militia. Officers of this force were to be elected or appointed according to later direction of the legislature. The governor, who was authorized to appoint an elaborate corps of aides-de-camp, had the power to "call forth the militia to execute the laws of the State, to suppress insurrections, and repel invasion." The constitution also provided that conscientious objectors could escape service if they paid for "an equivalent for personal service."[65]

In no section of the constitution did the power of the citizenry reflect itself more than in the formulation of the lengthy judicial article. The phraseology and provisions reflected the historic complaints, justified or unjustified, to Congress of the ineffectiveness, inadequacies, and inequities of the territorial judiciary. The constitution outlined in extensive detail a system of courts responsive to the will of the general assembly, almost to the point of wholesale legislative invasion of the judiciary. It provided for a supreme court, circuit courts, and a court in chancery, and it declared that no judge could serve who had attained the age of seventy. The general assembly elected the attorney general and as many solicitors as it deemed necessary.[66]

The two constitutions reflected a difference in attitude toward education. Mississippians devoted but three lines to education: "Religion, morality, and knowledge, being necessary to good government, the preservation of liberty, and the happiness of mankind, schools, and the means of education, shall for ever be encouraged in this state."[67] Conspicuously absent was a provision for financial support for public education at any level. By contrast, the drafting committee in Huntsville directed the Alabama general assembly not only to administer prudently the sixteenth-section lands preserved for support of education, but also to establish a "State University, for the promotion of the arts, literature, and science." Furthermore legislators were—as early as possible—to endow the university and provide for the "improvement and security" of the endowment.[68] This permanent provision seems to bear close kinship to the one in the Indiana Constitution in 1816. Mississippi, on the other hand, did not establish its state university until 1848.

Alabama's constitutional fathers directed the establishment of a state bank with as many branches as future general assemblies thought expedient. The state was to own two-fifths of the stock and exercise a proportionate amount of control and liability. Furthermore, no bank could begin operation until half the stock issue had been subscribed in gold and silver, the legislature could call in obligations at any time, and existing banks upon request might be absorbed into the public system.[69]

As was the case in Mississippi, the Alabama Constitution, completed on August 2, 1819, was transmitted directly to Washington without ratification by the people. Some four months later, Alabamians received a Christmas present from Congress in the form of statehood which became a reality on December 14, 1819. Actually Alabama had begun functioning as a state on August 2 when Governor Bibb, who considered congressional approval a certainty, forthwith organized the state government.[70]

The creation of the states of Mississippi and Alabama involved a rare complexity of human and political pressures. Large areas of both states remained virginal wilderness, even though expansion of settlement outran Indian treaty negotiations as well as the platting and sale of public lands. Alabama especially felt the impact of the panic of 1819 in its inceptive years. The establishment and control of banks under the constitutional mandate became as serious a political issue as it was a financial one. Paper money, inflation, and bank management all agitated the public mind. The banking issue grew into a struggle of private versus public controls, and resulted in a bitter factionalization of local politics.[71]

Admission of the two states in the southwestern corner of the young republic strengthened the national position of the South, but it also introduced a new and influential sectional force. Eyes of Northern politicians focused more intently upon the growing cotton-slave South with its peculiar, particular social and economic complexities. Without a doubt, the addition of four new proslavery Senators contributed significantly to the controversy over the admission of Missouri, and in this sense, the Old Southwest and its destiny seemed inextricably intertwined with that of the vast domain known as the Louisiana Purchase.

Within the states themselves, widening diversities of social, economic, and political interests and attitudes reflected the vagueness of the line of demarcation between the rising yeoman and planter classes. Recurring census reports revealed the progress of a cotton economy, an increasing slave population, and the expansion of an intensely rural subsistence agrarian economy. The historian is hard-pressed to identify when the Old Southwest frontier vanished. If the test of public land availability were used, then frontier conditions prevailed in some areas until well after 1890. Too, it would be equally difficult to draw an intelligible line between what was a staple cotton-plantation culture, and what, basically, was a rural small farmer backwoods society that reacted to public issues in the local and regional context of what soon would be labeled Jacksonian Democracy. Emergent political parties, however, had their central roots anchored rather deeply in the territorial era. Politically, after 1820, much of the Old Southwest underwent transformation from frontier to an Old South of antebellum distinction. Socially, it remained, to a large extent, the frontier.

12

Eclipsing Ancient Nations

"Removal was not rape. It was an exchange of land based on the premise that the two races could not live together, that the Indians occupied more land than they needed or would cultivate, and that the Indians, where they were, endangered the frontier and menaced not only settlers but the American nation itself. Removal involved consent, but it was a limited—if not distorted—kind of consent. . . . In theory, removal protected everyone: whites, the Indians who stayed, and those who removed. Everyone benefited."[1]

Every educated American will react to these thoughts of Robert V. Remini: some in agreement, others in violent disapproval. But they will react, and chances are their minds will turn to Andrew Jackson. Though the roots of the concept extend at least back to President Jefferson, no American is so closely identified with the policy of Indian removal as Jackson. Nor is any other the subject of such scholarly controversy.[2]

The controversy relates to Jackson's motivation rather than to his leadership in Indian removal. Few students of American history would quibble with Remini when he asserts that Jackson, "more than any other man . . . was responsible for the removal of the Indians to the remote reaches west of the Mississippi River."[3] Many, however, will disagree with Remini's conclusion that Old Hickory was not an "Indian hater." Until the 1970s, the majority of Americans, historians included, subscribed to the "devil theory" of interpreting Jackson's motivation. Simply put, hatred drove Jackson who supposedly felt that "the only good Indian is a dead Indian." Though such a simplistic view discredits one of America's greatest heroes and ignores the historic nuances of the Old Southwest, it was, nevertheless, standard academic fare for generations.

In 1969 revisionists such as Francis Paul Prucha convincingly repudiated this long-accepted belief.[4] Jackson's obsession, explain the revisionists, was for national security, and his hatred was of the British who annihilated his family and orphaned him at an early age. He was a fierce combatant intent on overwhelming his enemy, whomever he might be. Undeniably, Jackson also hungered for the status and honor that accompanied rank. And most assuredly he was determined to implement the removal of the Eastern Indians.

According to Prucha, Jackson's complex reasons were humanistic and legalistic. The dream of assimilation never materialized; protection of their enclaves was unfeasible; destruction was unacceptable. Hence, to Jackson, the only humanistic recourse was removal west of the Mississippi. There the conflict of state versus federal jurisdiction might be avoided. Because Jackson denied that the tribes constituted sovereign nations, they had no absolute title to their lands nor could they establish independent enclaves within states. So, Jackson's reasoning continued, Congress should rule them as it did the whites.[5]

Finally, according the revisionists, the record of Jackson's conduct during the Creek War, the War of 1812, and the Seminole War belies the charge of an inherent hatred for Indians. In those campaigns the general dealt with hostile as well as friendly Indians with justice, fairness, and humanity. On more than one occasion, he punished officers who violated their rights. Not only did he welcome Indians as allies, but the friendship established with a number of chiefs lasted a lifetime. Most often cited as evidence of Jackson's lack of racial hatred is his adoption of an infant boy, Lincoya, orphaned in battle, who was reared with Jackson's family at the Hermitage.[6] Perhaps his adoption of Lincoya symbolizes the paternalistic attitude that directed his approach to Indian affairs. If any single attitude of Jackson's stood out, it was paternailism, not hatred.[7] However, the jury is still out, so far as the revisionist case is concerned. The "devil theory," in the minds of the American public and of many scholars, still best explains Jackson's Indian policies.[8]

In one sense, Remini was right: "More than any other man," Jackson was responsible for removal of Indians to the west of the Mississippi. Yet in another, Remini was wrong: For Jackson was as much an implementor [reflector] as an instigator [a director] of western policies. He personified or epitomized the post–War of 1812 nationalistic, expansionistic West. He was their agent—an extremely powerful, effective agent, but nevertheless an agent.

The forces of expansionism had been throttled since the end of the French and Indian War. King George's Proclamation of 1763 deterred many pioneers, but others ignored his efforts to keep them out of the trans-Appalachian domain of the Five Civilized Tribes. The American War for Independence held some migrants back; others it encouraged. Meanwhile a Yankee schoolteacher invented an effective, easily replicated cotton gin. Now the cotton planters coveted Indian lands as did the cattle raisers and speculators. And foreign intervention by England and Spain legitimatized their surge into the Old Southwest. In the cause of national security and modified Puritanism, they poured southwestward, waving the flag of the United States and, figuratively speaking, banners of several sects of fundamental Protestantism. The land-hungry frontiersmen also resented Indian claims to such vast tracts in relation to their numbers—land on which they "saunter about upon like so many wolves and bares [sic]."[9]

Such were the expansionist forces of which Andrew Jackson was the agent, or, if you choose, the personification. One can only understand his actions in the context of *his* times, not *ours*.

Meanwhile, within the Indian nations of the Old Southwest, forces of cultural dissolution and deterioration set in motion by contact with Europeans had taken their toll. Weakened and divided, the tribes could not long withstand the pressures and bribes of the treaty commissioners representing the United States of America, more vibrant and confident than ever after defeating the British for a second time. It is doubtful that Washington officials realized the extent to which the long-standing "civilization" policy had succeeded.[10]

By the eve of removal, many of the tribal ways had been eradicated. To a large extent the plow had replaced the bow. Herds of cattle, swine, sheep, and goats grazed near the towns, and flocks of poultry pecked and scratched around the huts. Indeed, some of the herds of cattle were extensive and were tended by men on horses of superior quality. Exportation of beef, pork, and cotton was common. After the War of 1812, cotton had increased in importance within the Indian nations just as it did elsewhere in the South. In 1830, for instance, a government agent estimated that the Chickasaw would export a thousand bales.[11]

The tribesmen were developing an economic system modeled after that of the Anglo-Americans. With cash from their agricultural surpluses (and decreasing number of furs and skins) they purchased luxuries as well as necessities. There were some role changes, too. Men increasingly cultivated the fields so the women could spin, weave, sew, and tend to a widening range of housekeeping chores. Other aspects of the Anglo-American society were emulated, including the mode of dress and acquisition of African slaves in greater numbers.

To paint a picture of bucolic calm among the tribes during the pre-removal era, however, is to create a false image or to depict only the façade. Beneath the surface seethed destructive forces of discontent and dissent; neither the ethnic nor cultural homogeneity of their societies existed any longer, if they ever were truly homogeneous.

Now Native American society consisted of Indians, whites, Africans, and mixed bloods, and it was the growing dominance of the latter group which contributed most to the factionalism which characterized the tribes on the eve of removal. Europeans had lived among the Indians since the explorations of De Soto. Such "countrymen," however, were rare until the seventeeth century when the trade rivalry among the British, French, and Spanish intensified. Then their numbers began to significantly increase. All the while they took Indian wives, and because of the matrilineal social structure of the tribes, their mixed-blood progeny inherited the status of their mothers. It was not, however, until the end of the French and Indian War that the mixed bloods ascended in significant numbers to leadership roles.

With each year their presence and power increased, and by the time of removal, the more assertive mixed bloods formed an aristocracy in the tribes. Because they were bilingual, generally literate, and conversant with the ways of Europeans, Jeffersonian paternalism worked very much in favor of these descendants of Tories, traders, and retired soldiers. So much so that they soon acquired valuable farms, plantations, herds, and commercial enterprises of all sorts.

Social stress took its toll. Even before the ascendancy of the mixed bloods to political and economic leadership, the tribes had been splintered over international relationships. During the colonial period, much energy had been dissipated over pro-French and pro-British factionalism. Now, an even more emotional issue sapped their strength. Mixed bloods, numbering between one-fifth and one-fourth of the populations, controlled tribal politics and often used their power to economic advantage. Meanwhile their more reticent full-blooded kinsmen increasingly withdrew. Many of them lost leadership roles by default; others drowned their sorrows in drink.

To view the removal issue within the tribes in the simple terms of mixed bloods versus full bloods would be misleading. During the negotiation of cession treaties, many mixed bloods protected their considerable interests, and in a sense sold out their full-blooded relations. Others, however, fought removal with a vehemence. The growing rift between the mixed-blood factions became clearly evident in the years immediately following the Creek War. James Pitchlynn (son of John Pitchlynn), Middleton Mackey, and Edmund Folsom, for example, represented the pro-Jackson or pro-American faction of the Choctaw. On the other hand, Levi Perry and David Folsom, an active Presbyterian preacher, opposed removal. So from any perspective, removal defies simplistic analysis. It was not simply white versus Indians; nor was it mixed bloods versus full bloods. It was an unfathomable human problem that defies simple description.[12] While it would be inaccurate to suggest that any single motivation bound factions together during the removal debates, self-interest may have guided more people than any other factor.

Though they played no direct role in the removal controversies, the presence of African slaves had several significant influences on Native American societies in the Old Southwest—all of which ultimately affected the cultural dissolution of the tribes. Slavery heightened the aristocratic pretensions of the white countrymen and the mixed bloods who owned most of the blacks. Because slaves contributed to the improvement of properties, they enhanced the removal settlements in some cases, and their presence did increase the speed of role changes. The blacks, many of whom spoke English, also bridged the communicatioon gap, and in this manner increased the rate of acculturation. Finally, though not directly germane to removal, slavery greatly influenced the character of Indian society in the trans-Mississippi West during and after the Civil War.

Such was the life of the Native Americans at the time that Andrew Jackson inflicted his punitive document upon them at Fort Jackson—a document that marks one of the pivotal points in the entire history of the Indians of the Old Southwest and of the continent.[13] Not only was the Creek Nation shattered, but the United States was now headed rapidly down an irreversible course of obliterating the tribes as sovereign nations. With a few scratches of the pen at Fort Jackson, millions of acres of choice land awaited the auction gavel of the speculator. And this was only the beginning. Flushed with crushing victories over the Red Sticks at Horseshoe Bend and over the redcoats at the Crescent City, Jackson-led westerners did not relent until they had wrested from the Indians virtually every acre of their ancestral land in the Old Southwest.

The celebrations of the victories over the Creeks and the British had hardly subsided before commissions led by Jackson and his close associate, John Coffee, imposed cession treaties on the Cherokee, Chickasaw, and Choctaw in the fall of 1816.[14] Combining harsh threats with the bribery of important chiefs, Sharp Knife, Jackson's Indian name after the Fort Jackson Treaty negotiations, extracted millions of acres from the Cherokee and Chickasaw, and then Coffee, closely following Jackson's instructions, with little difficulty convinced the Choctaw to cede the balance of their land east of the Tombigbee. These three acquisitions, combined with that at Fort Jackson, opened to white settlement a strip hundreds of miles in width and depth.

National security as well as expansionism were apparently foremost on his mind as Jackson pressed the Indians for the huge concessions. "The whole southern country from Kentucky and Tennessee to Mobile has been opened up by the late treaties" proclaimed Jackson, who cited the many advantages offered by the acquisitions. In particular, he stressed the protection of the United States boundary with Spain. From the moment of Jackson's involvement in military and political affairs in the Southwest, he was constant in his strong desire for the expulsion of Spain from all of Florida.[15] It would be naive to believe that he was unaware of the economic boom the cessions would afford the land speculators, many of whom were his friends. The influx of as many settlers as possible, however, fitted into his obsession with security. Land speculation, for Old Hickory, was a "declining motive."[16]

Important as these 1816 treaties were, they pale in comparison with the one signed on July 17, 1817, with the Cherokee at Hiwassee, Tennessee. On that day a certain principle was applied for the first time. It was the removal of the Indians to the west of the Mississippi River. So, compared to the initial application of that principle, the fact that 2 million acres were added to the public domain was inconsequential, a fact acknowledged by the commissioners led by Jackson. "The cession of land is not important, but the Principle Established leads to great importance."[17]

Why was the "principle" first applied against the Cherokee, who in many ways were the most "civilized" of all North American Indians? The answer dates back to 1808 when the Cherokees agreed to exchange land east of the Mississippi upon the occupation of equal acreage in Arkansas. Though several thousand Cherokee had migrated to Arkansas in the meanwhile, no land was ceded to the Federal government in exchange. At Hiwassee in 1817, Jackson confronted leaders from both sides of the Mississippi not only with the issue of compensatory grants, and also with the proposition that the balance of the Cherokee migrate to Arkansas. Heads of households who chose not to leave would receive 640 acres each, but they henceforth would be subject to state laws.[18]

The chiefs balked, explaining to Jackson that the 1808 delegation to Washington had not been authorized to divide the Cherokee Nation. Besides, the purpose of their visit had been to wish President Jefferson well at the conclusion of his tenure in office. Jackson surmised that the

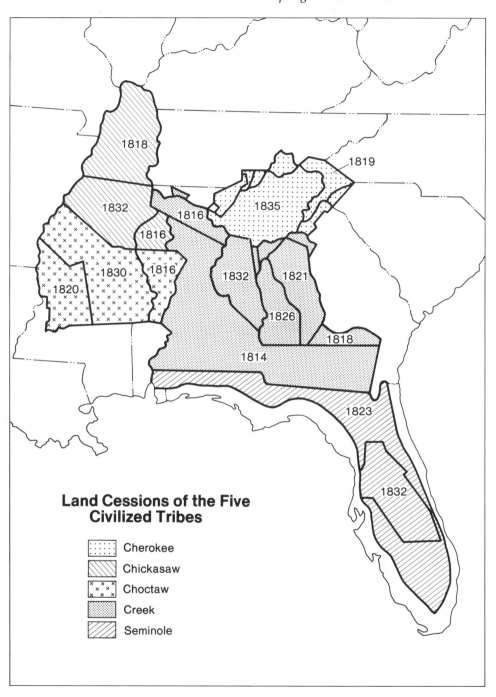

Land Cessions of the Five Civilized Tribes

Cherokee
Chickasaw
Choctaw
Creek
Seminole

mixed-bloods and evil white men were at the root of the resistance. But Jackson remained cool and collected. First, he forced individual chiefs, known to be friendly, to confirm the government's interpretation. Then Jackson stunned the headmen with an interrogatory. Were they prepared to do battle with him and suffer the same destruction as the Creeks? The opposition faded, and on July 8, 1817, the principle of removal became a precedent.[19]

The 1817 Cherokee treaty may have provided the precedent of removal, but it was the 1820 Treaty of Doak's Stand that provided the model of Indian removal.[20] Jackson was in a somber mood at that time as he traveled to the treaty site to the north of present-day Jackson, Mississippi, on the Natchez Trace. The Adams–Onís treaty, so vital to continued American expansion, awaited ratification in the Senate. He had played an active advisory role in developing the American position, especially relative to Texas. He favored Spanish retention of that province in order to keep distance between Americans and the Native Americans whom he was confident would be removed from the Old Southwest. Though his recent near censure for the invasion of Florida during the Seminole War added to his serious mood, the Missouri crises particularly troubled him. Division over slavery he could not control, but removal of the Indians to west of the Mississippi was a vital prerequisite to national growth and harmony, which he could effect.

Jackson's preoccupation with removal reflected the preferences of many westerners who coveted rich lands as the tide of migration rolled westward after the War of 1812. With the growth of the cotton culture, the rich river bottoms and delta lands were especially prized. Actually, his constituents probably were more selfishly motivated than was Jackson. Whatever the motives, the pressures were there.

The "Report of the Congressional Committee of Public Lands," chaired by Mississippi congressman George Poindexter, offers a good example of the attitude toward the Choctaw domain when it criticized the reluctance of tribal leaders to relinquish additional acreage in Mississippi. The committee, furthermore, recommended that the government not permit further emigration of Choctaw onto public lands west of the Mississippi without specific permission and took note of large parcels of unused land in their control. "The Choctaws possess the east bank of the Mississippi for a distance of near three hundred miles, which will remain an uninhabited wilderness for centuries to come, unless their claim is extinguished, and the country populated by the United States."[21] Then the point was made that so long as the Choctaw could hunt at will beyond the Mississippi they would never cede their eastern lands.

Jackson and his fellow commissioner, General Thomas Hinds, could hardly have agreed more with the Poindexter committee. The Choctaw must either consent to exchange their Mississippi lands for western preserves or be brought under the statutory jurisdiction of the newly formed state of Mississippi. The Choctaw, however, opposed both cession and/or exchange of land. Two of the elder chiefs, Mushulatubbee and Pushmataha, eloquently explained their predicament. "If a man should give one-half his garment, the remainder would be of no use; and take two fingers from the hand, the remainder would be of little use. When we had land to spare, we gave it, with very little talk."[22] Now they had no land to spare.

The dilatory manner in which the Choctaw responded to the treaty summons reflected their lack of enthusiasm for the expected message. The headmen had been propagandized against attending the council at Doak's Stand and it became necessary to send runners through the nation to urge the leaders to attend. When they did arrive, they were reluctant to assemble, preferring to play their skull-cracking stick ball than to listen to the patronizing talk of the white commissioners. Besides, they had heard it all before and they opposed its objective.

Another irritant to Jackson at first was the presence of the former agent to the Choctaw, Colonel Silas Dinsmoor, who had terribly upset Old Hickory in 1812 with his strict enforcement of passport regulations of the Natchez Trace. Had the popular Dinsmoor come to thwart the efforts of the commissioners? Why else, thought Jackson. As Hinds soon learned, however, the former agent attended in hopes that a cession treaty might include a reserve to indemnify him for loss of personal property at his agency years earlier. Dinsmoor's request was denied.[23]

After the ball games and a dance, the 500 or more representatives from the entire tribe gathered on October 10 to listen to Jackson's talk—one that was for him unusually long. The prelude was standard. Jackson delivered expressions of concern and sorrow from the President of the United States over the depraved state of many of their brethren, and he explained the wishes of the father in Washington to rectify the situation. He also repeated the familiar fear of the threat of Indian destruction by foreign powers invading the Mississippi Valley. In glowing terms, the commissioner described the wonders of the Arkansas lands and promised educational opportunities for all Choctaw youth so that they could better enjoy the rewards of civilization.[24]

Much of the contents of Jackson's message were true. American emigrants, crowding into the west, *were* demanding more land. So the government proposed a generous exchange of Arkansas land for a "slip of land" in Mississippi. "As your game is destroyed," Jackson warned, "you must cultivate the earth like your white brothers. You must also, in time, become citizens of the United States and subject to its laws."[25] The long speech contained a very simple message: Surrender your land in exchange for land across the river—or else!

The "slip of land" to which Jackson referred contained 5,000,000 acres—about one-third of the Mississippi lands still in Choctaw possession. Also, it was considerably better land than the Arkansas land. At least since the turn of the century, and perhaps before, bands of Choctaw had hunted and/or settled on the other side of the river. Thus the Choctaw were well acquainted with the region's shortcomings and were not to be hoodwinked by Jackson's rhetoric. Indeed, Jackson's old comrade in arms, Pushmataha, eloquently explained the reluctance of his people to accept the Arkansas land even in a two-for-one swap. When Jackson would not accept their objection to the poor quality of the region, they tried another tack. The Arkansas land was unacceptable because white settlers already occupied much of the area. The U.S. Army will drive them out, countered the general.[26]

For several days, the Choctaw debated among themselves. As his patience wore thin, Jackson warned them of the loss of American friendship and then threatened their nation with military destruction. Whereupon the Choctaw capitulated, and on October 18, 1820 they affixed their signatures to the document.[27] At Doak's Stand, the Choctaw ceded to the United States much of the region known as the Mississippi Delta—some of the most fertile farm land in North America. In exchange, they received nearly 13 million acres lying between the Arkansas and Red Rivers upstream from the Cherokee grant in what is now parts of southern Oklahoma and southwestern Arkansas. Although, in Article I, mention was made of the "grand and humane objects" of the treaty, the only provision that could be called either "grand" or "humane" was the establishment of Choctaw schools.

Settlers from over the Old Southwest, especially those in Mississippi, were jubilant over the terms of the treaty. The state demonstrated its appreciation by naming its new capital city on the Pearl River after Jackson and the county in which it was located after Hinds, and the Mississippi Senate and House of Representatives expressed their gratitude and praise in a joint resolution.[28] The cession did provide the State of Mississippi with the necessary room for settling its rapidly increasing population.

As a logical corollary to or continuation of the policy instituted by Jackson in the 1817 Cherokee cession, the Treaty of Doak's Stand constituted a blueprint for the complete dissolution of the Choctaw Nation east of the river. Furthermore it revealed an utter lack of knowledge on the part of Federal officials as to the spread of white settlements along the Arkansas River, a fact that the Choctaw were well aware of. Neither the War Department officials nor the treaty commissioners had familiarized themselves with available maps prior to the conference. In retrospect, the careless preparation for the treaty was more reprehensible than was the underlying philosophy.

Careless it was, indeed. The Choctaw objections at Doak's Stand based on the prior migration of white intruders to the proposed exchange lands proved well founded. The squatters had beaten the Choctaw to their newly acquired domain. Besides, the government was unaware of the value of some of it. Consequently, the ink was hardly dry before Secretary of War Calhoun proposed territorial adjustment, but the Choctaw refused to reopen negotiations in the field. Instead, they insisted on a trip to Washington. Permission was granted, and their delegation led by their beloved chief Pushmataha arrived in the District of Columbia late in 1824. It was a costly trip, for Pushmataha died on Christmas Eve in 1824. Two days later some two thousand mourners, including many Washington notables, attended his Washington burial with full military honors in response to his last wishes that "the big guns be fired over me."[29]

Though Pushmataha's death was a high price to pay, the trek to Washington proved worthwhile to the Choctaw Nation, which negotiated in 1825 an amendment to the Doak's Stand document. The disputed Arkansas land was exchanged for a tract located in present-day Oklahoma. In addition, the tribe received a perpetual annuity of $6,000 per year, an equal amount for sixteen years to support education, and other concessions.[30] This liberal settlement is attributed to the influence of a mixed-blood delegate, James McDonald, who had previously lived as a family member for four years with Thomas L. McKenney, formerly superintendent of Indian trade and now head of the new Office of Indian Affairs.[31]

While the delegation was in Washington, the Choctaw learned of President Monroe's message to Congress in which he recommended removal of all Indians to the western lands. Dismayed and distraught, the Indians sought and obtained an opportunity to respond before the Congress. Their spokesman was James McDonald who passionately delivered—and most likely authored—one of the most poignant statements ever made by the Native Americans of the Old Southwest. After a remarkable acknowledgement of the weaknesses of his people, he expressed an abhorrence of a forced removal to territory in the west. He then called upon the mercy of the American people and hoped that "our rights will be respected."[32]

Then the spokesman turned his attention to the social and political plight of the Choctaw remaining under the jurisdiction of the State of Mississippi which, as did other states in the region, denied Native Americans the rights due all "members of the human family." And even though they were "qualified by education," they could not hold public office, testify in court concerning their most precious interests, or serve as witnesses except against other Indians. The mixed-blood McDonald was at his most eloquent with his interrogatories.

> Can this be a correct policy? Is it just? Is it humane? . . . But the subject is a painful one, and we will dismiss it. The mist of prejudice is gradually vanishing before the light of reason, and enlarged sentiments of philanthropy begin to prevail. We leave the issue of the question to your wisdom and to the liberality of the south."[33]

Little did the sorely beset Choctaw delegation in Washington in 1825 realize that this truly "painful" question would be asked of the Old Southwest again and again in the future.

The Choctaw excursion of 1824–25 and the resulting treaty stands as the apex of the policy of enlightened moderation fostered during the eight-year term of Secretary of War John C. Calhoun. During his tenure emphasis was placed on education as an important means for the peaceful integration of the Indian into a new pattern of existence. In a sense, it was an extension of Jefferson's civilization policy in which both the Anglo-Americans and the Native Americans could move toward tolerance and understanding.

As the chief administrative officer of the War Department, Calhoun undeniably deserves considerable credit for the movement in that direction. Indeed, this credit was paid to him by the Choctaw delegation before they left Washington in February of 1825. It is easy, however, to become so enamored of well-known and romantic figures that the contributions of subordinates and lesser lights are ignored. Arthur H. DeRosier, Jr. provides an example of such oversight in his oft-cited study of the removal of the Choctaw, DeRosier pays great tribute to the roles of Pushmataha and Calhoun as the two "most eloquent spokesmen" of the "exponents of enlightened moderation" while ignoring the seminal role of Thomas L. McKenney and the leadership of James McDonald.[34] The latter figure, more than the popular Pushmataha, provided the moving force behind the delegation that negotiated the favorable treaty of January 20, 1825.

After Calhoun left the War Department, McKenney remained as head of the Bureau of Indian Affairs. So there was no abrupt abandonment of an enlightened approach, but there was a definite shift toward Indian removal in which McKenney participated. Though he befriended the Indians throughout his career he, like many others, became convinced of the wisdom and humanity of the removal policy. It was McKenney, for instance, who convinced the Choctaw, in a party led by Greenwood LeFlore, to at least explore the lands west of the river. The scarcity of water and wood, however, convinced LeFlore that he never wanted to abandon the remaining territory in Mississippi. Later, however, at the conference table his position altered considerably; most Choctaw might be removed, but LeFlore arranged to remain in Mississippi as a prosperous planter!

With the election of Jackson, many westerners expected immediate application of the removal policies expounded by him, and they were puzzled by the sympathetic tone of parts of his inaugural address. Could he be serious when he professed that "it will be my sincere and constant desire to observe toward the Indian tribes within our limits a just and liberal policy, and to give . . . humane and considerable attention to their rights and their wants. . . ."[35] Furthermore, President Jackson allowed McKenney to remain as head of the Bureau of Indian Affairs. He pacified the westerners, however, with the appointment of Tennessean John Eaton as Secretary of War. Before the year was out, they were no longer disappointed. In Jackson's first annual message he set forth his Indian policy: Remove voluntarily or be subject to state laws.

McKenney could only hope to palliate the downhearted, downtrodden Indians. Pressured by both state and Federal actions, the Choctaw vacillated and hesitated. Greenwood LeFlore was deposed, but shortly thereafter, he was restored as chief of the entire Nation—an unprecedented honor not even bestowed on the revered Pushmataha. This was good news for Jackson because LeFlore was now ready to press for removal providing he could protect his own personal interests and remain east of the river. For Jackson more good news soon arrived—Congress passed his removal act, which he signed on June 30, 1830.[36]

Although the Cherokee had long struggled against state's rights and removal pressures, the Choctaw tribe, so familiar to Jackson, would be the first to feel the combined legislative weight of the Federal and state governments.[37] In September of 1830, eight months after the Mississippi legislature had followed Georgia's lead and passed a law placing Indians under state jurisdiction, General Coffee and John H. Eaton, former Secretary of War, had met the Choctaw leaders at Dancing Rabbit Creek on the border of Noxubee and Winston Counties in central eastern Mississippi. Eaton was truculent and Jacksonian in his approach, telling the Indians pointedly that they either had to dispose of their lands and move west or fall under the control of the United States Army. Coffee was compassionate in his remarks. Former Indian factor and commissary to the meeting, George S. Gaines recalled that the Choctaw reacted angrily to Eaton's talk: "It filled them with surprise, astonishment, excitement, grief, and resentment. Not a single Choctaw favored the cession of the lands of the tribe. It had not a single advocate among them."[38]

No doubt the Indians were shocked at Eaton's tone, but they could hardly have been wholly surprised by his message. President Jackson had earlier informed the United States Senate, on May 6, that he had received by special messenger the general outline of an agreement drawn up by some members of the Choctaw Nation. In it, he said, the Choctaw agreed to cede their lands and to remove to the Choctaw territory on the Arkansas. He sought advice and suggestions from that body in the formulation of a treaty partly because the Indian spokesmen had asked that the preliminary agreement be submitted to the Senate. The President said that the Choctaw Nation was the largest and most powerful of the southern tribes. Although the cost of removal would be substantial, the government would quickly recover its investment from the sales of released lands. Above all the removal of the Indians would solve "the perplexing question involved in the present location—a question in which several States of the Union have the deepest interest, and which, if left undecided much longer, may eventuate in serious injury to the Indians."[39]

Commissioners Eaton and Coffee took to the Dancing Rabbit Council a treaty which had been formulated in Washington, and which in general terms had been sanctioned by the Senate. It was much too extensive and detailed to have been prepared in the Mississippi forest.[40] Various Indian groups, in defiance of the pro-removal chiefs, had earlier approved a threat of death to any chief who might be tempted to accept the government proposal. Spokesmen in the council were adamant, they would neither sign away their lands nor move the tribe to the West. General

Eaton again warned that they had no choice, and many of the Indians left the treaty ground in a fit of anger. The commissioners, however, held secret meetings with some of the chiefs, and after promising generous land allotments and other considerations, were able to secure agreement to the treaty.[41]

The most visible one of the cooperating chiefs was Greenwood LeFlore. Sharing with him as beneficiary of the terms of Section IV of the treaty granting four sections of land each, were Netackachie and the venerable Mushulatubbee. In addition to the Land, the three were also given annuities of $250 so long as they remained chiefs, except that Mushulatubbee's life annuity was increased to that amount.[42]

The heart of the Dancing Rabbit Creek Treaty was the clause by which the Choctaw Nation ceded "the entire country they own and possess east of the Mississippi River; and they agree to remove beyond the Mississippi River, as early as practicable. . . ." In extensive and specific guarantees the United States assured protection to its wards in transit and in their new settlements. Selected chiefs were to receive $500 annually for twenty years, the nation was to have free access to navigable streams, all former promises of annuities were to be combined with additional future payments, orphans were to be cared for, forty youth were to be chosen annually to be educated at government expenses, and a council house was to be paid for with public funds. Wagons and steamboats were to be made ready for the Choctaw's removal, and the people were to be subsisted for a year on corn, pork, and beef. Removal was to take place between 1831 and 1832.[43]

If some Choctaw chose to remain in their homeland as citizens of the state, they could do so by signifying their intention within six months to Choctaw agent William Ward. Each head of a remaining family was entitled to claim a section of land. Again the twenty remaining veterans who had served Anthony Wayne's army were to be paid annuities of twenty-five dollars. The treaty was signed on September 27, 1830, by Eaton, Coffee, 172 Choctaw, and eleven witnesses, including the Reverend Samuel A. Worcester and Indian agent William Ward.

For the Jackson Administration, the Dancing Rabbit Creek treaty was of tremendous importance in asserting the policy of removal. It was accomplished by much posturing and the manipulation of full-blood and mixed-blood political factions within the tribe. In all the delayed official planning, and the misery associated with the final emigration of the Choctaw, there were added the treacherous acts of William Ward in his failure to comply faithfully with the provisions of Section XIV which allotted land grants to those Indians who remained behind and accepted state citizenship. Ward kept highly defective records of these land requests and was later accused of corruption, venality, impudence, drunkenness, and general failure to preserve governmental integrity. Indeed, his utter lack of probity guaranteed a plethora of Choctaw legal claims against the United States for far into the future.

The decade following the signing the Dancing Rabbit Creek treaty in 1830 was one of unmatched drama and pathos in the history of relations between the American Indians and the United States government. Administration officials moved quickly to extract similar concessions from the remaining southeastern tribes. The Seminole and Creeks signed removal treaties in May of 1832; the Chickasaw did likewise in October of that year. The Cherokee, after a bitter heart-rending schism, acquiesced in the presence of military force in 1835. The day of removal had indeed arrived and the Jacksonians scurried to make the most of it. By 1840 sixty thousand members of the Five Civilized Tribes had completed their forced migration to the Indian Territory (now the state of Oklahoma).[44]

The Choctaw, who had signed the model removal treaties of Doak's Stand and Dancing Rabbit Creek, were the first to vacate their ancestral lands.[45] Though most of them emigrated with government supervision and assistance, approximately one thousand members of the tribe made their way independently to the Indian Territory. The first official Choctaw emigration was organized under the direction of George Gibson, commissary general of the U.S. Army. His careful logistical preparation was negated by the bickering and incompetence of civilian agents and army officers in the field. The resulting delays caused the first group of émigrés to suffer terribly from the unusually harsh winter of 1831–32. Gibson kept out civilian agents from the two subsequent removals, which proceeded more smoothly, but disruptive bureaucratic bungling and the 1832 cholera epidemic in Mississippi created much panic and pain. When the dreadful process ended, some 12,500 Choctaw were settled in the Indian Territory. Approximately 600 of the tribe remained in Mississippi—the majority of them residing on allotments of land granted by the treaty, a few living as vagrants.[46] Choctaw removal was far more costly both in financial and in human terms than the Jackson Administration had predicted. The expenditures, including the treaty, the emigrations, and the reparations, totaled in excess of $5 million, which was more than the government had planned to spend for the removal of all the eastern tribes.[47] Nevertheless, Jackson forged ahead with removal.

The removal of the Creeks involved the use of military force. As had the Choctaw, the Creeks had signed a number of cession treaties with the United States, but the Creeks were more deeply divided. The emergence of the Red Sticks and the Creek War illustrate the depth and pervasiveness of their tribal animosities. Though the Creeks, by the Treaty of Fort Jackson, had already paid a high price for their factionalism, they paid even more dearly for their persistent schism with the approach of removal. After William McIntosh violated Creek law by signing a cession treaty in 1825, he and some of his followers were murdered on orders of the Creek council. President John Quincy Adams in 1826 insisted on renegotiating this fraudulent treaty, which resulted in the emigration of only a few affluent mixed-blood families.

Subsequently, the Alabama legislature incorporated Creek lands into organized counties and extended the jurisdiction of state courts over the Indians. Pressures caused by these actions and by increasing numbers of intruders led the Creeks to sign in Washington in March of 1836, a quasi-removal treaty. While the Creeks ceded the remainder of their eastern lands, heads of families were to receive allotments of a half section of land which they could retain or sell. Ninety chiefs received parcels of a full section. The document, however, contained expressions of the government's desire that the Creeks join their brethren west of the Mississippi. As reasonable as this treaty appeared, it proved to be quite destructive. The government failed to keep its promise to protect the Creeks from rapacious intruders, and the Indians fell prey to outrageous intimidations and frauds. Conditions degenerated quickly. When violence erupted in the spring of 1836, Secretary of War Lewis Cass ordered the Army to subdue and remove the Creeks to the West. By July the military had restored peace and begun evacuating the Creeks. First to leave were the subdued warriors—handcuffed and chained—who were accompanied by their families. By early August, all of the hostile Indians had departed, and soon the friendly Creeks followed. Their route to the West was a circuitous one. After taking various trails to Montgomery, they embarked for the trip down the Alabama River to Mobile, over to New Orleans, and up the Mississippi River and its tributaries to their western lands. Of the 14,608 Creeks removed in 1836, the Army listed only 2,495 as hostiles.

Of all the southeastern Indians, the Chickasaw of northern Mississippi and northwestern Alabama experienced the least traumatic removal. They also obtained the most equitable financial return for their ceded lands. In 1816 and 1818 the Chickasaw had acquiesced to the sale of portions of their territory in Alabama, Tennessee, and Kentucky, but they were extremely reluctant to part with any additional acreage. In 1830 President Jackson personally negotiated a cession treaty at Franklin, Tennessee. Because it was contingent upon the Chickasaw approval of the western lands offered in exchange, however, the treaty became void after the Chickasaw exploratory expedition could not agree on a suitable location beyond the Mississippi. Meanwhile, the Mississippi Legislature extended state jurisdiction over the Indians, and whites increasingly intruded upon their land. After President Jackson plainly reiterated that their only hope of relief was relocation to the Indian Territory, the Chickasaw in October of 1832 agreed to the Treaty of Pontotoc Creek. It was generous by comparison with other Indian treaties. Each adult Chickasaw, in accordance with the size of his family, received an allotment ranging from one to four sections. The profits from the sale of these individual plots and from the unassigned or surplus tribal lands were to create a general fund of the Chickasaw Nation.

While the Mississippi lands were being surveyed and sold, a commission of Chickasaw searched for an acceptable location within the Indian Territory. The Federal government had always insisted that the Chickasaw should settle adjacent to the Choctaw. Finally, at Doaksville in the Indian Territory, the two tribes in 1837 agreed to the Chickasaw purchase of the western portion of the Choctaw lands. The emigration of 4,914 Chickasaw and their 1,156 slaves began forthwith. Perhaps not to the extent as some of their kinsmen, the Chickasaw nevertheless suffered pain and humiliation en route to their new national domain. In addition, some of the profits from the sale of their land disappeared into the pockets of unscrupulous supply contractors and corrupt bureaucrats. While it in no way compensated them for the trauma of removal, at least the Chickasaw began their relocated national life with a federal fund of some $3 million. From its interest, the Chickasaw could expect a per capita yield of $14 to $18, compared with the $2 to $5 per capita income for the Choctaw.[48]

Events surrounding the removal of the Seminole were as atypical as the rest of their tribal history. Best described as dissident, discordant Creeks who had amalgamated with several small Florida tribes, these people were not labeled as a separate tribe until the turn of the nineteenth century. Even though their land actually was not as valuable as that of the other southeastern Indians, the Federal government for seven years fought an expensive war to remove the Seminole from Florida. It is also ironic that despite the less desirable nature of their land, no other tribe in the region defended its territory as fiercely as did the Seminole. Rather than land, black slaves were at the core of the Seminole problem. White masters above the thirty-first parallel resented the fact that for decades fugitive slaves had sought—and found—a sanctuary in Florida. Indian removal provided white slave owners of Mississippi, Alabama, and Georgia a perfect opportunity to achieve three goals through removal of the Seminole: open new land for cotton and cattle; recover runaway slaves; and destroy an accessible refuge for escaped slaves.[49]

Though Indians throughout the Old Southwest owned African slaves, the Seminole attitude toward their black slaves differed. Slaves found their Seminole masters to be more tolerant and understanding—so understanding that the Seminole refused to cooperate with white masters who attempted to recover their chattels. Hence the white man's interest in Seminole removal actually related more to slavery than it did to land greed.[50]

By an 1823 treaty, the Florida Indians had agreed to reside on a reservation in central Florida and to return runaway slaves to their rightful owners. They did not fulfill these good intentions, however, and after the passage of the Indian Removal Act in 1830, pressures increased to have the Seminole relocated to the Indian Territory. The removal treaty signed by the Seminole in 1832 was contingent upon a tribal delegation inspecting and approving the western site. A delegation did sign an approval out in the Indian Territory, but a large faction of the Seminole considered the 1832 treaty null and void. War broke out after some Seminole murdered Indian Agent Wiley Thompson in late December of 1835. By the time of the conclusion of the war in 1842, over 1,500 American soldiers had lost their lives and the Federal government had spent $20 million. Such was the cost of removing some 2,800 Seminole to the Indian Territory. Several hundred irremovable Seminole remained in Florida.[51]

In terms of American dollars, the Seminole removal was the most costly; but in terms of Indian lives, the most costly was the removal of the Cherokee. There is an irony present in the loss of Native American life en route to the Indian Territory, but the maximum irony is in the loss of so many lives by the Cherokee who were considered by most observers to be the most civilized—in the terms of Jefferson's civilization policy—of all the American Indians.[52]

It is not generally recognized that by 1816 some 2,000 Cherokees voluntarily had migrated to Arkansas. In 1817 and 1819 the Cherokee had ceded parcels of their homeland in exchange for a tract of land between the Arkansas and White Rivers. While a majority of the Cherokee in the East staunchly opposed removal, nevertheless emigration had swelled the number in Arkansas to more than 6,000 by 1836. Conventional wisdom within the Jackson Administration attributed the anti-removal stance of Cherokee leaders to the influence of mixed-bloods, which probably was not the case. It was a mixed-blood on the other hand—a Major Ridge— who led the small pro-removal faction known as the "treaty party."[53] John Ross, another mixed-blood, headed the "anti-war party," which the majority of the eastern Cherokee supported.

Unable to successfully treat with the Ross faction, a Federal commissioner negotiated a treaty with Major Ridge at New Echota in northwestern Georgia in late December of 1835. By only one vote, the United States Senate ratified this treaty in which the Cherokee ceded their eastern lands for $5 million plus seven million acres of land north of the Arkansas River. Members of the treaty party then migrated to their new trans-Mississippi homes without incident. Virtually all the remaining Cherokee, however, signed a petition to Congress denouncing the validity of the New Echota document which John Ross had unsuccessfully attempted to renegotiate. Tensions mounted and Jackson ordered the military into the Cherokee country at the end of June in 1836. The Cherokee had given no signs of vacating their land by the treaty deadline of May 23, 1838, so the Administration ordered General Winfield Scott to proceed into the Cherokee country and organize the Indian's removal.

Official records indicate that General Scott insisted that his men carry out their orders in a humane and compassionate manner, but contemporary accounts show that in some cases the troops behaved cruelly. After John Ross saw that further delay was useless, he sought and received permission to oversee the emigration. In the fall of 1838, some thirteen thousand Indian emigrants, including the slaves, began their "Trail of Tears." For several thousand of them, however, it was a trail of death.[54]

The number of Indians who avoided removal from the Old Southwest may never be calculated exactly. Official accounts number them in the hundreds, but it is more likely that thousands managed to stay behind. Many of the Indians who remained east of the Mississippi eked out an existence as economic castaways—devoid of both state citizenship and tribal identity. Fortune was much kinder to others. Of those who stayed east of the Mississippi, a few endured as a proud minority who coped on the fringes of white society, but many of the mixed-bloods melded into the Euro-American majority.

Removal opened wide the door of land speculation, and a horde of opportunists and entrepreneurs rushed into the Old Southwest, seeking the rich cotton lands made available by the cessions forced upon the Five Civilized Tribes. Most of the ceded land was eventually purchased by yeoman farmers, but generally not before it had passed through the hands of speculators. In many instances, however, the speculators did not realize the degree of profit they had anticipated. Ironically, the lure of better land in Texas plus the 1837 panic with its ensuing economic depression caused a large number of land speculators to lose money instead of reap profits from the misfortune of Indians.[55] Indeed, many of the new owners of ceded lands, or their descendants, would eventually suffer through plummeting cotton prices and a devastating Civil War to emerge as an impoverished class. Of course, others prospered as did a number of the relocated Indians.

Removal ushered into the Old Southwest a period known as the "Flush Times," a heady transitional era which witnessed the coronation of King Cotton. Slavery in its most visible form—on the plantation—distracted the eyes of the maturing nation away from the frontier of the Old Southwest. Just as the varicolored frontier eclipsed the ancient nations, the peculiar institution eclipsed the frontier of the Old Southwest.

13

Conclusion

As complex as the other frontiers of the United States might have been, none was so multi-layered, multifarious, and marked by conflict as the Old Southwest. Its heritage of international and sectional rivalries matched in complexity the physiographical features of the region. Nature had provided an appropriate stage for such an assortment of national and ethnic settlers to make their appearances. The natural stage was a gigantic maze of waterways, valleys, and ridges bordered along the Gulf Coast by countless swamps, estuaries, bays, and barrier islands. Thousands of years before the intrusion of the Europeans, a large, diverse native American population already was on stage.

During the century prior to the American Revolution, France, Great Britain, and Spain engaged in a rivalry in the Old Southwest that continued until the conclusion of the War of 1812. European presence along the Gulf Coast did not disappear finally until the Adams-Onís (Florida Purchase) Treaty of 1819. Involvement of these international rivals greatly complicated relations of the Indian tribes with each other, with the European powers, and with the emerging United States of America. To a considerable degree, the continuing interference or meddling of France, Spain, and Great Britain in the affairs of the native Americans in the Old Southwest provided land hungry settlers and speculators with a tailor-made opportunity to propose and institute Andrew Jackson's Indian removal policy. Though it can be argued that removal was an inescapable eventuality in the Old Southwest, there is no doubt that the War of 1812 hastened the removal of the Five Civilized Tribes and unleashed an anti-Indian policy from which emerged post–Civil War reservations in the trans-Mississippi West.

Removal was not the only national Indian policy generated in the Old

Southwest. In a perverted way, the success of the Federal Factory System among the Indians there prompted fur magnates such as John Jacob Astor and William H. Ashley to lobby successfully for the abolition of the factory system. In some ways, the treatment of Indians in the Old Southwest prior to removal was atypical of subsequent policy and implementation. The early Federal Administrations dealt with the Native Americans as fairly and honorably as one could expect. The appointment of men of such good will, ability, and stalwart integrity as Benjamin Hawkins and Silas Dinsmoor stands as evidence of the sincerity of the early presidents of the United States in the design of Indian policy. Trans-Appalachian frontiersmen, however, dictated an alteration of this course by the end of the Madison administration.

Just as the presence of France, Spain, and Great Britain impacted directly and indirectly upon the lives of the Native Americans, intervention by these European powers also significantly affected the lives of Anglo-Americans in the Old Southwest. At times the loyalties of frontiersmen there wavered as they sought to take political and economic advantage of international events. In extreme cases, some Americans were tempted to align themselves with Spain. Aaron Burr and James Wilkinson merely represented the best known of the frontiersmen who entertained plans to achieve fame and fortune by establishing an independent nation on the flanks of the young Republic.

Compared with many nations of the world, the United States has enjoyed international borders that generally were free from conflict. Minor incidents occasionally arose on the Canadian and Mexican borders, and the United States inherited the Nueces–Rio Grande boundary dispute from the Republic of Texas. In the Old Southwest, however, one of the persistent problems from 1783 until 1819 related to the possession of Florida by Spain. As favorable and popular as was Pinckney's Treaty in 1795, the boundary established by it along the thirty-first parallel proved to be primarily a line of contention.

Residents of the Old Southwest loudly joined the outcry of discontented farmers of the upper Mississippi and the Ohio Valleys, which resulted in the Louisiana Purhcase. While this gigantic acquisition ultimately gave the entire nation a magnified sense of destiny, it did not resolve the tensions along the thirty-first parallel. Many land owners and claimants found their properties bisected by what they perceived to be a contrived and artificial line. Slave owners saw Florida as a haven for their escaped chattels, and nearly all Anglo-Americans blamed Indian unrest on a variety of foreign agents operating below the national border.

The Baton Rouge Rebellion of 1810, the short-lived Republic of West Florida, and the ensuing presidential proclamation ordering the forcible occupation of West Florida to the Perdido River illustrate well the uniqueness of the heritage of the Old Southwest, as do the filibustering activities of the Mobile Society directed by Reuben Kemper and Joseph Kennedy. Troubles spawned by Spanish control of West Florida intensified the uneasiness that characterized the Tombigbee settlements until after the War of 1812. Even without the Spanish presence in West Florida, however, the Tombigbee residents would have felt isolated, neglected, and endangered. In other words, sectional controversy would have existed within the sprawling Mississippi Territory, but the vestiges there of European empires considerably complicated every aspect of frontier life.

In a large sense, the active involvement of residents of the Old Southwest in the War of 1812 is another legacy of the presence of European powers there. Many of the frontiersmen in the Old Southwest eagerly participated in the precipitation of the War of 1812 with England, in the fighting of that war, and in the concurrent Indian hostilities known as the Creek War. Tecumseh and the Prophet stirred more unrest in the Old Southwest than is generally recognized. As was the case everywhere, the Old Southwest was not marked by unanimity of public opinion on the war issues. Some of the settlers profiteered from the hostilities by selling supplies and commodities to the British forces. Nevertheless, accounts of the causes and the battles of the War of 1812 often fail adequately to portray the significance of events in the Old Southwest.

The most common exception to this statement, of course, is the attention given to Andrew Jackson, whose career was intertwined with events in the Old Southwest. In the American myth, Jackson may be best known as an Indian fighter, but it was his victory over the British forces at New Orleans that provided him with a national popular mandate sufficiently strong to catapult him to the presidency. If Jackson hated any category of people, it was British nationals rather than Indians. His anti-British xenophobia was one of Jackson's strongest motivating forces. Regardless of the drive behind his rise to a hero of epic proportions, many of the most significant events in his family, military, and political lives related to the Old Southwest. It was in the Natchez District that Jackson married his beloved Rachel, and it was on the Natchez Trace that he acquired his most famous sobriquet, Old Hickory. Experiences in the Old Southwest molded some of the most controversial policies of his presidency—those relating to Indians, banks, and land.

Under normal circumstances, perfection of land titles can be complicated and drawn out, but on no other frontier did so many European powers leave such a tangle of land claims. To unravel the conflicting

French, Spanish and British claims would have tested the best legislative and judicial systems. The task, however, became almost insurmountable in the Old Southwest as a result of the antedated Spanish claims of the 1790s and the Georgia speculations of the 1780s and 1790s. While litigation of land titles was a ubiquitous problem across American frontiers, adjudication in the Old Southwest proved incredibly complex and lengthy. The experience in Mississippi Territory also demonstrated public demand for pre-emption laws. Settlers bombarded Congress with petitions requesting pre-emptive rights—petitions that often resulted in passage by Congress of special or local pre-emption acts.

All probems relating to land acquisition seem to have been exaggerated in the Old Southwest; the levels of speculative activities provide another case in point. Although the entire United States was a "land of speculation," the Old Southwest was the scene of the most grandiose schemes on record. As bold as it was, the 1785 Bourbon County fiasco paled in comparison to the 1789 and 1795 Yazoo schemes perpetrated by the Georgia legislature. While authors of basic textbooks often cite Fletcher *v.* Peck as a landmark supreme court decision affirming the sanctity of contracts, historians as noted in chapter 4 seldom stress sufficiently the proportions of the 1795 Yazoo fraud and the resulting nightmare of litigation.

One of the most interesting features of the Old Southwest is the Natchez Trace. Its history is the story of the flow of humanity into the farthest reach of the frontier of the young republic, and, in this sense, it constitutes a microcosmic picture of the region. Concern for national security— roused by the presence of European powers and populous Indian tribes— led to the authorization of this federal road to the nation's most distant and infant settlement. With the rapid growth of downriver commerce on the Ohio and Mississippi Rivers, gold-laden boatmen increasingly traveled the Natchez Trace as the route home to Tennessee, Kentucky, and points beyond. They were not alone. The whole cast of characters of the Mississippi Valley also marched the same route—robbers, rugged pioneers, fashionable ladies, shysters, politicians, soldiers, and men of destiny such as Aaron Burr, Andrew Jackson, and Meriwether Lewis.

Though reasons for immigration into the Old Southwest were as varied as the individuals who settled there, most of them followed dreams of "gitting land." Nameless squatters as well as scions of tidewater planters shared this common goal. In this sense, the frontier of the Old Southwest typified the national experience. In its social and economic complexities, however, the Old Southwest differed considerably. First of all, this frontier comprised such a wide range of racial and/or ethnic types—Caucasions of many European nationalities and religions, Africans, Native Americans, and an assortment of mixtures of the three types—that it defies calculation. Though the number and roles of mixed-bloods will never be accurately determined, mixed bloods nevertheless played a more significant role in both the Euro-American and Native American developments than has previously been recognized.

The spectrum of economic activities in the Old Southwest was also wide and diverse. Though the exact nature of the economic structure remains uncertain, it was not simply a division of pioneers into small farmers and large planters. Though some planters were present from the earliest colonial days, they did not become a dominant force until the opening of the Indian cessions. The less affluent Euro-American agriculturalists included a large proportion of Celtic-American herdsmen as well as English-American yeoman farmers. Also present were farmers of substance, typified by Gideon Lincecum. Scholars have yet to determine the economic relationships of these agriculturalists and the degree of upward mobility available to them. Recently, as discussed in Chapter 6, historians have begun to emphasize the significance of cattle raising in the Old Southwest and the antecedent role of that industry to the much publicized cattle kindgom of the post–Civil War trans-Mississippi West. In addition to the herders, farmers, and planters, smaller numbers of pioneers in the Old Southwest engaged in the manufacturing of naval stores and other timber products. Others made brick. Still others made their living from the sea. Finally, in the urban centers of Mobile, Natchez, and New Orleans, entrepreneurs engaged in a wide variety of commercial and financial businesses, and artisans plied their trades. Alabama developed a significant mining industry shortly after statehood, an industry that has grown steadily until recent times. In the late nineteenth and early twentieth centuries, timber barons made huge fortunes cutting millions of acres of virgin pine trees.

At least five major factors were responsible for the uneven flow of immigration into the Old Southwest. One was the controversy surrounding Spanish West Florida; another was the presence of four major Indian tribes and the extent of the domain claimed by them. The third and fourth were related: The War of 1812 and Indian removal. While the fifth factor—Eli Whitney's 1793 invention of an easily replicated cotton gin—had an immediate influence; it was particularly important in the rush of slave-owning planters into the rich lands ceded by the Indians in the decades following the War of 1812. Remarkably, cotton gins appeared in the Indian

Nations by the turn of the nineteenth century, and by the eve of removal a significant number of Indians, primarily mixed bloods, were slave-owning cotton planters.

Despite the presence and power of aristocratic planters, the Old Southwest had the same democratic flavor that characterized the other American frontiers. In their stately mansions, planter families undoubtedly socialized with their own kind and in their own style, but in the larger society democratic standards were imposed on everyone. The first state constitutions in Alabama and Mississippi reflected the established pattern of frontier liberalism. Both documents did, however, contain mild restrictions on the franchise and on qualifications for holding office. In 1832, Mississippians rewrote their constitution so that it would more nearly reflect the political reforms of the Jacksonian Era.

While equality characterized politics, society in the Old Southwest was far from homogeneous. In some ways, lifestyles were as diverse as the complexity of the genetic pools. No greater disparity could exist than that which distinguished the mansions of pretentious planters and merchants from the crude, ill-kept cabins of the Celtic herders. Except in pockets of civility in the urban centers and in plantation drawing rooms, the rough and tumble behavior so often associated with frontier life prevailed. It was not unusual that alcohol, tobacco, and profanity were used to excess. In the Old Southwest, more often than not, the code dictated that people should eat when they were hungry and drink when they were thirsty. They danced when they were merry, voted for candidates whom they liked best, and were ready to knock down anyone who questioned their right to do these things.

As did pioneers all across the United States, settlers in the Old Southwest worshipped as actively as they worked and played. The experiences of circuit riders and farmer-preachers in the Mississippi Territory differed little, it at all, from those of their counterparts in Illinois. As they were in Kentucky and on other frontiers, camp meetings were major events where noisy sinners "got religion" after desperate struggles with the Lord or the Devil—or both.

The similarities between the frontier of the Old Southwest and any other American frontier are striking. Historians, nevertheless, have generally read the Old Southwest out of the Turnerian model because of the existence of slavery. This tendency is puzzling because in the Old Southwest, as in other American territories, farmers were found on every rung of the economic ladder. In addition, there were on this frontier an abundance of cattle raisers who differed only in minor respects from the famous cowboys of Texas. Moreover, small farmers and herders owned slaves as well as did the planters. Undoubtedly slavery gave the frontier of the Old Southwest a unique quality, but its presence does not exclude the Old Southwest from the same frontier process that existed in the Old Northwest. Was a frontier with a "peculiar institution" a lesser frontier? Except for their ownership of slaves, the planters of the Old Southwest and the well capitalized wheat or corn farmers of the Old Northwest shared many frontier characteristics. It is interesting that, despite the practice of slavery in Texas, the cultivation of cotton there, and its role in the Confederacy, historians and the reading public view Texas as the West. Although everyone recognized that the first Texans were transplanted Southerners, nearly eveyone views the Old Southwest as more "South" than "West," implying of course that it was not really a frontier region.

It is the enduring sectionalism, so characteristic of the entire South, that distracts attention away from the frontier qualities of the Old Southwest—actually, from the entire Southern frontier. African slaves, just as their masters, were frontiersmen. Was a black man who floated down several rivers, who survived Indian attacks, and who endured all of the other privations of the trip any less of a frontiersman because of the color of his skin or the document that declared him a chattel? By the same token, was a wealthy person who carved a plantation out of the wilderness any less of a frontiersman than the herder or the yeoman farmer who lived on adjacent land?

Failure to recognize the Old Southwest as a frontier is particularly ironic because the frontier lingered longer in the Old Southwest than it did in any of the other so-called frontier regions. One could easily list a number of counties in Mississippi and Alabama, for instance, where life in the 1920s bore a stong resemblance to life a century earlier. An occasional railroad track, automobile, or telegraph line might reflect the only marks of the passage of a hundred years. In a few extremely isolated pockets, one could use World War II as the watershed.

Several factors may explain the enduring nature of the frontier of the Old Southwest. Much of it lay for years buried in a virgin forest, bound together by the powerful influence of isothermal lines. The river systems defied rapid internal commercial developments, and railroad lines did not develop significantly until well after the Civil War. Consequently, to a large extent, the region now known as the Old Southwest was isolated— socially, economically, and politically—and marked by localism until the mid-twentieth century.

Finally, recognition of the role of residents in the Old Southwest in the course of American empire is long overdue. Their participation in events that led to the Louisiana Purchase, the Baton Rouge Rebellion, the founding of the West Florida Republic, and the occupation of Spanish West Florida are clear indicators of the extent of their nationalistic fervor. The Old Southwest—particularly the Natchez District—was the base from which many filibusters departed for their forays into Mexico. Some of the same southwesterners who waved the lone star banner during the Baton Rouge Rebellion soon were in the midst of the revolution in Texas. It is not an overstatement to assert that the Old Southwest was an important incubator of Manifest Destiny, that expansionist fever so closely associated with the Mexican War and the United States' push to the Pacific Ocean.

Appendix

Time Line of Indian Agents and Government Officials

*Column headers (left → right): TREATIES, CESSIONS & EVENTS · Year · Creek Agent · Choctaw Agent · Chickasaw Agent · Territorial Secretary · Territorial Governor · Secretary of War · Secretary of State · President. The block at right is labeled **TERMS OF FEDERAL AND TERRITORIAL OFFICIALS**.*

TREATIES, CESSIONS & EVENTS	Year	Creek Agent	Choctaw Agent	Chickasaw Agent	Territorial Secretary	Territorial Governor	Secretary of War	Secretary of State	President
	1798						James McHenry	Timothy Pickering/ John Marshall	John Adams
	1799					Winthrop Sargent			
	1800		John McKee					James Madison	
Treaty of Fort Adams	1801			Samuel Mitchell	John Steele				Thomas Jefferson
Factory System	1802					W.C.C. Claiborne			
Hoe Buckintoopa; Louisiana Purchase *Cato West Acting Governor	1803				Cato* West				
	1804					Cato* West	Henry Dearborn		
Treaty of Mt. Dexter Signed	1805				Thomas Williams				
Burr Plot	1806	Benjamin Hawkins				Robert Williams			
	1807			William Hill	Cowles Meade				
Embargo Act Treaty of Mt. Dexter Ratified	1808		Silas Dinsmoor	Thomas Wright					
	1809				Thomas Williams		Thomas Williams		James Madison
West Florida Convention	1810					William Eustis		Robert Smith	
	1811			James Neely					
War of 1812	1812					David Holmes	John* Armstrong	James Monroe	
*Monroe Served as Interim Secretary Of War After Armstrong Fort Mims Massacre	1813			James Robertson	Henry Dangerfield				
Treaty of Fort Jackson (Creeks)	1814								
	1815		John McKee	William Cocke	Nathaniel Ware		William Crawford		
Treaty of Choctaw Trading House Treaty of Chickasaw Council House	1816								
	1817								

263

Notes

Chapter 1: "The lands here lie in a very curious manner"

1. George L. Prentiss, ed., *A Memoir of S. S. Prentiss* 2 vols. (New York, 1855), p. 95.

2. For an example of how the Old Southwest was viewed in the early nineteenth century, see Timothy Flint, *A Condensed Geography and History of the Western States, or the Mississippi Valley*, 2 vols. (Cincinnati, 1828); also useful are Rupert V. Vance, *Human Geography of the South* (Chapel Hill, 1935) and Almon E. Parkins, *The South: Its Economic–Geographic Development* (New York,1938); Arthell Kelly, "The Geography," Richard Aubrey McLemore, ed., *A History of Mississippi*, 2 vols. (Jackson, 1973), I, pp. 3–23; Ralph Cross, ed., *Atlas of Mississippi* (Jackson, 1974), pp. 2–21.

3. Nina Leftwich, *Two Hundred Years at Muscle Shoals* (Tuscumbia, Ala., 1935); J. Haden Aldredge, *History of Navigation on the Tennessee River System*, (Washington, 1937), House Doc. 254.

4. For an example of local resentment of Spanish interference with trade through Mobile, see "Judge Harry Toulmin to Delegate William Lattimore," December 6, 1805, Clarence Edwin Carter, ed., *The Territorial Papers of the United States*, V (Washington, 1937), p, 437 and Petition to Congress by a Convention East of the Pearl River," November 11, 1809. *Ibid.*, VI, pp. 26–30. (Hereafter cited as Carter, TP.); also, there are many references to problems of river trade in Isaac Joslin Cox, *The West Florida Controversy, 1798–1813* (Baltimore, 1918), for example, see p. 177.

5. "Toulmin to Lattimore," Carter, TP, V, pp. 435–36.

6. "Reclamation of Southern Swamps," *DeBow's Review*, 17 (1854), pp. 525–29.

7. "Postmaster Gideon Grainger to Judge Harry Toulmin," July 10, 1806, Carter TP, V, pp. 468–70; "Edmund P. Gaines to Secretary of War," January 29, 1808, Carter, TP, V, 598–602; William Darby, *The Emigrants' Guide to the Western and Southwestern States and Territories* (New York, 1818), pp. 114–18, 131–36.

8. William Richardson, *Travel Diary of William Richardson from Boston to New Orleans by Land in 1815* (New York, 1818), pp. 14–15.

9. John Pope, *A Tour Through the Southern and Western Territories of the United States of North America* (Richmond, 1792), pp. 24–31; Fortescue Cuming, *Sketches*

of a Tour to the Western Country—1807–1809 (Reuben Gold Thwaites, ed., *Early Western Travel, 1748–1846*, Cleveland, 1904; reprinted New York, AMS Press, 1966), pp. 284–95; Benjamin L. C. Wailes, *Report on the Agriculture and Geology of Mississippi* (Philadelphia, 1854), pp. 213–26.

10. William Darby, *A Geographical Description of the State of Louisiana, the Southern Part of the State of Mississippi, and the Territory of Louisiana*, 2nd ed. (New York, 1817), pp. 298–301, 323–26; Joseph F. Williams, *Old Times in West Tennessee* (Memphis, 1873), pp. 7–37.

11. "Ephraim Kirby to Thomas Jefferson," May 1, 1804, Carter, TP, V, pp. 322–26.

12. J. F. H. Claiborne, "A Trip through the Piney Woods," *Publications of the Mississippi Historical Society*, 9 (Oxford, 1906), p. 523.

13. Francis Harper, ed., *The Travels of William Bartram*, Naturalist's Edition (New Haven, 1958), p. 258.

14. *Ibid.*, p. 252.

15. *Ibid.*, p. 242.

16. *Ibid.*, pp. 164, 170–73.

17. Flint, *A Condensed Geography*, I, pp. 112–14.

18. Harper, *Travels of William Bartram*, pp. 52–54; Cuming, *Sketches of a Tour*, p. 304; "Our Southern Tormentor—The Mosquito," *DeBow's Review*, 19 (1855), pp. 171–85; Justus Wyman, "A Geographical Sketch of the Alabama Territory," *Publications of the Alabama Historical Society*, III (1899), p. 114

19. Cuming, *Sketches of a Tour*, p. 310.

20. Flint, *A Condensed Geography*, I, pp. 484–87.

21. For sources pertaining to the American Indians, see notes to Chapters 2, 7, 8 and 12.

22. "William Bowen to David Hughes," January 22, 1817, Carter, TP, XVIII, p. 49.

23. For one of the recent studies of the mixed bloods, see Samuel James Wells, "Choctaw Mixed Bloods and the Advent of Removal" (Ph.D. diss., University of Southern Mississippi, 1987).

24. Samuel Flagg Bemis, *Pinckney's Treaty* (Baltimore, 1926).

25. "Cotton and the Cotton Planters," *DeBow's Review* 3 (1847), p. 1.

26. Albert Burton Moore, *History of Alabama and Her People*, 3 vols. (Chicago and New York, 1927), I, p. 191. This excellent chapter is heavily laced with illustrative but anonymous quotations and embroidered with frontier figures of speech.

Chapter 2: Changing Empires

1. In no area of American history is there greater elusiveness of objectivity than in accounts of the Native American. The authors are acutely aware of this fact and call attention to Francis Paul Prucha's admonitions in "Doing Indian History," in Jane F. Smith and Robert M. Kvasnicka, eds. *Indian-White Relations: A Persistent Paradox* (Washington, 1976), pp. 1–10.

2. Robert S. Cotterill, *The Southern Indians: The Story of the Civilized Tribes Before Removal* (Norman, Okla., 1954), pp. 5–9. Statistics of the southern Indian population show wide variations. The census taker was unwilling to make a guess. In

1825 Thomas L. McKenney estimated there were 53,625 Indians in Georgia, Alabama, Tennessee, and Mississippi; 1313 in Louisiana; 5,000 in Florida and 18,917 in Arkansas, "Report, Office of Indian Affairs," January 10, 1825, *American State Papers* (hereafter cited as ASP), *Indian Affairs*, 8, p. 547. See also Henry F. Dobyns, *Native American Historical Demography: A Critical Bibliography* (Bloomington, 1976), for a comprehensive review of Native American demography.

3. John D. W. Guice, "Indigenous Prologue," in *Atlas of Mississippi*, ed. Ralph D. Cross (Jackson, Miss., 1974), pp. 24–28. The authors have drawn from a number of comprehensive histories of the southeastern Indians. For example, see Charles Hudson, *The Southwestern Indians* (Knoxville, 1976). Though many books on Native Americans have appeared in the last decade, several excellent bibliographical works are available. Three are: Dwight L. Smith, ed., *Indians of the United States and Canada: A Bibliography* (Santa Barbara, 1974); Francis Paul Prucha, *A Bibliographical Guide to the History of Indian-White Relations in the United States* (Chicago, 1977); ———, *United States Indian Policy: A Critical Bibliography* (Bloomington, 1977).

4. Arrell M. Gibson, *The Chickasaws* (Norman, Okla., 1971), pp. 4–7; Hudson, *Southeastern Indians*, p. 440.

5. Francis Paul Prucha, *American Indian Policy in the Formative Years: The Indian Trade and Intercourse Acts, 1790–1834* (Cambridge, 1962), pp. 27–37.

6. *Ibid.*, pp. 41–50. The new nation adhered to a policy of pacification.

7. ASP *Public Lands*, I, pp. 78–81; Charles C. Royce, *Indian Land Cessions in the United States* (New York, 1971), extract of *Eighteenth Annual Report of the Bureau of American Ethnology* (Washington, 1900), pp. 648–51; Charles J. Kappler, ed., *Indian Affairs: Laws and Treaties* (Washington, 1904), II, pp. 8–16. The excellent maps in Royce and the detailed treaty texts of Kappler dictate that both of these works be consulted on questions concerning treaties between the various tribes and the United States.

8. Secretary Henry Knox to Governor William Blount, April 22, 1792, quoted in Prucha, *Formative Years*, p. 41.

9. Prucha, *Formative Years*, pp. 43–50, 84–93; Edgar B. Wesley, *Guarding the Frontier: A Study in Frontier Defense from 1815 to 1825* (Minneapolis, 1935), pp. 35–41; Ora Brooks Peake, *A History of the United States Indian Factory System* (Denver, 1954), p. 2; *United States Statutes at Large*, vol. 1 (hereafter cited as 1 US Stat.), p. 443.

10. Peake, *Factory System* (Denver, 1954), pp. 10–25.

11. Prucha, *Formative Years*, p. 8.

12. *United States Statutes at Large* (Buffalo, 1962), vol. 7 (hereafter cited as 7 US Stat.), p. 24.

13. 7 *US Stat.*, pp. 42–43, Royce, *Cessions*, pp. 652–53, Kappler, *Treaties*, pp. 29–33.

14. 7 *US Stat.*, pp. 40–41.

15. *Ibid.*, pp. 56–59; Kappler, *Treaties*, pp. 46–50; Royce, *Cessions*, pp. 658–59.

16. Kappler, *Treaties*, pp. 51–55; Royce, *Cessions*, pp. 660–61, Plate CLXI.

17. Prucha, "Doing Indian History," p. 7.

18. Samuel J. Wells, "The Evolution of Jeffersonian Indian Policy with the Choctaws of Mississippi, 1800–1830" (Master's thesis, University of Southern Mississippi, 1981), pp. 9–11.

19. Dearborn to Dinsmoor, May 8, 1802, Clarence Edwin Carter, ed., *The Terri-*

torial Papers of the United States, V (Washington, 1937), p. 146. (Hereafter cited as Carter, TP.)

20. For Jefferson's long-held convictions on the educability of the Native Americans, see Thomas Jefferson, *Notes on the State of Virginia,* ed. William Peden (New York, 1954), p. 140.

21. Jefferson to Hawkins, February 18, 1803. *The Writings of Thomas Jefferson,* ed. Andrew A. Lipscomb (Washington, 1904), pp. 360–65.

22. For an example of this interpretation, see Arthur DeRosier, Jr., *The Removal of the Choctaw Indians* (Knoxville, 1970), p. 167.

23. Often cited as evidence of Jefferson's belief in removal is his letter to William Henry Harrison, Feb. 27, 1803, in *Documents of United States Indian Policy,* ed. Francis Paul Prucha (Lincoln, Neb., 1975), pp. 22–23. One of the most novel, interesting, and complex commentaries on the long-range impact of Jefferson's Indian policy is offered by Bernard W. Sheehan. Though Sheehan does not question the sincerity of Jefferson's motivation, he traces the seeds of Indian extinction to Jeffersonian paternalism. The Virginian's well-intentioned program of civilization of the natives, instead of leading to assimilation and absorption, contributed to their near annihilation, according to Sheehan. Bernard W. Sheehan, *Seeds of Extinction: Jefferson Philanthropy and the American Indian* (New York, 1973).

24. DeRosier, *Removal,* p. 167; Arrell M. Gibson, *The American Indian: Prehistory to the Present* (Lexington, Mass., 1980), p. 282; Michael D. Green, *The Politics of Indian Removal: Creek Government and Society in Crisis* (Lincoln, 1982), p. 47.

25. Robert B. Remini, *Andrew Jackson and the Course of American Empire, 1767–1821* (New York, 1977), especially Chap. 19.

26. Kappler, *Treaties,* pp. 55–56; Royce, *Cessions,* pp. 660–61.

27. Kappler, *Treaties,* pp. 56–58; Royce, *Cessions,* pp. 660–61, Plate CXLIII.

28. Kappler, *Treaties,* pp. 58–59; Royce, *Cessions,* pp. 662–63, Plate CXXII.

29. Kappler, *Treaties,* pp. 63–64; Royce, *Cessions,* pp. 662–63, Plate CXLIII.

30. Kappler, *Treaties,* pp. 69–70; Royce, *Cessions,* pp. 664–65, Plate CXLIII.

31. ASP *Indian Affairs,* II, pp. 697–98; Kappler, *Treaties,* pp. 73–74; Royce, *Cessions,* pp. 666–67, Plate CXXII; ASP *Indian Affairs,* I, October 18, 1805, p. 698. This became the famous "lost treaty" which later plagued the War Department. In 1824 Thomas Jefferson recalled its contents for John C. Calhoun. Calhoun to Jefferson, April 19, 1824, and Dearborn to Jefferson, April 14, 1804, ASP *Indian Affairs,* II, p. 511.

32. Kappler, *Treaties,* pp. 79–80; Royce, *Cessions,* pp. 668–69, Plate CLXI.

33. *Ibid.,* pp. 670–71; Kappler, *Treaties,* pp. 82–84.

34. Royce, *Cessions,* p. 671.

35. *Ibid.,* pp. 670–71; Kappler, *Treaties,* p. 84.

36. Lipscomb, 10, *Jefferson,* p. 362.

37. *Ibid.*

38. *Ibid.,* pp. 363–64.

39. *Ibid.*

40. Kappler, *Treaties,* pp. 85–86; Royce, *Cessions,* pp. 670–73.

41. The Republican stance against standing military forces must not lead one to erroneously assume that Jefferson was not staunch in his defensive posture. Indeed, his correspondence leads one to believe that he feared internal attack on republicanism from the "federal party," or "sect," as well as from foreign elements.

42. Lipscomb, *Jefferson*, 10, p. 360; 17, p. 373.

43. Dearborn to Robertson and Dinsmoor, March 20, 1805, ASP, *Indian Affairs*, II, p. 750.

44. Dearborn to Dinsmoor, August 29, 1805, Letters sent by the Superintendent of Indian Trade, 1807–1823, Record Group 75, National Archives, also available in microfilm publication M–16.

45. Often writers erroneously place Mount Dexter in the general vicinity of the Nanih Waiya mound, which is a few miles northeast of present-day Philadelphia, Mississippi, in Neshoba County. However, Henry Sales Halbert, nineteenth century educator and historian of the Choctaw, locates Mount Dexter in present-day Noxubee County just to the northeast of Neshoba County. See Folder 65N, Halbert Papers, Alabama Department of Archives and History; George S. Gaines, factor to the Choctaw, corroborates Halbert, "Gaines reminiscences," *Mobile Register*, 1872, Clippings File, J. F. H. Claiborne Letterbook E, Claiborne Collection, Mississippi Department of Archives and History. Cartographer John Melish agrees with Halbert and Gaines. See the 1818 Melish map of Alabama which includes the eastern edge of Mississippi.

46. Samuel J. Wells, "Rum, Skins, and Powder: A Choctaw, Interpreter and the Treaty of Mount Dexter," *Chronicles of Oklahoma* 61 (Winter 1983–84), p. 427. Most sources refer to Pitchlynn as a countryman, but it is not unlikely that he was a mixed blood.

47. W. David Baird, *Peter Pitchlynn: Chief of the Choctaws* (Norman, 1972).

48. For example, see Green, *Politics of Removal*, p. 47; Gibson, *Chickasaws*, p. 104. For a perspicacious treatment of this topic, see also Prucha, *Formative Years*, p. 88.

49. Lipscomb, *Jefferson*, 10, p. 370.

50. Lipscomb, *Jefferson*, 17, p. 374.

51. For example, see Thomas McKenny's instructions to Choctaw Factor George S. Gaines to raise the prices of supplies to the army 50 percent above those charged to the Indians. National Archives, Records of the Bureau of Indian Affairs, Record Group 75, Superintendent of Indian Trade, Letters Sent 1807–23, M16, Role 4, p. 401.

52. For a detailed view of Choctaw factory debts, see National Archives, Records of The Choctaw Trading House, 1803–24, Record Group 75. See also Secretary Dearborn's instructions to factor Peterkin, "The prices of the several articles of merchandise should be as uniform as possible, and to avoid disputes and ultimate losses, no credit should be given excepting in extraordinary cases and to men of note and distinction." in Dearborn to Peterkin, July 28, 1802, Letters Sent by the Secretary of War Relating to Indian Affairs, 1800–1824, National Archives.

53. ASP *Indian Affairs*, I, p. 748. The authors gratefully acknowledge that Samuel J. Wells called their attention to the questions raised by the timing of Jefferson's actions on the Mount Dexter treaty and to the tenor of his communications regarding it.

54. OED, *s.v. character*, 18.

55. ASP *Indian Affairs*, II, p. 698; Kappler, *Treaties*, 90–91; Royce, *Cessions*, pp. 668–672. For a discussion of Jefferson's strategy, see John Hawkins Napier, III, "The Gulf Coast: Key to Jeffersonian Empire," *Alabama Historical Quarterly* 33 (Summer 1974), pp. 98–115.

56. Kappler, 90–92; Royce, *Cessions*, p. 675; Meigs to unidentified correspondent, September 28, 1807, and to Dearborn, December 3, 1807, ASP *Indian Affairs*, II, p. 753.

Chapter 3: A Perimeter of Conflict

1. Lowell H. Harrison, *John Breckinridge, Jeffersonian Republican*, pp. 148–50; James Wilkinson to Juan Ventura Morales, July 6, 1803, Clarence Edwin Carter, ed., *The Territorial Papers of the United States*, V (Washington, 1937), pp. 219–21 (hereafter cited as Carter, TP.); W. C. C. Claiborne to Manuel de Salcedo, November 15, 1802, J. D. Richardson, *Messages and Papers of the Presidents*, I, pp. 348–50; Samuel Flagg Bemis, *Pinckney's Treaty* (Baltimore, 1926), especially Appendix No. 5 which contains the text of the treaty.

2. "Secretary of War to James Wilkinson," September 14, 1802, Carter, TP, V, p. 177.

3. See Arthur Preston Whitaker, *The Mississippi Question 1795–1803; A Study in Trade, Politics, and Diplomacy* (New York, 1934.

4. Carter, TP, V, p. 189.

5. 2 *U S Statutes*, pp. 139–46.

6. "Henry Dearborn to Silas Dinsmoor," May 8, 1802, Carter, TP, V, pp. 146–49. An enclosure ("copy of instructions to Several Indian Agents") defined more clearly the relationship between territorial governors and agents.

7. 2 *U S Statutes*, February 20, 1811, pp. 641–43, April 8, 1812, pp. 701–04, May 1, 1912, p. 734. Actually, Spain's claims were not finally extinguished until the Adams-Onís treaty of 1819.

8. Dunbar Rowland, ed., *Letterbooks of W. C. C. Claiborne*, V, *passim*; Isaac J. Cox, *The West Florida Controversy, 1798–1813* (Baltimore, 1918), pp. 388–436. Based on judicious, extensive use of Spanish as well as American primary sources, Cox's book remains as the authoritative work on this topic.

9. J. F. H. Claiborne, *Mississippi as a Province, Territory and State*, pp. 260–62; Cox, *West Florida Controversy*, pp. 152–63.

10. *Ibid.*, pp. 159, 163; "Claiborne to Casa Calvo," August 17, 1804, "Casa Calvo to Claiborne," August 11, 1804, Rowland, *Letterbooks*, II, pp. 308–10.

11. According to Isaac Cox, the stars of the flag carried by the Kempers were in a field of blue, but Stanley Clisby Arthur refers to "twin stars on a red union." The illustration of the "Kemper Brothers' Flag" in the Arthur book depicts four blue and three white horizontal stripes and two white stars in a solid field which is in the upper left corner of the flag. The two stars are aligned along an imaginary diagonal line running from the upper left corner of the field to the lower right corner. In other words, the stars are not side by side or on top of each other, but are placed diagonally. See Stanley C. Arthur's "The Story of the Kemper Brothers" (*St. Francisville (La.), Democrat*, July 8, 15, 22, 29, 1933, and Cox, *The West Florida Controversy*, pp. 155–56.

12. Cox, *The West Florida Controversy*, pp. 175–77.

13. Carter, TP, IX, 314–16.

14. *Ibid.*

15. Claiborne, *Mississippi*, p. 261; Cox, *West Florida Controversy*, pp. 165–67; Robert V. Haynes, "A Political History of the Mississippi Territory" (Ph.D. diss., Rice University, 1958), pp. 140–41. For testimony of several participants, see William Baskerville Hamilton, *Anglo-American Law on the Frontier: Thomas Rodney & His Territorial Cases* (Durham, N.C., 1953), pp. 245–49.

16. Connelley and Coulter, *History of Kentucky*, I, pp. 424–33.

17. "Claiborne to Casa Calvo," October 30, 31, Rowland, *Letterbooks*, II, pp. 382–84, November 8, 9, 10, 18, 22, III, pp. 5–23.

18. Thomas P. Abernethy, *The Formative Period in Alabama*, p. 9–12.

19. "Ephraim Kirby to Thomas Jefferson," May 1, 1804, Carter, TP, V, 322–26; "Claiborne to Madison," January 10, 1804, Rowland, *Letterbooks*, I, pp. 329–33; Cox, *West Florida Controversy*, pp. 150–78.

20. Carter, TP, IX, pp. 694–95.

21. Daniel Clark, *Corruption of Wilkinson*, passim; Cox, *West Florida Controversy*, pp. 284–308.

22. *Ibid.*

23. Daniel Clark, *Deposition of Daniel Clark, the Delegate in the House of Representatives from the Territory of Orleans*, pp. 6–8.

24. Cox, *West Florida Controversy*, p. 619.

25. *Ibid.*, pp. 334–41.

26. "Petition to Congress by a Convention East of the Pearl River," November 11, 1809, Carter, TP, VI, pp. 26–30. Undoubtedly the geographical designations "east of the Pearl" and "west of the Pearl" antedate their use in the 1803 Act establishing two land offices in the Mississippi Territory. The districts so designated were divided by the Pearl River, already known as the "halfway river." See "An Act Providing for the Disposal of Land South of the State of Tennessee," [March 3, 1803], Carter, TP, V, p. 195.

27. *Ibid.*

28. "Petition to Congress by Inhabitants of the Territory," Carter, TP, VI, pp. 253–57.

29. Cox, *West Florida Controversy*, pp. 313–25; for illustrations of the enmity toward French inhabitants of West Florida, see Grady Daniel Price, "The United States and West Florida, 1803–1812" (Ph.D. diss., University of Texas, 1939), pp. 87–88.

30. Cox, *West Florida Controversy*, pp. 325–28.

31. There was extensive correspondence between Governor Claiborne and various officials, including Secretary of State Robert Smith, on this subject, Rowland, *Letterbooks*, V, pp. 1–201.

32. "Membership of the West Florida Convention," July 26, 1810, Carter, TP, IX, p. 889; "Correct List of the Florida Convention," p. 895; "Audley Osborn to Claiborne," December 6, 1810, Rowland, *Letterbooks*, V, pp. 51–53.

33. Cox, *West Florida Controversy*, pp. 397–403; Stanley C. Arthur, *The Story of the West Florida Rebellion* (St. Francisville, La., 1935), pp. 89–108.

34. Arthur, *West Florida Rebellion*, pp. 107, 116.

35. Richardson, *Messages*, I, pp. 480–81.

36. *Ibid.*, p. 480.

37. "Claiborne to Secretaries of Treasury and War," December 24 & 28, 1810, "Claiborne to Secretary of State," August 28, 1810, "Holmes to Secretary of State," January 1, 1811, Carter, TP, IX, pp. 898, 903–14.

38. "Holmes to Secretary of State," Carter, TP, IX, pp. 909–14.

39. "Deposition of John Brewer and Richard Brashears," December 16, 1806, Carter, TP, V, pp. 481–82.

40. "St. Maxent to Sparks," June 25, 1810. *Ibid.*, VI, p. 77.

41. "Sparks to the Secretary of State," July 12, 1810. *Ibid.*, pp. 79–82.

42. *Ibid.*, p. 82.

43. "Toulmin to Madison," July 28, 1810. *Ibid.*, pp. 92–93.

44. "Holmes to James Caller," July 31, 1810. *Ibid.*

45. "Holmes to Toulmin," September 8, 16, December 26, 1810. *Ibid.*, pp. 113, 118, 166.

46. "Holmes to Vincente Folch," September 4, 1810. *Ibid.*, pp. 104–05.

47. "Holmes to Toulmin," September 8, 1810, "To James Caller, Joseph Carson, and James Patton," September 8, 1810. *Ibid.*, pp. 113–14.

48. "Toulmin to Madison," October 3, 1810, "To Captains of Militia," November 4, 1810. *Ibid.*, pp. 128–31.

49. "Toulmin to Madison," November 22, 1810. *Ibid.*, pp. 135–39.

50. Cox, *West Florida Controversy*, p. 470, citing Kemper to McMillan, November 23, 1810, West Florida Papers, MS., 53, 54, Library of Congress.

51. "Folch to John McKee," December 2, 1810. *Ibid.*, pp. 147–48; Cox, *West Florida Controversy*, pp. 462–75; "Robert Smith to Governor of West Florida," January 28, 1811, Carter, TP, IX, p. 922; "Secretary of State to General George Matthews and John McKee," January 26, 1811, Richardson, *Messages,* I, pp. 506–7, "To General Matthews," April 4, 1812, pp. 507–8, "To D. B. Mitchell, Governor of Georgia," April 10, 1812, pp. 508–9.

52. "Toulmin to Madison," December 12, 1810, Carter, TP, VI, pp. 152–58. *Idem.*, December 6, 1810, Carter, TP, VI, pp. 149–51.

53. *Ibid.*, November 22, 1810, pp. 135–39, November 28, 1810, pp. 140–43.

54. Carter, TP, VI, December 12, 1810, pp. 152–58; Cox, *West Florida Controversy*, p. 484. Toulmin mentions that Folch took ten to twelve prisoners, while Cox, using Spanish sources, sets the number at seven.

55. *Ibid.*, pp. 530–71.

56. "Secretary of War to Thomas Cushing," December 21, 1810, Carter, TP, VI, pp. 162–63.

57. "Cushing to Claiborne," January 8, 1822. *Ibid.*, pp. 167–68.

58. "Toulmin to Madison," February 27, 1811. *Ibid.*, pp. 179–80.

59. "Edwin Lewis to Secretary of State Robert Smith," February 15, 1812. *Ibid.*, pp. 265–67,

60. "Toulmin to Madison," February 17, 1812. *Ibid.*, pp. 268–71, "Toulmin to Graham," February 25, 1812. *Ibid.*, pp. 271–74, "Toulmin to Secretary of the Treasury," February 26, 1812. *Ibid.*, pp. 275–76, "Toulmin to Madison," March 2, 1812. *Ibid.*, pp. 276–79, James Caller to Madison," April 20, 1812, containing notations in the hand of Albert Gallatin. *Ibid.*, pp. 286–87.

61. Thomas D. Clark, ed., *A Description of Kentucky . . .*,[by Harry Toulmin] (Lexington, 1945), ix-xiii; Robert B. Haynes, "A Political History of the Mississippi Territory" (Ph.D. diss., Rice Institute, 1958), p. 137, n. 54, pp. 238–40; Leland L. Lengel, "Keeper of the Peace: Harry Toulmin in the West Florida Controversy, 1805–1813" (master's thesis, Duke University, 1962).

62. Much of this analysis reflects this views of Dr. G. Douglas Inglis of Seville, Spain, who has worked extensively in the Archivo General de Indias, and the authors gratefully acknowledge his assistance.

63. Thomas A. Bailey, "The Friendly Rivals: Bemis and Bailey," *The Society for Historians of American Foreign Relations Newsletter* X (March, 1979), p. 16.

64. This description of the capture of Mobile is based largely on Cox, *The West Florida Controversy*, pp. 609–22, and Peter J. Hamilton, *Colonial Mobile* (Boston and New York, 1897), pp. 409–15.

65. Cox, *The West Florida Controversy*. p. 618.

66. Hamilton, *Colonial Mobile*, p. 415.

Chapter 4: Land of Speculation

1. William Priest, *Travels in the United States of America: Commencing in the Year 1793 and Ending in 1797* (London, 1802), p. 132.

2. For a concise explanation of Georgia's claims, see William Estill Heath, "The Yazoo Land Fraud," *Georgia Historical Review*, 16 (December 1932), pp. 275–77.

3. For a more thorough treatment of British grants, see Clinton N. Howard, *The British Development of West Florida, 1763–1769* (Berkeley and Los Angeles, 1947); Cecil Johnson, "The Distribution of Land in British West Florida," *Louisiana Historical Quarterly*, 16 (October, 1933), pp. 539–53; ——, "Expansion in West Florida, 1770–1779," *Mississippi Valley Historical Review*, 20, (March 1934), pp. 481–96 (Hereafter cited as MVHR.); Mrs. Dunbar Rowland, "Peter Chester, Third Governor of the Province of West Florida under British Dominion, 1770–1781," Mississippi Historical Society, *Publications*, centenary series, 1 (1916), 405–28. Spanish reoccupation of West Florida is described in Robert V. Haynes, *The Natchez District and the American Revolution*, (Jackson, Miss., 1976).

4. Franklin L. Riley, "Spanish Policy in Mississippi after the Treaty of San Lorenzo," Mississippi Historical Society, *Publications*, 1 (1898), pp. 50–66; James M. Helms, "Land Tenure in Territorial Mississippi" (M.A. thesis, University of Virginia, 1954); William B. Hamilton, "American Beginnings in the Old Southwest, the Mississippi Phase" (Ph.D. dissertation, Duke University, 1938). Chapter 1 of the Hamilton dissertation, pp. 1–112, remains as one of the best treatments of land problems in Mississippi Territory.

5. Arthur Preston Whitaker, *The Spanish-American Frontier: 1783–1795: The Westward Movement and the Spanish Retreat in the Mississippi Valley* (Boston, 1927, Bison Reprint, Lincoln, 1969), pp. 55–58.

6. See Thomas P. Abernethy, *The South in the New Nation, 1789–1819* in *A History of the South*, Vol. 4, eds. Wendell Holmes Stephenson and E. Merton Coulter (Baton Rouge, 1961), pp. 74–101; Charles H. Haskins, "The Yazoo Land Companies," *Papers of the American Historical Association* 4 (October 1891), 61–103; Arthur P. Whitaker, "Documents: The South Carolina Yazoo Company," MVHR, 16 (March 1930), pp. 383–94; Heath, "The Yazoo Land Fraud."

7. Abernethy, *The South in the New Nation*, p. 79. For details of O'Fallon's operations, *ibid.*, pp. 79–85; see also Whitaker, *The Spanish American Frontier*, pp. 130–33,

140–44; John Carl Parish, "The Intrigues of Doctor James O'Fallon," MVHR, 17 (September 1930), pp. 230–63.

8. Whitaker, *The Spanish American Frontier*, p. 143; Parish, "The Intrigues of Doctor James O'Fallon," pp. 246–61.

9. Abernethy, *The South in the New Nation*, pp. 84–101; Haskins, "The Yazoo Land Companies," pp. 75–80.

10. *Ibid.*

11. *Ibid.* Also see Heath, "The Yazoo Land Fraud," pp. 278–81 and Haskins, "The Yazoo Land Companies," pp. 80–90. For numerous reports concerning the Yazoo frauds, see the ASP *Public Lands*, I. For the debate over the compromise settlement eventually passed by Congress in 1814, see *Annals of Congress*, 8 Cong, 1 and 2 Sess.

12. Absalom H. Chappell, *Miscellanies of Georgia, Historical, Biographical, Descriptive, Etc.*, (Columbus, Ga., 1928), p. 99, pp. 100–103.

13. *Ibid.*, p. 98.

14. Samuel B. Adams, "The Yazoo Fraud," *Georgia Historical Quarterly*, 7 (June 1923), p. 156.

15. *Annals of Congress*, 8 Cong., 1 Sess., p. 1140.

16. Thomas U. P. Charlton, *The Life of Major General James Jackson* (Augusta, Ga., 1809), pp. 206–9.

17. Abernethy, *The South in the New Nation*, p. 152; Haskins, "The Yazoo Land Companies," p. 86.

18. *Ibid.*, p. 88.

19. "An Act for the Government of the Mississippi Territory," Clarence Edwin Carter, *The Territorial Papers of the United States*, V (Washington, 1937), pp. 18–22. (Hereafter cited as Carter, TP.).

20. "Petition to Congress by Committee of Inhabitants," Carter, TP, 5, p. 83.

21. "An Act for the Government of the Mississippi Territory," Carter, TP, 5, pp. 18–22; "Georgia: Cession of Western Land Claims." *Ibid.*, pp. 142–46; for an analysis of the nuances of these developments, see Robert V. Haynes, "The Disposal of Lands in the Mississippi Territory," *The Journal of Mississippi History*, 24 (October 1962), pp. 226–52.

22. W. C. C. Claiborne to James Madison, Natchez, November 5, 1902, Dunbar Rowland, ed., *Official Letter Books of W. C. C. Claiborne, 1801–1816*, 1 (Jackson, Ms., 1917), pp. 219–20.

23. "An Act Providing for the Disposal of Land South of the State of Tennessee," March 3, 1803, Carter, TP, 5, pp 192–205; Helms, "Land Tenure in Territorial Mississippi," pp. 38–65.

24. "An Act for the Government of the Mississippi Territory," May 10, 1800, Carter, TP, 5, pp. 95–98.

25. Donald A. MacPhee, "The Yazoo Controversy: The Beginning of the 'Quid' Revolt," *Georgia Historical Quarterly* 49 (March 1965), pp. 23–43.

26. *Annals of Congress*, 8 Cong., 1 Sess., p. 1104.

27. *Ibid.*, 8 Cong., 2 Sess., p. 1032.

28. *Ibid.*

29. *Ibid.*, pp. 1121–26.

30. Jane Elsmere, "The Notorious Yazoo Land Fraud Case," *Georgia Historical*

Quarterly, 51 (December, 1967), pp. 425–42; C. Peter Magrath, *Yazoo: Law and Politics in the New Republic—The Case of Fletcher V. Peck* (Providence, R.I., 1966).

31. *Annals of Congress*, 13 Cong., 1 & 2 Sess., p. 1838.

32. 3 *U. S. Statutes*, p. 116.

33. Richard S. Lackey, "Credit Land Sales, 1811–1815: Mississippi Entries East of the Pearl" (M.S. thesis, University of Southern Mississippi, 1975), p. 113. In an exemplary piece of scholarship based on complete histories of 190 parcels of land, Lackey demonstrates that previous generalizations on the failure of the credit system were not supported by the experience in Mississippi Territory east of the Pearl. It took Lackey several years and thousands of hours to document his study which serves as a model for persons desirous of acquainting themselves with use of land records.

34. Executive Proclamation by Governor David Holmes, June 29, 1815 (Carter, TP, 6), p. 538. For a particularly entertaining letter from an illiterate squatter from "Munrow" County to President James "Maderson," see "Clabon Harris to the President." *Ibid*, pp. 647–48.

35. 2 *U. S. Statutes*, pp. 526, 765. Also, ASP *Public Lands*, I, p. 908.

36. Harry Toulmin to William Lattimore, December 6, 1805 (Carter, TP, 5), pp. 431–38; Thomas Rodney to C. A. Rodney, December 31, 1804, *Pennsylvania Magazine of History and Biography*, 44, No. 2 (1920), pp. 183–85.

Chapter 5: Wilderness Artery

1. Winthrop Sargent to Timothy Pickering, April 20, 1799, Dunbar Rowland, ed., *Mississippi Territorial Archives*, I, (Nashville, 1905), pp. 139–44.

2. Pickering to Sargent, May 20, 1799, Clarence Edwin Carter, ed., *The Territorial Papers of the United States*, V, (Washington, 1937), p. 57.

3. Julian P. Bretz, "Early Land Communications with the Lower Mississippi Valley," *Mississippi Valley Historical Review*, 13, (June, 1926), pp. 3–29; See Arminta Scott Spalding, "The Natchez Trace Parkway: A Study of Origins of an Interstate Federal Highway," (M.A. thesis, Stephen F. Austin State College, 1965), p. 6.

4. J. F. H. Claiborne, *Mississippi As a Province, Territory and State* (Jackson, 1880), p. 222; For an excellent treatment of the commercial growth of Natchez, see Michael F. Beard, "Natchez Under-the-Hill, 1790–1840: A Reinterpretation" (Honors thesis, University of Southern Mississippi, 1971), pp. 15–30; W. Wallace Carson, "Transportation and Traffic on the Ohio and the Mississippi Before the Steamboat" *Mississippi Valley Historical Review*, 7 (June, 1920), p. 34.

5. Extract from the speech of the Commissioners of the United States to the chiefs of the Cherokees assembled at Southwest Point, September 4th, 1801, ASP, *Indian Affairs*, I, pp. 656–57.

6. Commissioners James Wilkinson, Benjamin Hawkins, and Andrew Pickens to Secretary of War Dearborn, Chickasaw Bluffs, October 25, 1801, ASP, *Indian Affairs*, I, pp. 651–52.

7. See Chapter 2, pp. 31 above.

8. Dawson A. Phelps, "The Natchez Trace in Alabama," *The Alabama Historical Review*, 7 (January, 1954), pp. 22–41; Lena Mitchell Jamison, "The Natchez Trace:

A Federal Highway of the Old Southwest," *The Journal of Mississippi History*, 1 (April, 1939), pp. 82–99.

9. William Baskerville Hamilton, "American Beginnings in the Old Southwest: The Mississippi Phase" (Ph.D. dissertation, Duke University, 1938), pp. 157–66; For a comparison of the modern Natchez Trace Parkway and the historic Natchez Trace, including a thoroughly illustrated map, see Bern Keating, "Today Along the Natchez Trace," *National Geographic*, 134 (November, 1968), pp. 641–67.

10. Three decades ago Professor Francis Paul Prucha investigated the many facets of military roads in the Old Northwest. While no comparable study has been undertaken for the Old Southwest, it is clear that there also the role of the military in the construction of roads was critical. See Francis Paul Prucha, *Broadax and Bayonet: The Role of the United States Army in the Development of the Northwest 1815–1860* (Madison, Wis., 1953), pp. 131–48. Jefferson refers to the trace as a "military road" in "The President to the Postmaster General," July 18, 1806, Carter, TP, V, pp. 471–72.

11. W. C. C. Claiborne to James Madison, December 20, 1801, Rowland, *Territorial Archives*, I, pp. 363–64.

12. Francis Baily, *Journal of Tour in Unsettled Parts of North America in 1796 & 1797* (London, 1856).

13. Dawson A. Phelps, "Stands and Travel Accommodations on the Natchez Trace," *Journal of Mississippi History*, 11 (January, 1949), pp. 1–54; this excellent piece by Phelps, for years a historian for the Natchez Trace Parkway, is based on an exhaustive search of travel gazetteers, diaries and journals, and official records. Also see Phelps, "The Natchez Trace in Tennessee History," *Tennessee Historical Quarterly*, 13 (September 1954) pp. 196–203; the later piece contains considerable bibliographical data.

14. Many primary and secondary sources contain frequent references to mixed bloods on the trace. See Samual Wells, "Choctaw Mixed Bloods and the Advent of Removal," (Ph.D. diss., University of Southern Mississippi, 1987).

15. Phelps, "Stands and Travel," pp. 4 & 20.

16. *Ibid.*, p. 5.

17. S. F. Hildreth, "History of a Voyage on the Ohio and Mississippi Rivers, with Historical Sketches of the Different Points along Them," *The American Pioneer*, 1 (March 1842), pp. 140–45.

18. W. C. C. Claiborne to Daniel Burnet, April 27, 1802, Rowland, *Territorial Archives*, I, pp. 422–23.

19. *Ibid.*; also see Claiborne, *Mississippi*, pp. 226–28.

20. W. C. C. Claiborne to John McKee, June 29, 1802, Rowland, *Territorial Archives*, I. pp. 458–59.

21. Robert M. Coates, *The Outlaw Years: The History of the Land Pirates of the Natchez Trace* (New York, 1930), pp. 66 & 161–65; Jonathan Daniels, *The Devils Backbone: The Story of the Natchez Trace* (New York, 1962), pp. 114–24.

22. Erik F. Haites, James Mak, and Gary M. Walton, *Western River Transportation: The Era of Early Internal Development, 1810–1860*, The Johns Hopkins University Studies in Historical and Political Science, 93rd Series (Baltimore, 1975), pp. 21–3.

23. Hamilton, "American Beginnings," p. 164. Though he mentions no names, Hamilton clearly was reacting to a highly popular work by novelist Robert M. Coates, *The Outlaw Years*, published in 1930. For a commentary on this extremely readable work, see the 1986 University of Nebraska Press reprint with a foreword by John D. W. Guice. Ironically, Coates devotes nearly half of the book to John A. Murrell, who committed his most infamous acts in the years after travel on the trace had significantly declined. See James Lal Penick, Jr., *The Great Western Land Pirate: John A. Murrell in Legend and History* (Columbia, Mo., 1981).

24. Hamilton, "American Beginnings," p. 165.

25. Michael Francis Beard, "Frontier Port on the Mississippi: A History of the Legend of Natchez Under-the-Hill, 1800–1900" (M.A. thesis, Louisiana State University, 1981); see also, Beard, "Natchez Under-the-Hill, 1790–1840: A Reinterpretation (Honors thesis, University of Southern Mississippi, 1971). Beard's M.A. thesis is a penetrating and creative 205-page analysis of the rise and decline of the images and legends relating to Natchez Under-the-Hill. Not since the late William B. Hamilton has a scholar so thoroughly searched extant files of Natchez newspapers, and though Beard cites no statistics, he expressed this view in conversations with John Guice.

26. Claiborne, *Mississippi*. p. 228.

27. Beard, "Frontier Port on the Mississippi," pp. 22–53.

28. See, for example, Raymond Friday Locke, "The Natchez Trace: Road of Blood," *Mankind*, (1975) pp. 30–37.

29. Daniels, *The Devil's Backbone*, pp. 102–3; D. Clayton James, *Antebellum Natchez* (Baton Rouge, 1968), pp. 136–61.

30. Jamison, "The Natchez Trace," pp. 84–85; Bretz, "Early Land Communications," pp. 6–9; "Postal Schedule: Nashville to Natchez," Carter, TP, VI, pp. 404–5; see also Daniels, *The Devil's Backbone*, pp. 114–24.

31. Robert Green Hall, "The Natchez Trace: A Study in Transportation and Travel between the Early West and Southwest" (M. A. thesis, University of Wisconsin, 1914), pp. 41–42; Spalding, "The Natchez Trace Parkway," pp. 30–31; Daniels, *Devil's Backbone*, pp. 140–49.

32. Hamilton, "American Beginnings," pp. 167–71; W. A. Evans, "Gaines Trace in Monroe County, Mississippi," *Journal of Mississippi History*, 1 (April 1939), pp. 100–09; Arthur Dugan and J. H. Evans, "Gaines Through Eastern Clay County, Mississippi," *Journal of Mississippi History*, 1 (April, 1939), pp. 127–28.

33. Phelps, "The Natchez Trace in Tennessee History," p. 197.

Chapter 6: Rough Riders in the Old Southwest

1. J. F. H. Claiborne, "A Trip Through the Piney Woods," *Publications of the Mississippi Historical Society*, 9 (Oxford, 1906), pp. 514, 521–22, 530.

2. Frank L. Owsley, *Plain Folk of the Old South* (Baton Rouge, 1949), p. viii.

3. John Ray Skates, Jr., "In Defense of Owsley's Yeoman" in Frank Allen Dennis, ed., *Southern Miscellany: Essays in History in Honor of Glover Moore* (Jackson, 1981), pp. 3–15; here Skates speculates on reasons why historians downplayed

Owsley. Particularly interesting are his comments on the effects of Marxist interpretations and of emphases on minority history.

4. Lewis Cecil Gray, *History of Agriculture in the Southern United States to 1860,* Carnegie Institution of Washington Publication No. 430, 2 vols. (Washington, 1932), p. 1042, Table 53: Number of horses and mules, cattle, swine, and sheep in the Southern states, 1840, 1850, 1860.

5. Forrest McDonald and Grady McWhiney, "The South from Self-Sufficiency to Peonage: An Interpretation," *American Historial Review,* 85 (December 1980), p. 1099; Donald B. Dodd and Wynelle S. Dodd, *Historical Statistics of the South, 1790–1970* (University, Ala., 1973), pp. 4, 36.

6. Owsley, *Plain Folk,* pp. 47–48.

7. Frederick Jackson Turner, *The Frontier in American History* (New York, 1920), p. 16

8. Recently historians have argued that theories on the origins of the Texas cattle industry presented by Walter Prescott Webb in *The Great Plains* (Boston, 1931) were not only in error but that they also suppressed the study of cattle raising in the South. See John D. W. Guice, "Cattle Raisers of the Old Southwest: A Reinterpretation," *Western Historical Quarterly,* 8 (April 1977), pp. 167–87 and Terry G. Jordan, *Trails to Texas: Southern Roots of Western Cattle Ranching* (Lincoln, 1981). Jordan traces the diffusion of Anglo cattle herding from its "Carolina hearth" westward through the South into Texas and ultimately on to the high plains. Other scholars blame Frederick Jackson Turner for the relegation of the Southern herders by historians to such a minor role. See Forrest McDonald and Grady McWhiney, "The Antebellum Southern Herdsman: A Reinterpretation," *Journal of Southern History,* 41 (May 1975), pp. 147–66. In this article McDonald and McWhiney introduce their argument that the Scotch-Irish frontiersmen brought to the Southern frontier from the British Isles their centuries-old Celtic herding heritage. For further reading on their "Celtic thesis" which has generated considerable reaction, also see Grady McWhiney, "The Revolution in Nineteenth-Century Alabama Agriculture." *Alabama Review,* 31 (January 1978), pp. 3–32; Forrest McDonald and Grady McWhiney, "Antebellum North and South in Comparative Perspective: A Discussion," *American Historical Review,* 85 (December 1980), pp. 1150–66; ———, "Comparative History in Theory and Practice: A Discussion," *American Historical Review,* 87 (February 1982), pp. 134–37; Forrest McDonald and Ellen Shapiro McDonald, "The Ethnic Origins of the American People, 1790," *William and Mary Quarterly,* 3rd Series, 37 (April 1980), pp. 179–99; Grady McWhiney, *Attack and Die: Civil War Military Tactics and the Southern Heritage* (Univesity, Ala., 1982)

9. Statement of Gonzalo de Riber, Saint Augustine, May 17, 1567, Escribania de Camara, 154-A, fol. 1,322, Archivo General de Indias (AGI). The authors gratefully acknowledge the research assistance of Dr. G. Douglas Inglis, Seville, Spain, who provided material cited herein from the Archivo General de Indias.

10. Gray, *History of Agriculture,* I, pp. 55–57.

11. N. M. Miller Surrey, *The Commerce of Louisiana during the French Regime, 1699–1763,* Columbia University Studies in History, Economics, and Public Law, vol. 71, no. 1 (New York, 1916), p. 61.

12. Statement of Ezekiel Forman to Governor Estevan Miró [1791], Papeles procedentes de Isla de Cuba (PC), legajo (leg.) 120, AGI.

13. Winston DeVille, *Opelousas: The History of a French and Spanish Military Post in America, 1716–1803* (Cottonport, La., 1973), p. 6; William Darby, *The Emigrant's Guide to the Western and Southwestern States and Territories* (New York, 1818), pp. 76–77; Estwick Evans, *A Pedestrious Tour* (Concord, N.H. 1819), in Reuben Gold Thwaites, ed., *Early Western Travels, 1748–1846*, 32 vols. (New York, 1966), 8, pp. 313, 329–30.

14. William Baskerville Hamilton, "American Beginnings in the Old Southwest: The Mississippi Phase" (Ph.D. diss., Duke University, 1938), pp. 183–84 (date on title page is 1937, but the date of committee approval is January 14, 1938); Timothy Flint, *History and Geography of the Mississippi Valley* (Cincinnati, 1832), pp. 216–9; also see Clarence Walnorth Alvord and Clarence Edwin Carter, eds., *Journal of Capt. H. Gordon, 1766*, Collections of the Illinois State Historical Library, vol. 11 (Springfield, Ill., 1916), p. 307.

15. Charles W. Arnade, "Cattle Raising in Spanish Florida, 1513–1763," *Agricultural History*, 35 (July 1961), pp. 116–24; Joe A. Akerman, Jr., *Florida Cowman, a History of Florida Cattle Raising* (Kissimmee, Fla., 1976).

16. P. Lee Phillips, *Notes on the Life and Works of Bernard Romans*. Publications of the Florida State Historical Society, no. 2 (De Land, Fla., 1924), pp. 120–23.

17. Cecil Johnson, *British West Florida, 1763–1783* (New Haven, 1943), p. 170; Akerman, *Florida Cowman*, p. 12–13; Jordan, *Trails to Texas*, p. 42.

18. Census figures are from Papel procedentes de Isla de Cuba, Archivo General de Indias, in the following legajos: 1784: leg. 116; 1787: leg. 200; 1788: leg. 2361; 1792: leg 2353; 1794: leg. 31; Recensement du Poste de Oppeloussais, pour l'année de 1788, PC, leg. 2361, AGI. In 1799 one third of the cattle at the Rapides Post were in herds of 100 or more. See Winston DeVille, ed., *Rapides Post—1799* (Baltimore, 1968), pp. 3–8.

19. Padron del Districto de la Nueva Feliciana, July 14, 1798, PC, leg. 192, AGI. A 1797 census of the Tombigbee shows that forty of the fifty-four family units owned a total of 1292 head for a ratio of 4.72 cattle per person, 23.93 per family, or 32.40 per cattle-owning family; see Districto de San Estevan de Tombecbe, April 16, 1797, PC, leg. 64, AGI.

20. Relaciones of Eduardo Nugent and Juan Kelly, 1770, PC, leg 81, AGI.

21. Enclosure in Daniel Clark to James Madison, New Orleans, July 26, 1803, Consular Dispatches, New Orleans, 1798–1807, Microcopy T-225, Record Group 59, General Records of the Department of State, National Archives; Gray, *History of Agriculture*, I, p. 150, cities estimate as high as 300,000 by the turn of the century grazing on grass as high as a horse's back.

22. Lists for Washington County, 1804, Claiborne County, 1804, and Jefferson County, 1805: Auditors' Records, Series B. vol. 15, Territorial Archives; List for Adams County, 1805; Auditors' Records, Series A and B, vol. "Oversize," Territorial Archives; List for Washington County, 1805, and Wilkinson County, 1805; Auditors' Records, Series B, vol. 16; Territorial Archives, Mississippi Department of Archives and History, Jackson.

23. Hamilton, *Papers*, Box 144, Duke University Library. Because the territo-

rial archives in Jackson have been recatalogued, the citations on Hamilton's card vary from those in note 30, but unquestionably he handled the same documents.

24. Jordan, *Trails to Texas*, pp. 25–28.

25. Webb erred in his insistence that "American men began handling cattle on horseback" in Texas. Webb, *Great Plains*, p. 208.

26. Sandra L. Myers, "The Ranching Frontier: Spanish Instutitional Backgrounds of the Plains Cattle Industry," in *Essays on the American West*, ed., Harold M. Hollingsworth and Sandra L. Myers (Austin, 1969), pp. 19–39; Donald E. Worcester mentions the Spanish influence through Florida in "The Significance of the Spanish Borderlands to the United States," *Western Historical Quarterly*, 7 (1976), p. 6. Arnade, "Cattle Raising in Spanish Florida," *Annals of the Association of American Geographers*, 66 (1976), pp. 360–76.

27. Claiborne, "A Trip trough the Piney Woods," pp. 521–22; ———. "Rough Riding Down South," *Harper's New Monthly Magazine*, (June 1862), pp. 29–37. For other comparisons, see John Hedges Goff, *Retracing the Old Federal Road and Cow Punching in Old Georgia: Two Articles Relating to the Economic History of Georgia*, Emory University Studies in Business and Economics, no. 5 (Atlanta, 1950); Frederic Remington, "Cracker Cowboys of Florida," *Harper's New Monthly Magazine*, 91 (August 1895), pp. 339–45.

28. Hamilton, on p. 182 of his 1938 dissertation, concluded that cattle raising was a "more universal occupation than the raising of tobacco or cotton."

29. For example, see Gray, *History of Agriculture*, I, p. 150 and Jordan, *Trails to Texas*, p. 41.

30. John G. Clark, *New Orleans, 1718–1812: An Economic History* (Baton Rouge, 1970), pp. 158, 259–60. Clark's statements are not documented adequately; the size of the herds in the Opelousas and Atakapas regions as well as in the Natchez District do not substantiate his assessment of the meat consumption in New Orleans. However, in his letter to the author, Lawrence, Kansas, May 7, 1973, he indicates an awareness of the effect of market prices in the West Indies on the sale of cattle locally—i.e., cattle may have been shipped there instead of to New Orleans for domestic consumption.

31. Clarence Walnorth Alvord and Clarence Edwin Carter, eds., *Journals of Capt. H. Gordon, 1766*, Collections of the Illinois State Historical Library, vol. 11 (Springfield, Ill., 1916), p. 306; Peter J. Hamilton, *Colonial Mobile* (Mobile, 1897), pp. 258–59; Clark, *New Orleans*, pp. 56–57; *Mobile Commercial Register*, Dec. 16, 1822, p. 2.

32. Though some ship's manifests are in Record Group 36, National Archives, they appear to be incomplete. Undoubtedly, recently collected papers of Panton, Leslie, and Company at the University of West Florida contain information on this topic.

33. W. H. Sparks, *The Memories of Fifty Years* (Philadelphia, 1870), p. 333.

34. "Agreement," October 31, 1786, signed by Juan Joseph Martino and John Ellis calling for delivery in October 1787 of 66 two-year-old and 34 eighteen-month-old horned cattle, 5 two-year-old bulls, and a pair of working oxen four or five years old for $1,800. Copy of Spanish Translations, Natchez Records, Book D. 29, Hamilton Papers, Box 129.

35. "Agreement," between Paul Lafitte of District of Natchitoches and Stephen Minor, Commandant, Natchez Records, Book D, 33. Each man could choose an

expert to examine the cattle on arrival to determine them to be "free from all 'epidemic' or other diseases," and the animals were to be evenly divided by ages at two, three, and four years "upward." Estate Inventory Book, 1790–1800, Bisland (John and Family) Papers, Box 4, Department of Archives and Manuscripts, Louisiana State University Library.

36. Hamilton, "American Beginnings in the Old Southwest," p. 183.

37. Antonio deGrass to Samuel Kelly, Sandy Creek, November 27, 1803, Gras-Lauzin (Family) Papers, Box 1, Louisiana State University Library. Another indication of the fluctuation in prices is a sale of 2,019 head (about 1804) at $13 each, "Rodney's Notebook, 1806 Dec. 5, Sup. Ct. Cormeo *v*. Ellot [Ellet]," cited on note in Hamilton Papers, Box 144.

38. Libramientos paid at New Orleans for Natchez accounts, 1785–90, PC, leg. 282, AGI.

39. Mention is not made here of legislation and codes as indicators of social and economic history in general and the significance of the cattle industry in particular.

40. Typed copy of "Inventory of Estate of Isaac Guion," Box 54, Chancery Clerk's Office, Natchez, Hamilton Papers, Box 131, file "I."

41. Note citing Hanah Vousden *v*. Executors of William Vousden, Mississippi Territorial Supreme Court, May 26, 1808; reference simply lists source as Brown University Library, Hamilton Papers, Box 133; Hamilton, *Colonial Mobile*, p. 341.

42. Correspondence between Colonel Josef Ezpeleta and Capitán Manuel Caboello, January–March, 1781, PC, leg. 116, AGI. John Blommart in Account Current with Richard DeVall, [1781], PC, leg. 9-a, AGI; Carlos de Grande Pré to Estevan Miró, No. 240, May 6, 1782, PC, leg. 9-a, AGI; also letters to Miró No. 149, June 3, 1782 and No. 152, June 3, 1782, PC, Leg. 9-a, AGI.

43. Grimarest to Ferrer, March 26, April 9, and May 23, PC, leg. 116, AGI. Sale of beef to the British in indicated in Alexander Dickson, Manchac, to Charles de Grand Pré [Point Coupe], April 13, 1779, PC, leg. 192, AGI. The "customary price of 12 dollars per head" is mentioned in Patrick Strachen to Colonel Josef de Ezeleta, Tansa, June 18, 1780, PC. leg. 193-b, AGI. Louisiana, which was exporting cattle in 1777, by 1780 obtained permission for *Ganado Bacuno* (cattle) to be driven there from Texas; El Cavallero de Croix to Joseph de Gálvez, Arispe, No. 570, October 23, 1780, AGI, Audiencia de Guadalajara, leg. 267, AGI. The examination of John Brown taken before Jno. Blommart, Natchez District, December 20, 1780, PC, leg. 2359, AGI.

44. Petition of Inhabitants of Mississippi Territory *re* Indian Depredation, January 2, 1816, Private Claims, 13th Cong., 3rd sess., Records of the United States House of Representatives, Record Group 233, National Archives. Published as *Frontier Claims in the Lower South*, compiled by Richard S. Lackey with an Introduction by John D. W. Guice (New Orleans, 1977); Captain Samuel Manac, a friendly mixed-blood Creek, listed, in a similar petition, a loss of 700 cattle valued at $4,200 and 200 head of hogs valued at $860; see "Indemnity for Damages by Creek Indians," March 15, 1828, Twentieth Congress, first session, House Document No. 200, p. 8–11.

45. Thirty-three other claimants, without specifying the exact nature of their

losses, sought some $8,000 damages in this petition, mainly citing claims for lost stock without further description.

46. According to affidavit "P" included in this petition, Alexis Trouillet, a "free man of color" owned, if not all, at least a share of 130 head of horned cattle valued at $1,560.

47. For example, William and Jonathan Pierce, in their affidavit, listed cattle for roughly one-fourth of their nearly $10,000 loss, which included evidences of a multiple business operation.

48. Gary S. Dunbar, "Colonial Carolina Cowpens," *Agricultural History*, 35 (July 1961), p. 126, for comments on ownership of cattle on the frontier by Charleston merchants. Peter H. Wood, *Black Majority: Negroes in Colonial South Carolina From 1670 through the Stono Rebellion* (New York, 1974), p. 30.

49. Jacob R. Marcus, *The Colonial American Jew, 1492–1776*, 3 vols. (Detroit, 1970), III, pp. 534–35; ———, *Early American Jewry: The Jews of Pennsylvania and the South, 1635–1790* (Philadelphia, 1953), pp. 324–44.

50. Jordan, *Trails to Texas*, p. 50.

51. John Spencer Bassett, ed., "Major Howell Tatum's Journal While Acting Topographical Engineer (1814) to General Jackson Commanding the Seventh Military District," *Smith College Studies in History*, 7 (Northampton, Mass., 1921–22), p. 95.

52. For an argument for the accuracy of the term *ranch* in regard to Florida plantations, see William Theodore Mealor, Jr., "The Open Range Ranch in South Florida and Its Contemporary Successors" (Ph.D. diss., University of Georgia, 1972), pp. 34–47. One of the few historians of the South to use the term *ranch* is John Hebron Moore in his *Agriculture in Ante-Bellum Mississippi* (New York, 1958), p. 40.

53. Gray, *History of Agriculture*, I, p. 150; G. Douglas Inglis, "Anthony Hutchins: Early Natchez Planter," (M.A. thesis, University of Southern Mississippi, 1973), pp. 57–58.

54. Evans, *Pedestrious Tour*, p. 330.

55. See the "1775 map of Mobile Bay and the Mobile or Tombecbe [Tombigbee] River, showing the boundary of the Choctaw Indians between the Tombecbe and Pascagoula Rivers," C. O. 700, Florida, No. 51, Public Record Office, London. We credit Dr. G. Douglas Inglis for calling our attention to this map.

56. Lawrence Kinnaird, ed., *Spain in the Mississippi Valley 1765–1794*, in two parts, Annual Report of the American Historical Association, 1945, 3 vols. (Washington, 1946), III, pp. 305–11. Spanish census of 1792, PC, leg. 2, 353, AGI.

57. For detailed examples, see Guice, "Cattle Raisers of the Old Southwest," n. 68, pp. 183–84.

58. Robert William Fogel and Stanley L. Engerman, *Time on the Cross: The Economics of American Negro Slavery* (Boston, 1974), p. 42.

59. John S. Wilson, "Health Department," *Godey's Lady's Book*, 60 (February 1860), p. 178 cited in Sam Bowers Hilliard, *Hog Meat and Hoecake: Food Supply in the Old South, 1840–1869* (Carbondale, 1972), p. 42.

60. Hilliard, *Hog Meat and Hoecake*, p. 92.

61. Richard Parkinson, *A Tour of America in 1798, 1799, and 1800. Exhibiting Sketches of Society and Manners, and a Particular Account of the American System of Agriculture with Its Recent Improvements*, 2 vols. (London, 1805), p. 290 cited in Gray, *History of Agriculture*, I, p. 206.

62. Gray, *History of Agriculture*, p. 206.

63. McDonald and McWhiney, "The Antebellum Southern Herdsman," p. 154. Hilliard, *Hog Meat and Hoe Cake*, pp. 92–111.

64. McDonald and McWhiney, "The South from Self-Sufficiency to Peonage," p. 1103; ——, "The Antebellum Southern Herdsman," p. 159.

65. McDonald and McWhiney, "The South from Self-Sufficiency to Peonage," p. 1107.

66. Gray, *History of Agriculture*, II, Table 53, p. 1042.

67. Eben'r Ford to Thomas Ewbank, November 6, 1850, *Report of the Commissioner of Patents, for the Year 1850. Part II. Agriculture* (Washington, 1851), pp. 260–61.

68. Hamilton Papers, Box 144, citing "An abstract of manufactures, establishments, and manufactures within the Mississippi Territory taken from reports of the assistants employed in taking the census of [ ]" from a "Miscellaneous Almanack." Hamilton, a meticulous researcher, dated the recap 1812.

69. *New-Orleans Price-Current and Commercial Intelligencer*, vols. 4 and 5, 1825–27. A cursory survey of the weekly prices reported in this journal for dried and salted hides, horns, sole leather, upper leather, tanner's oil, and tallow indicates a lively market for these products during this period. Though he has not undertaken a statistical analysis of the data, colleague G. Douglas Inglis of Seville, Spain, concludes that a sizable shoe-manufacturing industry existed in New Orleans in the 1780s and 1790s, based on an unusually large number of cobblers listed on pertinent Spanish censuses. Inglis to author, June 7, 1976.

70. Hamilton, "American Beginnings in the Old Southwest," pp. 184–85.

71. McDonald and McWhiney, "The Antebellum Southern Herdsmen," p. 166.

72. Dunbar, "Cowpens," p. 130. Wood, *Black Majority*, p. 30.

73. Jordan, *Trail to Texas*, pp. 74, 143; Akerman, *Florida Cowman*, pp. 41.

74. Evans, *Pedestrious Tour*, p. 328; Darby, *Emigrant's Guide*, p. 77.

75. Order of Don Alexander O'Reilly. Here the term *tame* cattle is used, but throughout the colonial and early national periods the terms *neat, black,* and *horned* were used interchangeably, sometimes in tandem, such as "neat or black" cattle.

76. Philip Durham and Everett L. Jones, *The Negro Cowboys* (New York, 1965), p. 19. "Thus the story of the Negro cowboys began in Texas and the Indian Nations before the Civil War. There thousands of Negroes, most slaves, some free, learned to ride and rope and brand."

77. Michael F. Doran, "Antebellum Cattle Herding in the Indian Territory," *Geographical Review*, 66 (1976), pp. 48–58.

78. Arrell M. Gibson, *The Chickasaws* (Norman, 1971), pp. 227–28, 288; Akerman, *Florida Cowman*, pp. 20–22.

79. Hawkins, "Sketch of Creek Country," p. 93.

80. Dawson A. Phelps, "The Choctaw Mission: An Experiment in Civilization," *Journal of Mississippi History*, 14 (January 1952), p. 44.

81. Herbert Weaver, *Mississippi Farmers 1850–1860* (Knoxville, 1945), p. 13.

Chapter 7: Dance of the Prophets

1. Claiborne to Monroe," July 9, 1812, Dunbar Rowland, ed., *Official Letterbooks of W. C. C. Claiborne, 1801–1816*, VI (Jackson, 1917), pp. 127–28.

2. Rowland, *Letterbooks*. This is true of the correspondence contained in vol-

umes V and VI, 1811 and 1812. Also, see the correspondence of David B. Holmes for the same period in Clarence Edwin Carter, ed., *The Territorial Papers of the United States*, VI, (Washington, 1938).

3. *Annals of Congress*, 12th Congress, 1st Session, p. 326; 2 *U. S. Statutes*, p. 734; "Holmes to Wilkinson," October 19, 1812, Carter, TP, VI, pp. 328–29.

4. "Holmes to Wilkinson," *Ibid.*, p. 328.

5. *Ibid.*, p. 329.

6. "Holmes to Secretary of State," May 5, 1813, Carter, TP, VI, pp. 364–65; for an analysis of the roles of Great Britain and Spain in the War of 1812 in the South, see Frank Lawrence Owsley, Jr., *Struggle for the Gulf Borderlands: The Creek War and the Battle of New Orleans 1812–1815* (Gainesville, 1981), pp. 18–29.

7. James Wilkinson, *Memoirs of My Own Times*, 3 vols. (Philadelphia, 1816), I, pp. 507–8.

8. 2 *U. S. Statutes*, p. 734.

9. "Claiborne to Wilkinson," Rowland, *Letterbooks*, VI, pp. 216–17; "A Proclamation," March 15, 1813. *Ibid.*, pp. 232–33.

10. Thomas Robson Hay and M. R. Werner, *The Admirable Trumpeter*, p. 312; Peter J. Hamilton, *Colonial Mobile*, pp. 410–11; Wilkinson, *Memoirs*, I, p. 522.

11. Wilkinson, Memoirs, I, pp. 510–16; Hamilton, *Colonial Mobile*, pp. 411–14.

12. March 7, 1812, John Spencer Bassett, ed., *The Correspondence of Andrew Jackson*, I (Washington, 1926), pp. 220–21. He had written Thomas Jefferson earlier, November 6, 1806, that he would lead troops in the event of Indian war. *Ibid.*, I, p. 156.

13. "To George Campbell," January 15, 1807, Bassett, *Correspondence*, I, pp. 167–70; "To General Henry Dearborn," March 17, 1807. *Ibid.*, pp. 172–78; "Claiborne to Jackson," March 27, 1807. *Ibid.*, I, p. 179; Robert V. Remini, *Andrew Jackson and the Course of American Empire, 1767–1821* (New York, 1977), pp. 165–70.

14. *Ibid.*, pp. 170–71.

15. "Jackson's Announcement to His Soldiers," November 14, 1812, Bassett, *Correspondence*, I, pp. 241–42.

16. "Willie Blount to Jackson," December 31, 1812. *Ibid.*, pp. 252–53.

17. Remini, *American Empire*, pp. 172–74.

18 *Ibid.*, p. 174.

19. Because Russia and Spain were at this time allies, the Czar attempted to play the role of peacemaker between the United States and Great Britain. Hence Congress, which previously had seemed to favor an invasion of East Florida, now showed some hesitancy to risk war with Spain. "Armstrong to Jackson," February 5, 1813, Bassett, *Correspondence*, I, pp. 275–76.

20. "Claiborne to Jackson," March 15, 1813, Rowland, *Letterbrooks*, VI, p. 213.

21. "Armstrong to Wilkinson," May 27, 1813, Carter, TP, VI, p. 370.

22. As cited in Hamilton, *Colonial Mobile*, p. 415; "Armstrong to Wilkinson," May 22, 1813, Carter, TP, VI, p. 368.

23. "Claiborne to Simon Farve," August 4, 1812, Rowland, *Letterbooks*, VI, pp. 138–39; "To David Holmes," August 9, 1812. *Ibid.*, p. 151.

24. Secretary of War to Wade Hampton," July 20, 1811, Carter, TP, VI, p. 213; "Armstrong to Hawkins," April 26, 1813, *American State Papers, Indian Affairs*, I, pp. 840–41; "Hawkins to Big Warrior," April 26, 1813. *Ibid.*, p. 843.

25. "Hawkins to Doyell," March 25, 1813, *Ibid.*, p. 839.

26. "Mrs. Crowley's Deposition," August 11, 1812, Bassett, *Correspondence*, I, p. 225 nl; Frank Lawrence Owsley, Jr., *Struggle for the Gulf Borderlands: The Creek War and the Battle of New Orleans, 1812–1815* (Gainesville, Fla., 1981), pp. 15–16.

27. ASP, *Indian Affairs*, I, p. 813.

28. *Ibid*.

29. J. F. H. Claiborne, *Mississippi as a Province, Territory and State* (Jackson, 1880), p. 317.

30. *Ibid*. For a recent, balanced treatment of Tecumseh, see R. David Edmunds, *Tecumseh and the Quest for Indian Leadership* (Boston, 1984). For a thorough historiographical assessment of Tecumseh, see Edmunds, "Tecumseh, The Shawnee Prophet, and American History: A Reassessment," *Western Historical Quarterly* 14 (July 1983), pp. 261–76.

31. Owsley, Jr., *Struggle for the Gulf Borderlands*, p. 15, citing Deposition of Samuel Manac, Aug. 2, 1813, enclosure in Flournoy to Secretary of War, Aug. 10, 1813, National Archives, Letters Sent, Secretary of War, RG 107.

32. "Hawkins to Armstrong," July 28, 1813, ASP *Indian Affairs*, I, pp. 849–50. Numerous letters of Hawkins contain vivid descriptions of the Red Stick destruction of various Upper Creek towns; see ASP, *Indian Affairs*, I, pp. 848–53.

33. For an excellent commentary on the Cherokee perspective of the Creek War, see Thurman Wilkins, *Cherokee Tragedy: The Ridge Family and the Decimation of a People*, Second Edition Revised (Norman, 1986), pp. 52–80.

34. "Indemnity for Damages by Creek Indians," March 15, 1828, Twentieth Congress, first session, House Document No. 200, pp. 8–11.

35. "Holmes to Secretary of War," August 3, 1813, Carter, TP, VI, pp. 390–91; Albert James Pickett, *History of Alabama and Incidentally of Georgia and Mississippi, From the Earliest Period* (Birmingham, Ala., 1900), p. 518.

36. "Big Warrior to Hawkins," August 4, 1813, ASP *Indian Affairs*, I, p. 851.

37. "Hawkins to Armstrong," July 20, 1813. *Ibid*., p. 849; Owsley, *Gulf Borderlands*, pp. 24–30.

38. "Toulmin to Lattimore," December 1815, Carter, TP, VI, p. 586.

39. *Ibid*. Also see Leland L. Lengel, "The Road to Fort Mims: Judge Harry Toulmin's Observations on the Creek War, 1811–1813," *Alabama Review* 29 (January 1976), pp. 16–36.

40. "Flournoy to Armstrong," June 27, 1813. *Ibid*., p. 381.

41. "Holmes to the Secretary of War," July 27, 1813, Carter TP, VI, pp. 388–89.

42. "Holmes to the Secretary of War," August 10, 1813, Carter TP, VI, pp. 393–94.

43. Flournoy stood on his rank and orders, and undertook to treat raw backwoods militiamen like seasoned regulars. "Flournoy to Holmes," August 6, 1813. Ibid., pp. 397–98; "Holmes to Flournoy," November 3, 1813. Ibid., pp. 400–402.

44. Owsley, *Gulf Borderlands*, pp. 35–41; Richard H. Faust, "William Weatherford: A Case Study of a Man Dominated by Historical Events in the Creek Nation, 1780–1824" (Master's thesis, University of Southern Mississippi, 1973), pp. 37–42.

45. Owsley, *Gulf Borderlands*, p. 35; Faust, "William Weatherford," p. 42.

46. Owsley, *Gulf Borderlands*, p. 38, n. 35; Albert James Pickett, *History of Alabama*, p. 535. For a sketch of Fort Mims based on manuscripts belonging to General F. L. Claiborne, see *ibid*., p. 456.

47. Owsley, *Gulf Borderlands*, pp. 39–41; "Holmes to Flournoy," November 3, 1813, Carter, TP, VI, pp. 400–402; Claiborne, *Mississippi*, pp. 327–29.

Chapter 8: "Unnerve the Arm that Draws the Bow and Raises the Tommyhawk"

1. Henry Sale Halbert and T. H. Ball, *The Creek War of 1813 and 1814* (Chicago: Donohue and Henneberry, 1895); "Coweta Chiefs to Benjamin Hawkins," September 16, 1813, ASP *Indian Affairs*, I, p. 858; "Hawkins to Secretary of War," September 17, 21, 26, 1813. *Ibid.*, pp. 853–54.

2. Halbert and Ball, *Creek War*, p. 291; ASP *Indian Affairs*, 8, pp. 150, 291.

3. "Hawkins to Creek Chiefs," June 16, 1841, ASP *Indian Affairs*, 2, p. 845; "To Secretary of War," June 30, 1813. *Ibid.*, p. 849; "Andrew Jackson to Willie Blount," July 13, 1813. *Ibid.*, p. 850; "Hawkins to Secretary of War," August 23, 1813. *Ibid.*, pp. 851–52; "Hawkins to General Floyd," September 30, 1813. *Ibid.*, p. 845; Hugh M. Thomason, "Governor Peter Early and the Creek Indian Frontier, 1813–1815," *Georgia Historical Quarterly*, 45 (September 1961), p. 224.

4. There is substantial evidence of this fact in the two volumes of ASP *Indian Affairs*, and in the correspondence contained in the territorial papers of Mississippi and Alabama.

5. John D. W. Guice, "Face to Face in Mississippi Territory, 1798–1817," in *The Choctaw Before Removal*, ed. Carolyn Keller Reeves (Jackson, Miss.: University Press of Mississippi, 1985), pp. 157–80

6. Remini, *American Empire*, pp. 70–71.

7. "Andrew Jackson to George W. Campbell," October 15, 1812, John Spencer Bassett, ed., *Correspondence of Andrew Jackson* I (Washington, 1926–33), pp. 236–37; *Niles' Register*, 34, April 12, 1828, pp. 110–13; Bette B. Tilly, "The Jackson–Dinsmoor Feud: A Feud in a Minor Key," *Journal of Mississippi History* 39 (May 1977), pp. 117–31.

8. "Division Orders," November 1811, Bassett, *Correspondence*, 1, pp. 210–11; March 7, 1812. *Ibid.*, pp. 220–23.

9. Marquis James, *Andrew Jackson: The Border Captain* (Indianapolis: Bobbs-Merrill, 1933), pp. 149–54; "Division Orders," Bassett, *Correspondence*, 1, pp. 220–23.

10. Bassett, *Correspondence*, 1, p. 152.

11. "Armstrong to Blount," July 13, 1813. *Ibid.*, pp. 315–17.

12. "General Orders," September 19, 1813. *Ibid.*, pp. 319–20; "Blount to Jackson," September 24, 1813. *Ibid.*, pp. 320–21; *Statutes at Large*, 1, pp. 264–65. The War Department eventually sustained this notion by ruling that they had enlisted under the militia law of 1795. "John Armstrong to Jackson," January 3, 1814, Bassett, *Correspondence*, 1, pp. 432–33.

13. "Certificate of James Sitler," September 5, 1813, Bassett, *Correspodence*, 1, p. 317; "Thomas Hart Benton's Account of the Duel," September 10, 1813. *Ibid.*, pp. 317–18. Also see Robert V. Remini, *Andrew Jackson and the Course of American Empire, 1767–1821* (New York, 1977), pp;. 181–86 for a lively account of the duel and gunfight.

14. Bassett, *Correspondence*, 1, pp. 319–20.

15. "To Blount," October 13, 1813. *Ibid.*, p. 332.

16. J. F. H. Claiborne, *Mississippi as a Province, Territory, and State* (Jackson, Miss., 1880), pp. 327–30.

17. *Ibid.*, p. 328.

18. For a recent account of this action, see Owsley, *Struggle for the Gulf,* pp. 24–48.

19. A. J. Pickett, *History of Alabama,* pp. 574–76; Claiborne, *Mississippi,* pp. 331–32.

20. Thomason, "Governor Peter Early," pp. 224–25. See Owsley, *Struggle for the Gulf,* pp. 61–71.

21. Bassett, *Correspondence,* 1, pp. 482–94. Andrew Jackson made no mention of the weapons or the lack of weapons of the Creeks in his various reports of the Battle of Horseshoe Bend.

22. R. David Edmunds, *Tecumseh and the Quest for Indian Leadership* (Boston, 1984), pp. 187–212; see pp. 213–25 for a balanced retrospective commentary on Tecumseh.

23. Bassett, *Correspondence,* 1, pp. 482–94.

24. "Read, Mitchell and Company to Jackson," October 18, 1813. *Ibid.*, pp. 33–34. Throughout the Jackson correspondence for this period there is reflected deep concern about militia retirements. The law of Tennessee is vague, *Washington Republican,* October 17, 1813, p. 2; "Raulston to Jackson," October 18, 1813, Bassett, *Correspondence,* 1, p. 333.

25. Letters reflecting his discouragement were directed to Willie Blount, December 13, to John Armstrong, December 16, and to Rachel Jackson, December 19, 1813. *Ibid.*, pp. 390–92, 396–97, 400–01.

26. "Jackson to William B. Lewis," October 24, 1813. *Ibid.*, p. 336.

27. "Jackson to Troops," October 24, 1813. *Ibid.*, pp. 337–38.

28. "To Blount," November 14, 1813. *Ibid.*, p. 345.

29. "Coffee to Jackson," October 22, 1813. *Ibid.*, pp. 334–35.

30. "To Wealthy Residents," October 23, 1813. *Ibid.*, p. 335.

31. "Order to Coffee," November 2, 1813. *Ibid.*, p. 340; "Jackson to Blount," November 4, 1813. *Ibid.*, p. 341.

32. *Ibid.*, November 15, 1813, pp. 348–50.

33. "To John Cocke," November 16, 1813. *Ibid.*, pp. 353–54.

34. "Cocke to White," November 6, 1813. *Ibid.*, p. 342 n. 2.

35. "Blount to Jackson," November 7, 1813. *Ibid.*, p. 351 n. 2.

36. "Pinckney's Instructions to Jackson," November 16, 1813. *Ibid.*, pp. 352–53.

37. John Reid and John Henry Eaton, *The Life of Andrew Jackson* (University, Alabama, 1974, reprint), pp. 83–85.

38. For additional quotations from this letter plus an analysis of its contents, see Remini, *American Empire,* pp. 204–04. Remini cites this letter of Andrew Jackson to Willie Blount, December 29, 1813, in John Spencer Bassett, ed., *The Correspondence of Andrew Jackson* (Washington, 1926–33) 1, pp. 416–20.

39. "To Pinckney," January 29, 1814. *Ibid.*, pp. 447–54.

40. Remini, *American Empire,* pp. 209–10.

41. "To Pinckney," March 14, 1814. *Ibid.*, p. 481.

42. "To Rachel," April 1, 1814. *Ibid.*, pp. 492–93.

43. "Proclamation, Fort Williams," April 2, 1814. *Ibid.*, pp. 494–95.

44. "To John Armstrong," April 5, 1814. *Ibid.*, pp. 506–08.

45. Pickett, *Alabama*, pp. 592–93.

46. Fort Jackson provided the final link in a chain of posts connecting Tennessee and Georgia with the eastern half of Mississippi Territory.

47. Remini, *American Empire*, p. 218. For a highly romanticized account which has Weatherford, almost in the style of a knight, riding into camp on the same gray horse on which he leaped to freedom over a cliff, see Pickett, pp. 592–96; Weatherford's genealogy is clearly outlined in Richard H. Faust, "William Weatherford: A Case Study of a Man Dominated by Historical Events in the Creek Nation, 1780–1824" (Master's thesis, University of Southern Mississippi, 1973), pp. 15–20.

48. For excerpts from Jackson's moving orations to his army on their departure and to his fellow citizens on his return, see Remini, *American Empire*, pp. 220–21.

49. For recent, fuller accounts of the treaty process, see Remini, *American Empire*, pp. 220–33 and Owsley, *Struggle for the Gulf*, pp. 86–94.

50. "Pinckney to Hawkins," April 23, 1814, Bassett, *Correspondence*, 2, p. 1, n. 1.

51. "Jackson to Pinckney," May 18, 1814. *Ibid.*, pp. 1–4.

52. *Ibid.*, pp. 3–4.

53. *Ibid.*, pp. 4–5.

54. "To Armstrong," August 10, 1814. *Ibid.*, pp. 24–26.

55. Though this account is based on many of the same sources, readers are directed to the lengthy biographical treatment of the Fort Jackson scene in Remini, *American Empire*, pp. 225–31.

56. Remini, *American Empire*, p. 227.

57. ASP *Indian Affairs*, I, pp. 826–27; Charles J. Kappler, *Indian Affairs, Laws and Treaties*, 2, pp. 107–10; 7 *U.S. Statutes*, pp. 120–22.

58. *Niles' Weekly Register*, June 29, 1816, 10, p. 304.

59. "To Armstrong," August 10, 1814, Bassett, *Correspondence*, 2, p. 25. "To Armstrong," August 10, 1814, ASP *Military Affairs*, III, p. 792.

60. Owsley, *Struggle for the Gulf*, pp. 106–19; Remini, *American Empire*, pp 234–45. Though he treats the matter with an even hand, Owsley emphasizes the British recruitment of blacks—a move designed as much for its psychological impact as for the resolution of a manpower shortage.

61. "George F. Ross to Jackson," August 15, 1814, Bassette, *Correspondence*, 2, pp. 26–27; "To W. C. C. Claiborne," August 22, 1814. *Ibid.*, p. 27; "Claiborne to Jackson," August 24, 1814. *Ibid.*, pp. 29–30; "To Armstrong," August 5, 1814. *Ibid.*, pp. 30–31; "To Robert Butler," August 27, 1814. *Ibid.*, pp. 31–33; "To Blount," August 27, 1814. *Ibid.*, pp. 33–34; "From Claiborne," August 29, 1814. *Ibid.*, pp. 35–36.

62. "To Monroe," September 17, 1814. *Ibid.*, p. 51.

63. "To González Manrique," September 9, 1814. *Ibid.*, pp. 44–46.

64. "From Monroe," October 21, 1814. *Ibid.*, pp. 79–80.

65. Owsley, *Struggle for the Gulf*, pp. 120–26; William S. Coker, "How General Andrew Jackson Learned of the British Plans Before the Battle of New Orleans," *Gulf Coast Historical Review* 3 (Fall 1987), pp. 85–95.

66. The best description of Jackson's march from Mobile to New Orleans is in John Spencer Bassett, ed., "Major Howell Tatum's Journal While Acting Topo-

graphical Engineer (1814) to General Jackson Commanding the Seventh Military District," *Smith College Studies in History* VII (October to April, 1921–22).

67. This description of the Battle of New Orleans is based largely on the accounts in Owsley, *Struggle for the Gulf*, pp. 126–68 and Remini, *American Empire*, pp. 246–88.

68. For a detailed account of this action, see William S. Coker, "The Last Battle of the War of 1812: New Orleans. No, Fort Bowyer!," *Alabama Historical Quarterly* 43 (Spring 1981), pp. 42–63. Also see Owsley, *Struggle for the Gulf*, pp. 169–74.

69. Remini, *American Empire*, pp. 6–25.

70. The relationship of these two wars defies simple explanation. While the Creek War began largely as a separate conflict, in its final phase it became indistinguishable from the War of 1812, and in a sense the two became one.

Chapter 9: "Where smiling Fortune beckoned them"

1. W. H. Sparks, *The Memories of Fifty Years: Containing Notices of Distinguished Americans, and Anecdotes of Remarkable Men; Interspersed with Scenes and Incidents Occurring During a Long Life of Observations Chiefly Spent in the Southwest* (Philadelphia, 1870), p. 27.

2. *Census of 1800, 1810, 1820.* For an excellent overview of migration into the Old Southwest, see Charles D. Lowery, "The Great Migration to the Mississippi Territory, 1798–1819," *Journal of Mississippi History*, 30 (August 1968), pp. 173–92.

3. Lowery, "The Great Migration to the Mississippi Territory," p. 178, citing *Niles' Register*, 8, p. 38.

4. As pointed out in Chapter 3, Spain controlled the sparsely populated Gulf Coast until 1810. The coastal strip between the Pearl and the Perdido Rivers was not added to the Mississippi Territory until 1812.

5. *Census of 1800; Abstract of the Mississippi Territorial Census of 1810*, Record Group 2, Mississippi Department of Archives and History.

6. *Ibid.*

7. *Census of 1810*; Edward Chamber Betts, *Early History of Huntsville, Alabama, 1804–1870* (Montgomery, 1909), pp. 6–14.

8. *Census of 1810.*

9. Thomas P. Abernethy, *The South in the New Nation 1789–1819* (Baton Rouge, 1961), p. 465. The chapter entitled "The Great Migration," pp. 444–75, reflects Abernethy's considerable insight into the many forces at work in the Old Southwest.

10. *Censuses of 1800, 1810, 1820.*

11. Sparks, *Memories of Fifty Years*, p. 20.

12. William Baskerville Hamilton, "American Beginnings in the Old Southwest: The Mississippi Phase" (Ph.D. diss., Duke University, 1938), pp. 124–27; Robert V. Haynes, "Life on the Mississippi Frontier: Case of Matthew Phelps," *Journal of Mississippi History* 39 (February 1977), pp. 1–15. Hamilton's chapter on settlement, pp. 113–78, abounds in family names and bibliographical data.

13. Frank L. Owsley, "The Pattern of Migration and Settlement of the Southern Frontier," *Journal of Southern History*, 11 (May 1945), pp. 147–76.

14. Owsley, "The Pattern of Migration," p. 168. Owsley cites Vidal de la Blache's *Principles of Human Geography*, John M. Peck's *A New Guide for Emigrants to the*

West, and William Darby's *The Emigrant's Guide to the Western and Southwestern States and Territories.*

15. Owsley, "The Pattern of Migration," p. 172; Hamilton, "American Beginnings in the Old Southwest," p. 123. Hamilton, who wrote his dissertation a dozen years prior to the Owsley article, also uses the same Biblical analogy and provides illustrations of the practice.

16. James A. Tait to Charles Tait, December 15, 1817, Tait Papers, Alabama Department of Archives and History, cited in Owsley, "The Pattern of Migration," p. 173.

17. *Ibid.,* p. 169.

18. William O. Lynch, "The Westward Flow of Southern Colonists before 1861," *Journal of Southern History,* 9 (August 1943), pp. 303, 327.

19. *Compendium of the 1850 Census.*

20. For a detailed illustration of the heterogeneity of the Natchez District population, see Vernon Larry Walters, "Migration into Mississippi, 1798–1837" (M.A. thesis, Mississippi State University, 1969), pp. 61–76; see also Hamilton, "American Beginnings in the Old Southwest," pp. 123–59.

21. Judge Harry Toulmin to President James Madison, November 22, 1810, Clarence Edwin Carter, ed., *The Territorial Papers of the United States,* VI, (Washington, 1938), p. 136. (Hereafter cited as Carter, TP.)

22. Abernethy, *The South in the New Nation,* pp. 469–70.

23. *Ibid.*

24. Lynch, "The Westward Flow," pp. 316–17.

25. Gaius Whitefield, Jr., "The French Grant in Alabama, A History of the Founding of Demopolis," *Transactions of the Alabama Historical Society,* IV (Montgomery, 1904), pp. 321–55; Albert James Pickett, *History of Alabama and Incidentally of Georgia and Mississippi, From the Earliest Period* (1851; reprint ed., Tuscaloosa, 1962), pp. 623–33; Anne Bozeman Lyon, "The Bonapartists in Alabama," *Alabama Historical Quarterly* 25 (Fall & Winter 1963), pp. 227–41.

26. Frederick Jackson Turner, *The Frontier in American History* (New York, 1920), p. 16.

27. Timothy Flint, *Recollections of the Last Ten Years Passed in Occasional Residence and Journeys in the Valley of the Mississippi* (Boston, 1826), pp. 240–41.

28. Captain Basil Hall, *Travels in North America in the Years 1827–28* (3 vols.; Edinburgh, 1829), III, pp. 131–33.

29. Franklin L. Riley, comp., "Autobiography of Gideon Lincecum," *Publications of the Mississippi Historical Society,* VIII (Oxford, Miss., 1904), pp. 443–519; Mary H. Clay, "Gideon Lincecum, Southern Pioneer, 1793–1874" (M.S. thesis, Mississippi State College, 1953).

30. Riley, "Autobiography of Gideon Lincecum," p. 459.

31. *Ibid.,* p. 464.

32. *Ibid.,* p. 469.

33. Frank L. Owsley, *Plain Folk in the Old South* (1949; reprint ed., Baton Rouge, 1982), pp. 66–67.

34. A. C. Ramsey, *A sketch of the life and times of Rev. A. C. Ramsey as written by himself in 1879 at the age of 72, . . . Gadsden, Ala., September, 1879* edited as *The Autobiography of A. C. Ramsey* by Jean Strickland (Moss Point, Miss., no date).

Strickland, who purports to have copied verbatim the manuscript in the Alabama Department of Archives and History, provides documented genealogical and geographical notes, maps, and diagrams. Rather than a diary as catalogued in the archives, this fascinating account is actually a memoir.

35. Ramsey, *Autobiography*, p. 5.

36. *Ibid.*, p. 8.

37. Owsley in *Plain Folk*, pp. 67–73, cites only five moves.

38. Ramsey, *Autobiography*, p. 15.

39. *Ibid.*, p. 9.

40. For a classic description of frontier life in the Old Southwest shortly after the end of the War of 1812, see Ramsey, *Autobiography*, pp. 42–43. The final two-thirds of the Ramsey memoir pertains primarily to the development of Methodism in southeastern Mississippi. There are references, however, to other denominations.

41. Richard Haughton, "Influence of the Mississippi River upon the Early Settlement of its Valley," *Publications of the Mississippi Historical Society*, IV (Oxford, Miss., 1901), pp. 465–82. For a moving account by an elderly slave of a migration to the Natchez District from the Carolinas via the Holston, Tennessee, Ohio, and Mississippi Rivers, see Stark, *The Memories of Fifty Years*, pp. 304–5.

42. For a survey of early nineteenth century trails into the Old Southwest, see Genevieve Lois Maxon Stark, "Traces of Early Mississippi" (M.A. thesis, Mississippi State University, 1969); also see the chapter on routes of migration into Mississippi in Walters, "Migration into Mississippi," pp. 18–47.

43. Julian P. Bretz, "Early Land Communication with the Lower Mississippi Valley," *Mississippi Valley Historical Review*, 13 (June 1926), pp. 12–13. Though written over a half century ago, this solidly researched piece still deserves a prominent place in the historiography of the trails into the Old Southwest.

44. *History of Cosmopolite: Or the Writings of Rev. Lorenzo Dow: Containing His Experience and Travels, in Europe and America, up to Near His Fiftieth Year. Also, His Polemic Writings, to Which Is Added The "Journey of Life," by Peggy Dow* (Cincinnati and Philadelphia, 1857), p. 650. It is interesting to note that on the title page of this work appears this boast: "Sixth Edition Averaging 4000 Each."

45. *Ibid.*

46. *Ibid.*, p. 651.

47. Josiah Blakely to Abby (a niece in Connecticut), February 28, 1812, cited in Peter J. Hamilton, *Colonial Mobile* (New York, 1910), p. 407.

48. John Hedges Goff, *Retracing the Old Federal Road and Cow Punching in Old Georgia: Two Articles Relating to the Economic History of Georgia*, Emory University Studies in Business and Economics, no. 5 (Atlanta, 1950).

49. Stark, "Traces of Early Mississippi," pp. 5–18.

50. *Ibid.*, pp. 25–39.

51. Walters, "Migration into Mississippi," pp. 28–32.

52. Frances Cabaniss Roberts, "Background and Formative Period in the Great Bend and Madison County" (Ph.D. diss., University of Alabama, 1956), p. 139. Roberts illustrates the impact on American Revolutionary military service on migration by tracing the George Taylor family, pp. 150–52. Chapter III, "To The Land of Milk and Honey," pp. 137–75 abounds in family histories.

53. Surveyor Thomas Freeman to Secretary of Treasury Albert Gallatin, August 25, 1808, quoted in Roberts, "Background and Formative Period," p. 149.

54. *Ibid.*, pp. 204–05.

55. *Ibid.*

56. *Ibid.*, p. 205.

57. Many of the ideas expressed here result from the comments of Richard S. Lackey at a gathering of geneaologists in the Department of History, University of Southern Mississippi, April 18, 1981. Lackey, at the time of his death at the age of forty-one in 1983, was President of the Board for Certification of Genealogists. A fellow in the American Society of Genealogists who published widely in his field, Lackey served on several faculties, including the National Institute on Genealogical Research at the National Archives. The Lackey Collections, containing his genealogical library and his research materials, is housed in the McCain Library, University of Southern Mississippi, Hattiesburg.

58. See the file titled "Powe Family and Wayne County Migration," Lackey Collection, McCain Library, University of Southern Mississippi, for Powe genealogy and the notes used by Lackey in his presentation. Owsley not only emphasizes the practice of prospective migrants sending out advance scouts, but he also reinforces Lackey's observation of the tendency for communities from the East to replicate themselves on the frontier. See Frank L. Owsley, "The Education of a Southern Frontier Girl, Part I," *Alabama Review* 6 (October 1953), pp. 268–88.

59. Only by studying the particulars surrounding individual migrants and their extended families will accurate answers be formulated to questions of why frontiersmen migrated. By compiling and analyzing significant amounts of family data it may be discovered that some traditionally accepted reasons for migration stand the test of close scrutiny and others do not. For a provocative discussion of the relationship between historians and genealogists, see Elizabeth Shown Mills, "Academia *vs.* Genealogy," *National Genealogical Society Quarterly*, 71 (June 1983), pp. 99–106.

Chapter 10: Nabobs and Nobodies

1. While most of the large planters who migrated to the Old Southwest in the nineteenth century were part of the planter dynasty of the Old South, some of them had resided in the Natchez District during the periods of Spanish and English dominion.

2. William B. Hamilton, "American Beginnings in the Old Southwest: The Mississippi Phase" (Ph.D. diss., Duke University, 1938), p. 334. Based on meticulous, exhaustive research, Hamilton's 622-page study will likely stand unchallenged as the authoratative work on Mississippi Territory. Charles Sydnor, Hamilton's mentor at Duke University, emphasizes the cosmopolitan nature of Natchez in *A Gentleman of the Old Southwest Region, Benjamin L. C. Wailes* (Durham, 1938); William B. Hamilton, "The Southwestern Frontier, 1795–1817: An Essay in Social History," *Journal of Southern History*, 10 (November 1944), pp. 389–403.

3. While neither the Spanish nor the early United States censuses reveal places of origin of residents, many contemporary accounts refer to the presence of various non-Anglos. See, for example, Jacob Young, *Autobiography of a Pioneer: Or, the Nativity, Experience, Travels, and Ministerial Labors of Rev. Jacob Young, With Incidents, Observations, and Reflections* (Cincinnati, 1860), pp. 222–23.

4. James Hall, *A Brief History of the Mississippi Territory* (Salisbury, N.C., 1801), p. 41. Historians are unanimous in their concensus on the dominance of English culture in the Natchez region.

5. Hamilton, "American Begininnings," p. 136.

6. *Ibid.*, p. 265; D. Clayton James in *Antebellum Natchez* (Baton Ruge, 1968), p. 137, similarly suggests that social mobility was based on ownership of proeprty.

7. Dr. G. Douglas Inglis of Seville, Spain, who has exhaustively studied Spanish archival sources relating to Natchez, concludes that length of residency was considered a prestige factor by permanent settlers, and that after 1795 the older planters in the district constituted a separate type, if not class, of people. Another factor explaining the emergence of a planter class by the 1820s, in addition to the accumulation of wealth, was the aristocratic disposition of the loyalists and former British officers who migrated to the Natchez District during the revolutionary period. See "Yale's Loyalists," *Yale Alumni Magazine*, XXXIX (October 1975), pp. 21–22.

8. Though William B. Hamilton, whose dissertation was dated 1937 but signed by his committee on January 14, 1938, reflected an anti-Turnerian bias, he nevertheless was accurate when on p. 264 he wrote of the people in the Natchez District: "With a thoughtless stubbornness, they refuse to fall into the pattern which would delight a historian of the West."

9. Cenus of 1810. Mobile remained considerably smaller than Natchez until after admission of Alabama as a state in 1819.

10. Fortescue Cuming, *Sketches of a Tour to the Western Country, Through the States of Ohio and Kentucky; a Voyage Down the Ohio and Mississippi Rivers and a Trip Through the Mississippi, and Part of West Florida Commenced at Philadelphia in the Winter of 1807, and Concluded in 1809* (Pittsburgh, 1810), Reuben Gold Thwaites, ed. *Early Western Travel 1748–1846* (N.Y. 1966), vol. 4, p.. 320; Hamilton, "American Beginnings," pp. 356–57; In n. 163, p. 334 Hamilton cites a dozen descriptions of Natchez in travel accounts.

11. Act of Incorporation, March 3, 1809, Turner's *Digest*, p. 355.

12. Toulmin's *Digest*, p. 128; Act of December 9, 1809, Turner's *Digest*, p. 347; Act of January 17, 1814, *Ibid.*, p. 352; Warrant issued to Alex. Bailie for tending public nursery, January 5, 1818, List of Warrants, *Mississippi Republican*, March 19, 1818; D. Clayton James, "Municipal Government in Territorial Natchez," *Journal of Mississippi History*, 27 (May 1965), pp. 148–67. Pride of China trees, still common today in parts of Mississippi, are colloquially known as chinaberry trees.

13. J. F. H. Claiborne, *Mississippi As a Province, Territory and State* (Jackson, 1880), pp. 258–60; Sydnor, *Gentleman of the Old Natchez Region*, pp. 40–43. Sydnor asserts that Wailes authored the above cited passage for Claiborne. See *ibid.*, p. 41, n. 31. Though he counted only "thirty scattering houses" in Washington in 1808, Fortescue Cuming admitted that the dress of the ladies there was "tasty and rather

rich." Cuming, *Sketches of a Tour*, p. 319; Also see Guy B. Braden, "A Jeffersonian Village: Washington, Mississippi," *Journal of Mississippi History*, 30 (May 1968), pp. 135–44.

14. Intruders near the Great Bend of the Tennessee in the area which eventually became Madison County resembled the settlers above Mobile in type as well as in feelings of isolation and neglect; Ephraim Kirby to President Thomas Jefferson, Fort Stoddert, May 1, 1804, Clarence Edwin Carter, ed., *The Territorial Papers of the United States*, V (Washington, 1937), pp. 323–24. For a more sympathetic—and probably accurate—view of squatters, see Captain Basil Hall, *Travels in North America in the Years 1827–28*, 3 vols. (Edinburgh, 1829) III, pp. 354–55.

15. Copia de la Sta. Visita . . . en el año 1791, Archivo General de Indias, Seville, Spain, Santo Domingo, legajo 1436. (Hereafter cited as AGI).

16. Kirby to Jefferson, May 1, 1804.

17. Francisco Bellestre, Pascagoula to Maximiliana de St. Maxent, September 9, 1805, September 24, 1805, and October 9, 1805, AGI, Papeles de Cuba, legajo 142-A. (Hereafter cited as PC plus legajo number.) Testimony before Juan Bautista Pellerin, Bay St. Louis, June 4, 1809, AGI, PC, 63. Petition to Francisco Henreterio de Hevia, Pascagoula, 1810, *Ibid.*; Also see Claiborne, *Mississippi*, pp. 305–06.

18. Juan Bautista Pellerin, Pascagoula to Vicente Folch, May 2, 1806, May 14, 1806, and July 12, 1807, AGI, PC, 62; Testimony before Juan Bautista Pellerin, Bay St. Louis, June 4, 1809; Pellerin, Pass Christian, to Vicente Folch, October 22, 1809, AGI, PC, 63.

19. The complexities of these ties are treated in J. Leitch Wright, Jr. , *The Only Land They Knew: The Tragic Story of the American Indians in the Old South*, (New York, 1981), Chapters 10 and 11.

20. Censuses of 1801 and 1810, RG 2, MDAH; Census of 1816, Carter, TP, VI pp. 720, 730. Because of the statehood issue, the accuracy of the Census of 1816 remains suspect; Hamilton "American Beginnings," pp. 322–24; Charles S. Sydnor's *Slavery in Mississippi* (New York, 1933) remains the standard study of slavery n Mississippi; Numerous petitions and acts are extant in the Territorial Legislative Records, RG 5, MDAH. One of the most unusual relates to a black who fathered ten children by a white woman, RG5, vol. 14, MDAH.

21. Petition of William Barlow, December, 1814, RG 5–27; Terry L. Alford, "Some Manumissions Recorded in the Adams County Deed Books in the Chancery Clerk's Office, Natchez, Mississippi, 1795–1835," *Journal of Mississippi History*, 33 (February 1971), pp. 43–44.

22. Hamilton, "American Beginnings," pp. 136, 311–15.

23. Wright, *The Only Land*, p. 246.

24. Samuel J. Wells, "The Role of Mixed-Bloods in Mississippi Choctaw History," in Samuel J. Wells and Roseanna Tubby, eds. *After Removal: The Choctaw in Mississippi* (Jackson, Miss., 1986), pp. 42–55.

25. Kirby to Jefferson, Carter, TP, V, pp. 322–26 Kirby uses over a dozen disparaging terms in this oft-cited letter which scholars should use with care. Kirby was a disappointed, critically ill Connecticut Puritan who probably made little effort to understand the farmer-herdsmen from the interior of North Carolina, South Carolina, and Georgia. Besides, Kirby may have viewed them as Loyalists

or Tories so repugnant to a Revolutionary War veteran. Letters in the Kirby Paper, Duke University, abound in similar harsh denigrations. According to one legal historian, Kirby "died in the Alabama wilderness with a French grammar at his bedside." He was studying French in anticipation of an appointment to the supreme court of Orleans Territory. See Allan V. Briceland, "Ephraim Kirby: Pioneer of American Law Reporting, 1789," *Journal of American Legal History* 16 (October 1972), pp. 297–319.

26. Judge Harry Toulmin to William Lattimore, Fort St. Stephens, December 6, 1805, Carter, TP, V, p. 431.

27. As noted above in Note 25, it is likely that Kirby overreacted to the cattle raisers who clearly formed a "coarse" class of folk. Dr. Gideon Lincecum, who as a youth taught children reared "among the cows and cowdrivers" of Western Georgia, described them as "positively the coarsest specimens of the human family I had ever seen." in "Autobiography of Gideon Lincecum," *Publications of the Mississippi Historical Society*, VIII (1904), p. 459.

28. John B. Boles *The Great Revival, 1787–1805: The Origins of the Southern Evangelical Mind* (Lexington, Ky., 1972), p. 170. Boles, who offers the most sophisticated analysis to date of the complex origins of southern frontier revivalism, emphasizes the world view of these frontier people and their concept of the sovereignty of God.

29. Donald E. Byrne, Jr., *No Foot of Land: Folklore of American Methodist Itinerants* (Metuchen, N.J., 1975), p. 126.

30. "Deliverance from Dangerous Beasts." *Ibid.*, pp. 129–34. Folklore about the frightening packs of wolves is substantiated by an account of an escape from a dozen "gaunt and ravenous *wolves*" by historian J. F. H. Claiborne in "A Trip Through the Piney Woods," *Publications of the Mississippi Historical Society*, IX (1906), p. 532.

31. Lorenzo Dow, *History of Cosmopolite: or the Writings of Rev. Lorenzo Dow* (Cincinnati, 1857), p. 216.

32. Jacob Young, *Autobiography*, pp. 236, 242–43, 217; Thomas D. Clark, *The Rampaging Frontier: Manners and Humors of Pioneer Days in the South and the Middle West* (Bloomington, 1939), p. 142.

33. Walter Brownlow Posey, *The Development of Methodism in the Old Southwest: 1783–1824* (Tuscaloosa, 1933), p. 28; for an insightful autobiographical account, see W. H. Sparks, *The Memories of Fifty Years: Containing Brief Biographical Notices of Distinguished Americans, and Anecdotes of Remarkable Men; Interspersed with Scenes and Incidents Occurring During a Long Life of Observations Chiefly Spent in the Southwest* (Philadelphia, 1870).

34. Clark, *Rampaging Frontier*, p. 144.

35. "Gloster campground was scene of fiery weather, sermons," Jackson *Clarion-Ledger*, August 21, 1983, p. 11F.

36. Ray Holder, *William Winans: Methodist Leader in Antebellum Mississippi* (Jackson, Miss., 1977), p. 23.

37. For a typical and humorous account of dealing with disruptive rowdies, see Young, "Autobiography," pp. 291–92; Hamilton lamented that historians of the church in the Old Southwest had concerned themselves "mainly with estab-

lishing "firsts" rather than analyzing the effects of ideology and theology. See Hamilton, "American Beginnings," p. 324 and pp. 325–31.

38. John James Audubon, "The Squatters of the Mississippi" in *Delineations of American Scenery and Character* (New York, 1926), p. 137.

39. Hamilton W. Pierson, *In the Brush: Old-Time Social, Political, and Religious Life in the Southwest* (New York, 1883), p. 10. Pierson's observation is particularly intersting when viewed in the light of the continuous debate over the value of travel accounts as sources.

40. Claiborne, "A Trip Through the Piney Woods," pp. 515–16.

41. Grady McWhiney, *Cracker Culture: Celtic Ways in the Old South* (Tuscaloosa, 1987), pp. xiv–xviii.

42. *Ibid.,* p. 268.

43. *Ibid.,* p. 94.

44. Claiborne, "A Trip Through the Piney Woods," p. 533–34.

45. *Ibid.,* p. 533.

46. Pierson, *In the Brush,* pp. 47–59.

47. Ray Holder, *William Winans,* pp. 45–46.

48. Grady McWhiney, "Antebellum Piney Woods Culture: Continuity over Time and Place," in Noel Polk., ed., *Mississippi's Piney Woods: A Human Perspective* (Jackson, Ms., 1986), p. 48; Audubon, *Delineations,* p. 82.

49. Byrne, *No Foot of Land,* pp. 198–205.

50. Hamilton, "American Beginnings," pp. 358–59.

51. Silas Dinsmoor to Secretary of War Henry Dearborn, October 12, 1805, Robertson Papers, Tennessee State Archives.

52. Capt. B. W. Shamburgh to Major Thomas H. Cushing, Ft. Stoddert, December 1, 1799, Cushing Letter Book, Letters Received, Records of U.S. Army Commands, Vol. 402, RG 98, National Archives.

53. Claiborne, *Mississippi,* p. 528.

54. Address of Lewis Kerr to Mississippi Territorial House of Representatives, October 24, 1803, RG 5, vol. 14, Territorial Legislature file, MDAH; James, *Antebellum Natchez,* C. 10.; McWhiney, *Cracker Culture,* pp. 128–30.

55. Territorial statutes reflect repeated efforts to curb gambling by every imaginable means from fines, destruction of equipment, voiding of gambling debts, to the use of the militia by judges to enforce gambling laws, and an act that imposed a $20 fine for militiamen who refused to meet such a muster. For examples, see *Turner's Digest,* pp. 176, 235–36, 238, 241; James, *Antebellum Natchez,* pp. 259–60; Laura D. S. Harrell, "Horse Racing in the Old Natchez District," *Journal of Mississippi History* 13 (July 1951), pp. 123–37; ——, "Jockey Clubs and Race Tracks in Antebellum Mississippi, 1795–1861," *Journal of Mississippi History* 28 (November 1966), pp. 304–18.

56. McWhiney, *Cracker Culture,* p. 126.

57. *Ibid.,* p. 123.

58. William B. Hamilton, "The Theatre in the Old Southwest: The First Decade at Natchez," *American Literature,* 12 (May 1941), pp. 471–85; Joseph M. Free, "The Ante-Bellum Theatre of the Old Natchez Region," *Journal of Mississippi History,* 5 (1943), p. 14; Hamilton, "American Beginnings," pp. 366–69.

59. Hamilton, "American Beginnings," pp. 369–71.

60. *Ibid.*, p. 371.

61. *Ibid.*, p. 371–75.

62. Indispensable to a study of the intellectual trends in the Natchez District is Sydnor, *A Gentleman of the Old Natchez Region*, pp. 120–51.

63. Evon Orpha Moore Rowland, ed., *Life, Letters and Papers of William Dunbar of Elgin, Morayshire, Scotland, and Natchez, Mississippi: Pioneer Scientist of the Southern United States* (Jackson, Ms. 1930); Franklin L. Riley, "Sir William Dunbar: the Pioneer Scientist of Mississippi," *Publications of the Mississippi Historical Society,* II (1899), pp. 85–111; James R. Dungan, "Sir William Dunbar of Natchez: Planter, Explorer, and Scientist, 1792–1810," *Journal of Mississippi History,* 24 (October 1961), pp. 211–28; Arthur H. DeRosier, Jr., "William Dunbar, Explorer," *Journal of Mississippi History,* 25 (July 1963), pp. 165–28; ———, "William Dunbar: A Product of the Eighteenth Century Scottish Renaissance," *Journal of Mississippi History,* 28 (August 1966), pp. 185–227; ———, "Natchez and the Formative Years of William Dunbar," *Journal of Mississippi History,* 34 (February 1972), pp. 29–47.

64. Hamilton, "American Beginnings," p. 387. Because of the high value of slaves, one suspects that those slave owners who had confidence in vaccination had them vaccinated. It is unlikely, however, that many Indians were vaccinated.

65. Holder, *William Winans*, pp. 17, 21.

66. McWhiney, *Cracker Culture*, pp. 193–217.

67. Sydnor, *Gentleman of the Old Natchez Region*, pp. 120, 121–28.

68. Malcolm J. Rohrbough, *The Trans-Appalachian Frontier: People, Societies, and Institutions, 1775–1850* (New York, 1978), p. 117. Hamilton, "American Beginnings," pp. 281–82.

69. Michael Francis Beard, "Natchez Under-the-Hill: Reform and Retribution in Early Natchez" (unpublished manuscript, MDAH), citing Natchez *Ariel*, September 15, 1826.

70. Walter Blair and Franklin J. Meine, *"Mike Fink: King of Mississippi Keelboatmen* (New York, 1933), p. 264; for a thorough treatment of the legends of Mike Fink, see Walter Blair and Franklin J. Meine, *Half Horse Half Alligator: The Growth of the Mike Fink Legend* (Chicago, 1956).

71. For an example of the traditional view of the violence on the Southern frontier, see Everett Dick, *The Dixie Frontier: A Social History of the Southern Frontier from the First Transmontane Beginnings to the Civil War* (New York, 1948); McWhiney reinforces this view in his recently published *Cracker Culture.*

72. Michael Francis Beard, "Frontier Post on the Mississippi: A History of the Legend of Natchez Under-the-Hill, 1800–1900" (M.A. thesis, Louisiana State University, 1981); ——— "Natches Under-the-Hill, 1790–1840: A Reinterpretation" (Honors thesis, University of Southern Mississippi, 1971).

73. John D. W. Guice, "The Cement of Society: Law in Mississippi Territory," *Gulf Coast Historical Review,* I (Spring 1986), pp.76–99; David Bodenhamer, "The Efficiency of Criminal Justice in the Antebellum South," *Criminal Justice History: An International Annual,* 3 (1983), pp.81–95; "Law and Disorder in the Old South: The Situation in Georgia, 1830–1860," in Walter J. Fraser and Winfred B. Moore, eds., *From the Old South to the New: Essays on the Transitional South* (Greenwood Press, 1981), pp. 109–19.

74. For an account of one of the most violent outlaws in the Old Southwest

during the antebellum era, see John D. W. Guice, ed., *Life and Confession of the Noted Outlaw James Copeland* by Dr. J. R. S. Pitts (facsimile reprint of the 1909 edition with introduction and chronology, Jackson, Miss., 1980). Guice does not suggest that the career of Copeland supports the idea that violence and lawlessness was characteristic of the society at large.

75. Lincecum, "Autobiography," p 470.

76. Annette Kolodny, *The Land Before Her: Fantasy and Experience of the American Frontiers, 1630–1860* (Chapel Hill, 1984). One of the best works on nonplanter women is Keith L. Bryant, "The Role and Status of the Female Yeomanry in the Antebellum South: The Literary View," *Southern Quarterly—A Journal of the Arts in the South* 18 (Winter 1980), pp. 73–88.

77. Though they may encounter a paucity of sources, historians of the Southern Frontier should replicate the creative study of children in Elliott West, "Heathens and Angels: Childhood in the Rocky Mountain Mining Towns", *Western Historical Quarterly*, 14 (April 1983), pp. 145–64.

78. McWhiney, *Cracker Culture*, pp. 80–82.

Chapter 11: State-Making

1. "The President to Governor Williams," November 1, 1807, Clarence Edwin Carter, *The Territorial Papers of the United States*, V (Washington, 1937), p. 573. For the most scholarly and readable account of the Mississippi phase of the quest for statehood, see Robert V. Haynes, "The Road to Statehood," in Richard Aubrey McLemore, ed., *A History of Mississippi*, I, pp. 217–50.

2. "Petition to Congress by Inhabitants East of Pearl River" [May, 1809], Carter, TP, V. p. 733.

3. *Ibid.* p. 733.

4. *Ibid.* For a poignant expression of their grievances, see "Petition to Congress by a Convention East of Pearl River," November 11, 1809, Carter, TP, VI, pp. 26–31.

5. "Admission of the Mississippi Territory into the Union, " January 9, 1811, ASP, *Miscellaneous*, II, p. 129.

6. "Petition to Congress by a Convention East of Pearl River." [November 11, 1809], Carter, TP, VI, p. 27; *Annals of Congress*, 11th Cong., 2nd Sess., December 6, 1809, pp. 695–98.

7. Carter, TP, VI, pp. 26–31.

8. *Ibid.*, "Address by the Territorial Legislature to the President," November 22, 1809, p. 31.

9. "Memorial to Congress by the Territorial Legislature," [November, 14, 1811,] Carter, TP, VI, pp. 242–43.

10. 2 *U.S. Statutes*, pp. 69–70; "Georgia: Cession of Western Land Claims," Carter, TP, V, pp. 142–46; Secretary of State to Governor Claiborne, July 26, 1802, Carter, TP, V, pp. 156–58.

11. "Petition to Congress by Inhabitants of the Territory," [Referred December 27, 1811], Carter, TP, VI, 253–54; 2 *U.S. Statutes*, p. 734.

12. "Memorial to Congress by the Territorial Legislature," [November 9, 1812],

Carter, TP, VI, pp. 331–32; *Annals of Congress*, 12th Cong. 1st Sess., March 17, 1812, p. 1212.

13. "Admission of the Mississippi Territory to the Union, Communication to the House of Representatives," December, 17, 1811, ASP *Miscellaneous*, II, pp. 163–64.

14. "Memorial to Congress by the Territorial Legislature," [November 9, 1812], Carter, TP, VI, pp. 331–32.

15. *Annals of Congress*, 12th Cong., 2nd Sess., November 10, 1812, p.145, November, 24, 1812, p. 196, January 19, 1813, p. 55; 2 *U.S. Statutes*, p. 786.

16. "Memorial to Congress by the Territorial Legislature," [December 15, 1812], Carter, TP, VI, pp. 339–41.

17. *Annals of Congress*, 12th Cong., 2nd Sess., February 26, 1813, p. 109. In this reference Daniel Beasley is erroneously identified as Daniel Beverly.

18. "Petition to Congress by Inhabitants of the Territory," [October 10, 1814], Carter, TP, VI, pp. 449–52.

19. "Memorial to Congress by the Territorial Legislature," [December 23, 1814], Carter, TP, VI, pp. 481–82.

20. "Memorial to Congress by the Territorial Legislature," [December 27, 1814], Carter, TP, VI, pp. 484–87.

21. "Admission of the Mississippi Territory into the Union as a State," February 23, 1815, ASP *Miscellaneous*, II, pp. 274–75.

22. *Annals of Congress*, 13th Cong., 3rd Sess., January 21, 1815, p. 1085; *Annals of Congress*, 13th Cong., 3rd Sess., February 22, 1815, p. 1187–89.

23. Carter, TP, VI, p. 487, n. 22, n. 23.

24. "Petition to Congress by Inhabitants East of Pearl River," [Referred December 14, 1815], Carter, TP, VI, pp. 601–05.

25. "Petition to Congress by Members of the Territorial Legislature," [Referred February 15, 1816] Carter, TP, VI, pp. 655–56.

26. "Proceedings of a Convention," [October, 29, 1816]. *Ibid.*, pp. 708–17.

27. *Ibid.*, pp. 716–17.

28. "Secretary Ware to William Lattimore," November 15, 1816. *Ibid.*, pp. 719–20.

29. *Annals of Congress*, 14th Cong., 2nd Sess., December 9, 1816, p. 252. *Ibid.*, December 23, 1816. pp. 358–60.

30. *Annals of Congress*, 14th Cong, 2nd Sess., December 21, 1816, pp. 358–60; "Admission of Mississippi into the Union," December 23, 1816, ASP *Miscellaneous*, II, pp. 407–8.

31. "Memorial to Congress by the Territorial Legislature," [December 6, 1816], Carter, TP, VI, pp. 731–32; *Washington (Mississippi) Republican*, September 18, October 30, November 6, 13, December 11, 1816, January 8, 1817.

32. "Memorial to Congress by Members of the Territorial Legislature" [December 6, 1816], Carter, TP, VI, p. 733–34.

33. "Memorial to Congress by Members of the Territorial Legislature," [Referred January 8, 1817] Carter, TP, VI, pp. 744–46; *Washington (Mississippi) Republican*, January 22, 1817.

34. Proceedings of a Convention [Journal of a Convention of the Delegates of several Counties of the Mississippi Territory, begun and held at John Ford's on Pearl River, on Tuesday the 29th of Oct., 1816.], Carter, TP, VI, pp. 708–17; "Judge

Toulmin to H. B. Slade," January 16, 1817. *Ibid.*, pp. 748–49. A "Northern Republican" offered a lengthy discourse on the imbalance which would be created by the admission of two new slave states in the *Washington Republican*, March 19, 1817; William Lattimore presented a history of the division issues from 1803 to 1817. *Ibid.*, April 16, 1817.

35. *Annals of Congress*, March 1, 1817, 14th Cong., 2nd Sess., pp. 1282–84; 3 *U. S. Statutes*, pp. 348–49. *Ibid.*, pp. 371–73. Both Acts were printed by the *Washington Republican*, April 16, 1817. Mississippi was admitted to statehood on December 10, 1817, 3 *U. S. Statutes*, pp. 472–73.

36. Haynes, "The Road to Statehood," p. 246–47. Also see Franklin L. Riley, "Location of the Boundaries of Mississippi," *Publications of the Mississippi Historical Society*, III (1900), p. 167–84. As one can imagine, boundaries created extensive and often bitter arguments. Also see: "A Mobilian," *Washington Republican*, January 29, 1817 and William Lattimore's historical account. *Ibid.*, April 23, 1817. For other commentaries see: *Ibid.*, January 8, 22, 29, April 16, 23, 1817.

37. *The Journal of the Constitutional Convention of 1817*, reprinted in *Journal of Mississippi History*, 29 (November 1967), pp. 443–504; Winbourne Magruder Drake, "The Framing of Mississippi's First Constitution," *Journal of Mississippi History*, 29 (November 1967), pp. 301–27; Also see Richard A. and Nannie P. McLemore, "The Birth of Mississippi," *Journal of Mississippi History*, 29, (November 1967), pp. 261–69.

38. Drake, "The Framing of Mississippi's First Constitution," pp. 305–7; The commentray *re* the Mississippi Constitution of 1817 in this chapter agrees substantially with the Drake analysis.

39. *Ibid.*, pp. 311–27; *Washington Republican*, May 28, June 4, June 14, 1817.

40. Riley, "Location and Boundaries of Mississippi," pp. 175–81; *Statistical Abstract of the United States*, (Washington, 1930), p. 2.

41. *Mississippi Constitution of 1817*, Art. III. The full text of the constitution was published in the *Washington Republican*, August 23, 1817.

42. *Mississippi Constitution of 1817*, Art. IV.

43. *Ibid*, Art. V. For an analysis of problems relating to the Mississippi territorial judiciary, see John D. W. Guice, "The Cement of Society: Law in the Mississippi Territory," *Gulf Coast Historical Review*," 1 (Spring 1986), pp. 76–99.

44. *Mississippi Constitution of 1817*, Art. VI.

45. *Ibid.*

46. *Ibid.*, "Slaves."

47. *Ibid.*, Art. I.

48. Chilton Williamson, *American Suffrage from Property to Democracy 1760–1860* (Princeton, 1960), p. 210, quoting the *Worcester Spy*, which was quoted in *Albany Gazette*, October 11, 1817, 48; Drake, "The Framing of Mississippi's First Constitution" pp. 324–27.

49. *Washington Republican*, August 16, 1817; Drake, "The Framing of Mississippi's First Constitution," pp. 324–26.

50. Suanna Smith, "George Poindexter: A Political Biography," (Ph.D. diss., University of Southern Mississippi, 1980).

51. *Washington Republican*, August 16, 1817; "The Secretary of State to Governor Holmes," October 3, 1817, Carter, TP, VI, p. 805; *U. S. Statutes*, pp. 472–73.

52. Charles Royce, *Indian Land Cessions in the United States*, (Washington, 1900), Map 36.

53. *Annals of Congress*, February 4, 1817, 14th Cong., 2nd Sess, p. 100; 3 *U. S. Statutes*, pp. 371–73.

54. Albert Burton Moore, *History of Alabama and Her People*, (Chicago, 1927), pp. 133–35.

55. "Petition to Congress by inhabitants of the Territory" [No date], Carter, TP, Alabama, XVIII, p. 194.

56. *Ibid.*

57. "Memorial to Congress by the Territorial Assembly," [Referred March 10, 1818], *Ibid.*, pp. 268–71.

58. 3 *U. S. Statutes*, pp. 348–49.

59. "Memorial to Congress by the Territorial Legislature," [No date, 1819], Carter, TP, XVIII, pp. 459–61; "Abstract of the Territorial Census" [Taken in 1818], *Ibid.*, p. 462; *Senate Journal*, 15th Cong. 2nd Sess., p. 70; "J. W. Walker to Henry Clay," November 11, 1818, Carter, TP, XVIII, pp. 462–63.

60. *Annals of Congress*, December 18, 1818, 15th Cong., 2nd Sess., p. 75; *Ibid.*, January 12, 1819, p. 121; 3 *U. S. Statutes*, pp. 489–92.

61. The most concise and thorough account of the writing of the Alabama Constitution is in Malcolm Cook McMillan, *Constitutional Development in Alabama, 1798–1901; A Study in Politics, the Negro, and Sectionalism* (Chapel Hill, 1955), pp. 30–46. Also see Malcolm Cook McMillan, "The Alabama Constitution of 1819; A Study of Constitution-making on the Frontier," *Alabama Review* 3 (October 1950), 263–86.

62. Williamson, *American Suffrage*, pp. 217–18.

63. *Alabama Constitution of 1819*, Art. I, Art. VI.

64. *Ibid.*, Art. III, Art. IV.

65. *Ibid.*, "Militia."

66. *Ibid.*, Art. V.

67. *Mississippi Constitution of 1817*, Art. VI, Sec. 16.

68. *Alabama Constitution of 1819*, "Education."

69. *Ibid.*, "Establishment of Banks."

70. *Annals of Congress*, December 11, 1819, 15th Cong., 2nd Sess., p. 66; 3 *U. S. Statutes* pp. 608–09; Abernethy, *The Formative Period in Alabama*, pp. 45–47.

71. *Ibid.*, pp. 93–101.

Chapter 12: Eclipsing Ancient Nations

1. Robert V. Remini, *Andrew Jackson and the Course of American Empire* (New York, 1977), p. 336.

2. See Chapter 2, pp. 28–39 for a discussion of Jeffersonian Indian policy.

3. Remini, *American Empire*, p. 50.

4. Francis Paul Prucha "Andrew Jackson's Indian Policy: A Reassessment," *Journal of American History* 56, (December 1969), pp. 527–39; Richard H. Faust, "Another Look at General Jackson and the Indians of the Mississippi Territory,"

Alabama Review, 28 (January 1975), pp. 202–17; Bernard W. Sheehan, "Indian-White Relations in Early America: A Review Essay", *William and Mary Quarterly,* 3rd Ser., 26 (April 1969), pp. 268–86. All three authors cite numerous examples of works dominated by the "devil theory."

5. Prucha, "Andrew Jackson's Indian Policy," pp. 532–36.

6. Prucha, "Andrew Jackson's Indian Policy," pp. 529–31; Faust, "Another Look at General Jackson," pp. 208–15; Sheehan, "Indian–White Relations," pp. 269, 281. Sheehan absolves the white man of guilt by treating the demise of the Indian in terms of a cultural or societal clash. Because a process, not a person or persons, destroyed Native American society, it is impossible to assess guilt to Americans individually or collectively. Sheehan praises Prucha as the lone historian who recognizes removal as an extension of the civilizing process.

7. Remini, *American Empire,* p. 337; Prucha, "Andrew Jackson's Indian Policy," p. 537.

8. While he agrees substantially with Prucha, Remini concludes that Jackson was motivated more by his concern for his country's well-being than by what was best for the Indians. Ronald N. Satz, who disagrees with the revisionists on many points, suggests that the sources substantiate the traditional view of Jackson. See Satz, *American Indian Policy in the Jacksonian Era* (Lincoln, 1975) and ———, "Remini's Andrew Jackson (1767–1821): Jackson and the Indians," *Tennessee Historical Quarterly,* 38, (Summer 1979), pp. 158–66.

9. Petition to the President, September 5, 1810, Clarence E. Carter, ed., *Territorial Papers of the United States,* VI, p. 106.

10. For an excellent account of the Chickasaw on the eve of removal, see Arrell M. Gibson, *The Chickasaws* (Norman, 1971), pp. 138–57. While conditions in each tribe obviously varied, experiences of the other tribes in the Old Southwest were similar.

11. Gibson, *The Chickasaws,* p. 138. Cotton gins existed in the Indian nations as early as the turn of the century. John D. W. Guice, "Face to Face in Mississippi Territory, 1798–1817" in Carolyn Keller Reeves, ed., *The Choctaw Before Removal* (Jackson, Ms., 1985), p. 172; Daniel H. Usner, Jr., "American Indians on the Cotton Frontier: Changing Economic Relations with Citizens and Slaves in the Mississippi Territory," *Journal of American History,* 72 (September 1985): pp. 297–317.

12. Though the dominance of mixed bloods occurred earlier in some tribes than in others, by the time of removal it was prevalent among all of them. For an interesting new perspective of this much neglected topic, see Samuel J. Wells, "The Role of Mixed Bloods in Mississippi Choctaw History" in *After Removal: The Choctaw in Mississippi* (Jackson, Ms., 1986), pp. 42–55. Wells lists mixed bloods who signed the Treaty of Dancing Rabbit Creek as well as those granted land therein.

13. See chapter 8, pp. 148–50.

14. Charles J. Kappler, ed. and comp., *Indian Affairs: Laws and Treaties,* vol. 2 (Washington, 1904), pp. 133–37; Charles C. Royce, comp., *Indian Cessions in the United States,* reprint of 1900 edition, extract from 18th Annual Report, Bureau of American Ethnology (New York, 1971), pp. 682–84.

15. ASP *Indian Affairs,* II, Jackson to Crawford, November 12, 1816, p. 117; Remini, *American Empire,* p. 305.

16. Personal communication, Robert V. Remini to John D. W. Guice, August

25, 1980. Remini, several years after publication of *Andrew Jackson and the Course of American Empire,* reiterated in this letter his conclusion that by 1817 Jackson "no longer needed the satisfaction of personal financial gain," p. 332.

17. Commissioners to George Graham, July 8, 1817, Jackson Papers, Library of Congress.

18. Royce, *Cessions,* pp. 684–85; Remini, *American Empire,* pp. 332–35.

19. Royce, *Cessions,* pp. 684–85; Remini, *American Empire,* pp. 332–35.

20. From 1816 through 1837, at least two dozen treaties were signed with the Cherokee, Creeks, Chickasaws, and Choctaw—mostly involving either land cessions or clarifications thereof. Since the texts and summaries are readily available in Kappler and Royce, only those deemed most necessary to a comprehension of the removal process are discussed in detail here.

21. ASP *Indian Affairs,* II, pp. 180–81.

22. "Mushulatubbee and Pushmataha to the President," August 12, 1819. *Ibid.,* 230.

23. ASP, *Indian Affairs,* II, p. 243.

24. *Ibid.,* 235–37.

25. *Ibid.,* 236.

26. Gideon Lincecum, "The Life of Apushimataha," *Publications of the Mississippi Historical Society,* 9 (1906), pp. 466–72.

27. Royce, *Cessions,* pp. 700–03; Kappler, *Treaties,* pp. 191–95.

28. Arthur DeRosier, Jr., *The Removal of the Choctaw Indians* (Knoxville, 1970), pp. 67–8.

29. Herman J. Viola, *Thomas L. McKenney, Architect of America's Early Indian Policy: 1816–1830* (Chicago, 1974), p. 131.

30. Royce, *Cessions,* pp. 708–9; Kappler, *Treaties,* pp. 211–14.

31. Samuel J. Wells, "The Evolution of Jeffersonian Indian Policy with the Choctaws of Mississippi" (Master's thesis, University of Southern Mississippi, 1981), p. 48.

32. ASP *Indian Affairs,* II, p. 553.

33. *Ibid.*

34. DeRosier, *Removal,* 83–84. While DeRosier's was a pioneering study, discerning students will supplement his account with others. On this topic, for instance, they must read Herman Viola's *Thomas L. McKenny, Architect of America's Early Indian Policy: 1816–1830* (Chicago, 1974), to understand the role played by McKenney and others in fostering Indian removal. Also important is Ronald N. Satz's *American Indian Policy in the Jacksonian Era* (Lincoln, 1975).

35. Richardson, James D., comp., *A Compilation of Messages and Papers of the Presidents: 1789–1897* (Washington, 1896–99), II, p. 1001.

36. DeRosier, *Removal,* p. 114.

37. Volumes have been printed concerning the Cherokee struggle against pressures by state's rightists in Georgia and the removal which ensued. Since much of the Cherokee story is peripheral to the Old Southwest, only passing mention of it is made here. Within the boundaries of the Old Southwest the removal story is best understood by following the events relating to Choctaw removal.

38. Anthony Winston Dillard, "The Treaty of Dancing Rabbit Creek Between the United States and the Choctaw Nation in 1830," *Transactions of the Alabama Historical Society,* 3 (1898–99): pp. 99–106.

39. "President Andrew Jackson to the United States Senate," May 6, 1830, Richardson, *Messages*, II, pp. 478–79.

40. *Ibid.*

41. Dillard, *Dancing Rabbit Creek*, p. 29.

42. Kappler, *Treaties*, p. 313.

43. *Ibid.*, p. 311.

44. During the 1830s, the Federal government was also busy obtaining cessions from the Seneca, Ottawa, Winnebago, Sauk, Fox, and other tribes to the north. For details of those treaties as well as the ones discussed in this chapter, see Kappler, *Treaties*, pp. 310–478; Royce, *Cessions*, pp. 726–65.

45. For the most recent and authoritative synopsis of the removal of the Five Civilized Tribes, see Francis Paul Prucha, *The Great Father: The United States Government and the American Indians*, 2 vols. (Lincoln, 1984), 1, pp. 214–42. For a lengthy treatment, see Grant Foreman, *Indian Removal: The Emigration of the Five Civilized Tribes of Indians* (Norman, 1932). Foreman's descriptions of the conditions on the removal trail lack balance. For an account of Choctaw removal, see DeRosier, *Removal*.

46. Apparently the number of Choctaw who remained in Mississippi far exceeded the number officially recorded at the time of removal. See Samuel J. Wells and Roseanna Tubby, eds., *After Removal: The Choctaw in Mississippi* (Jackson, Miss., 1986).

47. For an account of the controversy over removal finances, see W. David Baird, *Peter Pitchlynn: Chief of the Choctaws* (Norman, 1972).

48. The best secondary work pertaining to the Chickasaw cession treaties and removal is Gibson, *Chickasaws*, pp. 158–215.

49. Francis Paul Prucha, *Sword of the Republic: The United States Army on the Frontier, 1783–1846* (New York, 1969), pp. 269–306.

50. Kenneth W. Porter, "Florida Slaves and Free Negroes in the Seminole War, 1835–42," *Journal of Negro History* 28 (October 1943), pp. 390–421; ____ "Osceola and the Negroes," *Florida Historical Quarterly* 33 (January–April 1955, pp. 235–39; ____"Negroes and the Seminole War, 1835–42," *Journal of Southern History* (November 1964), pp. 427–50.

51. For a full scholarly account of the Seminole War, see John K. Mahon, *History of the Second Seminole War, 1835–42* (Gainesville, Fla., 1967).

52. More has been written about the Cherokee than any of the other southeastern tribes. For a recent account, see Samuel Carter, III, *Cherokee Sunset, a Nation Betrayed: A Narrative of Travail and Triumph, Persecution and Exile* (Garden City, N.Y., 1976).

53. For a scholarly, yet sympathetic and well written history of the Ridge party, see Thurman Wilkins, *Cherokee Tragedy: The Ridge Family and the Decimation of a People*, 2nd ed. rev. (Norman, 1986).

54. For an excellent summation of the historiography of Cherokee casualties on the Trail of Tears, see Prucha, *The Great Father*, n. 58, p. 231.

55. Mary E. Young, *Redskins, Ruffleshirts, and Rednecks: Indian Allotments in Alabama and Mississippi, 1830–60* (Norman: University of Oklahoma Press, 1961).

Bibliography

Manuscript Collections

Alabama Department of Archives and History, Montgomery, Alabama
   The John Coffee Papers
   The Henry S. Halbert Papers
   The Albert J. Pickett Papers

Archivo General de Indias, Seville, Spain
   Papeles procedentes de la Isla de Cuba, Legajos 9-A, 31, 62, 63, 64, 81, 116,
      120, 142-A, 149, 192, 193-A, 193-B, 200, 267, 282, 2353, 2359, 2361.
   Audiencia de Santo Domingo, Legajo 1436

Duke University, William R. Perkins Library, Manuscript Department, Durham,
      North Carolina
   William Churchill Letters
   William B. Hamilton Papers
   Ephraim Kirby Papers
   William Law Papers
   George Poindexter Letters
   Samuel Steele Papers

Library of Congress, Washington, D.C.
   John Francis Hamtramck Claiborne Papers
   Correspondence of Andrew Ellicott
   Thomas Freeman Miscellaneous Manuscript Collection
   Papers of Thomas Rodney.

Louisiana State University Library, Department of Archives and Manuscripts,
      Baton Rouge, Louisiana
   John Bisland Papers
   Thomas Affleck Papers
   Nathaniel Evans Papers

David Hunt Papers
Gras-Lauzin Family Papers
William J. Minor Papers

Mississippi Department of Archives and History, Jackson, Mississippi
J. F. H. Claiborne Collection
Record Group 2: Territorial Governors
    Alien Enemies Law affidavits
    Bonds of tax collectors, sheriffs and Indian traders
    Census records
    Election returns
    Governors' correspondence and papers:
        Winthrop Sargeant, W. C. C. Claiborne, Cato West, Robert Williams,
            Cowles Mead, David Holmes
    Governors' executive journals and lettersbooks
    Indian Department journal
    Military records
    Passport affidavits
    Registers of civil and military commissions
    Secretary of territory letterbook
Record Group 3: Territorial Auditor
    Tax rolls
Record Group 4: Territorial Treasurer
    Reports of treasurer to legislature
Record Group 5: Territorial Legislature
    Acts and resolutions
    Assembly papers
    Bills introduced
    Council and House journals
    Petitions to General Assembly
Record Group 6: Territorial Court
    Case files and minute books

National Archives, Washington, D.C.
Record Group 59, General Records of the Department of State Consular Dispatches, New Orleans, 1798–1807, Microcopy T225
Record Group 75, Records of the Bureau of Indian Affairs
Letters Received by the Office of Indian Affairs, 1824–81, Microcopy M234
Letters Received by the Office of the Secretary of War Relating to Indian Affairs, 1800–1823, Microcopy M271
Letters Received by the Superintendent of Indian Trade 1806–24, Microcopy T58
Letters Sent by the Office of Indian Affairs, 1824–81, Microcopy M21
Letters Sent by the Secretary of War Relating to Indian Affairs, 1820–1824, Microcopy M15
Letters Sent by the Superintendent of Indian Trade, 1807–23 Microcopy M16
Records of the Choctaw Trading House, 1803–24, Microcopy T500
Register of Letters Received by the Office of Indian Affairs, 1824–80, M18

Record Group 98, Records of U. S. Army Commands
  Volume 401, Letterbook of Major Thomas Cushing, 1799, Letters Received
  Volume 402, Letterbook of Major Thomas Cushing, 1799, Letters Sent
Record Group 107, Records of the Office of the Secretary of War
  Letters Received by the Secretary of War, Registered Series, 1801–70, Micro-
    copy M221
  Letters Received by the Secretary of War, Unregistered Series, 1789–1861, Micro-
    copy M222
  Miscellaneous Letters Sent by the Secretary of War, 1800–1809, Microcopy M370
  Letters Sent by the Secretary of War Relating to Military Affairs, 1800–1889,
    Microcopy M6
  Letters Sent to the President by the Secretary of War, 1800–1863, Microcopy
    M127
  Confidential and Unofficial Letters Sent by the Secretary of War, 1814–47, Micro-
    copy M7

Public Record Office, London, England
  Colonial Office 700, Florida, No. 51

Tennessee State Library and Archives, Nashville, Tennessee
  Willie Blount Papers
  John Coffee Papers
  Andrew Jackson Papers
  Joseph McMinn Papers
  John Overton Papers
  Archibald Roane Papers
  James Robertson Papers
  John Sevier Papers

Tulane University, Howard-Tilton Memorial Library, New Orleans, Louisiana
  William C. C. Claiborne Papers

University of Southern Mississippi, Hattiesburg, Mississippi
  Richard Lackey Collection

Published Documents

Annals of Congress: 8th cong., 1st. sess.; 11th cong., 2nd sess. Bassett, John Spen-
  cer, ed. *Correspondence of Andrew Jackson.* 6 vols. Washington, 1926–33.
Bassett, John Spencer, ed. *Major Howell Tatum's Journal While Acting Topographical
  Engineer (1814) to General Jackson Commanding the Seventh Military District.* Smith
  College Studies in History, 7, Northampton, Mass., 1921–22.
Carter, Clarence E., ed. *The Territorial Papers of the United States.* Vol. 5: *The Territory of Mississippi, 1798–1817.* Washington, 1937.
———. ed. *The Territorial Papers of the United States.* Vol. 6: *The Territory of Missis-
  sippi, 1798–1817.* Washington, 1938.

————. ed. *The Territorial Papers of the United States.* Vol. 9: *The Territory of Orleans, 1803–1812.* Washington, 1940.

————., ed. *The Territorial Papers of the United States.* Vol. 18: *The Territory of Alabama, 1817–1819.* Washington, 1952.

Lackey, Richard, comp., *Frontier Claims in the Lower South.* New Orleans, 1977. Introduction by John D. W. Guice. Sworn statements with accompanying exhibits of sundry inhabitants of the Mississippi Territory, September-November, 1815, praying for relief from Indian depradations, 14th Cong., 1st sess., January 2, 1816, Other Select Committees, HR 14-F16.7. Record Group 233, House of Representatives, National Archives, Washington, D.C.

Lowrie, Walter, et al., eds. *The American State Papers: Indian Affairs,* vols. 1 & 2; *Miscellaneous,* vols. 1 & 2; *Public Lands,* vol. 1. Washington, 1832–61.

Richardson, James D., ed. *A Compilation of the Messages and Papers of the Presidents, 1789–1897.* 10 vols. Washington, 1896–99.

Rowland, Dunbar, ed., *Letterbooks of W. C. C. Claiborne,* 6 vols. Jackson, Ms., 1880.

————, ed. *Mississippi Territorial Archives, 1798–1803: Executive Journals of Governor Winthrop Sargent and Governor William Charles Cole Claiborne.* vol. 1. Nashville, 1905.

Toulmin, Harry. *The Statutes of the Mississippi Territory, Revised and Digested by the Authority of the General Assembly.* Natchez, 1807.

Turner, Edward. *Statutes of the Mississippi Territory; The Constitution of the United States, With the Several Amendments Thereto; The Ordinance for the Government of the Territory of the United States, North-West of the River Ohio; The Articles of Agreement and Cession, Between The United States and the State of Georgia; and Such Acts of Congress as Relate to the Mississippi Territory.* Digested by the Authority of the General Assembly. Natchez, 1816.

United States Census: 1800, 1810, 1820, and *Compendium of 1850 Census.*

United States Statutes At Large. vols 1, 2, 3 & 7.

Books and Articles

Abernethy, Thomas P. *The Formative Period in Alabama, 1815–1828.* Montgomery, 1822.

————. *The South in the New Nation, 1789–1819.* In *A History of the South,* Vol. 4, Edited by Wendell Holmes Stephenson and E. Merton Coulter. Baton Rouge, 1961.

Adair, James. *A History of the American Indians.* London, 1775. Reprint, New York, Promontory Press, 1986.

Adams, Samuel B. "The Yazoo Fraud," *Georgia Historical Quarterly,* 7 (June 1923): 155–65.

Akerman, Joe A., Jr. *Florida Cowman, A History of Florida Cattle Raising.* Kissimmee, Florida, 1976.

Aldredge, J. Haden. *History of Navigation on the Tennessee River System.* Washington, 1937, House Doc. 254.

Alford, Terry L. "Some Manumissions Recorded in the Adams County Deed Books in the Chancery Clerk's Office, Natchez, Mississippi, 1795–1835." *Journal of Mississippi History,* 33 (February 1971): 43–44.

Alvord, Clarence Walnorth, and Carter, Clarence Edwin., eds. *Journal of Capt. H. Gordon, 1766*. Collections of the Illinois State Historical Library, vol. 11. Springfield, Ill., 1916.

Arnade, Charles W. "Cattle Raising in Spanish Florida, 1513–1763." *Agricultural History*, 35 (July 1961): 116–24.

Arthur, Stanley Clisby. *The Story of the West Florida Rebellion*. St. Francisville, La., 1935.

Audubon, John James. *Delineations of American Scenery and Character*. Edited by Francis Hobart Herrick. New York, 1926.

"Autobiography of Gideon Lincecum." *Publications of the Mississippi Historical Society*, 8 (1904): 443–519.

Bailey, Thomas A. "The Friendly Rivals: Bemis and Bailey," *The Society for Historians of American Foreign Relations Newsletter*, 10 (March 1979): 12–17.

Baily, Francis. *Journal of a Tour in Unsettled Parts of North America in 1796 & 1797*. London, 1856.

Baird, W. David. *Peter Pitchlynn: Chief of the Choctaws*. Norman, 1972.

Baldwin, Joseph G. *The Flush Times of Alabama and Mississippi*. New York, 1853.

Bemis, Samuel Flagg. *Pinckney's Treaty*. Baltimore, 1926.

Betts, Edward Chamber. *Early History of Huntsville, Alabama, 1804–1870*. Montgomery, 1909.

Blair, Walter, and Meine, Franklin J. *Half Horse Half Alligator: The Growth of the Mike Fink Legend*. Chicago, 1956.

———. *Mike Fink: King of Mississippi Keelboatmen*. New York, 1933.

Bloom, Jo Tice. "Cumberland Gap Versus South Pass: The East or West in Frontier History. *Western Historical Quarterly*, 3 (April 1972): 153–67.

Bodenhamer, David. "The Efficiency of Criminal Justice in the Antebellum South." *Criminal Justice History: An International Annual*, 3 (1983): 81–95.

———. "Law and Disorder in the Old South: The Situation in Georgia, 1830–1860." In Walter J. Fraser and Winfred B. Moore, eds. *From the Old South to the New: Essays on the Transitional South* New York, 1981, pp. 109–19.

Boles, John B. *The Great Revival, 1787–1805: The Origins of the Southern Evangelical Mind*. Lexington, Ky., 1972.

Braden, Guy B. "A Jeffersonian Village: Washington, Mississippi." *Journal of Mississippi History*, 30 (May 1968): 135–44.

Bradley, Jared W. "William C. C. Claiborne, the Old Southwest, and the Development of American Indian Policy." *Tennessee Historical Quarterly*, 33 (Fall, 1974): 265–78.

Bretz, Julian P. "Early Land Communication with the Lower Mississippi Valley." *Mississippi Valley Historical Review*, 13 (June 1926): 3–29.

Briceland, Allan V. "Ephraim Kirby: Pioneer of American Law Reporting, 1789." *Journal of Amerian Legal History*, 16 (October 1972): 297–319.

Bryant, Keith L. "The Role and Status of the Female Yeomanry in the Antebellum South: The Literary View." *Southern Quarterly A Journal of the Arts in the South*, 18 (Winter 1980): 73–88.

Burnett, Edmund C., comp. "Papers Relating to Bourbon County, Georgia, 1785–1786." *American Historical Review*, Part 1, 15 (October 1909): 66–111; Part 2, 15 (January 1910): 297–353.

Byrne, Donald E., Jr. *No Foot of Land: Folklore of American Methodist Itinerants.* Metuchen, N. J., 1975.

Cain, Cyril Edward. *Four Centuries on the Pascagoula. Volume I: History, Story, and Legend of the Pascagoula River Country.* Privately published [No place cited], 1953.

———. *Four Centuries on the Pascagoula. Volume II: History and Genealogy of the Pascagoula River Country.* Privately published [No place cited], 1962.

Carson, W. Wallace. "Transportation and Traffic on the Ohio and the Mississippi Before the Steamboat." *Mississippi Valley Historical Review,* 7 (June 1920): 26–38.

Caruso, John Anthony. *The Southern Frontier.* Indianapolis, 1963.

Carter, Samuel, III. *Cherokee Sunset, a Nation Betrayed: A Narrative of Travail and Triumph, Persecution and Exile.* Garden City, NY, 1976.

Chappell, Absalom H. *Miscellanies of Georgia, Historical, Biographical, Descriptive, Etc.* Columbus, Ga., 1928.

Charlton, Thomas U. P. *The Life of Major General James Jackson.* Augusta, Ga., 1809.

Claiborne, J. F. H. *Life and Times of General Sam Dale, The Mississippi Partisan.* New York, 1860.

———. *Mississippi as a Province, Territory, and State.* Jackson, 1880.

———. "Rough Riding Down South." *Harper's New Monthly Magazine,* 25 (June 1862): 29–37.

———. "A Trip through the Piney Woods." *Publications of the Mississippi Historical Society,* 9 (1906): 487–538.

Clark, John G., *New Orleans, 1718–1812: An Economic History.* Baton Rouge, 1970.

Clark, Thomas D. *The Rampaging Frontier: Manners and Humors of Pioneer Days in the South and Middle West.* Bloomington, 1939.

———, ed. *Travels in the Old South: A Bibliography,* II, *The Expanding South, 1750–1825.* Norman, 1956.

Coates, Robert M. *The Outlaw Years: The History of the Land Pirates of the Natchez Trace.* New York, 1930.

Coker, William S. "How General Andrew Jackson Learned of the British Plans Before the Battle of New Orleans." *Gulf Coast Historical Review.* 3 (Fall 1987): 84–95.

———. "The Last Battle of the War of 1812: New Orleans. No, Fort Bowyer!." *Alabama Historical Quarterly,* 43 (Spring 1981): 42–63.

Cotterill, Robert S. "Federal Indian Management in the South, 1789–1825." *Mississippi Valley Historical Review,* 20 (December 1933): 333–52.

———. *The Southern Indians: The Story of the Civilized Tribes Before Removal.* Norman, 1954.

Cox, Isaac Joslin. *The West Florida Controversy, 1798–1813.* Baltimore, 1918.

Crane, Verner W. *The Southern Frontier,* Ann Arbor, 1956.

Craven, Avery. "The 'Turner Theories' and the South." *Journal of Southern History.* 5 (August 1939): 291–314.

Cuming, Fortescue. *Sketches of a Tour to the Western Country—1807–1809.* In *Early Western Travel, 1748–1846,* edited by Reuben Gold Thwaites. Cleveland, 1904, reprint New York, 1966.

Cushman, Horatio, B. *History of the Choctaw, Chickasaw & Natchez Indians.* Edited and introduced by Angie Debo. Stillwater, OK, 1962.

Daniels, Jonathan. *The Devil's Backbone: The Story of the Natchez Trace.* New York, 1962.

Darby, William. *The Emigrant's Guide to the Western and Southwestern States and Territories.* New York, 1818.

————. *A Geographical Description of the State of Louisiana, the Southern Part of the State of Mississippi, and the Territory of Alabama.* 2nd ed., New York, 1817.

Debo, Angie. *The Rise and Fall of the Choctaw Republic.* Norman, 1961.

DeRosier, Arthur H., Jr. "Natchez and the Formative Years of William Dunbar." *Journal of Mississippi History,* 34 (February 1972): 29–47.

————. *The Removal of the Choctaw Indians.* Knoxville, 1970.

————. "William Dunbar, Explorer." *Journal of Mississippi History,* 25 (July 1963) :165–85.

————. "William Dunbar: A Product of the Eighteenth Century Scottish Renaissance." *Journal of Mississippi History,* 28, (August, 1966): 185–227.

Dick, Everett. *The Dixie Frontier: A Social History of the Southern Frontier from the First Transmontane Beginnings to the Civil War.* New York, 1948.

Dillard, Anthony Winston. "The Treaty of Dancing Rabbit Creek Between the United States and the Choctaw Nation in 1830." *Transactions of the Alabama Historical Society,* 3 (1898–1899): 99–106.

Dobyns, Henry F. *Their Number Became Thinned: Native American Population Dynamics in Eastern North America.* Knoxville, 1983.

Dodd, Donald B., and Dodd, Wynelle S. *Historical Statistics of the South, 1790–1970.* University, Ala., 1973.

Doran, Michael F. "Antebellum Cattle Herding in the Indian Territory." *Geographical Review,* 66 (1976): 48–58.

Dow, Lorenzo. *History of Cosmopolite: Or the Writings of Rev. Lorenzo Dow: Containing His Experience and Travels, in Europe and America, up to Near his Fifteenth Year. Also, His Polemic Writings, to Which is Added the "Journey of Life" by Peggy Dow.* Cincinnati, 1857.

Drake, Winbourne Magruder. "The Framing of Mississippi's First Constitution." *Journal of Mississippi History,* 29 (November 1967):211–28.

Dunbar, Gary S. "Colonial Carolina Cowpens." *Agricultural History,* 35 (1961): 125–50.

Dungan, James R. "Sir William Dunbar of Natchez: Planter, Explorer, and Scientist, 1792–1810." *Journal of Mississippi History,* 24 (October 1961): 211–28.

Durham, Phillip, and Jones, Everett L. *The Negro Cowboys.* New York, 1965.

Edmunds, R. David. *Tecumseh and the Quest for Indian Leadership.* Boston, 1984.

————. "Tecumseh, The Shawnee Prophet, and American History: A Reassessment." *Western Historical Quarterly,* 14 (July 1983): 261–76.

Elsmere, Jane. "The Notorious Yazoo Land Fraud Case." *Georgia Historical Quarterly,* 51 (December 1967): 425–42.

Evans, Estwick. *A Pedestrious Tour.* Concord, N. H. 1819. In *Early Western Travels, 1748–1846.* Edited by Reuben Gold Thwaites. New York, 1966.

Evans, W. A. "Gaines Trace in Monroe County, Mississippi." *Journal of Mississippi History,* 1 (April 1939):100–9.

Faust, Richard H. "Another Look at General Jackson and the Indians of the Mississippi Territory." *Alabama Review*, 28 (January 1975): 202–17.

Flint, Timothy, *A Condensed Georgraphy and History of the Western States, or the Mississippi Valley*. 2 vols. Cincinnati, 1812.

———. *History and Geogaphy of the Mississippi Valley*. Cincinnati, 1832.

———. *Recollections of the Last Ten Years Passed in Occasional Residence and Journeys in the Valley of the Mississippi*. Boston, 1826.

Fogel, Robert William, and Engerman, Stanley L. *Time on the Cross: The Economics of American Negro Slavery*. Boston, 1974.

Foreman, Grant. *Indian Removal: The Emigration of the Five Civilized Tribes of Indians*. Norman, 1932.

Free, Joseph M. "The Ante-Bellum Theatre of the Old Natchez Region." *Journal of Mississippi History*, 5 (January 1943): 14–27.

Galloway, Patricia K., ed. *LaSalle and His Legacy: Frenchmen and Indians in the Lower Mississippi Valley*. Jackson, Ms., 1983.

Gibson, Arrell M. *The Chickasaws*. Norman, 1976.

———. *The American Indian: Prehistory to the Present* Lexington, Mass., 1980.

Goff, John Hedges. *Retracing the Old Federal Road and Cow Punching in Old Georgia*. Emory University Studies in Business and Economics. Atlanta, 1950.

Gratz, Simon, comp., "Thomas Rodney." *Pennsylvania Magazine of History and Biography*, 43 (1919): 1–23, 117–42, 208–27, 332–67; 44 (1920): 47–72, 170–89, 270–84, 289–308; 45 (1921): 34–65, 180–203.

Gray, Lewis Cecil. *History of Agriculture in the Southern United States to 1860*. Carnegie Institution of Washington Publication No. 430, 2 vols. Washington, 1932.

Green, Michael D. *The Politics of Indian Removal: Creek Government and Society in Crises*. Lincoln, 1982.

Guice, John D. W. "Cattle Raisers of the Old Southwest: A Reinterpretation." *Western Historical Quarterly*, 8 (April 1977): 167–87.

———. "The Cement of Society: Law in Mississippi Territory." *Gulf Coast Historical Review*, 1 (Spring 1986): 76–99.

———. "Face to Face in Mississippi Territory, 1798–1817." In *The Choctaw Before Removal*, edited by Carolyn Keller Reeves. Jackson, Ms., 1985.

——— "Indigenous Prologue." In *Atlas of Mississippi,* edited by Ralph D. Cross. Jackson, Ms., 1974.

Haites, Erik F.; Mak, James; and Walton, Garry M. *Western River Transportation: The Era of Early Internal Development, 1810–1860*. The Johns Hopkins University Studies in Historical and Political Science, 93rd Series. Baltimore, 1975.

Halbert, Henry Sale, and Ball, T. H. *The Creek War of 1813 and 1814*. Chicago, 1895.

Hall, Captain Basil. *Travels in North America in the Years 1817–2*. 3 vols., Edinburgh, 1829.

Hall, James. *A Brief History of the Mississippi Territory*. Salisbury, N.C., 1801.

Hamilton, Peter J. *Colonial Mobile*. Boston, 1897.

Hamilton, William Baskerville. *Anglo-American Law on the Frontier: Thomas Rodney & His Territorial Cases*. Durham, N.C., 1953.

———. "Politics in the Mississippi Territory. *Huntington Library Quarterly*, 11 (May

1948): 277–91. ———. "The Sources of History of the Mississippi Territory." *Journal of Mississippi History*, 1 (January 1939):29–36.

———. *Thomas Rodney: Revolutionary and Builder of the West*. Durham, 1953.

———. "The Southwestern Frontier, 1795–1817: An Essay in Social History." *Journal of Southern History*, 10 (November 1944): 389–403.

———. "The Theater in the Old Southwest: The First Decade at Natchez." *American Literature*, 12 (May 1941): 471–85.

———. "The Transmission of English Law to the Frontier of America." *South Atlantic Quarterly*, 67 (1968): 243–64.

Harper, Francis, ed. *The Travels of William Bartram*. Naturalist's Edition, New Haven, 1958.

Harrell, Laura D. S. "Horse Racing in the Old Natchez District." *Journal of Mississippi History*, 13 (July 1951): 123–37.

———. "Jockey Clubs and Race Tracks in Antebellum Mississippi, 1795–1861." *Journal of Mississippi History*, 28 (November 1966): 304–18.

Haskins, Charles H. "The Yazoo Land Companies." *Papers of the American Historical Association*, 5 vols., New York, 1891, Part 4:61–103.

Haughton, Richard. "Influence of the Mississippi River upon the Early Settlement of Its Valley." *Publications of the Mississippi Historical Society*, 4 (1901): 465–82.

Haynes, Robert V. "The Disposal of Lands in the Mississippi Territory." *Journal of Mississippi History*, 24 (October 1962): 226–52.

———. "Historians and the Mississippi Territory." *Journal of Mississippi History*, 29 (November 1967): 409–28.

———. "Law Enforcement in Frontier Mississippi." *Journal of Mississippi History*, 22 (January 1960): 27–42.

———. "Life on the Mississippi Frontier: Case of Matthew Phelps." *Journal of Mississippi History*, 39 (February 1977):1–15.

———. *The Natchez District and the American Revolution*. Jackson, Ms., 1976.

———. "The Revolution of 1800 in Mississippi." *Journal of Mississippi History*, 19 (October 1957): 234–51.

———. "The Road to Statehood." In Richard Aubrey McLemore, ed., *A History of Mississippi*, I, Jackson, Ms., 1973.

Hawkins, Benjamin. *A Sketch of the Creek Country, in the Years 1798 and 1799 and Letters of Benjamin Hawkins, 1796–1806*. 2 vols. in one. 1848. Reprint edition, Spartenburg, S.C., 1982.

Heath, William Estill. "The Yazoo Land Fraud." *Georgia Historical Review*, 16 (December 1932): 274–91.

Hildreth, S. F. "History of a Voyage on the Ohio and Mississippi Rivers, with Historical Sketches of the Different Points Along Them." *The American Pioneer*, 1 (March 1842):140–45.

Holder, Ray. *William Winans: Methodist Leader in Antebellum Mississippi*. Jackson, Ms., 1977.

Holmes, Jack D. L. "Cotton Gins in the Spanish Natchez District, 1795–1800." *Journal of Mississippi History*, 31 (August 1969):159–71.

Howard, Clinton N. *The British Development of West Florida, 1763–1769* Berkeley, 1947.

Hudson, Charles. *The Southeastern Indians.* Knoxville, 1982.

James, D. Clayton, *Antebellum Natchez* Baton Rouge, 1968.

James, D. Clayton. "Municipal Government in Territorial Natchez." *Journal of Mississippi History,* 29 (May 1965):147–67.

James, Marquis. *Andrew Jackson: The Border Captain.* Indianapolis, 1933.

Jamison, Lena Mitchell. "The Natchez Trace: A Federal Highway of the Old Southwest." *Journal of Mississippi History,* 1 (April 1939): 82–99.

Johnson, Cecil. *British West Florida, 1763–1783.* New Haven, 1943.

———. "The Distribution of Land in British West Florida." *Louisiana Historical Quarterly,* 16 (October 1933): 539–53.

———. "Expansion in West Florida, 1770–1779." *Mississippi Valley Historical Review,* 20 (March 1934): 641–67.

Kappler, Charles J., ed. *Indian Affairs: Laws and Treaties.* Washington, 1904.

Keating, Bern. "Today Along the Natchez Trace." *National Geographic,* 134 (November 1968): 641–67.

Kolodny, Annette. *The Land Before Her: Fantasy and Experience of the American Frontiers, 1630–1860.* Chapel Hill, 1984.

Leftwich, George J. "Some Main Traveled Roads, Including Cross Sections of Natchez Trace." *Publications of the Mississippi History Society,* 1 (1916): 463–76.

Leftwich, Nina. *Two Hundred Years at Muscle Shoals.* Tuscumbia, Ala., 1935.

Lengel, Leland. "The Road to Fort Mims: Judge Harry Toulmin's Observations on the Creek War, 1811–1813." *Alabama Review,* 29 (January 1976): 16–36.

Lewis, Marcus W. *The Development of Early Emigrant Trails in the United States East of the Mississippi River* Special Publications of the National Genealogical Society. No. 3, Washington, 1933.

Lincecum, Gideon. "The Life of Apushimataha." *Publications of the Mississippi Historical Society,* 9 (1906): 415–85.

Locke, Raymond Friday. "The Natchez Trace: Road of Blood." *Mankind: The Magazine of Popular History,* 4 (1975): 30–37.

Lowery, Charles D. "The Great Migration to the Mississippi Territory, 1798–1819." *Journal of Mississippi History,* 30 (August 1968): 173–92.

Lowry, Robert and McCardle, William H. *Biographical and Historical Memoirs of Mississippi.* 2 vols. Chicago, 1925.

Lynch, William O. "The Westward Flow of Southern Colonists before 1861." *Journal of Southern History,* 9 (August 1943): 303–27.

Lyon, Anne Bozeman. "The Bonapartists in Alabama." *Alabama Historial Quarterly,* 25 (Fall & Winter 1963): 227–41.

McDonald, Forrest, and McWhiney, Grady. "The Antebellum Southern Herdsman: A Reinterpretation." *Journal of Southern History,* 41 (May 1975): 147–66.

———, "Comparative History in Theory and Practice: A Discussion." *American Historial Review,* 87 (February 1982): 134–37.

McDonald, Forrest, and McDonald, Ellen Shapiro. "The Ethnic Origins of the American People, 1790." *William and Mary Quarterly,* 3rd Series, 37 (April 1980): 179–99.

McDonald, Forrest, and McWhiney, Grady. "The South from Self-Sufficiency to Peonage: An Interpretation." *American Historial Review,* 85 (December 1980): 1095–1118.

McLemore, Richard A. "The Division of Mississippi." *Journal of Mississippi History*, 5 (April 1943): 79–82.

———. "Factionalism, A Fruit of Spanish-American Rivalry on the Mississippi Frontier." *Journal of Mississippi History*, 6 (October 1944): 237–40.

McMillan, Malcolm Cook. "The Alabama Constitution of 1819: A Study of Constitution-making on the Frontier," *Alabama Review*, 3 (October 1950): 263–86.

———. *Constitutional Development in Alabama, 1798–1901: A Study in Politics, the Negro, and Sectionalism.* Chapel Hill, 1955.

MacPhee, Donald A., "The Yazoo Controversy: The Beginning of the 'Quid' Revolt." *Georgia Historical Quarterly*, 49 (March 1965): 23–43.

McWhiney, Grady. "Antebellum Piney Woods Culture: Continuity over Time and Place." In *Mississippi's Piney Woods: A Human Perspective*, edited by Noel Polk. Jackson, Ms., 1986.

———. *Cracker Culture: Celtic Ways in the Old South.* Tuscaloosa, 1988.

Magrath, C. Peter. *Yazoo: Law and Politics in the New Republic—The Case of Fletcher v. Peck.* Providence, R.I., 1966.

Mahon, John K. *History of the Second Seminole War, 1835–1842.* Gainesville, Fla., 1967.

Malone, Dumas. *Jefferson and His Time.* Vol. 4. *Jefferson the President, First Term, 1801–1805.* Boston, 1970.

Marcus, Jacob R. *The Colonial American Jew, 1492–1776.* 3 vols. Detroit, 1970.

———. *Early American Jewry: The Jews of Pennsylvania and the South, 1635–1790.* Philadelphia, 1953.

Mealor, W. Theodore, Jr., and Prunty, Merle C. "Open-Range Ranching in Southern Florida." *Annals of the Association of American Geographers*, 66 (1976): 360–76.

Mills, Elizabeth Shown. "Academia vs. Genealogy." *National Genealogical Quarterly*, 71 (June 1983): 99–106.

Moore, Albert Burton. *History of Alabama and Her People.* Chicago, 1927.

Moore, John Hebron. *Agriculture in Ante-Bellum Mississippi.* New York, 1958.

Napier, John Hawkins, III. "The Gulf Coast: Key to Jeffersonian Empire." *Alabama Historical Quarterly*, 33 (Summer 1974): 98–115.

Owsley, Frank L. "The Education of a Southern Frontier Girl, Part I." *Alabama Review*, 6 (October 1953): 268–88.

———. "The Pattern of Migration and Settlement of the Southern Frontier." *Journal of Southern History*, 11 (May 1945): 147–76.

———. *Plain Folk of the Old South.* 1949, Reprint, Baton Rouge, 1982.

Owsley, Frank L., Jr. *Struggle for the Gulf Borderlands: The Creek War and the Battle of New Orleans 1812–1815.* Gainsville, 1984.

Parish, John Carl. "The Intrigues of Doctor James O'Fallon." *Mississippi Valley Historical Review*, 17 (September 1930): 230–63.

Parkins, Almon E. *The South: Its Economic-Geographic Development.* New York, 1938.

Parkinson, Richard. *A Tour in America in 1798, 1799, and 1800. Exhibiting Sketches of Society and Manners, and a Particular Account of the American System of Agriculture with Its Recent Improvements.* 2 vols., London, 1805.

Peake, Ora Brooks. *A History of the United States Indian Factory System.* Denver, 1954.

Penick, James Lal, Jr. *The Great Western Land Pirate: John A. Murrell in Legend and History.* Columbia, Mo., 1981.

Phelps, Dawson A. "The Chickasaw Agency." *Journal of Mississippi History*, 14 (April 1952): 119–37.
———. "The Choctaw Mission." *Journal of Mississippi History*, 14 (January 1952): 35–62.
———. "The Natchez Trace in Alabama." *Alabama Review*, 7 (January 1954): 22–41.
———. "The Natchez Trace, Indian Trail to Parkway." *Tennessee Historical Quarterly*, 21 (September 1962): 203–18.
———. "The Natchez Trace in Tennessee History." *Tennessee Historical Quarterly*, 13 (September 1954): 195–203.
———. "Stands and Travel Accommodations on the Natchez Trace." *Journal of Mississippi History*, 11 (January 1949): 1–54.
———. "Travel on the Natchez Trace." *Journal of Mississippi History*, 15 (July 1953): 155–64.
Pickett, Albert James. *History of Alabama and Incidentally of Georgia and Mississippi, From the Earliest Period*. 1851, Reprint, Tuscaloosa, 1962.
Pierson, Hamilton, W. *In the Brush: Old-Time Social, Political and Religious Life in the Southwest*. New York, 1883.
Pope, John. *A Tour Through the Southern and Western Territories of the United States of North America*. Richmond, 1792.
Porter, Kenneth W. "Florida Slaves and Free Negroes in the Seminole War, 1835–1842." *Journal of Negro History*, 28 (October 1943): 390–421.
———. "Negroes and the Seminole War, 1835–1842." *Journal of Southern History*, 30 (November 1964): 427–50.
———. "Osceola and the Negroes." *Florida Historical Quarterly*, 33 (January-April 1955): 235–39.
Posey, Walter Brownlow. *The Development of Methodism in the Old Southwest: 1783–1824*. Tuscaloosa, 1933.
Prentiss, George L., ed. *A Memoir of S. S. Prentiss*. 2 vols. New York, 1855.
Priest, William. *Travels in the United States of America: Commencing in the Year 1793 and Ending in 1797*. London, 1802.
Prucha, Francis Paul. "Andrew Jackson's Indian Policy: A Reassessment," *Journal of American History*, 56 (December 1969): 527–39.
———. *American Indian Policy in the Formative Years: The Indian Trade and Intercourse Acts, 1790–1834*. Cambridge, 1962.
———. ed. *A Bibliographical Guide to the History of Indian-White Relations in the United States*. Chicago, 1977.
———, *Broadax and Bayonet: The Role of the United States Army in the Development of the Northwest 1815–1860*. Madison, Wi., 1953.
———. ed. *Documents of United States Indian Policy*. Lincoln, 1975.
———. "Doing Indian History." In *Indian-White Relations: A Persistent Paradox*, edited by Jane F. Smith and Robert M. Kvasnicka. Washington, 1976.
———. *The Great Father: The United States Government and the American Indians*. 2 vols. Lincoln, 1984.
———. *The Sword of the Republic: The United States Army on the Frontier, 1783–1846*. New York, 1969.
———. *United States Indian Policy: A Critical Bibliography*. Bloomington, 1977.
Ramsey, A. C. *A Sketch of the life and times of Rev. A. C. Ramsey as written by himself*

in 1879 at the age of 72, . . . Gadsden, Ala., September, 1879. Edited by Jean Strickland as *The Autobiography of A. C. Ramsey.* Moss Point, Ms., no date.

Remington, Frederic. "Cracker Cowboys of Florida." *Harper's New Monthly Magazine.* 91 (August 1895): 339–45.

Remini, Robert V. *Andrew Jackson and the Course of American Empire, 1767–1821.* New York, 1977.

Richardson, William. *Travel Diary of William Richardson from Boston to New Orleans by Land in 1815.* 1818, Reprint edition, New York, 1938.

Riley, Franklin L., comp. "Autobiography of Gideon Lincecum." *Publications of The Mississippi Historical Society.* 8 (1904): 443–519.

———. "Location of the Boundaries of Mississippi." *Publications of the Mississippi Historical Society,* 3 (1900): 167–84.

———. "Sir William Dunbar: The Pioneer Scientist of Mississippi." *Publication of the Mississippi Historical Society,* 2 (1899): 85–111.

———. "Spanish Policy in Mississippi after the Treaty of San Lorenzo." Mississippi Historical Society, *Publications,* 1 (1898): 50–66.

Robinson, W. Stitt. *The Southern Colonial Frontier, 1607–1763.* Albuquerque, 1979.

Rohrbough, Malcolm J. *The Trans-Appalachian Frontier: People, Societies, and Institutions 1775–1850.* New York, 1978.

Rowland, Dunbar. *History of Mississippi, The Heart of the South.* 2 vols. Chicago, 1925.

Rowland, Mrs. Dunbar. "Peter Chester, Third Governor of the Province of West Florida under British Dominion, 1770–1781." *Publications of the Mississippi Historical Society,* Centenary Series, 5 (1916): 1–183.

Rowland, Evon Orpha Moore, ed. *Life, Letters and Papers of William Dunbar of Elgin, Morayshire, Scotland, and Natchez Mississippi: Pioneer Scientist of the Southern United States.* Jackson, Ms., 1930.

Royce, Charles C. *Indian Land Cessions in the United States.* New York, 1971.

Satz, Ronald N. *American Indian Policy in the Jacksonian Era.* Lincoln, 1975.

———. "Remini's Andrew Jackson (1767–1821): Jackson and the Indians." *Tennessee Historical Quarterly,* 38 (Summer 1979): 158–66.

Sheehan, Bernard W. "Indian-White Relations in Early America: A Review Essay." *William and Mary Quarterly,* 3rd Ser., 26 (April 1969): 268–86.

———. *Seeds of Extinction: Jefferson Philanthropy and the American Indian.* New York, 1973.

Skates, John Ray, Jr. "In Defense of Owsley's Yeoman." In *Southern Miscellany: Essays in History in Honor of Glover Moore.* Edited by Frank Allen Dennis, Jackson, 1981.

Smith, Dwight L., ed. *Indians of the United States and Canada: A Bibliography.* Santa Barbara, 1974.

Sparks, W. H. *The Memories of Fifty Years: Containing Notices of Distinguished Americans, and Anecdotes of Remarkable Men; Interspersed with Scenes and Incidents Occurring During a Long Life of Observations Chiefly Spent in the Southwest.* Philadelphia, 1870.

Surrey, N. M. Miller. *The Commerce of Louisiana during the French Regime, 1699–1763.* Columbia University Studies in History, Economics, and Public Law, vol. 71, no. 1, New York, 1916.

Sydnor, Charles. *A Gentlemen of Old Southwest Region, Benjamin L. C. Wailes*. Durham, 1938.

———. *Slavery in Mississippi*. New York, 1933.

Thomason, Hugh M. "Governor Peter Early and the Creek Indian Frontier, 1813–1815." *Georgia Historical Quarterly*, 45 (September 1961): 223–37.

Tilly, Bette B. "The Jackson-Dinsmoor Feud in a Minor Key," *Journal of Mississippi History* 39 (May 1977): 117–31.

Turner, Frederick Jackson. *The Frontier in American History*. New York, 1920.

———. *The Significance of Sections in American History*. New York, 1932.

———. *The United States 1830–1860: The Nation and Its Sections*. 1935, Reprint, Gloucester, Mass., 1958.

Usner, Daniel H., Jr. "American Indians on the Cotton Frontier: Changing Economic Relations with Citizens and Slaves in the Mississippi Territory." *Journal of American History*, 72 (September 1985): 297–317.

Vance, Rupert V. *Human Geography of the South*. Chapel Hill, 1935.

Ver Steeg, Clarence Lester. *Origins of a Southern Mosaic: Studies of Early Carolina and Georgia*. Athens, Georgia, 1975.

Viola, Herman J. *Thomas L. McKenney, Architect of America's Early Indian Policy: 1816–1830*. Chicago, 1974.

Weaver, Herbert. *Mississippi Farmers 1850–1860*. Knoxville, 1945.

Wells, Samuel J. "The Role of Mixed-Bloods in Mississippi Choctaw History." In *After Removal: The Choctaw in Mississippi*, edited by Samuel J. Wells and Roseanna Tubby. Jackson, Ms., 1986.

———. "Rum, Skins, and Powder: A Chocaw Interpreter and the Treaty of Mount Dexter." *Chronicles of Oklahoma*, 61 (Winter 1983–84): 422–28.

Wesley, Edgar B. *Guarding the Frontier: A Study in Frontier Defense from 1815 to 1825*. Minneapolis, 1935.

Whitaker, Arthur Preston. *The Mississippi Question 1795–1803: A Study in Trade, Politics, and Diplomacy*. New York, 1934.

———. *The Spanish-American Frontier, 1783–1795: The Westward Movement and the Spanish Retreat in the Mississippi Valley*. Boston 1927. Reprint, 1969.

———. "Documents: The South Carolina Yazoo Company." *Mississippi Valley Historical Review*, 16 (March 1930): 383–94.

White, Richard. *The Roots of Dependency: Subsistence, Environment, and Social Change Among the Choctaws, Pawnees and Navajos*. Lincoln, 1983.

Whitefield, Gaius, Jr. "The French Grant in Alabama, A History of the Founding of Demopolis." *Transactions of the Alabama Historical Society*, 4 (1904): 321–55.

Wilkins, Thurman. *Cherokee Tragedy: The Ridge Family and the Decimation of a People*. 2nd rev. ed., Norman, 1986.

Wilkinson, James. *Memoirs of My Own Times*. 3 vols. Philadelphia, 1816.

Williamson, Chilton. *American Suffrage from Property to Democracy 1760–1860*. Princeton, 1960.

Winter, William F., ed. "Journal of the Constitutional Convention of 1817." *Journal of Mississippi History*, 29 (November 1967): 443–504.

Worcester, Donald E. "The Significance of the Spanish Borderlands to the United States." *Western Historical Quarterly*, 7 (January 1976): 5–18.

Wood, Peter H. *Black Majority: Negroes in Colonial South Carolina From 1670 through the Stono Rebellion.* New York, 1974.
Wright, J. Leitch, Jr. *The Only Land They Knew: The Tragic Story of the American Indians in the Old South.* New York, 1981.
"Yale's Loyalists." *Yale Alumni Magazine,* 39 (October 1975): 21–22.
Young, Jacob. *Autobiography of a Pioneer: Or, the Nativity, Experiences, Travels, and Ministerial Labors of Rev. Jacob Young, With Incidents, Observations, and Reflections.* Cincinnati, 1860.
Young, Mary E. *Redskins, Ruffleshirts, and Rednecks: Indian Allotments in Alabama and Mississippi, 1830–1860.* Norman, 1961.

Theses and Dissertations

Beard, Michael Francis. "Natchez Under-The-Hill, 1790–1840: Reinterpretation." Honors thesis, University of Southern Mississippi, 1971.
Beard, Michael Francis. "Frontier Port on the Mississippi: A History of the Legend of Natchez Under-The-Hill, 1800–1900." Master's thesis, Louisiana State University, 1981.
Briceland, Alan Vance. "Ephraim Kirby, Connecticut Jeffersonian, 1757–1804: The Origins of the Jeffersonian Republican Party in Connecticut," Ph.D. diss., Duke University, 1965.
Clay, Mary H. "Gideon Lincecum, Southern Pioneer, 1793–1874," Master's thesis, Mississippi State College, 1953.
Elliott, Mary J. "Winthrop Sargent and the Administration of the Mississippi Territory." Ph.D. diss., University of Southern California, 1970.
Faust, Richard H. "William Weatherford: A Case Study of a Man Dominated by Historical Events in the Creek Nation, 1780–1824," Master's thesis, University of Southern Mississippi, 1973.
Free, Joseph Miller. "The Theatre of Southwestern Mississippi to 1840." Ph.D. diss., Iowa State University, 1941.
Gillson, Gordon E. "The Development of a Military Frontier: The Story of Fort Adams and Its Hinterland." Master's thesis, Louisiana State University, 1954.
Hall, Robert Green. "The Natchez Trace: A Study in Transportation and Travel between the Early West and Southwest." Master's thesis, University of Wisconsin, 1914.
Hamilton, William Baskerville. "American Beginnings in the Old Southwest: The Mississippi Phase." Ph.D. diss., Duke University, 1938.
Haynes, Robert V. "A Political History of the Mississippi Territory." Ph.D. diss., Rice Institute. 1958.
Heidelberg, Nell Angela, "The Frontier in Mississippi." Master's thesis, Louisiana State University, 1940.
Helms, James M. "Land Tenure in Territorial Mississippi" Master's thesis, University of Virginia, 1954.
Inglis, G. Douglas. "Anthony Hutchins: Early Natchez Planter." Master's thesis, University of Southern Mississippi, 1973.

Lackey, William S. "Credit Land Sales, 1811–1815: Mississippi Entries East of the Pearl." Master's thesis, University of Southern Mississippi, 1975.

Lengel, Leland L. "Keeper of the Peace: Harry Toulmin in the West Florida Controversy, 1805–1813." Master's thesis, Duke University, 1962.

Mealor, William Theodore, Jr. "The Open Range Ranch in South Florida and Its Contemporary Successors." Ph.D. diss., University of Georgia, 1972.

Pershing, Benjamin H. "Winthrop Sargent: A Builder of the Old Northwest." Ph.D. diss., University of Chicago, 1937.

Price, Grady Daniel. "The United States and West Florida, 1803–1812." Ph.D. diss., University of Texas, 1939.

Roberts, Frances Cabaniss. "Background and Formative Period in the Great Bend and Madison County." Ph.D. diss., University of Alabama, 1956.

Smith, Suanna. "George Poindexter: A Political Biography." Ph.D. diss., University of Southern Mississippi. 1980.

Spalding, Arminta Scott. "The Natchez Trace Parkway: A Study of Origins in an Interstate Federal Highway." Master's thesis, Stephen F. Austin State College, 1965.

Stark, Genevieve Lois Maxon. "Traces of Early Mississippi" Master's thesis, Mississippi State University, 1969.

Waite, Mariella Davidson, "Political Institutions in the Trans-Appalachian West, 1770–1800." Ph.D. diss., University of Florida, 1961.

Walters, Vernon Larry. "Migration into Mississippi, 1798–1837." Master's thesis, Mississippi State University, 1969.

Wells, Samuel James. "Choctaw Mixed Bloods and the Advent of Removal." Ph.D. diss., University of Southern Mississippi, 1987.

Wells, Samuel James. "The Evolution of Jeffersonian Indian Policy with the Choctaws of Mississippi, 1800–1830," Master's thesis, University of Southern Mississippi, 1981.

Zahendra, Peter. "Spanish West Florida, 1781–1821." Ph.D. diss., University of Michigan, 1976.

Newspapers

New Orleans *Debow's Review.*
New Orleans *Louisiana Gazette.*
Natchez *Mississippi Herald and Natchez Gazette.*
Natchez *Mississippi Messenger.*
Natchez *Mississippi Republican.*
Natchez *Weekly Chronicle.*
New Orleans Price-Current and Commercial Intelligencer.
Baltimore *Niles Weekly Register.*

Index